GENDER, PLEASURE, AND VIOLENCE

NEW ANTHROPOLOGIES OF EUROPE
Michael Herzfeld, Melissa L. Caldwell, and Deborah Reed-Danahay, editors

GENDER, PLEASURE, AND VIOLENCE

The Construction of Expert Knowledge of Sexuality in Poland

AGNIESZKA KOŚCIAŃSKA

Translated by

MARTA ROZMYSŁOWICZ

INDIANA UNIVERSITY PRESS

This book is a publication of

Indiana University Press
Office of Scholarly Publishing
Herman B Wells Library 350
1320 East 10th Street
Bloomington, Indiana 47405 USA

iupress.org

Manufactured in the United States of America

Cataloging information is available from the Library of Congress.

ISBN 978-0-253-05308-4 (hardback)
ISBN 978-0-253-05309-1 (paperback)
ISBN 978-0-253-05310-7 (ebook)

First Printing 2021

CONTENTS

ACKNOWLEDGMENTS

I would like to sincerely thank everyone who made writing this book possible. This research was supported by a Marie Curie International Outgoing Fellowship within the Seventh European Community Framework Programme. I am particularly grateful to Magdalena Zowczak at the University of Warsaw and Michael Herzfeld at Harvard University for taking me and my project under their wings. I appreciate the helpful comments of the book's official and unofficial reviewers: Anna Wieczorkiewicz, Tomasz Wiślicz, Maria Dębińska, Magdalena Grabowska, Dorota Hall, and Magdalena Radkowska-Walkowicz. Special thanks go to Monika Płatek for her expertise and help with the legal elements in my research. I also thank the participants of the panel, "The Science of Sex in a Space of Uncertainty: Naturalizing and Modernizing Europe's East, Past and Present," which took place as part of the European Association of Social Anthropologists conference in Paris in July 2012—Agata Ignaciuk, Kristen Ghodsee, Agnieszka Weseli, Katarzyna Stańczak-Wiślicz, and Hadley Renkin—for the productive discussion about my presentation, in which I forwarded this book's main theses. Gratitude is also owed to all those who took part in other presentations of my research findings. I thank my colleagues and the students at the Department of Ethnology and Cultural Anthropology at the University of Warsaw for their insight and interesting questions. I thank Dorota Badzian, Agata Chełstowska, and Agnieszka Leszczyńska for their help in collecting data. I am grateful to Michał Buchowski, Danuta Duch, Anika Keinz, Ewa Klekot, Grażyna Kubica, Katarzyna Leszczyńska, Elżbieta Matynia, Lidia Ostałowska, Kateřina Lišková, Jill Owczarzak, Judith Okely, Frances Pine, Małgorzata Rajtar, Ann Snitow, Grzegorz Sokół, Karolina Szmagalska-Follis, and Carole Vance for inspiring conversations about my project and for their support and encouragement.

Special thanks go to all those who agreed to be interviewed and who served as my guides to the world of Polish expert knowledge of sexuality.

Finally, I would like to thank my friends and family for their faith in my capabilities. I thank Michał Petryk for his support, inspiration, and love.

The English-language version of this book would not have been possible were it not for the sympathy and determination of the editors of the New Anthropologies of Europe series, in particular Michael Herzfeld, on whose support and friendship I could count at all stages of my project. Heartfelt thanks go to Marta Rozmysłowicz for the effort she put into translating this book. I am also grateful to Jennika Baines of Indiana University Press for watching over the publishing process and to the directors of the University of Warsaw Press, Anna Szemberg and Beata Jankowiak-Konik, for their kindness during subsequent stages of this project. Many thanks to Agnieszka and Fredek Dzwonkowski for their hospitality and friendship, which allowed me to complete my work on the English version.

Small portions of this book were published earlier in the following articles of my authorship:

"Gender on Trial: Changes in Legal and Discursive Practices Concerning Sexual Violence in Poland from the 1970s to the Present," *Ethnologia Europaea* 2020, 50 (1): 111–127.
"Sex on Equal Terms? Polish Sexology on Women's Emancipation and 'Good Sex' from the 1970s to the Present." *Sexualities* 2016, 1–2:236–56.
"Feminist and Queer Sex Therapy: The Ethnography of Expert Knowledge of Sexuality in Poland." In *Rethinking Ethnography in Central Europe*, edited by Hana Cervinkova, Michał Buchowski, Zdeněk Uherek, 131–146. New York: Palgrave Macmillan; 2015.
"Beyond Viagra: Sex Therapy in Poland." *Sociologický časopis/Czech Sociological Review* 2014, 50 (6): 919–38.

Finally, I would like to thank the Polish Ministry of Science and Higher Education for supporting this project as part of the National Program for the Development of the Humanities (2018–2021; project no. 21H 18 0103 86; agreement no. 0103/NPRH7/H21/86/2018; amount 49 233 PLN).

NARODOWY PROGRAM
ROZWOJU HUMANISTYKI

GENDER, PLEASURE, AND VIOLENCE

Introduction

People are divided into two genders: male and female. The consequence of this division is sexuality, along with all the secondary effects, including erotic love. Sexology is the scientific study of all the consequences of . . . the division . . . into two genders for human development and health, for humans' harmonious co-existence with other humans and for their ability to form interpersonal relationships. . . . Sexology centers on . . . intimate life . . . in all of its . . . aspects: psychological, sociological, pedagogical, ethical-moral, legal, ethnographic, anthropological, biological, hygienic, religious and medical. The medical aspect is only one among many others, because sexology is interdisciplinary. The sexologist who does not know the other aspects of this science save for the medical is unable to determine the right diagnosis (because many interpersonal conflicts and disorders arise in the context of, for instance, differences in the socio-cultural background, or in the mode of upbringing), nor can he apply effective therapy. (Imieliński 1982, 7)

Kazimierz Imieliński wrote of gender, sexuality, and the science focused on their study. This physician founded the contemporary Polish school of sexology. He understood sexology to be interdisciplinary and placed sexuality in a psychological, sociocultural, and economic context. In writing and training future specialists, he referred to the experiences of his patients, from whom he drew his knowledge. Contact with patients also served as a strategy to legitimize that knowledge. Imieliński's approach differed fundamentally from that dominant in the second half of the twentieth century in the West, especially in the United States, where leading sexologists William Masters and Virginia Johnson (1966)—contemporaries of Imieliński—put clinical research above all else and examined sexual life outside of its actual context (I discuss this issue in chap. 1). The contribution of Masters and Johnson to the development of knowledge about the human sexual response is invaluable, just like their revolutionary research on women's sexuality. Nevertheless, the achievements of Masters and Johnson are criticized by North American feminist therapists and activists who see their studies as the source of today's commodification and biomedicalization of sexuality and therapy under the conditions of neoliberal capitalism. These feminists argue that Masters and Johnson ignored what Imieliński—whose work they might not be aware of—paid so much attention to: the cultural, social, economic, and political contexts of sexuality (see Tiefer 2001, 75–82).

Let Poland and the United States serve as examples of two systems: social-ist and capitalist (on sexuality in the context of socialism and capitalism and for a discussion of the most important literature, see Ghodsee 2018). In the narrative prevalent in public discourse—and, to a certain extent, in academic works—socialism denotes the absence of creativity. Accordingly, it was a to-talitarian system that fully determined the life of its citizens, and the history of Central and Eastern Europe after World War II is often understood through this lens. The intellectual accomplishments or progressive reforms of the pe-riod are hardly discernable in this framework. With all certainty, no success-ful sex life appears in the socialist foreground. In August 2017, a researcher of gender and sexuality in the region, Kristen Ghodsee (2017), wrote an opinion column for the *New York Times* in which she noted that although people suf-fered during socialism, it is worth remembering that not everything was bad at the time: women had more independence and thus more orgasms, and sexol-ogists proposed innovative methods of therapy. Ghodsee, who referred to my research presented in this book, caused a storm, especially on the West side of the already long-gone Iron Curtain. Outraged commentators, looking through the lens of totalitarianism, snickered at the idea of orgasms at the Gulag and argued that Ghodsee's text was an insult to Stalin's victims (Gutfeld 2017). In academia, attempts to draw attention to the emancipatory potential of state socialism, through study of women's agency or communist women's organiza-tions (see Daskalova 2007; Fidelis 2009, 2010; Ghodsee 2012*a*; Grabowska 2018; Lišková 2018) met severe criticism, and the researchers were proclaimed to be revisionists (Funk 2014). Accusations were launched despite years of research on gender and sexuality in the region aimed at showing the complexity of the situation, the destruction of stereotypes, and the search for alternative forms of modernity and agency (see, e.g., Owczarzak 2009*b*; Renkin and Kościańska 2016; on socialism as a modern project in the context of sexuality, see, e.g., Her-zog 2007). This rhetoric, rooted in the Cold War era, overlaps with preexisting ideas about Central and Eastern Europe as a space of sexual wilderness, non-modernity, and backwardness (Renkin 2016; see also Janion 2006; Wolff 1994). In contrast, such visions served and continue to serve the image of a modern, orderly, and progressive West (Renkin 2009). Furthermore, as Dagmar Herzog (2009) has shown, thinking about sexuality is dominated by the conviction re-garding continuous, unilinear progress based on the Western model (e.g., Alt-man 2001).

Such notions concern more than just sexuality and gender. Communism was perceived in this way not only in the West but also in the former Eastern Bloc. As anthropologist Michał Buchowski argued long ago, since the 1990s, the elites in Poland (and elsewhere; see Krastev and Holmes 2018) followed in step behind the West and capitalism, "orientalizing" (in the Saidian sense) all that was asso-ciated with communism and scolding societies for not being zealous enough in their strides toward attaining neoliberal standards. *Homo sovieticus*, a notion widely used by Polish sociologists, was characterized by anti-intellectualism, low productivity, and passivity (Buchowski 2006, 472).

2 *Gender, Pleasure, and Violence*

Since the early 1990s—that is, since the fall of socialism in Central and Eastern Europe—we have heard that we have to catch up with Europe, which appears as the epitome of normalcy. According to Ivan Krastev and Stephen Holmes (2018, 118), "For two decades after 1989, the political philosophy of postcommunist Central and Eastern Europe could be summarized in a single imperative: Imitate the West! The process was called by different names—democratization, liberalization, enlargement, convergence, integration, Europeanization—but the goal pursued by postcommunist reformers was simple. They wished their countries to become 'normal,' which meant like the West. . . . Imitation was widely understood to be the shortest pathway to freedom and prosperity." The end of socialism implies a return to normalcy, whatever that might mean. Either way, generally abstract and undefined Western values are placed at the top of the global hierarchy of values (Herzfeld 2004).

Work on this book was inspired by my refusal to accept a narrative that erases or simply ignores Imieliński and other Polish or, more broadly, Central European doctors, reformers, and thinkers in the dominant tale about the global past. This narrative has been dominant, at least until recently, in the social sciences and history (see, e.g., Zimmerman 2015; for new works on the history of sexuality in the region, see, e.g., Lišková 2018), and even more so in the public debate on progress. Breaking through this narrative is important both empirically and politically. As political scientists Krastev and Holmes (2018, 118) have shown recently, this sort of narrative has contributed to the victory of populism in Central and Eastern Europe:

What makes imitation so irksome is not only the implicit assumption that the mimic is somehow morally and humanly inferior to the model. It also entails the assumption that Central and Eastern Europe's copycat nations accept the West's right to evaluate their success or failure at living up to Western standards. In this sense, imitation comes to feel like a loss of sovereignty. Thus the rise of authoritarian chauvinism and xenophobia in Central and Eastern Europe has its roots not in political theory, but in political psychology. It reflects a deep-seated disgust at the post-1989 "imitation imperative," with all its demeaning and humiliating implications.

I hope that the history of Polish sexology might disrupt the dominant narrative about progress and time without creativity and serve to deorientalize Central and Eastern Europe. The accomplishments of Imieliński and of other Polish sexologists, like Zbigniew Lew-Starowicz or Michalina Wisłocka, challenge this orientalized vision of history and the need to imitate. These physicians founded an original school of thought and therapy that proposed solutions fundamentally different from those of their Western counterparts and that has stood the test of time. Today, voices critical of sexology according to Masters and Johnson are raised all over the world (see, e.g., Kaschak and Tiefer 2002; Tiefer 2001). These voices call for a sexology in the spirit championed by Imieliński.

Sexological works gained extraordinary popularity in Poland during the 1970s and 1980s. *The Art of Love* (*Sztuka kochania*) by sexologist and gynecologist

Michalina Wisłocka (1978) is said to have sold seven million copies (Izdebski 2016, 7). These books discussed issues directly related not only to sexuality but also to problems associated with gender, relationships, and attaining satisfaction in life. In their works, sexologists managed to deconstruct more than a single stereotype: they repeatedly stressed that masturbation is not a pathological act and that the clitoral orgasm fits within the norm. In recent years, they explained that homosexuality is neither a disease nor a form of pedophilia or zoophilia. They educated several generations of Poles, including the author of this book. I vividly remember my cheeks burning up as I read *The Art of Love* and *Sex on Equal Terms* (*Seks partnerski*; Lew-Starowicz 1983f), another highly popular sex manual in the late 1980s. In following the ideas of modern sex education propagated at the time by Polish sexologists, my parents kept these books out to encourage adolescent kids like myself to read them. It would not be an exaggeration for me to say that thanks to that reading, I could later undertake research on sexuality because I did not perceive this subject as shameful or lacking a conceptual apparatus.

Sexological works showed that sex serves not only the purpose of marriage and procreation (they also taught what to do for sex not to lead to procreation) but also pleasure, self-fulfillment, and health. They represented a counterbalance to the restrictive, Catholic approach to these issues.[1] The entire field of sexology displayed great merits in the struggle for the liberation of sexuality or *sexual reform*, a term that originates from the interwar tradition and to which Wisłocka (1978) and other Polish sexologists eagerly referred.

Nevertheless, I discovered another dimension to Polish sexological works. After more than twenty years, I took to examining these works anew as a person equipped with the tools to critically analyze discourses of gender and sexuality. It turned out that a pleasant, satisfying, and healthy sex life is subject to many restrictions, especially in the most popular literature from the 1970s and 1980s. Above all, traditional gender roles make for prerequisites, with sexual intercourse (penetration) involving a woman and a man as the foundation. I argue that because of these conditions, sexological discourse reinforces stereotypical ideas about gender and sexuality and naturalizes traditional gender roles through its definition of pleasant, healthy sex. It portrays women as the ones responsible for happiness in the family and for sex in marriage, without taking into account the structural limitations of their agency. Furthermore, sexological works also entered the space of violence and, in various ways, argued for the victim's joint responsibility alongside the perpetrator. There are no easy answers when it comes to sexuality, socialism, and emancipation.

The study of expert discourses of sexuality in socialist Poland, in the period of postsocialist transformation, and in the present contributes to destabilizing the narrative about progress. It shows that development is neither linear nor the same everywhere and that pockets of progressive (or otherwise) ideas might not develop simultaneously. Notably in the Polish case, the demands of sexual emancipation do not necessarily go hand in hand with women's equal rights. My research shows that these two spaces do not overlap at all. For example, the most important Polish book on sex, *The Art of Love* (Wisłocka 1978), says a lot about women's right to orgasm and gives practical tips on how to achieve it. Nonetheless, the main route that it forges towards sexual satisfaction entails a hierarchical relationship with the husband, regardless of the fact that the guide was written at a time when women's emancipation figured into official state policy (a similar process took place in Czechoslovakia in the 1970s; see Lišková 2018).

The transformation of 1989 brought diverse and often contradictory changes related to gender and sexuality. The institutionalized emancipation of women was definitively abandoned as a project (see, e.g., Gal and Kligman 2000; Pine 2001). Women were pushed out of the labor market and were primarily affected by the poverty brought on by economic transformation. Furthermore, reproductive rights were severely restricted. In the early 1990s, abortion was banned (Zielińska 2000), the state stopped subsidizing contraception and in vitro fertilization (Radkowska-Walkowicz 2013), and school sex education was gradually taken over by conservatives associated with the Catholic Church (Kościańska 2017; see also Mishtal 2015).[2]

At the same time, grassroots feminist movements thrived after 1989. Feminist activities contributed to positive changes in the approach to sexual violence by experts (i.e., lawyers and sexologists). Effectively, survivors received better treatment by the courts and by police interrogators and the physicians who examined them after rape. These changes are related directly to the activities of feminist organizations (before 1989, the communist Women's League was an active organization, but it was not interested in the problem of sexual violence). LGBTQ movements also developed after 1989 (under state socialism, they functioned in a very limited form and only during the last decade; Szulz 2017), demanding visibility and the right to civil partnership. Consequently, the Polish parliament had its first trans woman and outed gay man as members in 2011. Nevertheless, many homosexuals today believe that the time of socialism was better precisely because of the lack of visibility.[3] There is no doubt that the legal situation of trans people has deteriorated since 1989: before then, it was much easier to change one's legal name and gender than it is today. Furthermore, therapy and medical procedures associated with gender reassignment surgery are not financed by the state currently, whereas they were during socialism (more on this in chap. 2; see also Dębińska 2013; Kościańska 2017).

The nonlinear perspective might also highlight another issue of particular significance when it comes to Poland: the matter of the influence of the Catholic Church. Feminist and other literature often emphasizes that discrimination against women and restriction of reproductive and sexual rights are direct effects of the strong presence of the Catholic Church in Poland (e.g., Graff 2001; Mishtal 2015; Środa 1992, 2001). Catholicism is firmly rooted in the country, and especially after 1989, Church hierarchs worked more or less behind the scenes to institutionalize Catholic morality in Poland (Chełstowska et al. 2013). In the early 1990s, their efforts led to the criminalization of abortion; in recent years, they launched campaigns to discredit feminism, sex education, gender studies, and LGBTQ rights and tried to prevent Poland from ratifying the Council of Europe Convention on preventing and combating violence against women and domestic violence (Graff and Korolczuk 2017; Kościańska 2014b, 2016). But the influence of the Catholic Church cannot fully explain gender politics.[4] This becomes evident when the Polish case is compared with secular Czechoslovakia. Although sexology developed earlier there and generally had a different character (less oriented toward the humanities and more focused on research), some trends are common and involve understanding how a successful sex life relates to gender equality. Sociologist Kateřina Lišková (2016; 2018) has shown that in the 1950s, Czechoslovak specialists associated sexual pleasure with equality between women and men. In the 1970s, they advocated hierarchy in the relationship and traditional gender roles as the foundation of successful sex. Lišková links this turn of events with state policy and the changes that took place after the Prague Spring. During the first decades of communism, the state encouraged women to work and promoted communist principles of collectivism and gender equality. In the 1970s, as part of normalization, the regime sought to atomize society basing on the nuclear family. Effectively, gender equality discourse was replaced by a family-centered discourse, women's rights gave way to children's rights, and sexual pleasure became a byproduct of hierarchy in marriage. Sexologists argued, "Men and women are different and marriage only works if men are superior to women. If gender arrangements are different from this, women will suffer a pain similar to sexual dissatisfaction. It is the nuclear family and your spouse that are your only safe social bonds" (Lišková 2016, 212).

The case of Czechoslovakia, where neither the Catholic Church nor any other church wielded influence, can help illuminate what was happening at the time in particularly religious—as far as communist realities go—Poland. It would be difficult to talk about sexology in Stalinist times; however, if we look more broadly at the gender and sexuality issues in the late 1940s and early 1950s, the similarities with Czechoslovakia are striking. Gender equality was actively promoted by communists, so women were mobilized to enter the workforce (Fidelis 2010). Communist women's groups actively demanded the collectivization of housework (Grabowska 2018). My research on sex education (Kościańska 2017) also confirms the emphasis placed on collectivism and gender equality in that sphere. In the second half of the 1950s, cries were raised for gender equality. In a popular guide for young men, *What Every Boy Wants to Know* (*Co chce wiedzieć każdy chłopiec*), Janusz Łopuski (1957, 40–41)—apparently not a proponent of women taking up male professions—nevertheless argued that women's work is a necessity and that working women need to be treated with respect:

> You are now a young man, and men at times have a disrespectful, ironic attitude to women's work. When women were allowed to work in various professions in our country, which we can say with honesty, are not suitable for them, many girls rightly complained that instead of male advice and help, they get mockery and disrespect. It was not caprice that put the girl on the masonry scaffolding or on bricklaying in the streets, but hard necessity. These girls do not deserve to be mocked, but respected. When girls work side by side with boys, many of them think that they can be treated like candidates for satisfying their sexual needs. First a little affection,

then harassment, and once one of the girls gives in, comes the cynical opinion that all of them are the same. Instead of smothering girls with romance, boys should show their polite courtesy, because she is a friend and a companion of work, for whom it is more difficult than for a man to stand at the lathe or to lay bricks. And if it is more difficult for her, then for the same work she deserves greater respect.

This type of argumentation is not forwarded in subsequent decades. As I show (see chap. 4; Kościańska 2017), in the 1970s, the woman is associated with motherhood and the home space. We might try to explain this by the growing influence of the Catholic Church (Grabowska 2008; Kościańska 2018) or the efforts of the Communist Party to build good relations with the Church (Jarska 2019). But if we compare the Polish case with Czechoslovakia, it becomes clear that changes in the approach to gender equality in these countries are part of a wider trend in the Eastern Bloc that could be described as a push to abandon Stalinist gender equality politics.

In summary, in this book I focus on the specific Polish sexological discourse formed under socialism and currently. More generally, I study the expert discourse of sexuality because I also include in my discussion texts written by specialists from other fields. I examine the gender roles and models of sexuality constructed by this discourse, the mechanisms of their formation, and the various transformations, including the impact of factors like feminism and economic and political change.[5] This book is critical of sexological work; nonetheless, I wrote it in recognition of the achievements of the sexological field and its originality of thought, based on the assumption that the field is open to dialogue.

In following researchers of sexuality, particularly Michel Foucault (1978; see also Oosterhuis 2000; Vance 1989), I assume that expert discourse constructs sexual identities, behaviors, and feelings, as well as gender roles. It does so by naturalizing specific behaviors and identities and by associating given gender roles with a satisfying sex life. At the same time, this sort of knowledge is shaped by models present in a particular sociocultural context.[6] Thus, the history of expert knowledge of sexuality is also the history of sexuality. In analyzing expert literature, I try to answer the following questions: How does expert discourse define gender roles? How does it determine agency—that is, the range of possible actions and decisions available to women and men?[7] What kind of hierarchy of sexual behaviors and identities does it build? How does it relate to the sociocultural context in which it functions (mainly the problem of emancipation of women)? I also take a closer look at the process of constructing knowledge and consider the factors that shape its formation. I point to its nonlinear development and the role of knowledge production mechanisms, forged under socialism, in today's sexology. I juxtapose current developments with works from the 1970s and 1980s and point to both continuity and change. As for the issue of change, I consider the significance of feminism. I compare the development of sexology (and thus sexuality) in Poland and in the United States. The United States represents not only a reference point for sexologists around the world but also a force that shapes the global debate on sexuality. I examine two opposing dimensions of sexuality: pleasure and violence. My analysis concentrates on heterosexuality because the expert discourse on LGBTQ sexuality deserves a separate study and because the literature I studied was of a definitively heteronormative character. I write about homosexuality only to shed light on that heteronormativity (on the changing sexological approach to homosexuality, see Kościańska 2020; on transgender, see Dębińska 2013). Therefore, this book is a story about changes in sexology, and thus in sexuality, aimed at disrupting the dominant, unilinear narrative about Central and Eastern Europe as a nonmodern and backward space that should just catch up to the West.

Moreover, I deorientalize Central and Eastern Europe not only by showing sexology as an original, dynamically developing intellectual method but also by referring to theory forged in the region (on the status of anthropology in Central and Eastern Europe, see, e.g., Buchowski and Cervinkova 2015). When I analyze the processes of knowledge formation, I refer to *Genesis and Development of a Scientific Fact*, a treatise by Ludwik Fleck ([1935] 1979), a Polish Jew who lived in Lviv (currently in Ukraine) and wrote in the German language. His identity, interdisciplinary education, and rich intellectual horizons serve for a good reflection of the scholarly atmosphere in Central Europe at the time. Fleck was a doctor and a philosopher, inspired by the works of Émile Durkheim, from whom he borrowed the notion of collective representations. He also drew from the work of Lviv scholars like Kazimierz Twardowski and Kazimierz Ajdukiewicz. An important influence on Fleck was Leon Chwistek, a painter and "a constructivist logician and artist who wrote of 'the multitude of realities,' all of which exist with equal rights, contiguous to one another" (Schnelle 1986, 17–18). Chwistek was a childhood friend of Bronisław Malinowski and became friends with Fleck later in life.

Chwistek was not the only link between Fleck and Malinowski. As Roberto J. Gonzalez, Laura Nader, and C. Jay Ou have argued, the two scholars shared a precursory status in the anthropology of science. Whereas Malinowski was interested in the study of tribal cultures, Fleck was perhaps the first to have "by contrast, 'studied up' long before it was fashionable, spending much of his career in medical laboratories and hospitals with highly trained and specialized physicians and microbiologists" (Gonzalez, Nader, and Jay 1995, 877). Based on Durkheim's collective representations, Fleck coined the concept of the thought collective. He showed that scientific ideas are forged within collectives and are the effect of social and historical processes: "Fleck's originality stemmed from his willingness to question the dominant assumptions made by his contemporaries and his ability to cast a wide theoretical and conceptual net. Similarly, the strength of Malinowski's work was rooted in his criticism of the West through comparative studies of magic, science, and religion but also in the accessibility of his work to a wide audience. An anthropology of science informed by the work of both Poles might provide grounds for scholarly and public engagement with pressing contemporary issues of science and technology" (Gonzalez, Nader, and Jay 1995, 868).

Readers surely do not need to be reminded of Malinowski's contributions, though perhaps his Central European roots are worth mentioning (Flis 1988). Fleck, however, remains somewhat outside of the anthropological canon (although he did receive appreciation in science and technology studies [STS]; see Oudshoorn 1994). I approach Fleck's deliberations in a creative fashion, synthesizing his theory with the achievements of researchers in the field of gender and sexuality who represent various disciplines: the history of ideas (Foucault 1978), the history of sexuality (Oostehuis 2000; Terry 1999), STS (Clarke et al. 2010), and anthropology (Fishman 2004).

Chapter Outline

I start the book with a discussion of how the Polish school of sexology was formed. I examine its historical roots and specificity in comparison to developments in sexology elsewhere, mainly in the United States. I show the history of Polish expert discourse on sexuality. I focus on the particular character of sexology in the country, a result of the fact that sexologists interacted with patients and correspondents and drew on their experiences, creating their own interpretations of problems. My discussion of the historical development of sexology is aimed primarily at understanding what is happening now: How is scientific knowledge about sex formed today? How does the Polish school of sexology, in its specificity, interact with feminist ideas? How does sexology change with the global flow of knowledge and objects (in this case, pharmaceutical drugs; chaps. 1–2)?

Next, I turn to pleasure. I examine the conditions of pleasure, as prescribed by expert discourse. What kind of woman, and what kind of a man, enjoys a successful sex life? What constitutes "normal" and healthy sexual behavior? In this discussion, I use the concept of sexual hierarchy proposed by Gayle Rubin (1984). I also zero in on how sexologists approached women's emancipation. Did they understand the weight of this issue and women's double burden, an effect of state policy, that made women too busy and too tired for sex? The recipe prescribed by the experts to remedy women's problems was a return to the so-called traditional gender roles. Subsequently, I probe the influence of feminism on contemporary expert discourse.[8] I show that by adopting different strategies, feminists tried to deconstruct the heteronormative, patriarchal model of gender and sexuality. Their efforts brought a new response to women being overworked, equally so after 1989, and a new vision of female sexuality, agency, and gender roles (chaps. 3–5).

Finally, I take up the issue of sexual violence using the example of rape. I discuss how it was conceptualized in the sexological and legal discourse (chaps. 6 and 7). I show that in the analyzed expert literature, women's agency was equated with responsibility, with no consideration of structural limitations. Based on an analysis of expert discourse in the courtroom (chap. 8), I draw attention to the relation between the survivor's place in the sexual hierarchy and her ability to seek justice. In chapter 9, I present contemporary changes and the role of feminism. I am mainly concerned with defining the agency of women and men, the agency of victims and perpetrators, the meaning of suffering, the weight that feminists give to women's voices, and whether rape is understood as a sexual act or as an act of violence.

Research and Analyzed Materials

I collected materials for this book in the years 2008–12. The materials can be described as ethnographic (in-depth interviews and participant observation) or archival.

I conducted participant observation in the academic year 2011–12 at a state medical education center during training sessions for doctors, psychologists, and educators. Typically, courses lasted three days and involved the following issues: sexual disfunctions, forensic sexology, sexual orientation, and the latest developments in sexology. I obtained written consent from the course director to conduct participant observation. On every occasion, I informed course participants about the nature of my presence and asked whether they consented to it. Previously, in the 2008–9 academic year, I wanted to deepen my knowledge about sexuality, so I enrolled as a participant in the same series of training sessions (with the exception of classes on sexual orientation, which were not offered at the time) and obtained diplomas certifying their completion. Besides the course program, which I repeated after three years, I took part in training sessions on the sexuality of people with disabilities and on sexological diagnosis for psychologists.[9] It was then that the idea for this research was born. Because I participated in the training sessions twice, I could observe the changes that took place. These lectures were conducted by leading figures in Polish sexology and their assistants or former students.

In 2009 and in the 2011–12 academic year, I also conducted participant observation during selected classes for future sex educators at a state university. I obtained permission from the course lecturer (oral in 2009, written in 2011 and 2012), and I made sure to inform other participants about the nature of my presence and asked whether they consented to it. In 2011, I also carried out participant observation during a workshop on sexual violence at another state university. As elsewhere, I received written consent from the lecturer and oral consent from participants.

I attended conferences and debates on sexuality, in which experts were involved. At conferences, I registered as a participant and, if necessary, paid a conference fee. Once I presented a paper myself. Among the events, in which I took part, the following are worth mentioning:

- "Polish Sexology: 20 Years of the Polish Sexological Society," Sixteenth National Science and Training Conference (Warsaw, Hall of the Academy of Physical Education, October 21–23, 2011)[10]

- "Polish Sexology in the Past and in the Future," conference held in honor of the thirtieth anniversary of the Institute of Sexology and Pathology of Human Relations at the Warsaw Center of Postgraduate Medical Education (Warsaw, School of Medical Sexology and Psychotherapy, Medical Center for Postgraduate Education, Prof. W. Orłowski Independent Public Clinical Hospital, Main Hall, December 20, 2011)
- "4th National Debate on Sexual Health: The Sexuality of Poles 2011" (Warsaw, Marriott Hotel, November 23, 2011)
- "Prophylactics in Reproductive Health: The First Stages of Life" (Warsaw, Hall of the Warsaw Medical University, October 15, 2011)
- "Human Sexuality: Changes" (Krakow, Institute of Psychology, Clinical Section of the Student Psychological Society at the Jagiellonian University, March 23, 2012)
- "Woman and Man: Reproductive and Sexual Health" (Warsaw, Hilton Hotel, April 13–14, 2012)
- "Always on the Side of Women," Twentieth Anniversary of the Federation for Women and Family Planning (Warsaw, University of Warsaw, October 25, 2011, and Nowy Wspaniały Świat Café, October 29, 2011);
- Debates on the book *Sexual Harassment: Stupid Game or Serious Problem* (*Napastowanie seksualne. Głupia zabawa czy poważna sprawa*) by Anna Wołosik and Ewa Majewska (Warsaw, Maria Konopnicka and Maria Dulębianka Postgraduate Gender Studies at the Institute of Literary Research of the Polish Academy of Sciences, October 20, 2011; Gdańsk, "Nasza Przestrzeń" Foundation and "Na Styku" the Scientific Society of the Gdańsk University, December 2, 2011);
- Presentation of the Feminoteka Foundation's report, *End the Silence: Sexual Violence against Women and the Problem of Rape in Poland* (*Dość milczenia. Przemoc seksualna wobec kobiet i problem gwałtu w Polsce*) (Warsaw, Feminoteka Foundation and Cafe Kulturalna, Novermber 29, 2011)

I made use of my participation in these conferences and courses in several ways. First, they gave me insight into sexological knowledge today. I was able to learn about the most important debates and understand the perspectives of the lecturers, who were usually leading representatives of the field of sexology. Throughout this book, I use the knowledge gained during conferences and debates in the same way as knowledge drawn from written sources; I refer to specific lectures and courses. Second, I was able to trace what took place during these training sessions beyond the official program: I saw what the jokes were about, what was not said, and what elicited suggestive facial expressions. What was unsaid at times contradicted the official narrative. I also took part in countless informal discussions. Third, I was able to observe the reactions of other participants to see how they related, verbally and nonverbally, to the information presented and the sorts of questions they asked. Finally, course and conference participation allowed me to get to know the sexological social milieu to learn who is important in it, and which publications are considered significant. This last dimension determined the framework for the rest of my research, consisting of the interviews and archival investigation. People I met during the training sessions served as my "gatekeepers" to this community. Thanks to direct observations, I found out who generates the mainstream sexological knowledge and who opposes it. On this basis, I selected interview partners and determined the direction of library queries; I reached subsequent sources and people using the snowball method.

Following the knowledge and contacts I gained thanks to participant observation, I conducted and recorded twenty-seven in-depth interviews (two in 2009 and twenty-five in the 2011–12 academic year). In addition, eight interviews were conducted by my research assistant Agata Chełstowska. All interview partners were informed in detail about the nature of the interviews and agreed to participate in the study. With the exception of the two interviews from 2009, participants gave their consent in writing.

Interviews were conducted with experts who specialized in sex matters. They were sexologists, both doctors (four interviews) and psychologists (nine interviews with a total of ten people), sex educators (fifteen interviews), and people involved in providing support for survivors of sexual violence, who were mostly trained psychologists (seven interviews). The interlocutors (i.e., interview partners/interviewees) took various approaches to the issues discussed; they represented different generations and worked in large Polish cities. Some interviews concerned sensitive issues, and the interlocutors agreed to talk about them only on condition of guaranteed anonymity. To meet my obligations, I decided not to disclose their ages, genders, or the location of the interviews. Such information could serve to reveal their identities because the sexological community is so tight-knit that there would be no doubt as to who was talking. Therefore, the book does not contain a list of interlocutors. Interviews focused on experiences related to the interlocutors' work, the knowledge formation process, their views on sexuality, and their assessment of the dominant discourse of sexuality in Poland.

Another element of my research is the analysis of written sources. To understand how contemporary expert knowledge took shape, I decided to look into the past and examine the process of forming the Polish school of sexology. Many interlocutors invoked the achievements of Polish sexology in the 1970s and 1980s. Interviews, conferences, and training sessions allowed me to create a list of the most important Polish sexological publications—contemporary as well as those written over the past forty years. This list includes classic positions by Imieliński, Wisłocka, and Lew-Starowicz. Among contemporary works, I chose the very popular publications of Alicja Długołęcka and the books by Lew-Starowicz, published in recent years.

As mentioned, I used archival sources in the same way as other types of sources. I developed new research leads by, again, using the snowball method. Because the most important sexologists spoke out in the press, often writing regular columns and receiving many letters from readers to which they repeatedly referred in their texts, I decided to examine press articles as well.

I collected materials in two ways. First, I analyzed press clippings stored in the Archives of Modern Records (Telewizja Polska SA [Polish public TV], collection of press clippings, 1953–2009). The materials gathered in the archive allowed for a broad review of the press regarding the themes in which I was interested. The clippings included the daily press, weekly magazines, and monthly publications, both nationwide and regional, sorted by terms (I researched the following thematic files: sex, masturbation, rape, and Michalina Wisłocka). This gave me insight into the general tendencies of the changing discourse on sexuality. Second, I examined closely how experts spoke about sexuality in three journals: the student weekly *Etc* (*Itd*) (I studied all volumes from 1965 to 1990); the title published under socialism by the Polish Women's League and later privatized, *The Mirror* (*Zwierciadło*; editions from the years 1957–2012); and the journal of the Association of Polish Lawyers, *Law and Life* (*Prawo i Życie*; editions from 1965 to 2001).[11] The choice of these journals was dictated by different motivations. *Etc* was a student magazine that featured a column written by a sexologist (first by Imieliński, later by Lew-Starowicz) in each of its weekly editions from 1967 until the last issue in 1990. Other specialists (e.g., doctors) also frequently discussed topics related to sexuality in *Etc*. The weekly became famous for an important discussion on abortion in 1973. I chose *The Mirror* because of its association with the Polish Women's League. Because gender constitutes a basic subject of my research, I wanted to learn what the main organization concerned with the emancipation of women had to say about sexuality. Lew-Starowicz also ran a regular column in this magazine. I selected *Law and Life* because of the ongoing debates about sexual violence that were featured there. Analysis of only the press clippings already suggested this journal's leading role in this regard.

Finally, in developing the research leads that came up in interviews, training sessions, and the press, I decided to examine how expert discourse of sexuality—in this case, on sexual violence—translates into judicial practice. Many members of the sexological community serve as expert witnesses in the courts, and both mainstream expert and feminist interviewees were quite interested in the topic of violence. To this end, I analyzed thirty rape case files from 1981 to 2009 (ten cases for every decade). These materials come from a district court (formerly Voivodship) in a big city. I do not indicate the court, in which I conducted research, because I want to make every effort to fully safeguard the anonymity of the survivors. For this purpose, I also changed some details of the cases (I discuss the court trials in chap. 8).

In effect, materials obtained in a fundamentally different manner (ethnographic and archival) intertwine and complement each other in this book. I retrace the history of the Polish school of sexology in starting with the experiences of interlocutors and memories recalled during the training sessions. In my archival research, I develop the topics they discussed. When I write about the importance of patient experiences for the formation of expert knowledge, I also depart from participant observation, which suggested what to look for in the archival sources. At the same time, when it comes to certain issues, I rely almost exclusively on interviews and observations—for example, in discussing interactions between feminists and sexologists. This allows me to show the often informal nature of these contacts, which is, so important for the formation of knowledge. I use written sources to illustrate the results in the form of the transformation of discourse. In turn, the courtroom and the legal discourse of the 1970s and 1980s, contrary to today's discussions about rape, are depicted only on the basis of written texts: case files and publications. Again, the sources complement each other. I decided to use different sources at the same time to reflect the multidimensional character of the expert discourse analyzed and the various changes that it has undergone

Notes

1. Poland is a predominantly Catholic country, and even under socialism, especially in the 1970s and 1980s, the Catholic Church tried to wield control over the sexual life of Poles (more in Kościańska 2018).

2. Under socialism, abortion was easily accessible in Poland. The 1993 antiabortion law allows abortion only in three instances: when the pregnancy results form a crime such as rape or incest, when the pregnancy constitutes a threat to the woman's health and life, or when the fetus is seriously damaged. In today's Poland, it is extremely difficult for women to access legal abortion even in the three cases mentioned, as many gynecologists refuse to perform it on the ground of the so-called conscience clause.

3. This has been observed in the research conducted by the project team, "Cruising the 1970s: Unearthing Pre-HIV/AIDS Queer Sexual Cultures" (CRUSEV), of which I was a member (see, e.g., Burszta 2019).

4. It is worth remembering that the Catholic approach to gender and sexuality, and the opinions of the faithful on this subject, are varied and diverse (see, e.g., Peperkamp 2008; Kościańska 2012a, 2013, 2018). In addition, the Church's influence on sexual behavior is rather limited; for example, the Church strongly advocates against the use of contraception, other than so-called natural. As Zbigniew Izdebski has shown, the vast majority of Poles use contraception. This is clear, for example, in his 2005 survey of a sample of 823 men and 758 women who were asked about how they protected themselves from unwanted pregnancy in the past twelve months: 47.1 percent of men and 42.7 percent of women indicated a condom, and 23.2 percent of the male respondents and 24 percent of the female respondents marked that they used the pill. Methods approved by the Church were used much less frequently: calendar-based methods were used by 11.3 percent of men and 12.7 of women, whereas the temperature-based and the symptom-based and symptothermal methods were used by 1.8 and 3 percent of respondents, respectively (Izdebski 2012, 253).

5. This does not mean that no other factors shape gender roles and models of sexuality. In the Polish context, it is certainly the Catholic Church or, especially recently, the media. I exclude these issues from my analysis.

6. I draw on the considerations of Ludwik Fleck ([1935] 1979; see also Chauncey 1982/1983; Oosterhuis 2000; Terry 1999).

7. I discussed the concept of agency in my other works (Kościańska 2009a, 2009b).

8. I am deliberately not focusing on the 1990s, which deserve a separate discussion given their heterogeneity and constant changes. The economic and political transformation plowed through the organization of medicine and science, as well as through the publishing market. It reinforced the Church. The fierce abortion debate that took place in 1993 revealed the strong commitment of Catholic activists to issues related to sexuality and their extraordinary force of impact on state policy. The fall of the communist system opened

Poland up to Western ideas (which involved more translations and fewer Polish books) and products (the sex and pharmaceutical industry). In addition, although women's organizations existed in the 1980s, the feminist movement took concrete shape in the 1990s.

9. In the context of sexuality, an analysis of knowledge acquired during training sessions and conferences, in which the researchers were full-fledged, registered participants, was also conducted by Vance (1983) and Fishman (2004).

10. During this conference, I presented a paper entitled, "From Betty Dodson to Leonore Tiefer: Feminism and Sexology in the United States Since the 1970s to Present" ("Od Betty Dodson do Leonore Tiefer. Feminizm a seksuologia w Stanach Zjednoczonych od lat 70. XX w. do dziś").

11. This query was carried out by research assistants Dorota Badzian (*Etc.*, *Law and Life*, *The Mirror*) and Agnieszka Leszczyńska (*The Mirror*) based on my detailed instructions.

Part 1
Sexology and Society

1 | The Development of Sexology and Sexual Rights Activism in Europe and the United States

European Sexology and Sexual Emancipation Activism in Historical Perspective

Modern sexology was established in Europe with the publication of the first scientific and medical texts on sexuality in the second half of the nineteenth century.[1] Works by Richard von Krafft-Ebing (*Psychopathia Sexualis* [1886] 2011), Havelock Ellis (*Man and Woman* [1894] and *Sexual Inversion* [1897]), Magnus Hirschfeld (*The Transvestites: The Erotic Drive to Cross-Dress* [1910] 1991), and Sigmund Freud (*Three Essays on the Theory of Sexuality* [1905] 1949) described, categorized, and explained various sexual behaviors. With these publications, concepts that are common today, such as homosexuality, heterosexuality, transsexuality, pedophilia, sadism and masochism, fetishism, perversion, and exhibitionism, entered into usage. Years later, Michel Foucault (1978, 51–73) described what he considered the oppressive, early activity of sexologists in the context of changing forms of power and progressing medicalization. According to his concept, sexual medicine played a key part in the creation of subjectivities that served a new model of governing and economy.

In turn, Dutch historian of sexuality Harry Oosterhuis (2000) pointed to a somewhat different dimension of the studies conducted by the early sexologists. Training his focus on what was arguably the most important work published in the initial period of the discipline's development (i.e., Krafft-Ebing's *Psychopathia Sexualis*), Oosterhuis argued convincingly that the text cannot be interpreted as a mere catalog of sexual pathologies. His understanding was that Krafft-Ebing produced the work in response to the needs of his patients, effectively contributing to the process of creating sexual identities (14). *Psychopathia Sexualis* describes specific cases, with subsequent editions supplemented with new stories and testimonies. Once the book was published, Krafft-Ebing received mail from readers throughout Europe who learned that they were not alone in struggling with nonnormative sexuality. Although the prospect of a cure for their conditions, which he offered to his patients and readers, seems less than encouraging today, it was important at the end of the nineteenth century. Oosterhuis sheds light on factors that favored the creation of sexual identities in western Europe: the growth of individualism, capitalism, and urbanization. These developments allowed greater numbers of people to function beyond the traditional family and to regard their inclinations as a part of their new lifestyle (most of Krafft-Ebing's patients were recruited from this group; Oosterhuis 2000, 252). Sexual variance became more visible (253). Oosterhuis also calls attention to the role of romantic love; in the nineteenth century, romantic love gained prominence and effectively redefined the idea of marriage. Marriage gradually ceased to be a contract between families, with reproductive sexual intercourse as its only requirement. According to the new model, the bride and groom were expected to have mutual feelings for each other, which was not possible for everyone (e.g., homosexuals; Oosterhuis 2000, 231–40). As such, many people wanted to cure themselves of their "abnormal" inclinations. Discussing the case of a thirty-five-year-old homosexual, Krafft-Ebing wrote, "On the occasion of a consultation, in December, 1889, he asked me whether there were any means to bring him back to a normal sexual condition, since he had no real horror of women, and would very gladly marry" ([1886] 2011, 104).

In their work, Krafft-Ebing and other sexologists named and distinguished certain types of people. Previously, sexual acts did not define identity. Only with the publication of works like *Psychopathia Sexualis* did men who had relations with other men begin to be called *homosexual* and come to define themselves as such. In this way, according to Oosterhuis (2000), sexology contributed to the creation of sexual identities (e.g., gay and lesbian identity). It might also be argued that the rise of sexual identity was a condition for the creation of a movement to counteract discrimination on the basis of sexuality.

At the end of the nineteenth century, many physicians took part in what today would be called *sexual rights activism*. Throughout his entire life, for example, Magnus Hirschfeld contested Paragraph 175, which penalized homosexual relations in Germany. In 1897, Hirschfeld founded the first organization in the world to defend the rights of homosexual and transgender people, called the Scientific-Humanitarian Committee (Wissenschaftlich-humanitäres Komitee). He also initiated the World League for Sexual Reform, a movement that called for change in the approach to sexuality. Doctors and reformers associated with the league articulated their demands most coherently during the congress organized in London in 1929. These demands concerned gender equality in the political, economic, and sexual spheres; sex education; eugenic advice; access to abortion and contraception; and acceptance of sexual minorities and of the various forms of sex between consenting adults. Furthermore, they demanded legal divorce, recognition of the rights of illegitimate children and their mothers, prevention of venereal diseases and prostitution, a medical approach to sexual dysfunction, and an end to censorship (Bullough 1994, 62–75; Depko and Jędrzejewska 2008, 22; Gawin and Crozier 2006, 318; Wolff 1986, esp. chaps. 12 and 13).[2]

In partitioned Poland, doctors were not the only ones who wrote about sexual life.[3] Marital handbooks were published by the beginning of the nineteenth century. One of the first was *How to Have Happy Relations between Husband and Wife, or the Essential Virtues, Which Should Lead Them to This Aim* (*Sposób szczęśliwego pożycia między mężem i żoną czyli Cnoty istotne, które ich do tego celu doprowadzać powinny*), by Ignacy Lubicz Czerwiński (1817). There is an imprimatur on the last page of the book denoting that its contents were endorsed by the Catholic Church. Although the manual does not contain any strictly sexual advice, it bears some similarity to works published in the second half of the twentieth century. Lubicz Czerwiński (1817) addresses his writing to women: like some modern sexologists, he entrusted wives with the responsibility for marital happiness, the family, and the husband's well-being. Lubicz Czerwiński wrote, "She is destined by nature to alleviate her husband of his wild and crude self" (86). Bożena Urbanek (2004), a Polish historian, analyzed medical manuals focused on gender issues that were published in partitioned Poland in the nineteenth century. Her study shows that the authors of these manuals turned primarily to women and that women constituted the majority of readers (62, 71).[4] Urbanek points to the manuals' Christian character (63) and notes that in this period, men were advised moderation when it came to sex, whereas women were encouraged to help them. Only some authors saw the matter differently, arguing that men were capable of controlling themselves, whereas women were guided by emotions: Julian Weinberg noted that "a woman rather loves purely, a man out of calculation" (quoted in Urbanek 2004, 63). In the second half of the nineteenth century, new content appeared in the manuals (e.g., descriptions of sexual diseases, such as "male impotence"; Urbanek 2004, 69). The "psychological aspect of sexual intercourse" (70) had also been detected, and new publications began considering the achievements of various branches of medicine.

Sex manuals of the time were all written by men and from a man's perspective (Urbanek 2004, 71). According to Urbanek, "the image of women's sexuality was defined by men's wishes and desires" (71). The issue of women's pleasure and sexual autonomy appeared later, first in the feminist context and then in the medical context. At a women's congress in 1906, Zofia Nałkowska, a highly popular writer, was the first in partitioned Poland to draw attention to female sexual pleasure, triggering the indignation of many early women's emancipation activists (Sierakowska 2004, 367).

Various works that discouraged masturbation represent another type of nineteenth-century handbook on sexuality. Samuel Auguste Tissot's ([1760] 1832) famous treatise on the harms of masturbation, originally published in 1760, was translated into Polish and issued in 1802. Polish physicians also wrote on the subject, publishing texts such as *On the Effects of Self-Abuse (Onanism) and Nocturnal Emissions as Also Concerning Venereal Weaknesses (O skutkach samogwałtu [onanizmu] i zmazaniach nocnych jako też o słabościach wenerycznych)* by Antoni Stanisław Berger (1873; see Depko 2011). Publications of this sort appeared all over Europe (Laqueur 2003); they discussed the effects of masturbation, warned young people against it, and advised educators on how to maintain control over their pupils.

As for works that were strictly sexological, meaning those that examined various forms of sexual activity in the manner of *Psychopathia Sexualis*, a pioneer in this domain in Poland was Stanisław Kurkiewicz. A physician who liked to refer to himself as a *płciownik*, or genderist, Kurkiewicz authored a two-volume work entitled, *From Inquiries into Sexual Life (Z docieków nad życiem płciowym,* vol. 1 [1905], vol. 2 [1906]). Like other medical doctors, he devoted a great deal of space to the creation of new concepts in the Polish language. Thus, sexual perversion was known in his texts as *przewrotność płciowa*, which translates roughly as "gender-bending" (Kurkiewicz 1906, 245), whereas homosexuality was called *rówieśnictwo*, or "peer-hood" (594). Kurkiewicz seems to have been much less influential than the German, Austrian, and British stars of this emerging branch of medicine; this might explain why almost none of his innovative terminology survived the test of time in the Polish language. Magdalena Gawin and Ivan Crozier (2006) examined discourses on sexuality in the interwar period. Locating Poland in the international context, they gave credence to the leading Polish sexual reformist of the time, Tadeusz Boy-Żeleński, who argued that the partitions of Poland served to limit public interest in issues of morality because political matters were much more pressing at the time (Gawin and Crozier 2006, 324). It is worth noting, however, that sexological works were quickly translated into Polish. Krafft-Ebing's *Psychopathia Sexualis*, for example, was published in Polish only two years after the German-language edition was initially published in 1886.

It was only in the interwar period that the subject of sexuality began to be discussed, among others in *Literary News* (*Wiadomości Literackie*), dubbed by conservatives "the *Gynecological News*" (Chałupnik 2008, 346), or in the *Morning Courier* (*Kurier Poranny*) (Szpakowska 2012, 130).[5] Prominent Polish writers and poets such as Tadeusz Boy-Żeleński, Irena Krzywicka, and Maria Pawlikowska-Jasnorzewska, as well as other reformers, physicians, and progressive intellectuals, such as Justyna Budzińska-Tylicka, wrote about birth control, abortion, "inversion," and other issues related to sexuality.[6] They gave themselves up to, as Boy-Żeleński called it, "gynecological and social considerations" (1930, 135). The same milieu pushed for the establishment of the first conscious motherhood counseling center in 1931 (for discussion of this activity, see, e.g., Depko and Jędrzejewska 2008; Chałupnik 2008; Gawin and Crozier 2006, 324–33; Gawin 2009; Szpakowska 2012; Krzywicka 1998, esp. 234, who describes this event in detail in her autobiography).

In 1933, inspired by Hirschfeld's activities, the League for Moral Reform was established in Poland (the Polish League; Gawin and Crozier 2006, 325; see also Depko and Jędrzejewska 2008; Gawin 2009). Interestingly, Boy-Żeleński had already written about this initiative in 1930, using the phrase "sexual reform," but later, for strategic reasons, as can be assumed, he avoided the troublesome *s* word (Gawin and Crozier 2006, 326). The Polish League's demands differed somewhat from the demands formulated during the London Congress of 1929. Issues such as women's sexual pleasure, homosexuality, and the sexual norm did not appear there, though that did not mean that they were not discussed among the progressive circles of interwar Poland (Gawin and Crozier 2006, 326–28; see also Krzywicka 1998).[7] It is also worth noting that although doctors, scientists, and educators played key roles in the World League for Sexual Reform, the Polish League was mainly composed of novelists, poets, and other intellectuals. The roles of physicians, scholars, and educators were insignificant in the local context. This is partly conditioned by the fact that sexology in Poland was much less developed than in Germany or the United Kingdom during the interwar period (Gawin and Crozier 2006, 328).

Growing totalitarianism, especially Nazism, and the Second World War put a halt to the development of sexology and sexual reform on the old continent. Although sexology had developed primarily in Europe until the beginning of World War II, starting in the late 1940s, the United States took over leadership in the study of sex. North American research began to dominate world science; in recent years, it has also become an important reference point for Polish scholars. Today, the global hegemony of US sexology manifests itself in that specialists from different countries use guidelines developed by North American science, such as the classification system of the American Psychiatric Association, which also includes sexual problems. Likewise, the World Health Organization bases its definitions on those worked out by US experts and makes them binding throughout the rest of the world (Barker 2012). In writing about the specifics of the development of sexology in Poland, it is worth understanding how this discipline was shaped and came to function overseas.

Kinsey and Masters and Johnson: Mainstream Sexology in the United States

Absolutely groundbreaking for the development of sexology in the United States was the work of Alfred Kinsey and his collaborators Wardell B. Pomeroy, Clyde E. Martin, and Paul H. Gebhard: the so-called Kinsey reports.[8] Composed of two volumes, *Sexual Behavior in the Human Male* (1948) and *Sexual Behavior in the Human Female* (1953), each with more than eight hundred pages, the reports were based on a total of twelve thousand interviews and described in detail the sexual lives of white Americans.[9] Kinsey's interest in sexuality and, above all, his methodology, which consisted of amassing enormous amounts of data, sprung from his earlier passions. Initially, Kinsey specialized in zoology and lectured at Indiana University. Janice M. Irvine, in her in-depth study of the history of North American sexology, describes Kinsey's path to the study of sex:

> A taxonomist and collector par excellence, he had amassed over four million wasps during the course of his fieldwork. Kinsey's interest in the study of sexuality coalesced in the mid-1930 . . . As coordinator of a marriage course instituted at Indiana University in 1938, he was dismayed by the dearth of scientific literature on sex and his consequent inability to answer his students' questions. He was critical of all previous sex research as methodologically unsound or, in contrast to his own penchant for collecting, too narrow in scope. Thus he began compiling his own data, initially by taking the sexual histories of his students. (2005, 19)

The Kinsey reports differed from the works of the pioneers of European sexology, which tended to be catalogs of nonnormative sexual behaviors collected from the accounts of patients and readers. Kinsey's reports present a variety of sexual behaviors and reveal their quantitative dimensions. In so doing, the reports indicate the natural character of these behaviors, given their high prevalence. Although earlier sexological research focused on pathology, Kinsey sought out healthy norms and aimed at sexual emancipation: "When Kinsey proclaimed his 'objectivity,'" wrote Irvine, "he was eschewing both the moralism of religion and the pathologizing tendency of the social science" (2005, 20). His research proved that Americans engaged en masse in sexual behaviors considered abnormal. Kinsey normalized these behaviors: although he recognized the impact of social factors (e.g., class-based disparity), generally speaking, he considered statistically widespread behaviors to be natural. And because they derived from nature, neither law nor custom could ban them, he claimed. Included therein were homosexuality and extramarital relations.

Although Kinsey had his own distinct perspective on sexuality (he valorized diversity and frequent occurrence), he rarely expressed it directly. His research served to construct a certain model of sex research and a specific ethos of the sexologist. He believed that methodologically accurate research could provide objective scientific data and allow for understanding reality (Irvine 2005, 19). He rigorously selected and trained his research assistants. Kinsey required that his collaborators be happily married, which he saw as a necessary precondition to conducting interviews on such a difficult and embarrassing topic as sexual life. At the same time, he expected interviewers to be able to travel extensively (this excluded women, because as Kinsey argued, they could not both travel and maintain a happy relationship). Furthermore, interviewers had to hold a medical degree or doctorate and be able to communicate with working-class people. Kinsey gave them instructions on how to behave during interviews, including, for example, maintaining eye contact with the interviewees. Moreover, Kinsey's collaborators had to have been born in the United States and to understand North American culture. In addition, Kinsey never employed anyone with a strange ethnic name; he avoided Jews in particular, so as not to offend Protestants. In effect, the interviewers he hired were almost exclusively heterosexual male WASPs. In Kinsey's opinion, they exemplified US society and its morality, which, in his view, guaranteed obtaining objective data (2005, 24–5). He saw no other possible configuration. As Irvine wrote, "Although Kinsey noted that it was 'astonishing,' given the cultural taboo against revealing personal sexual activity, that anyone ever agreed to be interviewed, he did not believe the process would be enhanced if subjects were approached by a researcher from their own community. Against the need for women or black interviewers he argued that if one had to match interviewer and subject on the basis of sex or race, then one should also do so for other social groups, such as prostitutes—practice that he considered unworkable" (25).

Today in the fields of anthropology, sociology, and, above all, feminist and queer theory, questions about the researcher's positionality and the power relations in the process of knowledge production are analyzed in great detail (see, e.g., Haraway 1988; Reinharz 1992; Wyka 1993); however, Kinsey wrote in the 1940s, long before debates on these topics entered the social sciences. Kinsey believed in objectivism, which also had a political dimension: he believed that sex could be studied only by those with scientific legitimacy. Because of this contention, he decided not to engage politically. In so doing, he established the archetypal figure of the sexologist, uninvolved in social issues. This distinguished Kinsey significantly from European physicians like Hirschfeld, who dedicated themselves to fighting for sexual emancipation (Irvine 2005). Furthermore, before World War II, radical demands for sexual reform also had their advocates in both the medical and nonmedical milieus in the United States. For instance, at the Congress of the Sexual Reform League in 1928 in Copenhagen, among the delegate-representatives from the United States were Harry Benjamin, a sexologist and endocrinologist specializing in transsexuality, and Margaret Sanger, a feminist involved in the struggle for female sexual autonomy and "mother" of the contraceptive pill ("the pill"; Wolff 1986, 259; see also Oudshoorn 1994). Nevertheless, in the postwar period, North American sexologists were less involved with social issues related to sexuality, in part because of the conservative political climate and, in some ways, because of Kinsey's methodological approach.

Returning to the Kinsey reports, what did they say? Most important, as mentioned, they showed that white Americans, both women and men, indulged in sexual pleasures considered "perverted" or abnormal. According to Kinsey's test, "37 per cent of total male population has at least some overt homosexual experience" (Kinsey et al. 1948, 650), whereas 13 percent of women had achieved orgasm in a lesbian relationship (Kinsey et al. 1953, 475).[10] Kinsey and colleagues pointed to the prevalence of masturbation: 92 percent of men (1948, 499) and 62 percent of women (1953, 173) admitted to sexually stimulating themselves. Extramarital sex likewise turned out to be commonplace, with a third of the men (Kinsey et al. 1948, 585) and a quarter of the women (Kinsey et al. 1953, 416) studied taking part. Kinsey and colleagues also asked about zoophilia: 8 percent of men (1948, 670) and 3.6 percent of women (1953, 505) had some type of sexual contact with animals. Kinsey considered all of these practices simply as sex. He treated them on par with sanctified marital intercourse (also including various types of what he called "outlet," e.g., nocturnal male discharge and female orgasm during sleep). He analyzed each type of sexual outlet independently. For a unit of measure of sexuality, he took the orgasm, regardless of how it was achieved; this criterion was rather daring for the times, especially regarding women (Irvine 2005, 31).

The ubiquity of homosexual, extramarital, and solo sex was, for Kinsey, proof that these were natural behaviors. Similar conduct among other mammals and various customs among so-called primitive people further buttressed Kinsey's conviction. He repeatedly emphasized that such behaviors should not be stigmatized (Irvine 2005). In this sense, Kinsey's work contributed to changes in the approach to sexuality by revealing it as natural behavior and by tearing it away from the grips of pathologizing language used by other pioneers of sexology.[11]

In the context of my research, it is worth taking a closer look at Kinsey's approach to the sexuality of women and gender in general. As mentioned, Kinsey's research showed that women, like men, engaged in diverse sexual practices and that their behavior went beyond the ideal dominant in the conservative postwar United States. As a measure of women's sexuality, he took the orgasm, which was revolutionary; Kinsey leveled the "clitoral orgasm," which Freud considered immature, with the "vaginal orgasm." Thanks to his gigantic sample, he rendered the orgasm an objective fact and placed it at the center of the study of female sexuality. This choice had complex consequences, which I discuss later in this chapter. Kinsey's method of measurement and his results suggested similarity between women and men regarding orgasm. At the same time, because women had sex less frequently and less diversely than men, Kinsey concluded that they inherently had less "sexual capacity." He did not consider the cultural and social factors that might decrease women's interest in sex (Irvine 2005, 35). In this sense, he perpetuated stereotypes about sexuality. However, the analysis of nonbiological elements was not entirely foreign to Kinsey, as he did notice class disparities in sexual behavior among men.

It is also worth noting, in following Irvine (2005), how Kinsey's report on women was received. Both reports provoked outrage and were used in progressive milieus (e.g., in connection with activities aimed at depathologizing homosexuality; see Bayer 1981) and by conservative activists (in documenting societal moral collapse). Irvine argued that Americans were afraid of the results of Kinsey's study on women because it showed women to be sexual beings, the same as men, despite their lesser "potential." The volume on women proved more shocking than the volume on men. Irvine quoted a member of the US House of Representatives who argued that Kinsey "was . . . 'hurling the insult of the century' at American women and contributing 'to the depravity of a whole generation, to the loss of faith in human dignity . . . to spread of juvenile delinquency, and to the misunderstanding and confusion about sex'" (2005, 41). At the same time, Irvine considered Kinsey's report on women a lost opportunity. In the early 1950s, there was no feminist movement that could propagate and make political use of Kinsey's findings.

The path that Kinsey laid out was followed by obstetrician-gynecologist William Masters and his assistant Virginia Johnson. They did not, however, conduct statistical surveys. They gathered a group of volunteers (694 people for a study that resulted in the book *Human Sexual Response* [Masters and Johnson 1966] and 790 people for the second series of experiments described in their publication *Human Sexual Inadequacy* [Masters and Johnson 1970]; see also Robinson 1989, 133) who agreed to masturbate or to have sex in the laboratory while the two researchers measured their bodies' responses using a variety of instruments. It should be remembered that Kinsey had already watched people having sex, but given the conservative environment in postwar America, he did not publicly reveal this fact (Irvine 2005, 37). Masters and Johnson proposed the so-called linear model of sexual reaction, the same for both genders. This model included four consecutive phases: excitement, plateau, orgasm, and resolution (Masters and Johnson 1970). This scheme has dominated sexology for years. Later on, in collaboration with Helen Kaplan, they modified it slightly by adding to the female sexuality model a phase of desire preceding excitement (Nowosielski 2010, 101–2). It was not until quite recently that mainstream sexology began to see sexuality as multidirectional (e.g., the Rosemary Basson model from 2005; Nowosielski 2010, 104).

Masters and Johnson emphasized the sexual similarity of women and men even more than Kinsey did (Robinson 1989, 122). They argued that although technique might differ, the orgasm itself is always the same, and the orgasm constitutes the quintessence of sex. These researchers, like Kinsey, acknowledged orgasms achieved through clitoral stimulation and introduced the concept of the female multiple orgasm. Furthermore, because their books centered on sex therapy, they not only recognized masturbation as something natural but also stressed its importance in sex training. For them, masturbation was healthy and desirable, for both women and men. At the same time, Kinsey and especially Masters and Johnson located sex in marriage and considered it decisive for a well-functioning relationship (Irvine 2005).

The work of Kinsey and his associates and especially that of Masters and Johnson undergirded the authority of North American sexology and contributed to changing how sexuality was understood in the United States. Their work also set the tone for sexology all over the world for many years. They were referenced in western and eastern Europe, including in Poland (on which I focus), and outside the Euro-Atlantic context, for example, in China (see, e.g., McMillan 2006, 32–34). The American Psychiatric Association's (APA 2013) classification system of sexual dysfunctions is based on Masters and Johnson's research and in part on Kaplan's research: the 1980 *Diagnostic and Statistical Manual of Mental Disorders, Third Edition* (DSM-3), the 1987 revised version, the 1994 DSM-4 (Tiefer 2001, 76), and the revised version published in 2000. The DSM divides sexual dysfunctions into dysfunctions of desire, arousal, orgasm, and pain. Thus, Masters and Johnson's work continues to stimulate the understanding of sex today. In many places around the world, and certainly in the United States and in Poland, lectures in sexology usually start with references to the Kinsey reports and to Masters and Johnson's model of sexual response. Often their research is approached from a critical perspective. In May 2013, the DSM-5 was published and included dysfunctions of excitement and desire among women. This addition represented a delicate departure from the Masters and Johnson model because it is assumed that disorders can differ by gender and that sexual response is not always the same (APA 2013, 13).

Nevertheless, the approach described was not the only one existing in the United States. Irvine (2005) distinguished three competing orientations: medical (originating from the Masters and Johnson model), psychological (deriving from the movement of human potential), and sociocultural based on feminism and the LGBTQ movement.

Feminist Sexology in the United States

Masters and Johnson's work was initially well received by feminists.[12] Many appreciated the description of women and men as essentially similar in terms of sexuality. They valued Masters and Johnson's positive approach to sex, the way the duo wrote about masturbation, and the fact that they argued that proper stimulation of the genitals guarantees sexual satisfaction (Robinson 1989, 122, 140–41). Feminists positively assessed the egalitarian approach to orgasm achieved through clitoral stimulation, what Anne Koedt (1970) discussed in her classic essay, *The Myth of the Vaginal Orgasm*. In another important text of the period, *A Theory of Female Sexuality*, Mary Jane Sherfey (1970) praised the idea of female multiple orgasms that had been forwarded by Masters and Johnson.

Gradually, this initial enthusiasm turned into critique. An insightful, feminist reading of the works of Masters and Johnson (and of Kinsey and coworkers) shows certain limitations in their understanding of sexuality. Such a reading also draws connections between the approach they advanced and more recent developments, like the radical medicalization of sexuality and the pharmacologization of sex therapy. Basic critique of Masters and Johnson involves several related issues: the approach to sex as purely physical, the central role of the orgasm, overemphasis of the role of marriage, lack of critical reflection on the results of their study, presentation of study findings as fully objective, an overtly male perspective, omission of women's subjective experience, disregard of sociocultural conditions and power relations, the perception of male and female sexuality as fundamentally the same, and the consequences of the proliferation of their views. The latter point entailed the medicalization of sexuality and the forceful entry of the pharmaceutical industry into this sphere. These issues have come to constitute the pillars of the development of feminist sexology (see Irvine 2005; Tiefer 2000, 2001; New View Campaign 2000).

As Irvine (2005) rightly points out, similarity between women and men in the Masters and Johnson approach is rather trivial or even incidental. For example, Masters examined cases in which men had fallen victim to sexual assault. He claimed that their situation was identical to that of sexually battered women, even though he managed to find only eleven cases with male victims (Irvine 2005, 63). In perceiving the condition of women and men as the same, Masters and Johnson—like Kinsey before them—turned a blind eye to the cultural, social, political, economic, and relational limitations of sexuality; in a way, they understood sex in a vacuum (Tiefer 2000, 279; 2004, 774). Moreover, they did not propose any analysis of "male domination and heterosexism" (Irvine 2005, 62), and they did not see women's sexual problems as associated with such issues (Tiefer 2004, 774). Leonore Tiefer, a therapist and one of the leading figures of feminist sexology, has argued that Masters and Johnson's fixation on bodily responses along with their neglect of the contexts that shape both genders are visible at the linguistic level (803). In their work, cultural categories like *woman* and *man* appear only a few times, whereas for the most part, they use the biological terms *female* and *male*. This is also confirmed by the fact that in their original model, Masters and Johnson did not consider the issues of libido, desire, drive, or passion. Tiefer argues, "By omitting the concept of drive from their model, Masters and Johnson eliminated an element of sexuality that is notoriously variable within populations and succeeded in proposing a universal model seemingly without much variability" (590).

Tiefer (2001) examines these issues in connection with Masters and Johnson's methodology or, more precisely, their selection of the sample. They recruited people who had positive histories of masturbation (meaning orgasm) and were in successful relationships. Volunteers tended to be well educated and wealthy (a result of recruiting from the affluent neighborhoods surrounding campus and from the academic milieu). Findings that pertained to this group were extrapolated to reflect the whole population, despite the fact that Kinsey had already shown that class stratification mattered when it came to sex (Tiefer 2004, 616–20). Tiefer argues that Masters and Johnson's model should not be generalized because differences exist not only between women and men but also within each gender (Tiefer 2001, 78–79).

Another discrepancy between the feminist and the Masters and Johnson approaches to sexology relates to the issue of marriage. The research duo believed that successful sex was necessary for the well-being of a marriage. Kinsey also forwarded this belief, although he emphasized it to a much lesser extent (Irvine 2005, 38). Masters and Johnson's conservative approach also shines through in other matters; they disagreed with feminism and considered it dangerous. They saw women's emancipation as a road that led "through bed" and argued that "women's liberation in the bedroom was most important" (62). Finally, for Masters and Johnson, sex was something that occurred between a man and woman. Although a few of their volunteers were homosexual, a fact that they mention in their publications, the epitome of sex in the Masters and Johnson approach remains heterosexual contact. When AIDS made its appearance in the 1980s, Masters and Johnson praised marriage as the best means of combating the new illness (126–30).

As mentioned, Kinsey and coworkers, as well as Masters and Johnson were certain of their own objectivity. Their scientific credentials served an important strategic goal: the legitimization of the study of human sexuality. Both teams initially encountered a variety of difficulties like problems getting published, negative reviews by colleagues, and lack of funding. Ultimately, their research approach amounted to the almost complete exclusion of subjective experience (although in his volume on women, Kinsey did analyze some qualitative data such as memoirs; Irvine 2005, 31) that could have allowed for insight into sociocultural problems and power relations in sexual relationships. Their work set the stage for defining both healthy sexuality and therapeutic strategy, in which subjective experience was not taken into account. It was around these issues that an alternative feminist sexology began to arise.

The feminist movement took up the issue of sexuality starting in the 1970s (Chalker 2011). In San Francisco, the first feminist sex shop, Good Vibrations, opened its doors in 1977. Female pleasure and sexual self-awareness became topics of discussion at meetings organized by feminist consciousness-raising groups, a newly popular phenomenon in the United States at the time. A few to a dozen women usually gathered and talked about their gender-related experiences. Gradually, thanks to the work of Betty Dodson, an activist and an artist (and currently a certified sexologist), these meetings began to include matters of sex.

Women not only discussed their experiences but also learned about their own bodies; using mirrors, they examined their own genitals. Dodson taught women (and men over time) how to masturbate (Dodson 1974).

Two important feminist books on sex were published in this period: *The Hite Report* (Hite 1976) and *Our Bodies, Ourselves* (Boston Women's Health Book Collective 1971). The latter is a feminist guide to sexuality and the body, intended for women. It has come out in numerous editions, both in the United States and abroad, with about four million copies sold around the world (Radcliffe Institute for Advanced Study 2011). *The Hite Report* on the sexuality of women, written by Shere Hite (her report on men's sexuality was published in 1981), is based on dia-metrically different assumptions than the Kinsey report. Hite collected accounts from 1,817 North American women who responded to a survey that consisted of fifty-eight open-ended questions, distributed through women's organizations and the progressive press in 1972. Survey questions touched on a variety of sexual experiences. Hite asked if they were important; she welcomed comments and created space for adding what participants felt to be missing (Hite 1976, xii–xix, 425–435). She opened her report with the following words: "Women have never been asked how they felt about sex. Researchers, looking for statistical 'norms,' have asked all the wrong questions for all the wrong reasons—and all too often wound up telling women how they should feel rather than *asking* them how they feel. Female sexuality had been seen essentially as a response to male sexuality and intercourse. There has rarely been any acknowledgment that female sexuality might have a complex nature of its own which would be more than just the logical counterpart of (what we think of as) male sexuality" (xi, original emphases).

Hite (1976) managed to actually create space for women's voices. As she asked open-ended questions, her book is largely composed of citations. In her report, statistics do not serve the ends of constructing a norm. The report's contribution is of a completely different value. Hite presents the kinds of sex that women want, how they want to have it, what they do not like, and what they expect from their male and female partners. The respondents' answers show that many women do not achieve orgasm during intercourse (387–424). This issue was already known to researchers, as both the Kinsey team and Masters and Johnson had noted it in their studies. But it was Hite who drew attention to this fact, focusing on the subjective negative experiences of women during penetration (Irvine 2005, 113). She argued that in spite of this finding, Masters and Johnson nevertheless identi-fied "normal" sex with intercourse. Sexologists decried her research as unscien-tific. Virginia Johnson called Hite's report pseudoscience, and Kinsey's associate Wardell Pomey accused Hite of ideological, feminist bias. In 1976, Pomey wrote, "Although I am much in favor of women's lib in all its aspects, I do not favor biases or politics when they enter the portal of science" (quoted in Irvine 2005, 116). Quite visibly, the rhetoric of objectivity established by Kinsey (that neatly veiled the ideology hidden within) enjoyed a strong position in the scientific commu-nity in the 1970s. Hite's report was also criticized in Poland and accused of the same thing: ideology (e.g., Lew-Starowicz 1982*a*). Nevertheless, the most popular Polish sexologist of the 1970s, Michalina Wisłocka, expressed her compassion for Hite in an interview: "I feel sorry for Ms. Hite and her respondents, who see marriage only as an exchange of sexual services" (Różycki 1995, 159).

Contemporary feminist sexology has gone even further than did Hite by problematizing, for example, the issue of the central position of the orgasm. Tiefer (2001) and other feminist sexologists note that the universalization of the Masters and Johnson model has brought about the fusion (in both sexology and popular thought) of pleasure with orgasm. Tiefer (2001, 82) calls this the "tyranny" of orgasm. Such an approach makes it impossible to recognize other forms of pleasure and other routes to reaching it than physical stimulation. Meanwhile, notes Tiefer (2004, 791), numerous studies, including meta-analyses, indicate that women perceive emotional issues to be just as important as the orgasm. Therefore, measuring pleasure by means of the orgasm, along with the sexual response cycle described by Masters and Johnson, deprives women of their voice (Tiefer 2004, 794; for other examples of critique of the approach to female orgasm, see Jackson and Scott 1996; Lloyd 2005; Potts 2000).

Viagra and the Biomedicalization of Sexuality: Feminist Therapists Respond

In the second half of the 1990s, a new generation of prescription drugs became available on the market: phosphodiesterase type 5 inhibitors, or pills for erectile dysfunction, the most famous of which is Viagra. Gradually, selective serotonin reuptake inhibitors—antidepressants like Prozac that were introduced onto the market in the 1980s—began to be used off-label to treat premature ejaculation.[13] Viagra, Prozac, and other brands of similar drugs completely revolutionized the world of sexology. First of all, they changed the balance of power within the discipline. Doctors were given an effective tool to fight the most common sexual ailments, and their role in the sexological community was undeniably strengthened. Patients all over the world preferred to get a prescription (despite the fact that the drug was initially very expensive) rather than undergo long-term psychological therapy (see also Tiefer 2006; E. Johnson 2008, 34). At the same time, medical researchers began to work more with the pharmaceutical industry (Fishman 2004).[14] Second, the new prescription drugs changed the concept of the relationship. Previously, erectile dysfunction and ejaculation disorders were treated in couples therapy, with sets of appropriate physical and psychological exercises offered to patients.[15] With drug therapy, men are no longer dependent on their partners (see E. Johnson 2008, 41–42). Third, in following the principle that women and men are identical in terms of sex, pharmaceutical companies began the search for a drug that could successfully treat sexual dysfunctions among women.[16]

The emergence of these new medical products, often called "lifestyle drugs," figures into the process of the (bio)medicalization of sexuality. In my analysis, this long-term process represents an extremely important consequence of Kinsey's reports and, above all, of Masters and Johnson's studies. Rendering sex objective, presenting it as natural, and identifying it with the orgasm launched a process that eventually led to the introduction of drugs for the treatment of sexual problems. Remedies in the form of Viagra arise from a certain definition of sexuality, and campaigns and advertising materials aimed at increasing their sales serve to reinforce this picture (Åsberg and Johnson 2009; Fishman and Mamo 2001).[17]

The medicalization of sexuality, the development of medical control over the sphere of sexuality, and the emergence of new drugs to improve sexual life are not isolated phenomena. In the United States and many countries around the world, these phenomena are part of the medicalization of various areas of life, particularly the medicalization of mood. In the past, psychology or religious discourse maintained authority over areas of life like mood and sexuality. Various phenomena regarded today as diseases were previously perceived as natural processes (see, e.g., Jacyno 2007; on medicalization, see Zola 1972, 1991; Conrad 1979, 1992; and Clarke, Mamo, et al. 2010; on the medicalization of mood in Latvia, see Skultans 2007; in the United States and Western Europe, see Rose 2006). Numerous studies of the medicalization of mood have shown that North Americans increasingly express their concerns in medical terms, which is likely related to the growing power of the pharmaceutical industry (see Clarke, Mamo, et al. 2010; Rose 2006).[18]

Michel Foucault (1978, 139; see also Foucault 1979) has shown how new, dispersed forms of power that involved disciplining the body—"an anatomo-politics of the human body" and "a biopolitics of the population"—developed starting in the eighteenth century in European societies. The scientific and medical discourses played a key role in the process of shaping subjectivities and societies. Applying such a perspective to the North American context, Adele E. Clarke, Janet K. Shim, and colleagues (2010b, 47) define medicalization as "the processes through which aspects of life previously outside the jurisdiction of medicine come to be constructed as medical problems." The authors analyze the development of medicine in the United States, with an emphasis on historical fluctuations. The period from 1890 to 1945 was characterized by the professionalization of medical and nursing care. New professions, new social forms (e.g., hospitals and clinics), and new technologies and drugs appeared at this time. After World War II, medicine embraced new spheres because of rapid growth in the "production of medical knowledge and clinical interventions" (50). Issues that had previously been considered moral, legal, or social entered into the purview of medicine (Clarke, Shim, et al. 2010a, 1). Beginning in the 1970s, a new line of disorders entered the medical lexicon, such as *posttraumatic stress disorder* (PTSD), *premenstrual syndrome* (PMS), and *attention deficit hyperactivity disorder* (ADHD). American sociologists observing the institutional expansion of medicine called it "medicalization" (Zola 1972) and "medical social control" (Conrad 1979; discussed in Clarke, Shim, et al. 2010b, 51).

Clarke, Shim, and their collaborators (2010b, 51) argue that a significant change took place in the mid-1980s: a transition from medicalization to biomedicalization. Medicine was increasingly more important in the context of culture, society, politics, and the economy. People started to internalize medical language and use it to express their problems more frequently than before (on psychiatry, see also

Rose 2006, 479–81). For Clarke, Shim, and colleagues (2010*b*, 47), biomedical-ization denotes "the increasingly complex, multisited, multidirectional processes of medicalization that today are being both extended and reconstituted through the emergent social forms and practices of a highly and increasingly technosci-entific biomedicine." They see this as a manifestation of the process of transition from modernity to late or postmodernity: "The shift to biomedicalization is a shift from enhanced control over nature (i.e., the world around us) to the harness-ing and transformation of internal nature (i.e., biological processes of human and nonhuman life-forms), often transforming 'life itself.' Thus it can be argued that medicalization was co-constitutive of modernity, while biomedicalization is also co-constitutive of postmodernity" (52).

Biomedicalization is closely associated with scientific inventions, new social forms, the commodification of health, and techniques of self-control. It creates new identities and subjectivities, at both group and individual levels. The prefix *bio* has a strictly Foucauldian connotation here, referring to biopolitics and bio-power (Clarke, Shim, et al. 2010*a*, 4–5). Furthermore, insofar as medicalization implied the control of disease, biomedicalization entails the transformation not only of medicine but also of the body, and not only with the final aim of healing but also of perfecting the body along the way (2). According to Clarke, Shim, and their coworkers (2010*a*, 1–2; 2010*b*, 52), biomedicalization consists of five related processes: (1) changes within the scope of biopolitical economics (privatization and the domination of corporations; commodification of health and disease; nontransparent links between knowledge, technology, services and capital); (2) a focus not only on illness but also on health and its optimization through "techno-science" (interference in lifestyle); (3) "techno-scientification" of medical practice (e.g., the impact of the invention of Viagra on sexology); (4) changes in the pro-duction, distribution, and consumption of biomedical knowledge (especially the role of information technology and the internet); and (5) transformations of bod-ies, groups, and identities through techno-science.[19]

In the context of my research, two points are of particular importance. The first regards the production and distribution of knowledge. Modern develop-ment of medicine was characterized by the flow of knowledge from top to bottom (doctors and medical researchers produced medical knowledge and only they had access to it). Contemporary (i.e., postmodern) knowledge is produced by various entities and is distributed beyond the world of experts through the mass media and the internet. Consequently, it seems that a sort of democratization has taken place within the sphere of medical knowledge. However, Clarke, Shim, and coworkers (2010*b*, 74) draw attention to a somewhat different dimension of this process. They note that although access to knowledge is indeed more democratic, the information offered might turn out to serve the interests of industry. For ex-ample, content on a website about sexual problems faced by women, set up by two celebrities of American sexology, the Berman sisters (Laura, a psychologist, and Jennifer, a urologist), indirectly advertises drugs to improve sexual performance. Furthermore, the sister team conducts research on behalf of one of the biggest pharmaceutical companies, also by means of their website. People who visit the site are asked to take part in the research (for an analysis of this website and the sisters' media presence, see Fishman 2004, 202–7). Their activities also shed light on another aspect of biomedicalization: the co-optation of knowledge and practices generated by social movements. Clarke, Shim, and coworkers (2010b, 76) point to the appropriation of the achievements of the women's health movement (e.g., counseling for women) and gay activism (e.g., approach to HIV/AIDS) by biomedicine (exemplified by institutions such as the US Food and Drug Administration [FDA]). The Berman sisters also appropriate the achievements of feminism by calling on women's right to pleasure in the aims of increasing drug sales. In this sense, the feminist approach to sexuality is seized by medical discourse and loses its emancipatory potential. Finally, in an article ending the collection of texts on biomedicalization, Clarke (2010, 402–3) asks whether this phenomenon has occurred in other countries. Has it occurred in Poland, and if so, what does that mean for sexology and feminism? I return to this question later in the book, especially in chapter 5.

Also of note is the already mentioned shift in sexual therapy caused by the invention of Viagra and other drugs for the treatment of erectile dysfunction. This shift serves as a fitting example of the biomedicalization process. A technological invention changes medical practice to shape new forms of subjectivity, identity, and interpersonal relations (E. Johnson 2008).[20]

Feminists called attention to the medicalization of sexuality in the 1970s (see, e.g., Boston Women's Health Book Collective 1971). The biomedicalization that followed incited a new wave of feminist mobilization around sexuality. After the great success of Viagra, pharmaceutical companies wanted to market its equivalent for women. Viagra itself and other drugs were tested. This research went hand in hand with the idea that women's sexual dysfunctions can be easily overcome with the appropriate pharmaceuticals (medical researchers who worked with pharmaceutical companies took part in these trials; see Fishman 2004). Ultimately, there was an attempt in the United States to register a testosterone patch that supposedly raised libido, but the FDA rejected the application (as a result of Tiefer's campaign; see Canner 2009). The drug was successfully registered in the European Union. Regarding feminist activity in this area, perhaps the movement's most important manifestation was the New View Campaign, established in 2000 and active until 2015. Its founder and driving force was Leonore Tiefer. Feminists associated with this group promoted an approach to sexuality that considered cultural and social factors. They were involved in the education of therapists, monitored the activities of the pharmaceutical industry, and engaged in the social study of sexuality (New View Campaign 2017; Fishman 2004). They called attention to the fact that research on drugs for the treatment of women's sexual dysfunctions involves a variety of procedures that aim at changing the understanding of women's sexuality to include the idea of these disorders. In following the ideas forwarded by Masters and Johnson's studies, pleasure equals orgasm; as such, it is both purely physiological and universal. Therefore, women who have problems reaching orgasm or who show little interest in sex are abnormal, unhealthy, and necessarily unhappy.

In 2000, New View activists came out with a manifesto (New View Campaign 2000). In it, they protest against the activities of the pharmaceutical industry and the medical researchers who collaborate with industry on inventing "Viagra for women." New View was based on a critique of the approach to sexuality presented above, as defined in the classification system of the American Psychiatric Association (DSM-2 to -4). New View activists pointed to three mistaken assumptions: uniformity of female and male sexuality, uniformity of all women's experience of sexuality, and absence of consideration for the impact of social factors. They also presented positive perspectives on sexuality that support diversity and position sex in a sociocultural context. According to New View, the best example of this sort of approach is the declaration of sexual rights adopted by the World Sexual Congress in 1999, which includes the freedom to express sexuality; freedom from coercion, exploitation, and abuse; the right to autonomy, bodily integrity, and security; the right to privacy, equality, and pleasure; the right to the emotional expression of sexuality; the right to form and end relationships; freedom of reproductive choice; and the right to information based on scientific research, sex education, and access to (sexual) health services.[21]

The group of women therapists and researchers from New View questioned the legitimacy of the classification of disorders in the DSM (specifically the disorders of desire, arousal, orgasm, and pain) and proposed an alternative classification. They divided problems (they did not use the word *disorder*) into those that are (1) socially, culturally, politically, or economically conditioned; (2) associated with relationship issues and the partner; (3) psychologically conditioned; and (4) medically conditioned (New View Campaign 2000).

Regarding the first category, the manifesto's authors (New View Campaign 2000) pointed to issues such as ignorance resulting from the lack of sexual education, inadequate health care, restrictions related to the lack of vocabulary allowed to describe feelings and needs, the lack of information about biological human variability in the course of life, and the "lack of information about how gender roles influence men's and women's sexual expectations, beliefs, and behaviors," the lack of knowledge about birth control, deficiencies in the prevention and treatment of sexually transmitted diseases, and trauma caused by violence. In addition, they called attention to the avoidance of sexual contact because of feelings of failure to meet sociocultural ideals of beauty, uncertainty about sexual orientation or shame associated with having socially problematic desires or fantasies, or belonging to a group representing values other than the dominant. They also pointed to the lack of time and burnout associated with too much responsibility at work and in the family.

In the second category, New View activists distinguished sex avoidance associated with fear of a partner, abuse on his (or her) part, unequal footing in the relationship, lack of trust and understanding, and dissonance in the needs of the individuals concerned. Furthermore, they pointed to loss of sexual interest resulting from conflicts involving money, other family members, or traumatic experiences, such as the death of a child. Sex drive may wane along with a partner's health or sexuality-related problems.

The third category consists of sexual aversion associated with bad experiences in the past, personality problems, and depression or states of panic. In addition, a partner might cease sexual contact because of the fear of pregnancy, disease, or bad reputation, among others.

The fourth category discussed "pain or lack of physical response during sexual activity despite a supportive and safe interpersonal situation, adequate sexual knowledge, and positive sexual attitudes" (New View Campaign 2000). These types of problems may arise from neurological, neurovascular, hormonal, or vascular disorders; pregnancy-related issues; sexually transmitted diseases; side effects of prescription drug use; or medical malpractice.

Although this group of activists was successful in blocking the registration of the testosterone patch in the United States and contributed to changing the understanding of sexuality, there is no dialogue between feminist advocates and medical researchers engaged in testing new drugs who perceive sexuality in only physiological terms.[22] Many sexologists ostensibly declare support for the emancipation of women, or at least for the emancipation of their sexuality (Virginia Johnson, the Berman Sisters). But feminist sexology in the United States has evolved in opposition to both the mainstream and medicalization. Medical sexology and feminism constitute separate thought collectives, in the sense of Fleck ([1935] 1979), with little room for dialogue. In the meantime, medical sexology has tended to instrumentalize certain elements of feminism by pulling them out of their original context to aid its own purposes. As I demonstrate in this book, in Poland, relations between feminism and sexology took a completely different trajectory. In effect, the biomedicalization of sexuality is hardly as pervasive in Poland as in the United States.

Notes

1. This does not mean that there was no interest in sexuality. In European culture, it can be traced back to antiquity (see, e.g., Bullough 1994; Imieliński 1982; Laqueur 1990).

2. In addition to the publications, which I reference here directly, extensive literature is available on the beginnings of sexology (for a collection of articles discussing the early development of sexology, see Bland and Doan 1998a; for an anthology of early sexological works, see Bland and Doan 1998b; on Ellis, see Robinson 1989; for a feminist critique of early sexology, see Jackson 1987; on the role of early sexology, see Weeks 1985, chap. 4; on sexology in the context of sexual rights, see Katz 1995; on sexology in the Soviet Union, see Bernstein 2007; Healey 2009; Kon and Riordan 1993, esp. chap. 7; and Shcheglov 1993; on Czecholovakia, see Lišková 2018; on sexology in Japan and European influence on it, see Frühstück 2003; on Great Britain, see Fisher and Funke 2015; Hall 1991; and Porter and Hall 1995; on the United States, see Melody and Peterson 1999; on the relationship between early sexology and racism, see Bauer 2017; Beccalossi 2018; and Somerville 1994; on global flows of sexological knowledge, see Bauer 2015; and Fuechtner, Haynes, and Jones 2018).

3. At the time, Poland did not exist as an independent nation-state.

4. According to Urbanek (2004, 63n5), twenty-one such works appeared in the nineteenth century.

5. In the years 1932–34, ten issues of *Literary News* came out with a supplement called "Conscious Living" that focused entirely on issues of reproduction and sexuality (Szpakowska 2012, 132–35).

6. *Inversion* implied feeling like a person of the opposite sex and, consequently, having sexual interest in people of the same sex. Interestingly, today, *homosexuality* denotes sexual interest in people of the same gender.

7. By the time the Polish League was formed, homosexuality was no longer penalized in Poland.

8. I base my discussion of the work of Kinsey and Masters and Johnson on Irvine (2005) and Robinson (1989).

9. Contrary to what is often claimed, the reports do not describe all Americans; they contain no mention of African Americans or any other ethnic minority (Irvine 2005, 25).

10. Based on these studies, Kinsey argued that homosexuality and heterosexuality form a continuum and proposed his famous scale to classify individuals according to their sexual behavior.

11. Paul Robinson (1989) draws attention to the fact that, to some extent, Havelock Ellis also did so. It is worth noting that already at the turn of the twentieth century, Magnus Hirschfeld referred to the quantitative data he had collected to argue against the laws that prohibited homosexual practices in Germany (Wolff 1986).

12. It would be a stretch to paint an image of a unified American feminist approach to sexuality. In principle, we can distinguish two groups. At the beginning of the twentieth century, Margaret Sanger had advocated for the sexual autonomy of women (Coates 2008). Sanger identified as a feminist and was active in the field of reproductive rights. She founded the first Planned Parenthood clinic in Brooklyn and significantly contributed to making the pill available to women (Oudshoorn 1994). The tradition begun by Sanger was continued by sex-positive feminists, such as Betty Dodson, Shere Hite, and Leonore Tiefer, whom I discuss later, and by activists and scholars involved in advocating against the penalization of pornography, such as Ann Snitow and Carole Vance (see, e.g., Vance 1984a; Vance and Snitow 1984; FACT Book Committee 1986). Other feminist groups approached the issue of sex with reserve and demanded, for example, the prohibition of pornography, seeing it as a cause of rape (antipornography feminists included, e.g., Catherine MacKinnon and Andrea Dworkin [1997]). The diversity of feminist approaches to sexuality is thoroughly discussed, for example, in the volume edited by Stevi Jackson and Sue Scott (1996).

13. *Off-label* or unlicensed use denotes treating ailments with drugs that are not registered for that purpose.

14. In the United States, relations between doctors and pharmaceutical companies are strengthened by the fact that public funding for research is very limited. In Europe, research receives significant funding from taxes distributed through, for example, European Union grants.

15. Masters and Johnson contributed significantly to the development and dissemination of this method of treatment.

16. Although Masters and Johnson contended that women and men experience different sexual dysfunctions (Irvine 2005, 165), it was their own approach to sexuality that incubated the idea that women and men experience fundamentally the same sexual dysfunctions (just as they experience sex in the same way). If sexual dysfunctions are the

same among women and men, then they can be treated using the same methods, regardless of cultural, social, and other aspects.

17. Advertising of prescription drugs directly addressed to patients, or, rather, consumers, was allowed in the United States in the 1980s.

18. The World Health Organization's (WHO's) 2001 report, "Mental Health: New Understanding, New Hope" (Bruntland 2001) and other sources based on research in various social contexts indicate the increasingly frequent occurrence of mental health disorders. The WHO warns that these disorders may concern up to 25% of the world population. Nikolas Rose (2006, 467–69) notes other studies showing that at some point in their lives, more than 26% of the population of the United States and more than 27% of the population of the European Union experience mental illnesses understood according to the DSM-4 definition. Rose also shows that the consumption of antidepressants is growing rapidly. In the period from 2000 to 2002, for example, the number of antidepressants prescribed to people under the age of nineteen increased significantly: in Germany by 13%, in the United States by 30%, in Spain by 48%, in Brazil by 49%, in Argentina by 54%, in Mexico by 56%, and in Great Britain by 68% (Rose 2006, 473). According to official data, in the United States in the years 2000–2001, 8.3% of doctor visits by young people (aged fourteen to eighteen years) ended with the prescription of psychotropic drugs to treat ADHD (Rose 2006, 474). This state of affairs is in part related to the expansion of pharmaceutical companies (see also Lakoff 2004, on Argentina during the 2001 financial crisis; Skultans 2007, on the situation in post-Soviet Latvia). Nevertheless, according to Rose, the increases in the number of illnesses and the consumption of drugs are primarily due to the change in the way we express dissatisfaction and social problems. Psychiatry is a new discourse and a new method of articulation; it has replaced religion and psychology (Rose 2006).

19. Clarke, Mamo, et al. (2010) understand the term *techno-science* following Bruno Latour (1987, chap. 4), who defines it as a combination of science and technology while emphasizing the interpenetration of these spheres and the role of various factors, including the nonhuman (e.g., pharmaceutical drugs), on the development of science.

20. On men, see Fishman and Mamo (2001); on women, who have the "right" to (i.e., duty of) a successful sex life and who should do everything in their power (self-control) to achieve it, see Canner 2009. In the last few years, a departure from medicine can be observed in sexual therapy. Many doctors are increasingly less enthusiastic about drugs, including those intended for the treatment of sexual dysfunctions (see, e.g., Morgentaler 2003; on Sweden, see Åsberg and Johnson 2009; E. Johnson 2008, 42–44).

21. The universal declaration of sexual rights was adopted at the World Congress of Sexologists in Hong Kong in 1999, and in 2002 it received the approval of the World Health Organization. The Polish text of the declaration, translated by Zbigniew Lew-Starowicz (2002*a*), is available on websites of Polish feminist organizations, such as the SPUNK Modern Education Foundation (https://spunk.pl), or the Federation for Women and Family Planning (www.federa.org.pl). The declaration was revised in 2014 and is available on the World Association for Sexual Health website (http://www.worldsexology.org/resources/declaration-of-sexual-rights/).

22. For example, the activist film *Orgasm Inc.* (Canner 2009) was screened in San Francisco in April 2011 as part of a conference of the Society for the Scientific Study of Sexuality. The film portrays Tiefer's campaign against the medicalization of sexuality and excessive cooperation with the pharmaceutical industry. The documentary was warmly received, and it was accompanied by many lectures in the feminist spirit. But the

medical researchers present at the conference who were associated with the new drug trials and who advocate a strictly medical approach to sexuality simply did not attend the film screening or the feminist presentations. In fact, they just did not respond to the criticism that was directed at their approach. Historically, Carole Vance (1983) has described the same lack of dialogue in the context of the 1970s.

2 | The Polish School of Sexology

After World War II in Poland, the first sexological institution was established in 1957. A few years after Kinsey published his reports, a group of doctors and educators reactivated the movement for conscious motherhood and its clinics, founding the Boy-Żeleński Society for Conscious Motherhood. The organization's name indicated continuity with the interwar activity. As before the war, the society struggled for what we would call today *sexual and reproductive rights* and placed them in the social context, including issues like women's emancipation and cultural and legal reform. Among the founders was Michalina Wisłocka, author of the most famous Polish book on sex. In an interview shortly before her death, she confessed, "I adored Boy-Żeleński, I thought he was a genius when it came to the popularization of contraception" (Wisłocka 2004). The society drew inspiration not only from the interwar tradition of sexual reform (Gawin 2009) but also from regular contact with the International Planned Parenthood Association. During socialism, the society was the leading organization focused on the promotion of contraception and sex education (for more, see Ignaciuk 2019; Kuźma-Markowska 2013).

In the following decades, the organization underwent name changes. First, Boy-Żeleński's name was removed. Next, in following world trends, the society was renamed the Family Planning Society and then the Society for Family Development (for clarity hereafter, I simplified the organization's name to the Polish Planned Parenthood Association [PPPA]). According to one of my interlocutors, a sexologist of the older generation, this last name change was implemented under pressure from the state authorities who did not want to aggravate the Catholic Church. For years, the organization's president was Mikołaj Kozakiewicz, professor of education, birth control activist, sex educator, and politician. The association ran counseling centers, organized various forms of sex education, trained sexologists and educators, and integrated the sexological milieu. The doctors and therapists interviewed for my research agreed that the training offered by the association was very progressive under communism and contributed greatly to the development of sexology and sex education in the country. Although the organization continues to exist to this day, my interview partners stressed that its period of greatness had passed.

From the beginning, sexology developed in sync with the association. With time, its orbit also came to revolve around the sexology institutes first opened at the Krakow Medical Academy and then at the Warsaw Center of Postgraduate Medical Education. Kazimierz Imieliński, Michalina Wisłocka, and Zbigniew Lew-Starowicz contributed significantly to the development of this discipline in postwar Poland. Their exceptional involvement is confirmed both in the analysis of Polish sexological publications and my fieldwork. The majority of sexologists interviewed for this project named Imieliński, Wisłocka and Lew-Starowicz as their role models and the most involved in the development of the discipline. Although great differences might seem to divide these three doctors—Wisłocka wrote primarily for women; Imieliński focused on the education of specialists, the development of the discipline, and the conduct of science more so than the others; and Lew-Starowicz is of a completely different generation—together they form what I call the "Polish school" of sexology. What the three have in common is an interdisciplinary approach, orientation toward patients (as a method of collecting material and choosing topics for publication and, at the same time, a strategy for the legitimization of knowledge), a popularizing and educational mission, and a shared context of work as state socialism mixed with Catholic morality.[1] This last common factor does not mean that the Polish school of sexology was created in isolation. Polish sexologists knew and took into account the work of non-Polish scholars like Masters and Johnson, but they placed it in an interdisciplinary and particular sociocultural context. They formed a separate thought collective (Fleck [1935] 1979) and came up with their own specific approach. In the following sections, I discuss how the Polish school of sexology was founded and developed in the special context of general reluctance on the part of both the state authorities and the Church. I also examine the approach to gender and sexuality that the school espoused.

Kazimierz Imieliński: The Rise of the Polish School of Sexology and Its System of Training Physicians and Therapists

The foremost figure of Polish postwar sexology, Kazimierz Imieliński (born 1929, died 2010), represented the tradition derived from the interwar period. Imieliński was the first in Poland to obtain the title of specialist in sexology (in 1963) and to habilitate in the field.[2] He also founded the first strictly sexological centers: the Institute of Sexology at the Medical Academy in Krakow in 1973 and the Institute of Sexology and Pathology of Human Relations at the Warsaw Center of Postgraduate Medical Education in 1981 (Depko 2010, 22; Imieliński 1985b, 115). At these centers, specialists trained to work as sexologists, conducted scientific research, and treated patients.[3]

Imieliński graduated in 1954 from the Medical Academy in Krakow and took up a position at an internal medicine clinic (Imieliński 1974a). In an interview he gave to the weekly magazine *Itd* (*Etc*) in 1967, he talked about his first encounter with sexology in 1958:

> I was on a fellowship in Cologne and I had the sincere intention of continuing with internal medicine. Work at the clinic did not absorb me completely, so I had a lot of free time. Being a workaholic by nature, I spent my time off at the library and it was there that I came across sexological publications.[4] This field of medical science was at the time very little known in Poland, and even less popular. This gave me a kick: transfer it to the Polish terrain and contribute to the popularization of, in the end,

a non-trivial piece of knowledge about human beings. After returning home, I asked again for a scholarship, this time in the field of sexology, and I ended up getting my specialization at the Gdańsk Clinic for Psychiatric Disorders under the supervision of Prof. T. Bilikiewicz. (Imieliński 1967c, 10)

Imieliński managed to do more than just transfer sexology to Poland: he contributed to the formation of a dynamic, homegrown school of sexology, distinct from other traditions, especially, that in the United States. How does Imieliński differ from North American sexologists? His students claimed that Imieliński stood out because of his attempts at humanizing medicine, which he saw as a solution to medicine's suffering from an inability to cope with the human soul (Wasilewski and Dulko 2011; see also Imieliński et al. 1997). The basic features of the Polish school of sexology—an interdisciplinary approach, a patient orientation, and a popularizing mission—derive from this attitude. It would be a mistake to overlook the connection between this fact and the scholarly background of Imieliński's teachers: Kazimierz Dąbrowski and Tadeusz Bilikiewicz. Both were not only medical doctors but also philosophers and scholars with broad academic horizons rooted in the interwar tradition. Imieliński was also influenced by developments in Polish humanist psychiatry (see, e.g., Kępiński 1988; Maciuszek 1996). Moreover, like his teachers and other influential Polish sexologists, Imieliński embraced the intellectual ethos in which physicians and the elites in general were obliged to educate members of the lower social strata.

From the beginning, Imieliński saw human sexuality as multifaceted and thus requiring a holistic approach. This was how sexology as a discipline was to approach sexuality. In the already quoted interview, Imieliński explained (1967c, 10), "It is believed that sexology is a highly narrow specialization. This is a huge misconception. Needless to say that it is closely related to medical disciplines such as psychiatry, neurology, urology . . . but please note links of sexology to disciplines which are not part of the natural sciences: to pedagogy, law, psychology, and even someone could insist—to theology. And in this, let the Bible be my witness."

Such was the approach that Imieliński passed on to the next generation of sexologists and that he had pursued since the establishment of the Department of Sexology in Kraków. One of Imieliński's first interns, Stanisław Dulko, recalled that during the internship in Kraków, his teacher also saw to his cultural education: Imieliński asked his local coworkers to take the young doctor from Warsaw under their wing. In this way, Dulko spent all his afternoons and evenings learning about the intellectual and artistic life of Kraków, which at the time was Poland's capital of the arts (Wasilewski and Dulko 2011).

This model of sexological practice and training developed fully in the 1980s alongside the Institute of Sexology and Pathology of Human Relations at the Center of Postgraduate Medical Education in Warsaw. How did this approach figure in the daily work of the institute? Imieliński was an excellent organizer. The commitment of his team, which included the physicians Wiesław Czerniekiewicz, Stanisław Dulko, and Wiesława Sokołowska-Rucińska and the assistant Grażyna Jędrzej, to the idea of developing a research treatment center and institutionalizing sexology went far beyond their formal duties. As Imieliński (1985b, 115) wrote, "We started from scratch. We had a lot of enthusiasm and we knew what we wanted." Having discussed the matter collectively, Imieliński and his colleagues agreed on what the center should look like:

> The Institute is to be adapted to its activities and to the specificity of people who suffer from emotional and sexual disorders, as well as marital and family conflicts. Because patients consider these types of disorders as their most intimate secrets, they should be provided appropriate treatment conditions. We have therefore resigned from a typically medical interior for a more "homey" atmosphere at the Institute. The aesthetically pleasing, or "warm" style of the offices reduces emotional tension and stress in people who come to reveal their intimate problems; this creates conditions for good contact, which facilitates diagnosis and therapy. (115)

Imieliński's team insisted on the institute's autonomy from the hospital and on doing things the unorthodox way. The latter was a necessity in the early 1980s, as the doctors soon discovered:[5]

> The "insurmountable" difficulties showed up already in the first days, when we were clearing debris from the walls we had removed. There was a shortage of bricks and cement to erect new walls separating the Institute from the rest of the building (and the need to isolate our patients, due to the nature of their disorders, was an indispensable condition for the good functioning of the Institute). There were no materials in the Hospital's warehouse and you could not buy them anywhere. . . . Then Czernikiewicz remembered that he had some bricks and cement left over after a recent renovation at his own house. He paid out of his own pocket to have these materials brought over. He donated them for the Institute's use and the wall was built. (115–16)

During this period, wrote Imieliński (1985b, 117), physicians worked so hard that the construction workers who were remodeling the center brought them cookies so that they would not be hungry. After completing renovations, the team began assembling the furnishings, which required traveling around Poland to purchase equipment, sewing curtains, and buying necessary supplies using their private funds.[6] Imieliński recalled, "Finally, I had to officially prohibit paying for small repairs or investments with private money. . . . I write about this to give the atmosphere of those days; great enthusiasm, commitment and dedication to the cause on the part of all the Institute's employees" (117). The library was opened thanks to book donations, and film projections were made possible because of a donated VCR. The institute opened March 30, 1981.

Imieliński was a demanding boss and teacher. To this day, his students and colleagues recall that they were not allowed to be late to work or to a lecture. These principles were clearly articulated: "We started by introducing the unconditional requirement of formal discipline, where work began at 8 o'clock and not 5 minutes after 8 o'clock. . . . I had to be hard and consistent. In an era of frivolous attitudes to work, it was a tough school" (Imieliński 1985b, 118–19). He insisted on the proper treatment of patients: "'Training' also involved teaching politeness, kindness, and respect for other people. It applied to all employees but particularly those with whom patients had first contact, which required an especially high level of tact, subtlety, and consideration" (119). Imieliński wanted all his staff, as he put it, to speak "the same language" (118), even more so as new people joined the team. Twice a week employees took part in meetings devoted to discussing specific cases and world sexological literature. They diagnosed patients together; every patient was assigned both a physician and a psychologist. Imieliński noted that the diagnostic process lasted from six to fourteen hours, whereas treatment usually took from eight to thirty hours (119). Imieliński defined the specifics of sexology in clear terms: "we deal with the nooks and crannies of the human psyche, not with human genitals" (119). He saw the human psyche broadly—he noticed the external elements that influenced it, and he believed that the sexologist should know not only medicine and psychology but also sociology, pedagogy, ethics, law, and so on (119).

Based on these assumptions, Imieliński set up a sexology training program that attracted students from all over Poland. The program reflected how its founder saw the specifics of a sexologist's work. Imieliński also published works that served as teaching materials for successive generations of Polish sexologists. At the core of this curriculum lies *An Outline of Sexology and Sexual Medicine* (*Zarys seksuologii i seksiatrii*; Imieliński 1982) and a three-volume compendium edited by Imieliński, the titles of which reflect his interdisciplinary interests: *Biological Sexology* (*Seksuologia biologiczna*; Imieliński [1980] 1985c), *Cultural Sexology* (*Seksuologia kulturowa*; Imieliński [1980] 1984a), and *Social Sexology* (*Seksuologia społeczna*; Imieliński [1977] 1984b).

The institute also spearheaded scientific research. Its employees presented their data at home and abroad (mainly in the countries of the Eastern Bloc but also in the United States).

In retrospect, interviewees who collaborated or studied with Imieliński in the 1980s particularly appreciated the interdisciplinary nature of his work. A doctor who was a student of Imieliński's spoke of two primary aspects of his interdisciplinary approach: one within the scope of medicine, where sexology includes psychiatry, endocrinology, gynecology, and urology, and the other comprising "elements such as psychology, sociology, pedagogy, law, philosophy, ethics, cultural studies, art broadly defined, film and musical creativity, poetry, sculpture, painting, history, history of civilization, history of ideas, and the history of human thought." The interlocutor observed that "a philosophical approach intertwines with religious and theological aspects." In practice, extensive cooperation with representatives of the mentioned disciplines included invitations to participate in seminars and to give lectures. The institute even employed a priest in the 1980s, Dr. Stefan Kornas, who provided pastoral support to people preparing for gender reassignment surgery (Wasilewski and Dulko 2011).[7] My interview partners emphasized that Imieliński attached great importance to psychology. As mentioned, in the United States, medical and psychological approaches were in conflict. In Poland, psychology has always been and remains an integral part of sexology. The psychologists with whom I spoke pointed to Imieliński's role in including psychology within mainstream sexology in Poland. Were it not for him, they told me, as psychologists they could not also be sexologists.

Orientation toward patients, another aspect of Imieliński's Polish sexology, was linked closely with the interdisciplinary perspective and consisted of both elevated standards of courtesy and his holistic, time-consuming approach. Above all, patient orientation involved considering the patient's own experiences in shaping both practice and sexological theory. Masters and Johnson recruited fully sexually able volunteers, whereas Imieliński based his understanding of sexology on the experiences and narratives of the patients with whom he had contact in his daily medical work and on the feedback he received from people who read his works and listened to his lectures. In this way, he followed suit with the many German-speaking masters of sexology before him, with Krafft-Ebing at the forefront. This does not mean that he did not know North American research; it simply was not the basis of his work. Many years before Masters and Johnson proposed sexual therapy involving couples, Imieliński and his teacher Bilikiewicz had already developed a similar method. They used it with success and described it in their writing (Imieliński 1974a).

The last feature of Imieliński's approach to sexology, the popularization of knowledge, is closely related to the previous two. According to Imieliński, the road to sexual health leads through education. Apart from medical and scientific work, Imieliński was engaged in consciousness-raising activities. He authored numerous educational works (including *Man and Sex* [*Człowiek i seks*; Imieliński 1985a] and *Eroticism* [*Erotyzm*; Imieliński 1970]), as well as a guidebook (*Sexual Life: Psycho-hygiene* [*Życie seksualne człowieka. Psychohigiena*; Imieliński [1965] 1967a). He toured the country lecturing and was published in the popular press—for example, in the student magazine *Etc*, which reprinted sections of his books, including *The Intimate Life of Man* (*Życie intymne człowieka*; Imieliński 1974b) and *Eroticism* (1970). The extent to which he avowed the belief that knowledge is key is evident in his article for *Etc*: "In love we are illiterate as we have never learned the rules, by which it is governed" (Imieliński 1967a, 14), suggesting a need for education in love and sexuality. This theme recurs in other articles in which Imieliński discusses specific cases and shows the main problem to be lack of knowledge. For example, he reassured his female patients and readers who were worried that orgasm induced by clitoral stimulation was abnormal (Imieliński 1967b). Like other doctors, therapists, and researchers,[8] Imieliński linked knowledge with pleasure and recognized the dissemination of the former as the responsibility of sexologists. Based on this understanding, there is no satisfaction without knowledge; this interpretation suggests that in Western civilization, only modern medicine liberates sexuality from the yoke of limitations levied by Christianity and tradition. Such a vision of progress participates in the construction of a particular type of subject by means of sexological discourse (Foucault 1978). As I have tried to show by juxtaposing the development of sexology in Poland and in the United States, such progress could have different trajectories.

Michalina Wisłocka and Her Sexual Revolution

In an interview just before her death, Michalina Wisłocka (2004; born 1921, died 2005) claimed that her book *The Art of Love* sold seven million copies. This information is reiterated in many other places, including the publisher's websites.[9] Wisłocka never explained how she got this information, and it seems rather inflated. That is also how some of the interviewees see it: "Michalina exaggerated a little," said one, a sexologist of the older generation. Nevertheless, *The Art of Love* played an important role in shaping the sexual landscape of the Polish People's Republic and revolutionized the way Poles thought about sex. Its significance was confirmed in a poll by the weekly *Politics* (*Polityka*), in which the book was voted among the most important of the socialist period (Pietkiewicz 2005).[10] A bookseller once told me that after the poet Wisława Szymborska won the Nobel Prize for Literature in 1996, people came en masse to his shop to buy books by Michalina Wisłocka. Although their names sounded similar in Polish, Wisłocka's work was commonly discussed and thus more familiar to people than Szymborska's celebrated poetry.

The Art of Love, like Wisłocka's other texts, fits into the basic assumptions of the Polish school of sexology. Wisłocka's work is interdisciplinary and places sex in a broad context based on the experiences of patients. Although she had scientific aspirations, Wisłocka wrote in a way that was accessible not just to specialists; it had a popularizing and educational function.

What is *The Art of Love* about? What kind of vision of sexuality and gender does the author propose? What was her sexology? What controversies accompanied the book's publication? And how was it received by readers and experts alike?

Above all, like Imieliński, Wisłocka centered her work on contact with patients. In the introduction to *The Art of Love*, she wrote that her book was based on experience gained over the course of fifteen years of medical practice. This involved conversations with women, who, incidentally, generally adored her (Laszuk 2011). In the book's first edition, Wisłocka mentioned that she conducted interviews with five thousand gynecological patients and one thousand sexological patients (Wisłocka 1978, 10). Furthermore, Wisłocka's research included letters addressed to the Correspondence Clinic at the PPPA and to the monthly *Health* (*Zdrowie*) as well as purely scientific work (she was fascinated by cytological and hormonal research) and her popular writing experience.[11] "I fought tooth and nail for civilized emotional and sexual life," she wrote (9), implying her activities associated with the PPPA, which included public lectures on topics related to sexuality.[12] The advice she was able to give in this manner included sexual difficulties, contraception, and various ailments. As a gynecologist, Wisłocka spoke mainly with women, but she addressed the book to "both sexes" (10). Already, in the beginning of *The Art of Love*, it is apparent how the author understands the role of women in a relationship: "I do not think this attitude represents a negative side of the book because I am convinced that women hold love and the quality of the emotional life of the family in their hands" (10).

The Art of Love addresses sexual development, hormonal activity, the psyche and physiology of women and men, the anatomy of the genitals, sexual initiation, masturbation, orgasm, relations between the sexes, sexual health, contraception, and love.[13] As Wisłocka confessed in an interview given to *The Mirror*, a magazine published by the Communist League of Polish Women (on the league, see, e.g., Nowak 2009; Grabowska 2018), she was guided by the principle that "sexology is a matter of body, spirit and mind; I would even say it is more a matter of the psyche than of the body" (Wisłocka 1979). The chapter called "Monotony: The Enemy of Love," in which readers could find an "overview of basic sexual positions," spawned the greatest interest and the most controversy. Descriptions were accompanied by drawings: a white silhouette of a woman and a black silhouette of a man in the sexual act, along with sketches illustrating how the penis penetrates the vagina in a given position. Some more recent editions (Wisłocka [1978] 1995) were enriched with photographs. For her part, Wisłocka supplemented subsequent editions with the latest medical discoveries, mainly in the field of contraception.

The Art of Love is much more than a catalog of sexual positions. Wisłocka wrote a lot about love and marriage, relations between women and men, and about gender roles in general. Insofar as the book is revolutionary in its candor on matters of sex, it recycles tired stereotypes when it comes to gender roles. For Wisłocka, femininity goes hand in hand with motherhood, the family, passivity, and self-control when it comes to sexual matters. In contrast, she associates masculinity with the public sphere, formal employment, an active lifestyle, and a lack of self-control in sexual matters. What more, Wisłocka sees the emancipation of women as potentially harmful to bedroom relations. She defines sex as intercourse between men and women: "Finally, at the end of the long and work-intensive process of developing affection comes love for a member of the opposite sex. The love between a man and a woman becomes the synthesis of all forms experienced before—it is the desire and realization of a physical and emotional union" (Wisłocka 1978, 22). There is scarce reference to homosexuality in *The Art of Love*.[14] Later in the book I analyze how Wisłocka understood gender and sexuality and how she approached feminism. Because *The Art of Love* was a revolutionary text that electrified public opinion and induced hostility on the part of the medical establishment, the censors, and the Church, and because the publication of the book was accompanied by numerous controversies, I would like to take a closer look at how the book came to be published and at how it was received.[15] The various challenges that Wisłocka overcame illustrate the social climate in which sexology developed in Poland.

Although the book was written in the first half of the 1970s, it came out in 1978. Fragments were printed earlier in the magazine *Perspectives* (*Perspektywy*). What was the fate of *The Art of Love*? In many interviews, Wisłocka alleged that the first obstacle to publication was that the manuscript had been negatively evaluated by sexology and education specialists. She claimed that Kozakiewicz and Imieliński wrote unflattering peer reviews of the book, accusing her of debauchery: "The author must take into account the culture and traditions of

Polish society. In all popular world literature I have never seen over 100 pages about sex and orgasm. The author herself gets off on writing these mouthwatering stanzas" (quoted in Pietkiewicz 2005). Her critics also reproached her for engaging in pornography, which was illegal in Poland under socialism: "The book requires a reduction of chatter and hedonism, which emanate erotomania. The author will have to defend herself against allegations of pornography under the guise of information [in our cultural context]" (quoted in Pietkiewicz 2005).[16] According to Wisłocka, it was these reviews and not political motivations that delayed the book's publication. When asked in an interview, "Were the communists afraid to release *The Art of Love*?" Wisłocka (2004) replied, "It wasn't the communists who were afraid, but the competition. That no one would buy their books anymore, once mine came out. Four long years it was held under arrest at the Central Committee of the Communist Party: that was the result. The communists didn't give a shit about genitals. They cared that Mr. Kozakiewicz said that the book could not come out, and that the second sexologist, Mr. Imieliński, agreed."

Łukasz Szymański, an editor at Iskry, the press that eventually published the book, saw the matter differently. He suggested that the communists may well have been afraid; they did not want to turn the nation's attention away from more important issues, like building socialism. In addition, they did not want to risk conflict with the Church, which, it was assumed, would not be pleased with the book (Szołajski 2001). Many sexologists interviewed for this research were of a similar opinion. A sexologist of the older generation told me:

> Under socialism . . . sex was treated as . . . well . . . sex, sexual behavior, or sexological knowledge was treated as something strange, something unnecessary, something funny, intimate, it varied. The first books to come out, like *The Art of Love* by Dr. Michalina Wisłocka . . . the ordeal that woman had to go through to get that book published, because books like that didn't exist, it was something new. We live in a Christian culture, and the Church . . . according to the Church's teachings, sex is dirty, evil and only meant for procreation, which is why it shouldn't be talked about at all. . . . Because of this, the Church's teachings influence both politicians and everything else.

These concerns turned out to be unwarranted, at least in part. Wisłocka herself claimed that the Church was not out to undermine her (see, e.g., Wisłocka 2004), although some conservative Catholics certainly did not value her work. Among this group was doctor and writer Kinga Wiśniewska-Roszkowska, who published extensively on sexuality and authored such books as *Asceticism, Morality, Health* (*Asceza, moralność, zdrowie*; Wiśniewska-Roszkowska 1980; Chałupnik 2008, 425, 427; Wisłocka 2004). Nevertheless, many Catholic critics were favorable to *The Art of Love* because of Wisłocka's emphasis on love, although at the same time they criticized her for promoting the use of contraception (see, e.g., Dominican priest Władysław Skrzydlewski's statement in Szołajski [2001]). Sometimes their attitude was neutral, as in the case of the lectures on contraception, which often ended in argument. As Wisłocka (2004) would say, "And the priest just sat there and smiled mysteriously." On numerous occasions, Wisłocka (1997) affirmed that she was not an anti-Catholic (she considered herself a Protestant). In the latter half of the 1980s, for example, she took part in a discussion on the subject of a progressive handbook on sex education written by Wiesław Sokoluk, Dagmara Andziak, and Maria Trawińska (1987). Referring to a statement made by Magdalena Rulska from *Sztandar Młodych* (*Youth Banner*, a popular daily addressed to young people), who was conducting an interview with Wisłocka, that "the book is criticized for violating moral regulations, also those of the Catholic faith," Wisłocka (1987) responded:

> In writing such a book, it is necessary to take into account that violating these rules will result in a sea of protest. Taboo topics are: premarital intercourse, contraception in all its varieties, and youth masturbation. I could be accused of criticizing the handbook for taking up matters that I did not care to ignore in my own book. But what is allowed the author in his own book, which anyone can read or reject at will, should be treated with immense care and prudence in a handbook that is obligatory reading for school children. And here both parents and the Catholic Church, which has many followers in this country, should be taken into consideration.

Furthermore, in her book *Success in Love* (*Sukces w miłości*; Wisłocka 1993b), Wisłocka limited contraception to the so-called natural methods approved by the Church. She commented on this in an interview: "The chapter on contraception, here a nod to the Catholic Church, only discusses biological methods. This choice was made with the youth in mind, who can learn a lot about love from the book" (Wisłocka 1993a).[17] The book's publication coincided with what was probably the hottest moment in the Polish debate on birth control, ultimately culminating in significant restriction in access to abortion.

Returning to the 1970s, Wisłocka (2004) herself confirmed that the authorities had various reservations as to her book, *The Art of Love*:

> When the book finally made it to the censorship, the censors said the pictures of the sex positions were too big, and they were the size of postcards. We made them smaller and smaller, and finally they were the size of a postage stamp. Whenever I made them smaller, it wasn't enough, they needed to be even smaller. And it went like this on and on. In the end, when they were so small, that you couldn't tell which was the woman, and which was the man, I said to our graphic artist: "Color in the men black and the women white, or vice versa, so that you can see whose legs, whose hands, because all this together is good for nothing." He did it, and indeed the drawings are very legible. Then they started asking: "But why a white woman with a Negro?" That was the biggest complaint. . . . Once the censorship agreed, stamp and seal, *The Art of Love* was supposed to come out in three months. And then suddenly, out of the blue, several men in strange top hats, like in a movie, paid a visit to the Iskry publishing house. They ordered the director to close the premises and started a search of the office desks, one by one. They came to the editor, Mrs. Męcina, and as she had her mind in the right place, she asked the Censorship Office

for two sealed copies. They gave her two, one she hid deep in the safe, the other one was in a drawer. "Please, return the sealed document." They decided that they got everything. She took a big risk, if they had found the second copy.

At last, however, the story continued:

> A new director came to the publishing house Iskry. And my friend Rysio Wiśniowski, a young socialist activist, but also a journalist, said to me: "You know, I know this gentleman, we went to school together, I'll talk to him. The book is great, maybe before he catches on, he'll release it." The new head of the publishing house went to see the minister and told him: "It's a quiet book for married couples, so that they get informed and won't go at it fists and all, bla, bla, bla." And the minister said: "Here on the cover you will put a groom in a bow tie and a bride in a veil and it will be a pair of newlyweds. And they will not say that it is so debauched, because if it's for married couples, then it's for married couples." (Wisłocka 2004)

Indeed, the cover of the first edition (Wisłocka 1978) portrays a pair of newlyweds. Only the editions from the 1980s were adorned with a woman and a man in a more erotic pose. A careful reading of the book shows, however, that the cover proposed by the communist authorities more accurately reflected its actual line. In the book, Wisłocka often addresses married couples, proposing solutions aimed at breaking, as she calls it, boredom in marriage.[18] Iskry's new director, Łukasz Szymański, already referred to earlier in this text, claimed that the book was finally accepted for publication because he managed to convince Jerzy Łukaszewicz, the press and propaganda secretary of the Central Committee, to have his wife read *The Art of Love* (Szołajski 2001).

When the book finally came out, the entire print run of one hundred thousand copies sold out immediately.[19] Allegedly, pirated copies were available for purchase before the book's publication (Szołajski 2001). Even colleagues found it difficult to get a copy of the book, recalled one interviewee who worked at the PPPA in the 1970s: "I remember myself standing in line to buy the book at Uniwersus [one of the biggest bookstores in Warsaw at that time]. . . . I remember going there, I bought books for the clinic and we sold them, patients and other people who came by would buy them. . . . There was a separate stand [at Uniwersus], downstairs in the lobby where they only kept Wisłocka's books and they sold like fresh buns, a line of twenty people, it went fast."

It is worth adding that *The Art of Love* was also popular because of the way it was written. Wisłocka put a lot of effort into making sure the book was an accessible read. In one interview she said, "I remember when I finished *The Art of Love*, I took the manuscript to Melchior Wańkowicz [a widely-read Polish writer and journalist]. . . . I wanted him to tell me whether the book had a warm feminine feel, or if it was cold, indifferent. He wrote to me, 'The book is written in beautiful, popular language.' I was a little angry. I thought, By *popular language* does he mean what is spoken on the street? We checked the dictionary with a friend: *popular language* means living modern language. Oh, I got unnecessarily upset" (Wisłocka 2004).

The book was held in high esteem not only by colleagues from the PPPA but also by journalists. *Politics* magazine published a review by Dariusz Fikus, entitled "Van de Velde in Polish Wearing a Skirt" (Fikus 1979). The review is generally very positive. The critic emphasized that Wisłocka shows readers how to talk about sex, which is necessary because once there were only manuals for those in love (available in the houses of the prewar intelligentsia), not for those interested in sexuality; today, even the mainstream press in the United States discusses homosexuality. But at times, wrote Fikus, Wisłocka says too much: "For as long as Dr. Wisłocka is talking about orgasm . . . I am impressed, but when she tries to leave the gynecological office and the bedroom, her reflections become rather shallow." For example, Fikus noted, when she advises against nonmarital sex, "if she wants to give moral guidance on the margins of her handbook *The Art of Love*, she has to rise to a slightly higher level." He concluded, "Wisłocka is undoubtedly a Van de Veld of our time, not an Erich Fromm." This last remark must have irritated Wisłocka, as she kept asserting in her interviews that she wrote about love and eroticism, not about sex. Fikus also did not like the graphic art. His review served to confirm the book's popularity; just a few months after publication, it was only available on the black market, for 600 Polish zlotys (the price listed on the cover of the first edition was 56 zlotys). Meanwhile another reviewer, Zbigniew Iwanicki, writing in *New Books* (*Nowe Książki*), praised what Fikus did not like: "A proper positioning of sexuality in our lives as a whole distinguishes *The Art of Love* from guidebooks of the 'gymnastics-performance' sort" (Iwanicki 1979).[20] "Personally," Iwanicki said, "I highly appreciate the book in question because it delves deeply, above all, into the 'margins of the techniques of sexual life' (an important element of lasting love in contemporary times). This indicates more than just the author's extensive professional knowledge. It suggests wisdom, which is the result of many experiences, observations, reflections, and responsibilities that serve to develop a rare coherent structure of values. Only in such circumstances does sexuality not become the mere illusion of liberation, ominous of hidden troubles and disasters (of the personal sort, for the married couple, and in the family)."

To this day, many sexologists and commentators on social life in Poland emphasize that Wisłocka revolutionized the approach to sex in the country. On June 30, 2011, the anniversary of Wisłocka's birthday, leading Polish sex researcher and educator Zbigniew Izdebski unveiled a memorial plaque in Warsaw's Old Town: "Michalina Wisłocka, MD, gynecologist and sexologist, lived in this house. Author of the book *The Art of Love*. The most renowned advocate of sexological knowledge and pioneer of infertility treatment in Poland. She taught people happy love." The ceremony presented an opportunity to discuss Wisłocka's legacy. Some called attention to the fact that the knowledge forwarded by Wisłocka has since become partly obsolete; however, experts—including my interview partners, who are sexologists of different generations—agree that she played a revolutionary role in matters of sexuality. One, a gynecologist and sexologist in his fifties, asserted, "I am of the generation where *The Art of Love* flourished, that is, it was . . . a somewhat underground publication, something that was passed from hand to hand under the tables . . . and from this we . . . learned sexuality, and had any idea about sexuality, about intercourse, but . . . it is . . . a popular publication, more popular than scientific, more fiction than science, but that didn't matter."

Similarly, Zbigniew Lew-Starowicz, in a comment shortly after Wisłocka's death, wrote, "There is no other person in Poland who has given people as much happiness as Michalina Wisłocka. She always thought about others in terms of love and happiness. She treated sex in the same way" (quoted in ij 2005). To this day, sexologists mention Wisłocka on many occasions. For example, the Fourth National Debate on Sexual Health, organized and opened by Zbigniew Izdebski, began with a tribute to the author of *The Art of Love* and the assertion that, thanks to her, Polish women learned about sex (field notes, November 21, 2011; for sexologists' contemporary comments on Wisłocka, see, e.g., Laszuk 2011; Dąbrowa 2011).

The publication of *The Art of Love* was also met with contempt. Some readers considered the book to be incompatible with socialist ideology. A letter to *Politics* magazine read: "A valid detachment from the rigor of religious ethics does not always entail a rapprochement with socialist ethics. In following Wisłocka, it leads to gravitation towards another extreme, liberalism, or hedonistic bourgeois ethics" (quoted in Kubczak 1986).

As mentioned before, despite the fact that the book in its entirety came out only in 1978, fragments were published in the popular press in the early 1970s. Already back then, Wisłocka prompted a scandal by calling marital obligation "a little game in a bed." Outraged readers flooded the mailboxes of the editorial staff: "I am kindly asking you to answer, what right this lady has to refer to the most transcendent issues as great and attractive fun" (letter quoted in Pietkiewicz 2005); and, "Currently, standing on the brink of my life, I finally understand why juvenile detention centers and prisons are filled to the brim with Polish youth, the future of the nation. I understand how, with the help of the anti-Christ, the young people of our Polish Land are being corrupted. Today, I thank God that moral ethics and subtlety were instilled in me" (quoted in Kubczak 1986). Readers also addressed their letters of indignation to *Politics*: "We raise our children to be good and righteous citizens of the fatherland. Many mothers are outraged at the mass media, overflowing with instructions for how to 'play in bed.' We will deal with this ourselves." Some readers believed that young people were not interested in sex: "Young people are not interested in the art of loving which distracts them from their studies, sports, technical interests, model-building, and other civilized activities" (quoted in Kubczak 1986). In turn, Lew-Starowicz thought that *The Art of Love* was "too bold for those times" (MKA 2005).

In 2016, Poland rediscovered Wisłocka. A new edition of *The Art of Love*, complete with beautiful graphic design, was released by a leading Polish publisher. A new introduction was written by Zbigniew Izdebski, and thanks to his efforts, a film was made about the book's history. The film portrays an alleged behind-the-scenes theme related to the book's publication. According to the producers' interpretation, the book was allowed to come out because the wives of the

Communist apparatchiks (who were Wisłocka's patients) threatened their husbands that they would go on sex strike. The film also shows Wisłocka as a women's emancipation activist and the mother of Polish feminism (Sadowska 2017). I have a lot of sympathy for this type of approach as I likewise try to shed light on the achievements of Polish sexology in this book. Nevertheless, such a portrayal is quite problematic, especially because Wisłocka approached equality between the genders with considerable reserve. The new edition of the book and the premiere of the film were accompanied by a dynamic advertising campaign that showed the guidebook as necessary and up-to-date. Unfortunately, no room was left for any critique or in-depth evaluation of Wisłocka's legacy.

Zbigniew Lew-Starowicz: Sexology and the Postsocialist Transformation

Zbigniew Lew-Starowicz (born in 1943) personifies today's institutionalized sexology in Poland. President of the Polish Sexological Society, until recently he also headed the Polish Society of Sexual Medicine.[21] Lew-Starowicz is in charge of sexology education at the Center of Postgraduate Medical Education in Warsaw (the state medical education program) and its Medical Sexology and Psychotherapy Institute (formerly the Institute of Sexology and Pathology of Human Relations, established by Imieliński). He is a national consultant on sexology—that is, he oversees sexological practice in Poland.[22] Furthermore, Lew-Starowicz supervises psychotherapy for sexual disorders and serves as an expert witness in criminal and civil matters. In addition, he teaches future sexologists at two Warsaw universities: the Academy of Physical Education and the University of Economics and Human Sciences. He has published numerous scientific publications, including academic textbooks (e.g., Lew-Starowicz and Skrzypulec 2010; Lew-Starowicz 1985a, 1988e). Lew-Starowicz completed his medical studies in Łódź at the Military Medical Academy (no longer in operation) in 1966. In the years 1962–63, he attended lectures held by Imieliński (Lew-Starowicz 2011b). In 1981, he defended his doctorate, and in 1986, he completed his habilitation with a thesis on sexuality and relationships among alcohol and pharmaceutical drug addicts (Lew-Starowicz 1984c).[23] He is a sexologist, a psychiatrist, and a psychotherapist. For decades he worked at the clinic run by the PPPA. He is currently the director of the Lew-Starowicz Therapy Center (http://lew-starowicz .pl/), which he opened in partnership with his son, Michał.

Sexology, according to the professor, whose career spans two decades of socialist and two decades of postsocialist Poland, is very much in line with the Polish school of sexology. Although none of the books he wrote attained such great readership as *The Art of Love*, Lew-Starowicz's books were and continue to be widely read. In the 1980s, *Sex on Equal Terms* (Lew-Starowicz 1983f) came out in four editions, with one hundred thousand copies each. Successive generations learned about sex from Lew-Starowicz's articles, published in magazines addressed to various groups of readers: students read him in *Etc*, youth read him in *Together* (*Razem*), women read him in *Zwierciadło* (*The Mirror*), and residents of rural areas followed him in *Cultural Weekly* (*Tygodnik Kulturalny*). To this day, the professor is regularly asked for commentary by the media and publishes extensively; for instance, in 2011–12 he published four popular books about sexuality (*On Women* [*O Kobiecie*], 2011*a*; *On Men* [*O Mężczyźnie*], 2012*b*; *On Love* [*O Miłości*], 2012*c*; and *A Lion in the Bedroom* [*Lew w Sypialni*], 2012*a*). Just like *The Art of Love*, Lew-Starowicz's texts addressed to the general public are written in a manner that is accessible to laypeople and discuss not only the problems but also the benefits associated with sex. In a 1969 interview for *Etc*, he said, "It is necessary to disseminate knowledge about the nonpathological, positive facts, about long-term relationships, about the ones that are successful and happy" (Lew-Starowicz 1969*b*, 14).

From the beginning, Lew-Starowicz's approach was interdisciplinary and holistic. This is easily discernible in his cycle of articles written for *Etc*. A text from 1970, entitled "The Nature of the Sex Drive," was written because Lew-Starowicz was concerned about the letters he had been receiving from readers and about the questions he was asked during his meetings with students. He wrote, "Sexual drive is isolated in the consciousness of some people from activities of the highest sort: those intellectual, emotional, and aesthetic. Boiling sex down to impulsive-hormonal reactions not only distorts its nature, but in consequence may lead to a condescending stance on sex, as an activity of a lower sort." (Lew-Starowicz 1970*a*, 14). In another article he defines the sexual act in a similar spirit:

> The love game is the stage preceding the sexual act, which is an extremely complicated and complex construction, an activity that encompasses the entire psychophysical personality. Unfortunately, for some people the act is only a means to discharge their excitement and to satisfy their momentary desires. What motivates initiating a love game before the act is also often immature. Some are steered by curiosity, while others by situations which oblige a display of "male" behavior or "proof of love." Meanwhile, love should be the sole motivation; the desire to fuse, to give yourself to another person, to sink in inconceivable oneness. The act should serve as the crown reward of developed psychic ties, an expression of the desire to enter the world of another human being. (Lew-Starowicz 1971*a*, 14)

Lew-Starowicz makes references to both Ovid and Masters and Johnson as sources of his knowledge. Other sources include science, the arts, and various cultural contexts, and in his texts he often uses examples from other parts of the world or historical periods (see, e.g., Lew-Starowicz 1991).

The most important sources of Lew-Starowicz's knowledge are his patients and the many people who have written letters to him over the years. Lew-Starowicz refers to their experiences in his writing and teaching and in treating patients. He examines his patients' experiences with scientific scrutiny, classifying and analyzing the problems for which people come to see him. For example, his book *The Treatment of Functional Sexual Disorders* (*Leczenie czynnościowych zaburzeń seksualnych*), addressed to physicians of various specializations, is an analysis of "a population of 660 patients diagnosed with sexual neuroses and

120 patients diagnosed with neuroses accompanied by sexual disorders, both of which were part of the author's research program in 1970–1982" (Lew-Starowicz 1985a, 5). As he wrote, the book is based on both "world sexological literature" and the "the author's own experience": "Many methods of patient examination and treatment, along with scales of measurement, assessments of treatment effectiveness, and prognosis were presented in an altered version, with the option of putting them to use in outpatient settings so as to facilitate the doctor's work" (5).

Furthermore, in an article published in the *Sexological Review* (*Przegląd Seksuologiczny*), Lew-Starowicz and his team analyzed the problems for which young patients (aged fourteen to thirty-one years) came to him in the period from 2004 to 2010 (Szymańska, Lew-Starowicz, and Mastalerz 2012). Although some patients complain that Lew-Starowicz spends too little time on their ailments or gives bad advice, Lew-Starowicz maintains the belief that physicians should approach their patients' problems in a holistic manner.[24] He encourages his students to do so as well. For Lew-Starowicz, a holistic approach sometimes requires painstaking maneuvers. For example, to diagnose some patients in the 1980s, Lew-Starowicz insisted on learning their reactions to different forms of sex. For this purpose, he decided to show them pornographic images; however, these images were banned in state-socialist Poland. Lew-Starowicz obtained a special permit and was allowed to lend appropriate diagnostic materials from customs warehouses where so-called *świerszczyki* (pornographic magazines) were confiscated from Poles returning from the West (field notes from trainings and conferences in the 2011–12 academic year).

Lew-Starowicz used the letters he received from his readers as another source of data. He subjected these letters to systematic examination. For example, he regularly published meticulous analyses of what he called the "population of letter authors" in *Etc* magazine. In addition, his lectures were often based on specific examples, devoid of statistical significance. He also published a book composed almost exclusively of texts sent in by his readers (Lew-Starowicz 1989a).

Under socialism, he cooperated to a certain extent with the Catholic Church. He held meetings with students at the Catholic University of Lublin. He edited a Polish translation of Paul Chauchard's (1972) work on Catholic sexual ethics, entitled *Sexual Life* (*Życie seksualne*). Privately, he maintained a friendship with influential Catholic physician Kinga Wiśniewska-Roszkowska, whom he appreciated for her medical work despite the fact that publicly, he was its harsh critic (Lew-Starowicz 2011b). She was, in turn, an unforgiving critic of his work.[25] Today, during his courses and lectures, Lew-Starowicz emphasizes the negative influence of the Church on issues of sexuality in Poland—for example, in stonewalling efforts to introduce sex education in schools.[26]

In the 1990s, Lew-Starowicz began collaborating with pharmaceutical corporations by conducting both clinical and statistical research on their behalf (see, e.g., Lew-Starowicz 2002b). Nevertheless, despite this cooperation and in contrast to many of his North American colleagues, he has continued to emphasize the nonphysiological sources of sexual disorder, including among men. During one of his lectures, for example, he told the audience that the great enthusiasm that met the invention of drugs for treating erectile dysfunction in 1998 brought about oversight of the psychological aspects of sexuality. He has maintained for years that these aspects must be taken into account (field notes, February 2, 2012). During the workshops for future specialists where I conducted participant observation, Lew-Starowicz frequently called his students' attention to the importance of the psychological, social, and cultural conditions of sexuality. On one occasion, he organized a medical seminar (participating doctors received credits needed to obtain their medical specialization) at which one of the invited lecturers was a famous historian, Tadeusz Cegielski, who gave a talk on historically changing approaches toward beauty and the body.[27]

With the comprehensive approach, Lew-Starowicz was able to overcome many stereotypes in his publications. His 1985 book *Mature Sex* (*Seks dojrzały*) examines the sexuality of people who have already experienced parenting and are approaching meno- or andropause (Lew-Starowicz 1985e). In *Atypical Sex* (*Seks nietypowy*), Lew-Starowicz (1988d) describes various sexual behaviors without needless judgment. In addition, among his former students are doctors who approach their patients' problems by taking into account economic, social, and cultural factors (see, e.g., Blajer 2011). One of Lew-Starowicz's former students, Alicja Długołęcka, is also a leading figure of feminist and queer sexology.[28] At the beginning of the 1990s, she conducted the first Polish research on lesbian sexuality (see, e.g., Długołęcka, 2005, 2019; Długołęcka and Engel-Bernatowicz 2008). She currently studies women's sexuality in general (Długołęcka and Reiter 2011), with a more specific research focus on the sexuality of women with damaged spinal cords (Długołęcka 2011a, 2011b). She runs educational workshops addressed to young people, lesbians, and women with disabilities. Feminist and queer-oriented young therapists and sex educators emphasized in interviews that her lectures and books were the basis of their education. Lew-Starowicz has more than the odd sexist or homophobic comment on record (I discuss his approach to gender and sexual orientation in detail later), for which he is sometimes criticized by feminists (see, e.g., Keszka 2011). Nevertheless, it is obvious that Długołęcka draws extensively on his work (e.g., in defining relationships based on equal terms; Długołęcka and Reiter 2011, 16–17) and that her approach is also part of the Polish school of sexology.

Changes in Polish Sexology

Lew-Starowicz became the leading figure of Polish sexology just about the time of the postsocialist transformation. Sexuality began to appear more frequently in the media in this period. Pornography was legalized, and sex shops started opening up. Polish society began professing different values, and gender roles slowly started to shift; LGBTQ rights activism started and became increasingly visible (on sexuality under socialism, see, e.g., Fidelis 2009; Kościańska 2017; Tomasik 2012; on the transformation therein, see, e.g., Fiedotow 2012; Marody and Giza-Poleszczuk 2000; Owczarzak 2009a; Szpakowska 2003). In 1990, the World Health Organization removed homosexuality from its list of diseases

(*International Classification of Diseases, Tenth Revision* [ICD-10]). Patients who found themselves in the rat race began to turn to sexologists with a whole new array of problems. In addition, since 1989, health-care services underwent multiple revolutionary reforms, many of which were at least indirectly related to sex. At the beginning of the 1990s, abortion was almost completely banned, whereas contraception, in vitro fertilization, and gender reassignment therapy were no longer covered by the state. The opening of the borders brought in the pharmaceutical industry, for which Poland was not only an attractive market but also a place to test drugs (on drug tests in Poland, see Petryna 2009). Initially with varying results but with a steadily more authoritative voice and greater determination, the Catholic Church began to take on matters of sex. The ban on abortion was certainly its brainchild (see, e.g., Zielińska 2000). Furthermore, the Church took active part in the sex education of youth, almost entirely taking over this domain in Polish schools (see, e.g., Ponton 2009). Nevertheless, research continues to show that Poles are rarely guided by Catholic sexual ethics in their daily lives (see, e.g., Izdebski 2012, 253, 275). A few years after the fall of socialism in Poland, sexology around the world was changed by Viagra. How did Polish sexology fare in this period? To what extent did it succumb to global trends dominated by researchers from the United States? To what extent did it maintain its specific, interdisciplinary character?

Many experts interviewed for my research, especially those of the older generation, are convinced that the 1980s were the golden period of Polish sexology. They also assert that this period is now long gone. They link this with the medicalization of sexology and the expansion of the pharmaceutical industry. In effect, they argue, patients are only offered drug therapy, and sexual dysfunctions are considered to be purely physiological. Nonetheless, although they praise Viagra, some interviewees are aware of the existence of other methods and use them in their own medical work. As one of them, a middle-aged doctor, explained, "We have an effective tool, we write a prescription, and generally in most cases we are able to help. Things have gotten a little bit easier for us, but of course it would be a sin to say that this is all sexology is about. . . . Apart from pharmacological methods, there are also behavioral methods, psychological methods, and methods that just help us anyway," such as slimming down or quitting smoking, since erectile dysfunctions are often a side effect of other health problems.

Yet changes in the treatment of sexual dysfunction cannot be associated only with the invention of Viagra. They are also related to changes in the way specialists are trained. Under socialism, the state financed educational activity, such as what Imieliński was engaged in, and intellectual exchanges with other socialist countries (e.g., with Czechoslovakia, where sexology was exceptionally vibrant; see Lišková 2018). This changed dramatically after 1989. As one interview partner, a physician and former student of Imieliński, put it, "There was a fundamental difference, after the change of the socioeconomic formation in the 1990s; our regular exchanges, the Polish-Czechoslovakian conferences ended, because there was no one to pay for them, the hospital said it would not give us money to send a delegation . . . and we had to look for sponsors." Pharmaceutical companies seemed like natural donors, but the use of their resources aligned with organizational changes in the discipline: "They did not want psychologists, they had no interest in philosophers, sociologists, educators, ethics experts, moralists, art historians, God knows what. They were only interested in those who could write out a prescription." Changes in funding went along with changes in the understanding of sexuality, gender, and methods of therapy. One could expect models similar to those dominant in the United States, which, after the fall of cooperation within the Eastern Bloc, came to be the fundamental reference point for many sexologists.

How did it come to be that sexology developed differently in state-socialist Poland? Why were there no studies in Poland like those conducted by Masters and Johnson in the United States or other clinical trials that, with minor exceptions, are still not conducted today? Intuitively, two answers arise. First, there was no funding. Second, such studies conflicted with socialist or Catholic modesty. But perhaps answers should be sought elsewhere: when asked about these issues, a physician with many years of experience, answered, "because that's commercial." "Why did the West not follow Poland's lead?" wondered the physician-sexologist (interestingly, differently from the classic narrative on the East and West, he put Poland as the blueprint) and went on to explain, "Because it was already more commercialized there, funds were allocated for specific tasks, goals." It was the pharmaceutical industry that had the greatest funds. He concluded, "They envied us," sexologists in the United States envied us—that is, researchers and therapists from the Eastern Bloc who together educated themselves in interdisciplinary sexology.

The Polish sexological tradition has turned out to be quite resistant to market influences. Psychology still plays an important role, although the therapists I spoke with constantly pointed to the destructive influence of the pharmaceutical industry on sexology and the ever-diminishing importance of psychological therapy therein. Yet during my research, I met many doctors who consider not only psychological but also economic factors. Consideration of cultural and religious issues is standard practice because these conditions are believed to affect gender and sexuality. This does not mean that Polish sexology is imbued with feminism and free of heterosexist stereotypes (these will be discussed in the next chapters). Nonetheless, Polish sexology developed a specific approach to sexuality, an alternative to that proselytized by the Church, distanced from market mechanisms, and—thanks to its interdisciplinary character—open in some extent to feminism and queer theory. I discuss the latter aspect in detail in the following parts of the book, where I argue that feminism and interest in sexuality ranging beyond the heteronormative has been developing in full swing in Polish sexology today. This development has not always occurred in opposition to the mainstream—a fact that also has to do with the interdisciplinary and patient-oriented approach of Polish sexology. In comparing sexology in the United States and Poland, it could be argued that they represent two separate paths of development. In the United States, the medical model supported by the pharmaceutical industry, according to which women and men are basically physiologically similar, is dominant. At the same time, this model competes with the psychological approach and with approaches that grew out of feminism and LGBTQ activism. In Poland, the medical approach is intertwined with the psychological and, to some extent, with the feminist and the queer.

Notes

1. Others also played an instrumental role in the rise of the Polish school of sexology. Important herein were the achievements of Mikołaj Kozakiewicz (mentioned earlier) and Andrzej Jaczewski, author of numerous books for youth. Presently, the most important figures in this discipline include Maria Beisert, a Poznań-based psychologist; Zbigniew Izdebski, an expert on the sexuality of Poles; Alicja Długołęcka, a feminist educator; and Andrzej Depko, a progressive physician who is often featured in the media.

2. Interestingly, this was also the first formal sexological title to be given in the world because Poland was the first country to establish sexology as a medical specialization (Imieliński 1974a). In Czechoslovakia, for example, although sexology was institutionalized in 1921 with the founding of the Institute for the Study of Sexual Pathology in Prague, it became a medical specialization in postgraduate education in the mid-1970s. "The full integration of sexology into the health care system was completed in 1981 when the Ministry of Health, supported by the World Health Organization, legislated sexology as a part of health care services" (Lišková 2018, 16).

3. Lectures in sexology were offered already in the 1960s, at the Military Medical Academy in Łódź, where Lew-Starowicz studied.

4. During his stay in Germany, Imieliński did not focus solely on the study of classical German works in sexology. Despite the meager funding he received, he also had the opportunity to observe sexology in practice. In another interview, also for *Etc*, Imieliński confesses that during his stay in Cologne, he hitchhiked to Frankfurt to visit the Sexology Department there (Imieliński 1974a).

5. In the early 1980s, martial law was imposed in Poland, and this resulted in major economic crisis. Consumer goods, including food, were difficult to obtain.

6. Under socialism, many physicians ran private or semiprivate practices, which brought them earnings significantly above average.

7. The institute's cooperation with the clergyman ceased with the fall of socialism: the sexologists no longer had the financial means to employ him (Wasilewski and Dulko 2011).

8. Hanna Malewska, a social psychologist, was also convinced of the link between the lack of science-based knowledge and sexual dissatisfaction. In the mid-1960s, she and her team interviewed 800 patients of gynecological clinics. Their research showed the participants to have limited knowledge about sexuality and reproduction (Malewska 1969, 97–100).

9. The website of the Czarna Owca publishing house (formerly Santorski i s-ka), where entirely new copies of *The Art of Love* are still available for purchase, states, "About 7 million copies of *The Art of Love* were sold in Poland, not counting the pirated reprints."

10. *Politics* is an influential liberal weekly published continuously since 1957.

11. The book also includes autobiographical elements, to which Wisłocka admitted only years later (Szołajski 2001; see Wisłocka 1998, 2004).

12. These activities can indeed be called "fighting": "Crowds of women came. They had nowhere to go for contraception . . . in the 1950s, a rural club near Warsaw. They

invited us with Professor Lesiński [another member of the PPPA]. I was saying that they should have as many children as necessary: to have interrupted sex or to use condoms. Those who came were there to oppose us and wanted to throw at us the rotten things they had prepared earlier. Professor Lesiński was a hardline party member and the Communist Youth Union members who had invited us led us out the back door, because it would have ended in a scandal. When I toured through the villages of Rzeszowszczyzna [southeast Poland], they warned me that the priests would eat me. There was always a priest in attendance; it never happened that one would not come. The local doctor too. And who had his way with us? The doctor, not the priest. The priest never spoke, while the doctors performed the abortions on the girls and did not want any competition like us" (Wisłocka 2004).

13. I concentrate on *The Art of Love* because of its extraordinary popularity. It is worth remembering, however, that Wisłocka is also the author of many other publications on these topics, both books and articles, which, for the most part, she wrote in a similar spirit.

14. It must be remembered that at that time, the World Health Organization still considered homosexuality to be a disease, and the American Psychiatric Association had just removed it from its list of disorders (in 1973).

15. Under state socialism, before publication, each text had to be checked by a censor for its adherence to socialist doctrine and morality.

16. Wisłocka refers to these quoted comments in a few interviews, but I was unable to find the reviews in their original sources.

17. This does not mean that Wisłocka shared the Catholic approach to contraception and abortion. She was most actively engaged in promoting various forms of contraception. She also devoted a lot of space to the matter in her writing, including in *The Art of Love*. Although she advocated against abortion, considering it the worst solution, she believed that it should nonetheless be legal and generally available (see, e.g., Wisłocka 1978 and subsequent editions; Różycki 1995, 90–98; Dąbrowa 2011).

18. In this respect, the author is not different from the mainstream of American sexology of this period. As I mentioned, Masters and Johnson also put marriage at the center.

19. The authorities forced the publisher to write on the editorial page that the book had a print run of ten thousand copies (Szołajski 2001).

20. *New Books* is a monthly review of new book publications that has come out continuously since 1949.

21. In the world of health and therapy, professional associations perform important functions, including determining who can be considered a specialist. The affiliation itself serves to authenticate a member. As such, membership does not come easily, and interviewees for my research claim that some applicants are refused. The Polish Sexological Society, an organization open to physicians, psychologists, and, to some extent, representatives of other disciplines (within its ranks, the organization has a few educators and even an engineer), issues sexology certificates for psychologists. The Polish Society of Sexual Medicine recommends doctor's offices. Membership in either translates to greater earnings for doctors and therapists.

22. The tasks of national consultants are regulated by the Regulation of the Minister of Health regarding national and county consultants from 2002, modified in 2005 and 2007. See OJ 02.188.1582, Dz.U. 05.158.1333, Dz.U. 07.23.143; see also Polish Ministry of Health 2018.

23. In the Polish higher education system, the habilitation degree follows the PhD.

24. Some of the interviewees called attention to the issue of patients' complaints.

25. I have discussed exchanges between them elsewhere (Kościańska 2012*b*).

26. Lew-Starowicz wrote about his relations with the Church in his autobiography (Lew-Starowicz 2013).

27. Second International Medical Congress, "Woman and Man: Reproductive and Sexual Health," Warsaw, Hilton Hotel, April 13–14, 2012.

28. By feminist sexology, I understand sexology based on the achievements of diverse social movements and academic discussions that aim at women's emancipation. I understand queer sexology as based on the study of nonnormative sexuality, queer theory, and the achievements of the LGBTQ movement.

Part 2
Pleasure: Toward Good Sex

3 | Sexuality and Scientific Knowledge

Sexology and the Formation of Discourse of Sexuality

In state-socialist Poland, sexology played an important role in the process of constructing sexuality. It also served as the primary source of modern knowledge about sexuality. Pornography, today widely available around the globe as a transmission channel of patterns of sexual behavior (Attwood 2005), was illegal under socialism. Although pornography was smuggled in from the West and produced in Poland, its reach was limited: in the 1970s, Poles—unlike Americans—could not see productions like *Deep Throat* on the big screen (Nijakowski 2010, 211–212, 200–201). Communist censorship effectively restricted explicit sexual content, seeing it as a manifestation of moral decline typical to the capitalist West. Only implicitly sexual erotica was permitted, and pornography was not allowed to be shown at all. Sexologists often mention an anecdote about working as an expert witness in state-socialist Poland: they were frequently asked to indicate whether material that had been detained at the border was pornographic or erotic.[1]

Also subject to censorship restrictions, Polish cinema of the period was conservative on sex-related matters. There were no local versions of *Barbarella* or *Emmanuelle*.[2] The same was true of literature.[3] Knowledge about sexuality could be passed on in the private sphere, where parents instruct their children. However, as research showed, this form of knowledge transmission was also limited (Malewska 1969, 43–49). When it came to sex education in schools, the situation changed frequently (Dąbrowska 2012, 154–161; Kościańska 2017). Theoretically, sex education had been offered in Polish schools since the 1960s. Despite the existence of an official curriculum, each school had its own ideas about how to teach sex education, and it was not until the mid-1980s that a handbook was introduced. It is worth adding that in comparison to the majority of handbooks approved by the Polish Ministry of Education today,[4] the socialist sex education handbook was quite daring. It discussed issues like sexual positions and erogenous zones, orgasm, and masturbation (Sokoluk, Andziak, and Trawińska 1987; see Kościańska 2017).

An examination of the weekly student magazine *Etc* (published from 1960 to 1990) illustrates the general silence around sex, as well as the role of sexology in opening discussion of the issue. Initially, very little space in the magazine was allowed for sex-related topics. In 1965, for example, only four articles touched on sexuality, and none could be included in the educational category. In the article, "Do Youth Know How to Have Fun?" the journalist Marek Ołdakowski (1965) describes various student pastimes, including "ballets," which make for, according to the author, the most "perverted and disgusting" kind of party. Ołdakowski says that during such events, professional playboys would use tricks (e.g., confessing their love and riding around in their cars) to lure female students from their dormitories—lonely girls from small towns and villages who were lost in big-city academic centers. Ballets end tragically for the girls: "In the morning, they sneak back in to their dorms. After great love and the car, only the dark circles under their eyes remain as well as trauma for a long, long time, sometimes even for a lifetime" (7).

The other three texts from 1965 focus on the West. Two, written by the journalist Andrzej Łarski, refer to the moral decline of young people in Sweden ("'Mascots' and Marlon Brando and Sex," Łarski 1965a) and in France ("French Youth 'Without Prejudice,'" Łarski 1965b). Both articles combine an excess of freedom (in the sphere of sex, among others) and prosperity with the growth of juvenile delinquency, alcoholism, and a plague of venereal diseases. The last three phenomena were all present in Poland at that time, despite the fact that people there could only dream about freedom and material goods, but *Etc* did not mention that. Nevertheless, it is worth noting that in the days of censorship, writing about what was happening in the West often served as a means of smuggling other content to the readers.[5] Being critical of events taking place on the other side of the Iron Curtain was conducive to getting published. Particularly remarkable in this sense is the text about Sweden. The author juxtaposes the moral decline (exemplified by boys dressing as girls and female students demanding instructional sex courses) with what he calls "sexual politics" and "a propaganda campaign about sex." He notes, "I share the opinion of some that by allowing young people wide sexual awareness, the Swedes forgot about such important factors as civilized customs, not to mention that the detachment of sex from the sphere of emotions can prove detrimental to the delicate mindset of minors" (Łarski 1965a, 12).[6] As we will see later, linking civilization with sexuality is an important theme in Polish sexological writing. The last article from 1965 on sex examined Italian cinema and its erotic scenes ("Pornography in Italian Film" [A.P. 1965]). In 1966, only two articles in *Etc* touched on matters of sexuality. Both focused on the United States and the United Kingdom, where, as we learn, sex had made its way into art and film ("Sex in the Age of Space Vehicles" [J.W. 1966] and "Eros in Polyester" [K.J. 1966]).

In summary, throughout the 1950s, the 1960s, and, to a certain extent, the 1970s, sexuality was hardly ever talked about in terms of positive patterns of behavior (see, e.g., Malewska 1969; Szpakowska 2003). The press limited itself to sporadic references to sexuality or to reports about moral decline in the West and sometimes in Poland (Fidelis 2010, esp. chap. 5). Studies based on a variety of sources—for example, Hanna Malewska's (1969) qualitative research from the mid-1960s, Małgorzata Szpakowska's (2003) analysis of letters and diaries from that same period, or Mira Marody and Anna Giza-Poleszczuk's (2000) research on the women's press from the 1970s—confirm the general lack of information on sexuality and the conservative climate of the period (Chałupnik 2008, 422–23). At the same time, materials examined by these authors affirm a broad yearning for knowledge on the subject (see, e.g., Szpakowska 2003, 73–82). This gap was filled in by sexological publications, which became increasingly popular starting in the late 1960s.

The year 1967 brought dramatic changes in the situation at *Etc* magazine. The editors of the weekly introduced a new column entitled "Intimate Life" and entrusted its authorship to sexologist Kazimierz Imieliński, who would write about sex, often referring to his patients' problems.[7] By 1969, *Etc* featured two new series on matters of sex: "The Two of Us through Life," and then "Eroticism of 20th Century Man" (based on the book *Eroticism* [Imieliński 1970]). Imieliński published in *Etc* for almost three years. At the end of 1969, the column was taken over by the young Zbigniew Lew-Starowicz, at the time a physician at the start of his career, who would run it until the last edition of the weekly in 1990. From the beginning, both sexologists received countless letters from their readers (see, e.g., editorial commentary on the article by Imieliński [1967d]), to which they tried to respond in the column in *Etc*. Lew-Starowicz discussed these letters, for example, in two articles written in 1973. During the first three years, as many as 1,560 letters were sent to the magazine (Lew-Starowicz 1973d, 1973e). These letters, and other contacts with readers, became the basis of many sexological works. Often the sexologists' texts would begin by citing from the letters. Other times, they would start with a sentence addressing an issue raised by readers, patients, or audiences at open seminars. In this way, popular sexologists like Lew-Starowicz and Imieliński filled in the sexual gap in state-socialist Poland and educated subsequent generations of Poles about sex. Nevertheless, as I show below, this was not a simple flow of knowledge from experts to readers but rather a dialogue among doctors, patients, and readers. The result was the sexological works read by the masses. These texts defined "good" and "bad" sex and the gender roles that determine it.

Constructing Scientific Knowledge of Sexuality: Interactions and Agency

Historians of sexuality have assessed the social role of sexology in Western culture in various ways. Until the 1970s, the narrative of progress dominated. In this perspective, sexological knowledge contributes to liberating sex. Thanks to this knowledge, people began to see positive value in sex and began to enjoy it because they were able to overcome the limitations imposed by Christianity (see Robinson 1976; for a discussion of this narrative, see Waters 2006, 50–53). This is usually how sexologists themselves, both Polish and foreign—including the people I interviewed for my research—see the matter.

This story about the history of sexology was questioned by Michel Foucault (1978, esp. the chapter "Scientia Sexualis"). Foucault wrote that the science of sex was "a science subordinated in the main to the imperatives of a morality whose divisions it reiterated under the guise of the medical norm" (53) and "became associated with an insistent and indiscreet medical practice, glibly proclaiming its aversions, quick to run to the rescue of law and public opinion, more servile with respect to the powers of order than amenable to the requirements of truth"

(54). Foucault proposed a radically constructivist theory of sexuality, according to which sex and sexuality are products of history, whereas expert knowledge is a tool of power that generates sexual subjects. In modern power over life, as described by Foucault (1978, esp. the chapter "Right of Death and Power over Life"), the science of sexuality appears as a disciplinary force and is at the center of the power-knowledge system. Modern power is exercised over the body: "We . . . are in a society of 'sex,' or rather a society 'with a sexuality': the mechanisms of power are addressed to the body, to life, to what causes it to proliferate, to what reinforces the species, its stamina, its ability to dominate, or its capacity for being used. Through the themes of health, progeny, race, the future of the species, the vitality of the social body, power spoke *of* sexuality and *to* sexuality" (147; original emphasis). In this approach, the science of sex takes an important place in forming, disciplining, and naturalizing subjects: "It is through sex—in fact, an imaginary point determined by the deployment of sexuality—that each individual has to pass in order to have access to his own intelligibility . . . to the whole of his body . . . to his identity" (156–57). Sexuality is thus at the nucleus of contemporary identity, and expert discourses are responsible for its construction (on the mechanisms of constructing subjects, see Foucault 1979, 1983; for a discussion of Foucault's contributions to the study of sexuality, see Cocks and Houlbrook 2006, 6–11).

Does understanding sexuality as a political "deployment" and a product of history, and the science of sex as an instrument of power, not serve to exclude the body from analysis (Foucault 1978: 151)? Foucault answers this question convincingly:

> The purpose of the present study is in fact to show how deployments of power are directly connected to the body to bodies, functions, physiological processes, sensations, and pleasures; far from the body having to be effaced, what is needed is to make it visible through an analysis in which the biological and the historical are not consecutive to one another . . . but are bound together in an increasingly complex fashion. . . . Hence I do not envisage a "history of mentalities" that would take account of bodies only through the manner in which they have been perceived and given meaning and value; but a "history of bodies" and the manner in which what is most material and most vital in them has been invested. (151–52)

Foucault also challenges the existence of sex as a category. He asks, "This materiality that is referred to, is it not, then, that of sex, and is it not paradoxical to venture a history of sexuality at the level of bodies, without there being the least question of sex? After all, is the power that is exercised through sexuality not directed specifically at that element of reality which is 'sex,' sex in general?" (Foucault 1978, 152). In his answer, he topples the universality of the category of sex: "It is precisely this idea of sex in itself that we cannot accept without examination" (152). He goes on to argue that, starting in the nineteenth century, "one sees the elaboration of this idea that there exists something other than bodies, organs, somatic localizations, functions, anatomo-physiological systems, sensations, and pleasures; something else and something more, with intrinsic properties and laws of its own: 'sex'" (152–53). In this approach, a certain reversal takes place: discourse on sexuality does not derive from sex, a natural category, being at its center. On the contrary, it is discourse on sexuality, medical knowledge included, that produces the category of sex. Foucault notes, "We must not make the mistake of thinking that sex is an autonomous agency which secondarily produces manifold effects of sexuality over the entire length of its surface of contact with power. On the contrary, sex is the most speculative, most ideal, and most internal element in a deployment of sexuality organized by power in its grip on bodies and their materiality, their forces, energies, sensations, and pleasures" (155).

Foucault's reflections give special weight to knowledge about sexuality: this knowledge produces sexuality, subjects, and sex itself. Since the publication of the first volume of *The History of Sexuality* (the first French edition came out in 1976), many scholars have continued his research, adopting a more or less radically constructivist orientation (Vance 1989). Some researchers of sexology, recognizing Foucault's understanding of the importance of scientific knowledge of sexuality, have paid special attention to the process of its formation. They have shown that Foucault allowed no space for individual or collective agency. Both experts (sexologists) and entire populations appear to him as passive individuals and groups. Harry Oosterhuis (2000), who draws from Foucault's constructivism, has examined the process of the development of knowledge about sexuality, taking Richard von Krafft-Ebing, a pioneer of this discipline, as an example. Oosterhuis's research shows that this Viennese doctor maintained constant dialog with his patients and readers. The problems with which they came to see him laid the foundation for the sexual classifications that Krafft-Ebing established. His main work, *Psychopathia Sexualis*, is a collection of cases that, together, form a catalog of "deviations." Krafft-Ebing's readers from all over Europe shaped their identities based on what they learned from his work. They were grateful to the author: thanks to his work, they realized that they were not alone in experiencing sexual problems. Others wrote to him begging for help because, for example, they wanted to marry but were afraid of the opposite sex (see Krafft-Ebing [1886] 2011, 99–102). Oosterhuis examines the interactions between Krafft-Ebing and his patients and readers. He points to the active roles of both parties in forming knowledge of sexuality: "By publishing his patients' letters and autobiographies and by quoting their statements verbatim, Krafft-Ebing enabled voices to be heard that were usually silenced" (Oosterhuis 2000, 195). Oosterhuis also notes that *Psychopathia Sexualis* showed subjective experience and the manifold meanings attributed to sexuality, giving the work a truly polyphonic character (195). In addition, Oosterhuis argues that, contrary to popular thought, Krafft-Ebing avoided generalizing and classifying (195), and the accounts published in his work often contained social messages. For example, a homosexual writer said, "I think that sexual contact between two people of the same sex is at their individual discretion, without legislations having any right to interfere" (quoted in Oosterhuis 2000, 196).

George Chauncey (1982/1983) trains his focus on a different dimension of the interactive nature of knowledge about sexuality. In an article on the concept of feminine sexual "deviation" in the United States between the 1880s and the 1920s, he argues that scientific knowledge on this subject came about as a result of new social phenomena. It became the medical community's response to women's questioning of the Victorian gender order (140). Doctors at the time associated the increasingly frequent occurrence of "inversion" with feminist rejection of motherhood. Chauncey presents the views of William Lee Howard, a physician who maintained in 1900 that "the progeny of the woman who 'prefers the laboratory to the nursery . . . are perverts, moral or psychical.' By forsaking their proper social role . . . these 'emancipated' women produced effeminate sons and masculine daughters" (141). Chauncey's work demonstrates that a conservative approach to social change (e.g., antifeminism) can manifest by means of sexological discourse.

The process of the development of knowledge of sexuality based on dialogue is also well illustrated in the book by Jennifer Terry (1999), *An American Obsession: Science, Medicine, and Homosexuality in Modern Society*. The anthropologist examines research on homosexuality conducted in 1935 by the Committee for the Study of Sex Variants in New York. The project was directed by psychiatrist George William Henry. Terry notes that the project, in accordance with the spirit of the era, was aimed at solving social problems (in this case, homosexuality) through scientific knowledge (178). The study could be easily understood as a tool for repression because it conceptualized homosexuality as a disease indicative of inadequate social adjustment. Furthermore, the study used highly stereotypical definitions of masculinity and femininity. Homosexuals were thought to have transgressed the boundaries of gender, and the root causes of their "otherness" were sought, for instance, in gender role disorders among their closest relations (211). As Henry explained, the project was of a practical character and aimed to help "doctors and scientists in identifying and treating patients who suffered from 'sexual maladjustment'" (quoted in Terry 1999, 191). Interestingly, however, "the study was flexible enough to allow its subjects to give rich accounts of their experiences. . . . Researchers wanted to know what sex variants had to say for themselves, believing their impressions and histories would offer useful clues as to the causes of sex variance" (178).

Many members of the New York homosexual community saw potential benefits in participating in Henry's research. They believed that the research could help them defend themselves against growing aggression directed at their communities (Terry 1999, 190) and propagate tolerance (221). In addition, they liked the ambiguous term "variance" (221). In effect, more than one hundred people volunteered to talk about their sexual and emotional lives (190). They also agreed to be examined in detail by an entire team of scientists who were also interested in probing such matters as the structure of genital organs.

From my point of view, the most interesting part of Terry's (1999) reflections relate to the "game" in which the research subjects engaged the scientists.

Terry departs from Foucault's notion of reverse discourse (223). In *The History of Sexuality*, Foucault (1978, 101–2) wrote:

> There is no question that the appearance in nineteenth-century psychiatry, juris-prudence, and literature of a whole series of discourses on the species and subspecies of homosexuality, inversion, pederasty, and "psychic hermaphrodism" made possible a strong advance of social controls into this area of "perversity"; but it also made possible the formation of a "reverse" discourse: homosexuality began to speak in its own behalf, to demand that its legitimacy or "naturality" be acknowledged, often in the same vocabulary, using the same categories by which it was medically disqualified. There is not, on the one side, a discourse of power, and opposite it, an-other discourse that runs counter to it. Discourses are tactical elements or blocks operating in the field of force relations; there can exist different and even contra-dictory discourses within the same strategy; they can, on the contrary, circulate without changing their form from one strategy to another, opposing strategy.

Terry (1999) introduces the term "variant subjectivity" (223) based on Fou-cault's assumption that sexual "Others" employ medical classifications for their own use. However, a fundamental difference exists. Terry explains, "I do not assume that, in expressing their variant subjectivity, the subjects merely 'reversed' medical discourse. For one thing, the subjects spoke in a language that had mul-tiple sites of origin and enunciation, including, importantly, the subcultural practices they shared as dissenters from normative regimes of sex, gender and sexuality. For another, they understood medical discourse as a powerful mode for understanding themselves and for achieving some measure of dignity and respect. Moreover, they, like previous generations of sex dissenters, played a sig-nificant role, whether intentionally or not, in shaping the terms according to which homosexuality was understood" (223).

Terry (1999) also notes that interviews published in the work summarizing the results of the study show that the research subjects had agency in this process. They wanted to understand their own desires. They also managed to introduce their vocabulary to the work (225). Effectively, Terry suggests that extending Fou-cault's discussion of power to include resistance is more than just reversed dis-course. In her opinion, power is not, as Foucault claimed, all-encompassing and leaving no space unattended by its watchful eye. The study participants were able to introduce elements of their own subculture and experience, thus altering the study. Terry notes that for Foucault, power is dispersed and exercised at the micro level. In his perspective, doctors have no power over patients, as "power circulates between them" (225). Terry also points out that the doctors themselves—Henry, the principal investigator, in particular—functioned in a complex reality and had their own interest in changing the perception of homosexuality. Ultimately, the study's findings came about as the effect of interplay between the research sub-jects and the scientists.

What was this like in practice? As already mentioned, the researchers ini-tially embraced a stereotypical approach to gender that, for example, associated femininity with gentleness and motherhood (Terry 1999, 211). Terry examines the case of a pair of white women described in Henry's work: violinist and composer Ursula W. and sculptor Frieda S. (226–27). She shows how the couple breaks stereotypical thinking about gender because, in their take, femininity is associated with aggression. In describing Frieda, Ursula says, "She's tiny and very feminine, a fine artist, very virile and aggressive, my equal in aggressiveness and not at all possessive" (quoted in Terry 1999, 226).

Negotiation between different actors leading to the development of knowledge does not just concern the sphere of sexuality. Ludwik Fleck ([1935] 1979), the Lviv-based precursor to research on the social construction of science and, above all, medicine, had written about this phenomenon already in his famous 1935 treatise, *Genesis and Development of a Scientific Fact*. Fleck illustrated the ways in which nonscientific knowledge—what he calls "pre-ideas," implying elements of culture or of common knowledge—make their way into science.[8] Fleck argues that scientific ideas arise as a result of continuous interaction between individual thought collectives representing different thought styles. Fleck uses these terms in a specific sense: "If we define 'thought collective' as *a community of persons mutually exchanging ideas or maintaining intellectual interaction, we will find by implication that it also provides the special 'carrier' for the historical development of any field of thought, as well as for the given stock of knowledge and level of culture*. This we have designated *thought style*" (Fleck [1935] 1979, 39; original emphasis).

Such thought collectives can be teams of doctors working together and basing their knowledge on the same sources, patients from various social groups, feminists working toward the sexual emancipation of women, or religious activists. There is constant exchange among them: "The complex structure of modern society results in multiple intersections and interrelations among thought collectives both in space and time" (Fleck [1935] 1979, 107). According to Fleck, every such intersection "always results in shift or a change in the currency of thought" (109), implying that while certain claims might gain legitimacy, others might lose it altogether.

Thought collectives play a fundamental role in the process of the development of knowledge (Fleck [1935] 1979). Fleck said, "In comparative epistemology, cognition must not be constructed as only a dual relationship between the knowing subject and the object to be known. The existing fund of knowledge must be a third partner in this relation as a basic factor of all new knowledge" (38). This third partner, current knowledge, has a social dimension: "Cognition is therefore not an individual process of any theoretical 'particular consciousness.' Rather it is the result of a social activity, since the existing stock of knowledge exceeds the range available to any individual. The statement, 'Someone recognizes something,' . . . is therefore incomplete. [It] demands some . . . supplement as, 'on the basis of a certain fund of knowledge,' or, better, 'as a member of a certain cultural environment,' and, best, 'in a particular thought style, in a particular thought collective'" (38–39).

Thus the thought collective constitutes the third component. It is closely associated with thought style, or the way of thinking particular to a given group (collective; Fleck [1935] 1979). Such an approach allows for understanding of *thinking* itself as a social activity:

> Like any style, the thought style also consists of a certain mood and of the performance by which it is realized. A mood has two closely connected aspects: readiness both for selective feeling and for correspondingly directed action. It creates the expressions appropriate to it, such as religion, science, art, customs, or war.... We can therefore *define thought style as* [the readiness for] *directed perception, with corresponding mental and objective assimilation of what has been so perceived.* It is characterized by common features in the problems of interest to a thought collective, by the judgement which the thought collective considers evident, and by the methods which it applies as a means of cognition. The thought style may also be accompanied by a technical and literary style characteristic of the given system of knowledge. (99; original emphasis)

In this approach, social relations among particular groups shape the way in which reality is perceived and categorized. In effect, they construct scientific knowledge. What is more, a defined constellation of thought styles and collectives makes certain judgments seem obvious or natural (Fleck [1935] 1979, 107). In other words, Fleck presents the emergence of scientific facts as the result of social interactions and contacts between scientific disciplines (collectives of scientists representing various disciplines). He also takes into account cultural factors and common knowledge, or folk models.[9] Research conducted from a feminist perspective has shown the latter to be particularly important when it comes to exceptionally strongly naturalized issues of gender and sexuality (Vance 1989). For example, Nelly Oudshoorn (1994) argued that the process of the development of the birth control pill was based on representations of the female body, whereas Emily Martin (1991) posited that biological knowledge conceptualizes the egg and the sperm as woman and man. Analyzing the work of sexologists John Money and Anke Ehrhardt, Rebecca Jordan-Young (2010) showed that stereotypical thinking about gender characteristics (associating women with passivity and the private sphere and men with activity and the public sphere) was not in any way questioned during their research on sex difference.[10] Moreover, in a classic essay on the formation of anthropological knowledge (to some extent, Polish sexologists collect materials in a manner typical to the social sciences), Sylvia Yanagisako and Jane Collier (1984) argued that ethnographers conducting research on gender-related topics like kinship tended to adopt Western classifications as natural, not recognizing their cultural component.

In following the path set out by Fleck, Oosterhuis, Terry, Chauncey, and others, I assume that patients and correspondents are agents (Giddens 1984, 5–16), active in the process of knowledge construction. Their activity goes beyond Foucault's reverse discourse: they introduce new concepts to scientific discourse while challenging and reinterpreting existing categories. Other important actors in this process are various groups and movements—namely, Fleck's thought collectives, such as feminist or religious communities—that negotiate emerging knowledge. The entire process takes place under specific cultural conditions expressed by all actors involved, including the doctors and scholars themselves, who are also active agents.

In the context of my research on sexology and, more generally, on expert discourse, this multidimensional and multisubject process leads to the scientific definition of good and bad sex and to changes within these classifications. I take the terms *good* and *bad* sex from Gayle Rubin (1984).

Rubin (1984) proposed the concept of sexual hierarchy in her famous essay, "Thinking Sex": in a given society, certain sexual behaviors are defined as "good" and others are considered "bad." In the United States in the early 1980s, when Rubin forged her classification, "good" sex, or what was considered natural and normal, was understood as heterosexual, marital, and monogamous relationships that took place at home. Sex for money, along with intergenerational, sadomasochistic, and fetishist relations defined "bad" sex, or what was considered "perverse" and abnormal (Rubin 1984, 281, diagram). Religion, science, psychology, and medicine (mainly psychiatry and sexology) as well as common knowledge and popular culture engender these hierarchies. According to Rubin, medical hierarchies are visible in disease classification systems like the DSM, in which behaviors classified as disorders, such as fetishism, are also considered bad and unnatural and are slated for disapproval (280).

I depart here from Rubin's sex hierarchy to examine the mechanisms of its formation within expert discourse. I also consider how particular types of sex pass from one category to the other. Based on the achievements of scholars like Fleck, Oosterhuis, and Terry, I show the hierarchy of good and bad sex to be dynamic. I point to processes—debates in the sexological milieu, awareness of patients' needs, and discussions with representatives of different fields or thought collectives that result from the interdisciplinary and humanities-oriented specificity of Polish sexology—and actors that bring about change and factors that consolidate the status quo. These factors are both institutional (e.g., the conditions that must be met by future sexologists) and noninstitutional (e.g., jokes or gestures during sexological classes). I discuss the sources of expert knowledge. I also slightly broaden the category of good sex. Rubin (1984) associates it with the healthy, the natural, the normal, and "the blessed." In analyzing my research materials, I came to the conclusion that another feature is worth adding to this "positive" collection: satisfaction. Polish sexologists often link what is healthy with what is pleasant. This tendency probably derives from the emphasis they place on the importance of sex for a successful family life and the self-fulfillment of the individual, which in turn positively affects the family (see, e.g., Lew-Starowicz 1983f; Wisłocka 1978).

In this examination, I underscore the role that gender plays in sexual hierarchy, based on my analysis of the collected material. In the major sexological works (Wisłocka 1978; Lew-Starowicz 1983f), healthy and satisfying sex correlates with appropriate gender roles. Accordingly, good sex is possible if women are women and men are men. Disturbance of this order leads to sex problems. When it comes to gender, I am primarily interested in men's and women's agency:[11] What spaces, forms of action, and decisions are available to women and to men? Which of these paths lead to good sex? In following the relationship models presented in sexological works, for example, does the emancipation of women go hand in hand with a successful sex life? Can a woman who speaks directly about her expectations count on a happy relationship? Who can initiate sex and be active during its course? Who is responsible for sex and the relationship, and how does this responsibility manifest itself? What must be done to meet this responsibility?

In the following chapters, I examine sexological publications and discuss the sexological path to healthy, natural, and pleasant sex—meaning good sex. What conditions must be met, according to the experts, to enjoy a successful sex life? In short, I am interested in the experts' recipe for pleasure. An important component is gender or, more specifically, appropriate gender roles. Both pleasure and what is considered normative refer to gender, which constitutes the main theme of my discussion. Successful, healthy, and safe sex depends to a large extent on behavior proper to one's gender. I also examine the process of the formation of sexological knowledge and situate it in a social, cultural, and political context. I show the hierarchy of good and bad sex as dialogic and dynamic. Finally, I point to the main actors involved in establishing, consolidating, transforming, and legitimizing sexual hierarchy.

Analyzed Archival Materials

The sexological section of the magazine *Etc* represents the best example of the exchange of ideas between physicians and patient-readers, as well as other experts. Imieliński and, later, Lew-Starowicz discussed various sex-related matters in *Etc* and responded to their readers' letters. Imieliński ran the sex column from 1967 to 1969, at which point Lew-Starowicz took over. Initially, Lew-Starowicz's column was called, "Answers from a Sexologist." The series comprised 160 articles in total, all of which were written in reply to letters or groups of letters. In 1973, in response to the needs of readers, a new regular column, "Art of Love," was featured. In the column's opening article, Lew-Starowicz wrote, "Letters are increasingly coming in to the editorial office demanding a regular column about the themes of sexual, marital and family life" (1973j, 20). Although topics for the column were chosen by its author, the needs of the readers were not left out: "More personal contact with readers will be maintained in the already established practice of posting responses at the end of the article, as well as through individual reply to relevant and important questions. The column itself also expresses the need to respond to some questions addressed to the editors and the author, and it has been arranged with this purpose in mind. The new column includes five major sections . . . the propaedeutic of marriage, the nature of marriage and family, sexual issues and love art, problems, conflicts, pathology and issues of parenthood" (20).

Answers at the end of the column looked as follows and usually encouraged readers to see a specialist: "Mr. Jerzy S. from Poznań: the wife should see a sexologist, in this case the difficulties experienced during intercourse are not the effect of body structure" (Lew-Starowicz 1973i, 14)[12] or "'Unhappy student' should get in touch with a plastic surgeon, only this type of specialist can help" (Lew-Starowicz 1973k, 22). Sometimes, the doctor would assign reading material: "To Mr. Antoni B. from Zakopane, I recommend reading *Problems in Sexology* (3 volumes published by PZWL) and a systematic reading of *Family Problems*, a bimonthly by the Polish Planned Parenthood Association. You will find interesting materials there" (Lew-Starowicz 1973k, 22).

In 1975, *Etc* magazine included another column, entitled "The Sexologist's Advice," that continued until 1990. Letters from readers were again featured at the beginning of each article. The impulse for writing other articles was also, for example, the publication of interesting scientific research or questions asked by participants during a lecture session. Sometimes, at the end of an article, Lew-Starowicz would provide brief answers to specific problems, recommend specialists, and suggest reading.

In *Etc*, Lew-Starowicz practically had a free hand. Editors usually did not put pressure on him, although at times "signals" were sent down from above to encourage or discourage writing about certain topics. Interestingly, the issue of the Catholic Church was particularly sensitive. As Lew-Starowicz told me in an interview, "The authorities did not want to engage in an ideological war over sex. Sometimes . . . when there was temporary hostility and they wanted . . . to stick it to the Church, signals were sent that constraints were loosening up on writing, that you could write about sensitive topics . . . but because more often than not they got along, you had to reckon with that. . . . You had to know that you couldn't just go around writing revolutionary slogans."

During all the years that Lew-Starowicz authored the column in *Etc*, the censor representing the official state policy intervened only on three occasions.[13] These interventions concerned the question of clergymen and their sexuality, abortion, and sex communes, which is not surprising in light of the interview excerpt above.[14]

Publications written by the two leading figures of Polish sexology, Imieliński and Lew-Starowicz, have much in common. Both doctors tried to respond to the needs voiced by their patients and lecture participants. Lew-Starowicz, who wrote especially for *Etc* magazine, also tried to reply to the concerns of his readers, who sent him countless letters. In an interview accompanying the publication of the first "episode," Imieliński (1967c, 10) discussed the genesis of the articles for the column:

Ordinary. Very ordinary. Because of morals, traditions and very few publications, or very naive publications on human intimate life, these issues, so important to human life, have not yet been the subject of exhaustive and wide-ranging study. I want to fill in this gap as much as possible. I think I don't need to convince you that there is a need for this type of reading material. Besides, my conviction was confirmed by the huge turnout I had at all my lectures on the subject. I must add that I gave the lion's share of the lectures to student youth. Further, I will also add that my book is an attempt to answer collectively the questions that I received by the dozens during each lecture. These questions allowed me to select from a huge material the topics of greatest interest to my audience, mainly students. I would like to emphasize once again that it was the most grateful audience, so to them, discussions with them, which often lasted long into the night, I owe a lot to them when it comes to the book. An interesting fact: as a result of one such discussion, a small center was opened at the student dormitory in Jelonki, where once a week advice is given on intimate topics, and now female students from the student dormitory on Karolkowa street are trying to open such a center.

Imieliński's method may raise some doubts: did students really have the audacity to ask publicly about the most embarrassing and stigmatized issues, like those related to sexual orientation? But since the talks went on "long into the night," perhaps they also included private consultations. Either way, both Imieliński and Lew-Starowicz opened themselves up to the needs of their patients and readers.

Besides the sexology section in *Etc*, my analysis centers on other selected publications by Lew-Starowicz. As already mentioned, he published in many other magazines, including *Together*, *The Cultural Weekly*, and *The Mirror*. Below I refer to his articles in this last magazine, published by the League of Polish Women. I examine his flagship publication, *Sex on Equal Terms* (first edition 1983; Lew-Starowicz 1983*f*) and lesser known but important books like *Homosexuality* (*Homoseksualizm*; Lew-Starowicz and Lew-Starowicz 1999) and *Atypical Sex* (Lew-Starowicz 1988*d*). It is worth noting, however, the overlap of the contents of Lew-Starowicz's articles for various magazines and his sex manuals. Some articles published in *Etc* were republished in a slightly changed form in *Sex on Equal Terms* and other advice manuals (e.g., Lew-Starowicz 1980*a*, 1980*b*).

I also examine the writing of Michalina Wisłocka. Her *The Art of Love* (Wisłocka 1978) is another important source of knowledge. As mentioned in the previous chapter, Wisłocka likewise drew from the experiences of her patients. In an interview for *The Mirror*, she said, "Over the course of my work in the clinic, I encountered frigid women, women who were on infertility treatment, women who had huge sexual needs and who were in need of protection against unwanted pregnancy. This was a huge opportunity for me to collect data. Each patient had her own broad statistical chart with various data. Thus the book, for which I collected materials over a period of ten years, is a history of a few thousand women who came to see me in my 'room in the attic'" (Wisłocka 1979, 14).

Finally, albeit to a lesser extent, I inspect Imieliński's publications, which were also attuned to the concerns articulated by his patients and readers. Imieliński's work had a more scientific character and did not gain such wide popularity as the writing of Wisłocka and Lew-Starowicz.

Notes

1. I heard this story several times during the trainings and conferences in which I participated as a part of my research.

2. Anna Misiak (2006) writes about censorship in film in detail.

3. Zuzanna Grębecka, who analyzes youth literature published under state socialism, calls attention to its prudishness: "Erotica and interest in even innocent manifestations of sexuality are usually stigmatized. For as long as possible, love should remain platonic and crossing the next barriers of intimacy should be problematic" (2012, 136). Furthermore, an interest in sex is characteristic of negative protagonists (137).

4. In Poland, primary and secondary education is state regulated.

5. Sexually transmitted diseases were dealt with as an issue starting in the years 1968–69, with a series of articles in *Etc* (1968, nos. 43–44 and 46–50; 1969, nos. 1–11 and 14–18) by Jerzy Suchanek, director of the Municipal Hospital of Dermatology.

6. Civilized customs (*kultura* in Polish). While *kultura* means literally "culture," in this context it has an additional, specific meaning and refers to proper, "civilized" behavior that was promoted by the state as an important part of state-socialist modernization. I explain this in detail in chap. 4.

7. In the first article (Imieliński 1967e), we read that the column was made up of excerpts from a new work by Imieliński entitled *Secrets of Intimate Life*. In fact, the articles came partly from his book published a few years later, *The Intimate Life of Man: Psychophysiology* (1974b).

8. Or "pre-scientific ideas," as they have been called by Nelly Oudshoorn (1994, 10), who transferred Fleck's considerations to the field of gender studies.

9. Numerous historians and theoreticians continued the research that Fleck had initiated, primarily Latour (1987) and Kuhn (1962), as well as Hackett et al. (2008).

10. Other examples of feminist studies of science include Fine (2010), Fishman (2004), Freidenfelds (2009), Lloyd (2005), and Richardson (2010).

11. By *agency*, I mean all the forms (e.g., actions, speech) of an individual's ability to decide about her own fate and the shape of the world around her. I assume that the scope and form of agency are limited by cultural, social, and political factors. I wrote in detail about agency in the context of gender previously (Kościańska 2009a, 2009b).

12. This type of response to letters appeared sporadically in earlier articles.

13. Lew-Starowicz (2013, 162) also writes about his experiences with censorship in his autobiography.

14. It is worth noting that the sexologists' articles stand out clearly from other texts in *Etc* and letters sent in to the editorial office. They feature hardly any ideological communist propaganda, typical to this period, such as the cliché, "An honestly working man is of the highest value to the socialist system" (Cybulski 1973, 34).

4 | "Civilized" Sex and Gender Relations under Socialism

Normal, Civilized, and Mature Sexual Intercourse

In the sexological writing of the 1970s and 1980s, good sex was synonymous with "civilized and cultured sex" (*seks kulturalny*). As discussed already, an important feature of the vision of sex proposed by Imieliński, and later Lew-Starowicz, was its context—a perspective of sexuality beyond the body. Such a perspective is also evident elsewhere, beyond Lew-Starowicz's definitions of sex drive and the sexual act cited in chapter 2. Their approach to sex, health, and what constitutes the norm is perfectly reflected by the often used concept of *kultura seksualna*, which can be translated literally as "sexual culture" in English. The term, however, understood quite differently than in contemporary, mainly Anglo-Saxon publications, in which "sexual cultures" denotes "the multiplicity of contexts and social worlds" in which sexual practices and experiences occur (Weeks 2011, s.v. "sexual cultures"). In Polish sexology, this concept implies "civilized" sex. Such an understanding was also popular in a different socialist context: the Soviet Union. As Michele Rivkin-Fish (1999, 803) notes:

> Many of the key themes in contemporary sex education projects have their roots in discourses on "moral education" [*vospitanie*], and "sexual moral education" [*polovoe vospitanie*] that were created by the Soviet state during Stalinism. Under the repressive conditions of that era, the moral education of the population became a constant focus of state ideology. Moral education involved teaching and modeling the behaviors consistent with a "proper upbringing," captured in the notion of "culturedness" [*kul'turnost'*]. To advance "culturedness" among the population, state bureaucrats and medical experts launched a massive attack on disorder, dirt, and indecency portrayed as interchangeable categories in favor of order and hygiene as the paths to health and moral purity. These qualities came to symbolize the basic requisites for the "high level of culture" associated with a "civilized," urban life under modernity. They were advocated incessantly in the state's universalizing, disciplining projects for *vospitanie*, which became the exclusive form of knowledge transmission in health education texts for popular consumption.

This category of "culturedness," of being civilized and cultured, also often appears in Poland and is directly connected to socialist modernization.[1] The notion also covers sexuality. Lew-Starowicz begins an article from 1970 entitled, "Technique or Civilized/Cultured Sex," by quoting his readers' questions. Monika Z. from Gorzów Wielkopolski in western Poland wrote to the sexologist: "Much is said about the need for a civilized sexual act. What is it basically about? Is this the same as technique or is it something else?" (quoted in Lew-Starowicz 1970n, 14). In what follows, the sexologist summarizes the letters he received and meetings he had with readers: "The expression 'intercourse technique' arouses objection among a large number of readers. In discussions, the sexologist faces accusations that this expression exposes the intimacy of intercourse, strips it of feelings, reduces it to some sophisticated game, dominated by heartlessness, showing off manual skills, where quality turns into quantity and human values disappear, where Eros begins to lack imagination, emotions, and spontaneity" (14).

Immediately afterward, he adds that others "posit accusations concerning the reverse: an excess of spiritualization, too much talk, moral restriction, embarrassment, and too little information about the particular techniques of different positions" (Lew-Starowicz 1970n, 14). He points out that this was also recently discussed in the magazines *Perspectives* and *Politics*. Lew-Starowicz himself thinks that successful sex is more than intercourse technique and refers to his medical experience: "At the clinic, most patients experience trouble less so due to a lack of knowledge of erotic technique. The problem is rather the low level of culturedness in sexual contacts. Despite the lack of specialized publications in the field of 'technique,' I notice that many couples are well acquainted with the matter. They reach perfection on their own, guided by mutual tastes, and a desire to diversify their sexual experience, they discover the sphere of sex and its individual character" (14).

In Lew-Starowicz's (1970n, 14) opinion, the publication of a catalog of sexual positions could have negative consequences: "Sex would lose its intimate character, emotional quality, honesty and directness." He then moves on to the question of what is "civilized" and "cultured": "Civilized/cultured sex takes on the task of humanizing the sex drive" (14). According to Lew-Starowicz, civilized sex is a part of human culture in general: "It is based on the whole system of values, relations with others, and the concept of love" (14). He describes it in greater detail as follows:

Civilized sex includes, among others:

1. Knowledge about gender psychology, the influence of intercourse on personality, physiology, anatomy, pregnancy prevention, and the course of a pregnancy.
2. The ability to establish contact and get to know another human being: getting to know his/her mental world, the style of their sexual needs and desires, meeting the rules and requirements they put forward.
3. Exhibit syntonic behavior, or the ability to simultaneously experience a common mood or feeling, and to empathize with the current emotional state of a partner.
4. Awareness of a hierarchy of values, proper positioning of sex in one's own life as well as our shared life.
5. Engage in the sexual act in accordance with the desires and preferences of the other person, this is particularly important for women, for whom the world of Eros is more complex in both a physiological and a psychological sense.
6. The development of an individualized style of intercourse, based on mutual preferences and abilities, and not as a copy of currently popular patterns.

7. The ability to engage in dialog, and change your erotic behavior if it does not bring your partner pleasure. The willingness to sacrifice your own egotism for the sake of the common good.
8. Avoid approaching erotica in a formalized manner, as a duty or obligation. Rather, give it a joyful character, of a shared experience, full of devotion to the other person.
9. Keep intercourse attractive (by means of proper personal hygiene, dress, a pleasant atmosphere preceding intercourse, an extended period of foreplay, diversifying intercourse in relation to the duration of the marriage).
10. Interval breaks in having intercourse are important so as to increase the desire of Eros and practice self-control as well as attentiveness. (Lew-Starowicz 1970n, 14)

These points (save for the last) are mentioned again in Lew-Starowicz's (1973b, 1973c) two-part article, "Civilized Sexual Relations." This time, he adds: "Another element of civilized sexual relations are the positions" (Lew-Starowicz 1973b, 20). He complements his considerations with descriptions and drawings of these positions, including a diagram of how the penis penetrates the vagina (Lew-Starowicz 1973c). He also encourages readers to focus on what the other person feels and experiences (Lew-Starowicz 1973b). The concept of civilized and cultured sex figures as a staple throughout Lew Starowicz's articles in *Etc.*[2] It was also elaborated on by Imieliński. Earlier in the magazine, Imieliński wrote about civilized and emotional sex, as well as about civilized married life, combining these concepts with the notion of being civilized—"courteous, polite, helpful, patient, understanding, and of a kind disposition" (Imieliński 1969, 14)—and open to the other person (although the article is seemingly addressed to both genders, Imieliński encouraged mainly women to be understanding of their partners' behaviors, such as betrayal). Imieliński (1969, 15) emphasized the importance of being civilized and cultured in marriage and in functioning as a member of society: "Civilized and cultured sexual contacts are essential in marital relations. Lack thereof impairs the fulfillment of one of the most important of human needs that is sexual need. This makes married life extremely difficult or impossible. A low level of sexual culturedness and not getting full sexual satisfaction manifests itself outside in the form of mental tension, irritability, explosions, etc. It leads to quarrels, tensions and the disintegration of relations between spouses. This looks like a 'mismatch of characters' and is judged as such by the outside. Meanwhile, sexual deficiency is an important factor conditioning their behavior."

In turn, Michalina Wisłocka (1978, 9) began her most widely read work with a story of her struggle for "culturedness in feelings and sex." For these authors, civilized or cultured sex denotes appropriate behavior in the bedroom but, above all, effectively leads to harmony in the relationship and in society. Sexuality is perceived holistically, as should be treatment. Sexual technique alone is not enough; a single formula does not exist. Imieliński (1967f, 185) wrote that uncivilized and uncultured men mean problems for women—thus the need for civilized sex, or a whole set of relations and attitudes, that go beyond purely physiological matters. What is civilized is healthy and pleasant for everyone; therefore, civilized sex embodies the norm—that is, good sex, using Rubin's (1984) terminology.

Civilized sex is strongly associated with heterosexual intercourse. In the already quoted article, "Civilized Sexual Relations" (Lew-Starowicz 1973*b*, 1973*c*), we find not only illustrations of positions and penetration but also advice on the significance of foreplay before sexual intercourse: "this strengthens the sensual and psychological bond" (1973*b*, 20). The sexologist warns, however, that "not all sexual positions correlate with a high level of culturedness in sex, some of them excessively focus on sexual stimuli, in effect towering over the partner" (20). Accordingly, three variants of positions termed "normal" were drawn and described (Lew-Starowicz 1973*c*, 20), all involving a woman lying on her back and a man on top of her. Civilized sex thus designates the heterosexual, emotional, and marital "penetrational" norm, the latter element being additionally accented using drawings of how the penis penetrates the vagina. Anything that went beyond the norm was considered uncivilized and uncultured (i.e., bad sex, in Rubin's [1984] terminology). This is well illustrated in articles describing behaviors that represent the latter category.

A 1970 article entitled "French Love" is an interesting example of the use of the concept of civilized sex. Readers asked Lew-Starowicz, "What do you think about so-called French love?" J.S. from Łódź wrote: "I heard about it for the first time from my friends who were spitting and turning away at the thought of it. I myself have found out that many couples do it. I make this kind of love with my boy. Initial resentment and disgust turned into a beautiful feeling. I feel now that we can't do without it. French love arouses great excitement in us and I feel much more pleasure in intercourse itself. I am afraid, however, that this might be the first step to various sexual deviations." Meanwhile, another reader also signed J.S. from Lublin demands an explanation of the "problematic of sophisticated 'French love.'" He asks, "Is it a perversion? What spurs the inclination to engage in this form?" (Lew-Starowicz 1970*f*, 14).

The expert begins by explaining, "So-called French love (oral sex, fellatio) is based on using the mouth instead of a woman's vagina. Close to this concept is also cunnilingus" (Lew-Starowicz 1970*f*, 14).[3] Next he posits that, with the exception of the latest versions, most medical textbooks classify oral sex as a sexual perversion. He clearly sets the boundaries of the norm: "It is necessary to strictly separate the two functions of oral sex: as a form preceding intercourse itself and as a form of intercourse. In the latter case, categorization as pathology is obvious" (14). The sexologist goes on to discuss the causes:

1. Sophistication of foreplay. This may be due to a dulling of the senses. . . . It would seem here that everything is within the normal range, but a more precise analysis indicates that in most cases, the partner is reduced to an instrumental role, meaning that sex as an aim dominates over his being and the act acquires the characteristics of egocentric contentment for two.
2. Anxiety among women (fear of defloration, pregnancy, or intercourse itself). Oral sex is a form of defense, a means to ease tension.
3. Extension of self-abuse, already similar in form to oral sex.
4. Hypochondriac tendencies, a sense of low sexual worth. Oral sex is supposed to unleash a sense of security, improve self-confidence, and strengthen one's sense

of self-esteem. A mechanism of overcompensation can also be observed. Herein, this form is placed above the normal, by for example preaching opinions about its extraordinary value. Some exhibit snobbish self-satisfaction in engaging in a "higher" form of sexual culturedness, almost an elite group.

5. Overcoming the feeling of sexual impotence among men. . . . Oral sex is supposed to eliminate fears and in this way, a substitute function is accepted as the fundamental.
6. Disorders associated with hidden or overt psychosexual disorders: agalmatophilia, exhibitionism, sadism, masochism, homosexuality, fetishism. . . .
7. Some unattractive women who lack femininity, who are tormented by jealousy . . . who desire rivalry in life and who want a partner at all costs become convinced that French love can be their chance at success. As we can see, closer analysis . . . does not lead to a particularly positive assessment thereof. (Lew-Starowicz 1970f, 14)

At the end, the sexologist returns to the question of what is "civilized" and "cultured": "Using the argument of a higher level of culturedness in sexual relations is most often a camouflage of the above-mentioned motives. This cannot be approved of in our region because the state of hygiene is still too low and regular sexual relations still too uncivilized. Each case of oral sex qualifies rather for examination and possible treatment" (14).

As we will see later, civilized and cultured sex appears in various other contexts in which sexual behavior is not fully accepted. It is worth noting that when writing about highly civilized or uncivilized sex, just like when writing about the norm, Lew-Starowicz is also guided by his readers' opinions. In the 1985 article "Oral Sex" (Lew Starowicz 1985d) or the 1987 three-part text "Oral Fondling" (Lew Starowicz 1987c, 1987d, 1987e), he discusses "French love" in a completely different spirit. Later on, Lew-Starowicz revealed that when he first wrote about oral sex in 1968, he caused "a storm and numerous letters dragged me through the mud" (1985e, 23). As such, the 1970 pathologizing article quoted earlier was probably a reaction to this state of affairs. Nonetheless, in Sex on Equal Terms, he notes, "French love, or oral-genital sex, is an abnormal phenomenon only when it is the only form of achieving orgasm" (Lew-Starowicz 1983f, 317). In so doing, he returns, in a slightly more delicate manner, to his arguments from 1970, once again placing sexual intercourse (penetration of the vagina by the penis) at the top of the sexual hierarchy.

Another category determining good sex is maturity. In the article, "Attitudes Toward Sexual Practices," Lew-Starowicz (1973l, 14) discusses different attitudes toward sex while defining the norm and what constitutes pathology. He distinguishes eight attitudes: (1) the primitive (a biological approach "exhibits no psychological bond or sense of community, there is an awareness of complete separation, alienation, indifference and even sometimes disregard for the sexual partner"; very frequent, even among 50% of young people), (2) the quantitative (similar to the primitive, it is about attaining "a maximum number of relations per unit of time"), (3) the "cool-sex" (sex without love, perceived as an autonomous sphere), (4) the Manichean ("sex is an expression of lower drives"), (5) the indifferent (duty), (6) the sophisticated ("sexual attraction is highly valued," so much so that "it implies a permanent state of want"), (7) the perverse (intercourse in forms "that indicate deviation from the state of psychosexual norm"), and (8) the mature ("based on treating the sexual act as a joyful fusion, a unification of partners in love with each other"). Only the last attitude is considered right (14). All the others raise objections and are causes or symptoms of disorders. A similar argument appears in the article dated to that same year, entitled "Sexual Needs" (Lew-Starowicz 1973*m*). Here, the need to "make another person happy, give yourself to him, be fascinated by him, the need to immortalize the bond, thus we reach the layer of love that releases altruism, creativity, fertility" (20)—in other words, what translates to "maturity"—is of greatest value.

An excerpt from *Sex on Equal Terms* is another example of equating maturity with the norm. Lew-Starowicz (1983*f*) notes that there are many ways to define the norm. One way is by defining what is good for the relationship, which may seem like an equality-based approach. He adds, however:

> This type of criterion turns out to be very complex, but it advances harmony among the biological, cultural, social and ethical factors of human development. In this perspective, it appears that the criterion of the norm cannot be determined by the subjectivism of the partners. For example, if we take a successful sadomasochistic relationship with good sexual adaptation, their sense of satisfaction does not determine the concept of the norm. The thing is that the sadistic and masochistic traits present, however they may complement the relationship, are deepened and consolidated. The development of the partners' personalities has been directed towards cementing certain features. The relationship, although internally mutually satisfying, does not make for a union of mature persons who help each other in mutual development, but for a union of people stuck inside a circle of their own tendencies. (Lew-Starowicz 1983*f*, 57)

In my analysis, I am interested not only in conversations between sexologists and their patients but also in what is unspoken, namely, in implicit definitions of the norm. I look for meditations on its meaning by reading in between the lines and by putting together different statements. In trying to capture what is not named or articulated explicitly, I use the methodology proposed by researchers writing from the perspective of queer theory (Somerville 1994, 247–50). I examine how good sex is defined in writing on issues that are considered somewhat pathological, as in the case of the article about French love. In addition, issues of civilized sex and maturity emerge. A special place in my analysis is reserved for considerations of nonreproductive practices, including masturbation, clitoral orgasm, homosexuality, and contraception, which showcase the centrality of heterosexual intercourse but also openness to the partner. These deliberations exemplify the thesis forwarded by Judith Butler (1991), who, in analyzing the methods of the formation and preservation of heteronormativity, showed that heteronormativity needs homosexuality in order to exist. Butler argues against recognizing heterosexuality as the source from which homosexuality originates (see also Tin 2012).

Masturbation and the Clitoral Orgasm[4]

From the outset of the sex column in *Etc* magazine, many male readers and some female readers were concerned about the issue of masturbation.[5] W. from Wrocław wrote to doctor Lew-Starowicz: "a friend of mine told me with all certainty that self-abuse is bad for you.[6] I, however, am of a different opinion. In this situation, I ask that you resolve the dispute" (quoted in Lew-Starowicz 1969*a*, 14). K. from Gliwice asked, "Does frequent self-abuse accelerate or delay ejaculation and does it lead to infertility?" (14). The woman from Warsaw, who signed her name with the initial S., seems more liberated: "I often practice self-abuse in the evening. My girlfriends say that it is necessary for a normal level of self-confidence. Is this true?" (14). Lew-Starowicz starts off decisively. Masturbation is a global phenomenon, he notes, citing statistics. In case these failed to convince everyone, he adds, "Medical works suggest that self-abuse is not harmful to health" (14). He places the problem somewhere else instead. Problems are associated with the fear of masturbation because it can bring about neuroses. In another, somewhat later text, he argues that this may lead to an "onanistic complex," which involves "the belief that self-abuse always carries pathological consequences that impede or seriously hinder the sexual act" (Lew-Starowicz 1974*b*, 20). Similarly, in the article "Masturbation and Impotence," Lew-Starowicz (1984*a*) takes up the issue of masturbation and its association with the inability to have sex because of erectile problems. The sexologist settles his readers' worries by writing that such is not always, necessarily, the case. Nonetheless, his readers are left with certain fears, which remained a recurrent aspect of his articles on the subject.

Notably, in the first text about one-on-one sex published in *Etc*, Lew-Starowicz (1969*a*) argued against excess, which he characterized as a display of weak will and of the "'eroticization' of the psyche." Moreover, "Self-abuse cannot be explained by the need to discharge excess sexual energy because the body is such a perfect structure that it is able to manage itself by, for example, unloading this excess in the form of nocturnal emissions" (14). Lew-Starowicz was thus inclined to view masturbation as not completely natural:

Further consequences of self-abuse are:

- The perpetuation of the state of an eroticized psyche;
- The development of an egocentric attitude towards sexual life, which implies striving for satisfaction at the expense of a partner, thus hindering the development of common sexual experiences;
- Lowered mental efficiency, concentration skills, attention, weakened will power, self-control and energy;
- The emergence of the belief that sex equals power that cannot be resisted (a belief that often leads to a lowered sense of self-esteem);
- Premature ejaculation, excessive excitement and nervousness. (14)

In the end, the expert reassures his readers, "The phenomenon of self-abuse must be approached realistically, in considering its causes and effects, without getting down or depressed, but by starting to work on yourself instead. In case of failures, seek the advice of a sexologist" (14).

Lew-Starowicz's 1973 article on the subject is written in a similar vein. The sexologist notes that he still receives "many letters asking for an explanation of the possible consequences of self-abuse" (Lew-Starowicz 1973n, 20). He reveals that "many patients remain convinced that self-abuse in their youth triggered their sexual problems in the present." Such an approach, notes the expert, represents an attempt to qualify masturbation as either "normal or pathological behavior." The sexologist explains that "there are various forms and reasons for self-abuse." In effect, at times, masturbation constitutes correct behavior, while at others it is incorrect. He presents in points the same issues as in his article from 1969 (20). Another text on masturbation from this period is entitled "Mutual Self-Abuse" (Lew-Starowicz 1972c, 14). This time, readers ask about doing it together. A married couple from Lublin, who already have two children and do not want anymore, share their doubts: "In the so-called dangerous period, we avoid *normal sexual intercourse* and instead have sex in such a way that by the mechanical stimulation of our sexual organs we reach orgasm. We are afraid, however, that this unusual way may lead to neurosis or other psychiatric disorders in the future" (Lew-Starowicz 1972c, 14; emphasis added).

Halina, another reader from Łódź, complains that her "partner is so focused on the genital organs" that she feels herself to be only taking part in his own self-gratification. "Is this self-abuse?" she asks (Lew-Starowicz 1972c, 14). Lew-Starowicz answers in a similar tone as before. Self-abuse is not a pathology and does not lead to neuroses, but it is a manifestation of a low level of culturedness in sexual life—an immature form of sex. Furthermore, he says, "Mutual self-abuse contradicts the basic aim and sense of sexual contact" (14). In following the spirit of the Polish school of sexology, the expert perceives sex as something that goes beyond a purely physiological act: "In this style of sexual act the goal is sexual satisfaction as the outcome of intense sensory arousal brought on by mechanical stimulation, while in love art fondling is more important, while satisfaction is its natural result. In this way, the means overshadow the ends and therefore in this form of intercourse there is never true satisfaction of complex sexual needs. This type of sex culminates with the residue of dissatisfaction and among some people even reluctance towards the partner. Mutual self-abuse unravels rather than strengthens the bonds between partners" (14). Finally, Lew-Starowicz (1972c, 14) concludes that collective self-abuse "forms a disposition towards sexual betrayal, because partners have automatized sex that is instrumentalized and not related to their mutual mental needs, or emotions."[7]

His 1981 article entitled "Self-Abuse as Healing?" (Lew-Starowicz 1981a) begins by citing questions from readers who want to know whether it is true that masturbation can have therapeutic value: "Why do sexologists recommend self-abuse to those who have unsatisfied sexual needs? Is there no other way if you don't have a partner?" (23). Another reader mentions an example from an American sexology textbook that depicts "self-abuse as the most effective treatment for many sexual disorders." The sexologist corroborates that scientific views on the subject have changed and that masturbation is considered a form of treatment. But he distinguishes *self-abuse* (the term used by readers) and *autostimulation*. Self-abuse is associated with a "substitute means of satiating sexual needs, the aim of which is to achieve a state of sexual fulfillment" (23). In contrast, autostimulation implies "unblocking the emotions associated with your sexuality, getting to know how your own body reacts and accepting it" (23). In therapy, this second form leads to "accepting the partner's touch" (23). If we take into account this distinction, masturbation continues to be stigmatized to a certain extent. For example, therapeutic autostimulation is not recommended for people "with auto-erotic tendencies (excessive concentration on their own sexual reactions, turning their own SELF into an erotic object)," which carries the risk of "possible adverse conditions for intercourse, where self-abuse serves for an escape from actually meeting a partner" (23).

A 1983 article entitled "Masturbation" (Lew-Starowicz 1983c) presents a gentle take on autostimulation and clearly separates completely harmless adolescent or substitutive masturbation from its neurotic and pathological forms, which appear to be problematic. Although the article discusses the therapeutic application of masturbation, some techniques are portrayed as having implicitly negative effects: "Various techniques used by women can lead to the development of an 'orgasmic path,' or a stereotype of sexual arousal. In such cases intercourse with a real partner does not lead to orgasm, despite efforts on his part. Some techniques, like mutual masturbation, can lead to the development of homosexuality, as well as vulgarity in matters of sexuality and gender" (23).

Lew-Starowicz's (1983f) reflections on sexual fantasies in *Sex on Equal Terms* are maintained in a similar spirit. Ideas accompanying masturbation can affect sexual behaviors and preferences, "leading to the development of different types of deviation. Many researchers look for the genesis of, for example, homosexuality, exhibitionism, threesomes, and etc. in masturbation. I must admit that I was also able to identify such a mechanism among many of my patients" (75). Sexual fantasies can alter sexual expectations: "If, for example, while masturbating a young man cultivates his sexual fantasies, outlining in detail his own behavior and that of his partner, and imagines a specific type of a woman's construction, then this encoded sexual reaction may be so strong that the sexual satisfaction he experiences with his partner is considerably less fulfilling than during self-abuse, or it might not exist at all" (75). This in turn brings about various complications in the relationship.

A 1989 article presents masturbation "in the East" in an entirely different manner (Lew-Starowicz 1989b). This time Lew-Starowicz points to the advantages of masturbation, especially for women: "Masturbation among female members of the cultures of the East, apart from an increase of yin energy, also serves the development of the ability to control sexual reactions, teaches them about their bodies and their sexual physiology; it serves for a source of erotic self-knowledge"

(14). Lew-Starowicz also turns to what a few years earlier had been called "mutual self-abuse" and exemplified uncivilized sex:

> We come across . . . descriptions and engravings of heterosexual masturbation where the partners stimulate each other using oral-genital caressing (without the ejaculation of semen). It was believed that in this way women received yang energy from men, which would be transformed into yin energy and in this form it would return to men. In taking the yin energy from women, men would increase their own, while her part of it would turn into yang energy. Beyond this exchange of energy, heterosexual masturbation was also associated with mutual taming, a sort of sexual training for later sexual intercourse. It also played a role in mystical experiences and meditation. (14)

Despite a somewhat orientalizing approach to the East, evident here as in many similar accounts thoroughly deconstructed by Edward Said, the reference to images strongly rooted in the *Arabian Nights* or the *Kama Sutra* serves to show the cultural dimension of sexual constraints in Polish society. But even here, despite a positive approach to autostimulation, the author once again discusses it in relation to successful sexual intercourse—in this case, as a pit stop before the real thing. Although he generally depicts masturbation as harmless, in most articles he approaches it with a certain distance, as if ultimately it could be a detriment to sex for two (by an inappropriate conditioning of the orgasmic path, excessive eroticization, the tendency to betrayal or premature ejaculation). Thus he places masturbation in opposition to "normal" sexual acts (this term is also used by readers) and classifies it as uncivilized sex. In so doing, he strengthens the central position of intercourse, implying the supreme role of marriage and procreation (identified with civilized and cultured sex).

These same texts address the importance of women getting to know their bodies through masturbation. In an article for *The Mirror*, the sexologist refers to research that found "women who have experience with masturbation tend to orgasm more frequently during intercourse with their partners" (Lew-Starowicz 1985b, 12). In another text for *Etc*, Lew-Starowicz claims that these experiences might actually prove useful during intercourse itself: "Optimal stimulation of the clitoris by a partner requires gaining entry to a certain programmed code. Often, men need women to help them understand these conditions" (Lew-Starowicz 1987f, 23). The second part of the quoted article describes various ways to stimulate the clitoris (Lew-Starowicz 1987g). The piece also mentions that some women might want to "finish" on their own, if the man is unable to do so, "which may negatively affect her attitude toward the partner" (Lew-Starowicz 1987f, 23). As such, women's individual stimulation of the clitoris during intercourse is considered "correct": "For some women, conditions that arise during masturbation require their application also during intercourse with a partner. It happens that during intercourse women stimulate their own clitoris, because the partner's attempts proved ineffective. This type of intercourse is most natural and should not cause any concern" (Lew-Starowicz 1985b, 12).

If we compare this approach with the portrayal of masturbation in general (associated by default with men), known to trigger all sorts of problems and fortified with many "buts," the positive recognition of female autostimulation is striking. Even the previously stigmatized "orgasmic path" (Lew-Starowicz 1983c) seems no longer problematic: women can rouse the clitoris on their own during intercourse. Such positive recognition of female masturbation can be explained by sexologists' openness to the concerns of patients and readers (Imieliński 1967f, 161; Lew-Starowicz 1987f, 1987g) who, unable to achieve orgasm in a different way, wrote to him complaining about their husbands' reactions. Paradoxically, this links with "intercourse-centrism": clitoral stimulation functions here in a different context than, for example, for American feminist sexologists like Hite (1976), who perceived it as an autonomous space of women's pleasure. Yet for Polish sexologists, the conviction that male partners should make sure that their female partners experience pleasure or should understand the needs of the opposite sex ultimately led to an appreciation of clitoral stimulation. This makes for a subtle "breach" to holding intercourse as the desirable norm. Imieliński also took part in this process. In his *Sex Life*, in the chapter on "Technique of Sexual Intercourse," he notes that some women only achieve orgasm by stimulating the clitoris. According to Imieliński, this lies "within the normal range" (Imieliński 1967f, 158). He recognizes, however, that this matter may fuel marital disagreement, and he cites the story of a twenty-six-year-old patient:

> During foreplay her husband caressed her erogenous zones as well as the clitoris. This evoked strong sexual arousal. But when he was doing "immissio," he would stop teasing the clitoris and then her excitement would gradually fall. She would never climax. She was constantly irritated, and as time passed, she became increasingly reluctant to have sexual intercourse. Once during intercourse she held her husband's hand on the clitoris after "immisio." She climaxed then. The husband, however, believed that this way of inducing orgasm was "unnatural" and a "sexual deviation." He tried to make her feel guilty that she had not warned him that she was "sexually perverted" because he might not have married her if he had known. Under her husband's influence, the patient transformed and came to believe herself that she was actually a sexual degenerate. (Imieliński 1967f, 161–62)

Conflict in the marriage gradually intensified and even when the clitoris was stimulated, the woman gradually stopped experiencing pleasure and began to feel fear. "She wanted to commit suicide. . . . She believed that her sex drive and its 'deviation' were the cause of her unhappiness. She came to the Clinic asking for help, because she could not continue living in such a state," says Imieliński (1967f, 162). He summarized the case: "Her husband's inadequate level of awareness and his treatment of a completely normal, physiological symptom as a sexual deviation led to the occurrence of serious tensions in the marriage and to the wife's aversion to sex" (162). This approach does not imply that the sexologist sees the orgasm achieved by the stimulation of the clitoris as an autonomous form of sexual pleasure. He notes only that it is "natural" and consistent with physiology and that the husbands of women who only climax in this way should simply fondle the clitoris during intercourse; their doing so will ensure happiness and harmony in the relationship (161).[8]

Lew-Starowicz also received letters from women who were able to orgasm only through stimulation of the clitoris. His unswerving reaction to such letters was to reassure these women that such habits are natural and common. At times, he also discussed appropriate techniques (see Lew-Starowicz 1970a, 1981b). In the following example of a dialogue between the doctor and a reader, Jadzia begins her letter by using sexological classification, which she probably learned having read countless articles in *Etc* on the subject: "I am a young married woman and I belong to the group of women with a clitoral type of orgasm" (quoted in Lew-Starowicz 1987f, 23). Next she describes her marriage:

> My husband knows about it, but he doesn't know how to arouse me. He gets tired and annoyed quickly, he keeps asking me, am I coming close to orgasming? It infuriates me because I get distracted. When I talked to him about it, he said that I'm built wrongly, because after a moment of arousal he stops feeling my clitoris and thinks it is underdeveloped. . . . I suggested that he read something about it. He declared that he couldn't find a description of the technique of stimulation anywhere. Such reading is impractical, he said. It's difficult for me to lead him by the hand. I think that a real man should get to know his partner. When I talked to my girlfriends about it, they said that men don't know how to satisfy women and that's why we have to help ourselves during intercourse or after. I don't like the idea; I want my husband to do it. How should the clitoris be stimulated? Maybe some backward types will get all roused up again that such advice is technical sexology, but these sorts of problems can really break a marriage and disappoint people. (23)

It is difficult to draw conclusions based on two stories, but it is also impossible to ignore the difference between this letter and the case described by Imieliński more than twenty years before. There is no sense of aberration, the wife does not believe something to be wrong with her, and instead, she urges her husband to learn about her body.[9] Still, clearly evident here is the reader's belief in the importance of clitoral stimulation for a successful marriage: the reader does not think so much about her own pleasure but rather about marital relations.

In one way or another, sexologists underscored that the clitoral orgasm is not pathological and that women have the right to feel pleasure. As one more example, the 1970 article entitled, "Love Art," begins with quotes from two letters. W.S. from Ostróda in northern Poland wrote as follows to Lew-Starowicz: "I've been married for two weeks. From the very beginning, our sexual life has not been successful. Before the wedding, I thought it was temporary, that later everything would be back to normal. Unfortunately, I still get no satisfaction. Everything is very quick, my husband can't get me aroused. He claims that I'm frigid because I don't react as fast as he does" (quoted in Lew-Starowicz 1970a, 14). Kama from Warsaw directly addresses the issue of clitoral orgasm: "We've been having sex for a year. I was always able to achieve satisfaction, but then my husband decided that I should orgasm during intercourse, and not like before, through stimulation of my clitoris. He claims that before it was wrong and that now I have to 'switch' to the new form of sex" (quoted in Lew-Starowicz 1970a, 14). The sexologist's reply starts off very firmly: "In both cases, the husbands should be the ones to undergo treatment or schooling." He continues the thought, once again returning to the question of marriage: "There still remain, unfortunately, similar cases when men, having misconceptions about the art of love, unilaterally achieve satisfaction through intercourse. Many women are not able to achieve sexual satisfaction due to the fault of their own partners. Only some of them, by chance, are able to open their eyes to the importance of technique in intercourse. By that time, a marriage is close to breaking up" (14).

The issue of the clitoral orgasm was also taken up by Wisłocka in *The Art of Love*, although in a rather different fashion: "The clitoral orgasm determines the halfway point between fondling in the initial stage of love, when men are front and central, and intercourse with the full experience of it lived together" (1978, 250). Wisłocka criticized Masters and Johnson, as well as Kinsey, for the primacy that they attributed to pleasure achieved in this manner. In her opinion, the fact that they did not recognize the centrality of the vaginal orgasm derives from their having ignored the subjective experiences of women. The agency of female patients in the process of shaping knowledge serves as an instructive example: for Wisłocka, women's stories are of greater value than research conducted by North American scientists based on large research samples.

Wisłocka (1978) argues that in the course of their lives, women develop the ability to experience clitoral-vaginal orgasm during intercourse. If this does not happen, "they return to masturbatory practices or encourage their husbands to stimulate the clitoris so that they are able to orgasm outside of intercourse" (262). This occurs because of "a fixation of the clitoral reflex, as a result of which women remain at this stage of sexual development." According to the gynecologist, such a state of affairs may lead to the disbanding of a marriage; therefore, she proposes a solution: "I developed a therapeutic method that allows women to transfer sexual sensitivity also to the vagina and to gradually achieve full clitoral-vaginal orgasm during intercourse" (262).

It is worth adding that Wisłocka (1978) became interested in this problem in response to the difficulties reported by her patients: "I recall a very nice thirty-year-old female physician, who loved and was loved in return by her husband, who came to me clearly distraught: 'I love my husband very much and we fit together exceptionally well as a married couple, but when I read books like the stories written by Boccaccio, I realize that there is something I've been missing in my life because I have never experienced full pleasure during intercourse. . . . I've orgasmed many times, because my husband takes care to satisfy me. But it has never been our shared experience'" (263). On doctor's orders the patient exercised her "vaginal muscles" and introduced new positions, thanks to which she learned to experience orgasm simultaneously with her husband: "When she came to say goodbye, she declared . . . that now she feels like a one-hundred-percent-woman" (264).

Thus, Wisłocka proposes a slightly different solution to her patients' problems. She neither normalizes nor pathologizes the clitoral orgasm. Rather, seeing it as a threat to marriage and linking it with immaturity, she proposes a technique that allows her patients to experience orgasm during intercourse.

On the whole, the most important Polish sexologists of this period point to the inferiority of masturbation and clitoral orgasm in comparison with heterosexual intercourse. In effect, they contribute to strengthening the position of the latter at the top of the sexual hierarchy. Some of Imieliński's and Lew-Starowicz's (but not Wisłocka's) considerations about the clitoral orgasm constitute the only exception. These replies came in response to the difficulties experienced by their patients but, in the end, were intended for the good of the marriage. Wisłocka, in turn, degraded ways of achieving pleasure other than through intercourse, claiming that they jeopardize marital life.

Contraception

Another issue that readers asked for expert advice about was contraception. S.A., a reader from Warsaw, wrote to Lew-Starowicz (1971*b*, 14): "What is contraception like in practice? Are there effective methods and completely ineffective ones? What methods are available in our country? Is contraception itself a desirable and necessary phenomenon?" In his answer, the sexologist begins by stressing the complexity of the matter. He reminds readers of the issues that he has already discussed in other articles, such as abortion, which, interestingly, he considers to be a contraceptive method.[10]

In his article, Lew-Starowicz (1971*b*) focuses on what he describes as the social meaning of contraception and a presentation of available methods. He notes that birth control is widely accepted all over the world and encourages readers to use it: "Human beings, due to their reason, and the responsibility they hold for themselves, their families and the social good, should manage fertility and avoid recklessness in dealing with the forces of nature" (14). He adds that contraception does not challenge the idea of motherhood; rather, contraception connotes a rational approach to motherhood. Nevertheless, the expert points to certain abuses:

> While methods of pregnancy prevention have given human beings the opportunity to eliminate the fear of unwanted pregnancy, they have also fueled selfish behavior among many people. Families with only one child prevail in large metropolitan areas and many remain deliberately without children. From a social perspective and from the point of view of the principles of mental hygiene, this is an undesirable phenomenon. Conscious childlessness in a situation where proper conditions exist for child rearing is not only a distortion of the concepts of love and motherhood, but in the long run, works against the spouses themselves (an examination of divorce statistics should suffice). (14)

According to the expert, having only one child is also problematic: "Families with only one child do great harm to their children. Although only children possess an intellect that does not deviate from the norm, their emotional and social development is often immature: egocentric and narcissistic attitudes tend to prevail" (14).

Fertility must thus be managed reasonably but not egotistically. The sexologist goes on to share his thoughts on various methods of contraception, based on his work with patients at the Polish Planned Parenthood Association (PPPA) outpatient clinic. He considers that women overly believe in the effectiveness of the pill and downplay its harmful side effects. He complains that they do not learn about their own cycles because they want easy-to-use contraception. Interestingly, the last point he makes in the article directly concerns religious issues, a rare theme in sexological publications but one that suggests the Church wielded influenced in this sphere: "Among over 70% of the faithful, there is an evident lack of acceptance and knowledge of the *Humanae Vitae* encyclical" (Lew-Starowicz 1971*b*, 14; on Lew-Starowicz's approach to *Humanae Vitae*, see Kościańska 2018). Despite announcements, the article provides little information about actual methods of birth control.

In another article from the same year, Lew-Starowicz (1971*c*, 14) again discussed the rationality of using contraception and introduced a kind of gradation: "The most primitive people in terms of the degree of sexual awareness usually exhibit a completely careless attitude to the possibility of getting pregnant. The termination of pregnancy is also popular as a method of prevention. People with a higher degree of sexual awareness make attempts to use such methods of preventing pregnancy as coitus interruptus, or mechanical and chemical means. People with the highest degree of sexual awareness use the temperature method."

Lew-Starowicz (1971*c*, 14) goes on to outline the tragic state of education in this field: "The majority of society is deprived of factual, scientific information." Nevertheless, he does not seize the opportunity to make use of his own weekly publication in the student magazine toward this end. Instead, he limits himself solely to general comments on the effectiveness, side effects, and the influence of contraception "on mental harmony and the sexual bond between partners" (e.g., in his opinion, coitus interruptus causes neurosis).

In a different article on the side effects of selected contraceptives such as IUDs (intrauterine devices) and hormonal pills,[11] Lew-Starowicz (1983*d*) strongly discouraged young women and those without children from using these methods. Letters from three such readers provide a pretext—one, Katarzyna, wrote, "I have been taking oral hormone pills for 3 years, since I started having intercourse. I hear different opinions on this subject and I'm afraid of the side effects. The gynecologist, who has been prescribing me the pill from the beginning, is always trying to calm me down, and after seeing him I do feel calmer, but later the doubts come back. Should I take them or not?" (quoted in Lew-Starowicz 1983*d*, 23).

The expert suggests that the pill might have negative effects on future motherhood. He extensively quotes Michalina Wisłocka, who discouraged girls from taking the pill because of health risks, and at the end adds, "Various scientific reports have shown that young women who take hormonal contraceptive pills experience changes such as in body shape (narrow hips), psychosexual state (sexual immaturity, disorders of the libido) and of character (aggression)" (Lew-Starowicz 1983*d*, 23).[12]

In general, the sexologist advocates the use of contraception—its use represents one of the requirements of civilized and cultured sex—but he has reservations. Contraception should not imply childlessness or the reduction of family size, and young women who have never given birth should be particularly careful about these matters (excluding teen sex). Finally, he links the use of contraceptive pills with immaturity and the loss of womanly features, especially among youth. As such, his texts contribute to reinforcing the position of heterosexual procreative intercourse at the top of the sexual hierarchy. This time, a new argument is added and comes to the forefront: fertility. Accordingly, contraception does not serve women's independence or pleasure—for which Margaret Sanger, "mother" of the contraceptive pill, fought (Coates 2008; Oudshoorn 1994). In this take, contraceptives serve reasonable procreation (for more on the pill in the Polish context, see Ignaciuk 2014, 2016, 2019).

Homosexuality

Writings about homosexuality similarly contributed to reinforcing the sexual hierarchy (for more on homosexuality and sexology in state socialist Poland, see Kościańska 2020; Szulc 2017). Arguments about (im)maturity and (the lack of) fertility were likewise employed in this context.[13] In an article from 1970, entitled "Lesbian Love," Lew-Starowicz (1970g) addresses the issue of relationships between women in a generally positive manner. He deliberates on their origins since the times of Sappho and lauds their longevity. He discusses in detail the causes of the formation of the homosexual orientation. In the end, however, he notes, "After all, the lesbian relationship is a deformation of libido and sexuality. It distorts the proper direction of the sex drive, which steers towards the heterosexual relationship and procreation. You can experience intense emotional and erotic states in lesbian love, but this does not constitute normal development of personality, which needs the conjugation of male and female traits, their coexistence and the broadening of the horizons of thought to the psychophysical world of the other gender. Treatment is possible and effective" (Lew-Starowicz 1970g, 22).

Another article from the same year examines love between men. It starts off by quoting some dramatic letters from homosexual readers. J.B. from Wrocław wrote, "Homosexuality is the most horrific sexual deviation. I experience it myself, and I consider it to be my life's tragedy. . . . Life has become such a burden to me that I cannot see any reason, for which I should like to continue it. . . . Can homosexuality be cured? I'm sure the answer is 'no.' . . . Why do I have a hard time finding women attractive?" (quoted in Lew Starowicz 1970d, 14).

The sexologist emphasizes that the letter authors really suffer and feel fear. He talks about the universality of this "disorder of normal development" and discusses the causes. Finally, he assures his readers that the condition can be treated. In both articles, sex between persons of the same sex is characterized as incomplete, immature, and nonreproductive. It is worth noting, however, that these texts date from the time when both the American Psychiatric Association (depathologization in 1973) and the World Health Organization (depathologization in 1990) considered homosexuality a disease.

An approach that mixes a certain level of understanding for homosexuals with a clear stance on homosexuality as a transgression of the norm, along with an insistence on the possibility of treatment, is also evident in other articles published in *Etc* (e.g., Lew-Starowicz 1978*b*).[14] In the 1980s, although the World Health Organization (WHO) continued to recognize homosexuality as a disease, the contrary was increasingly argued by many physicians. Lew-Starowicz (1988*d*, 120) did the same, for example, in his book *Atypical Sex*. Here, he places emphasis on the fact that homosexuals are exposed to various forms of aggression and lack wider social acceptance. He points to the complexity of the matter (117–122) and discusses issues such as the attitude of the Catholic Church (121) and difficulties in relations between parents and homosexual children (121). He speaks of therapy aimed at affirming sexual orientation by both a homosexual person and his or her community (121). He also mentions treatment aimed at changing one's sexual orientation but limits his discussion to specific conditions including being a member of the clergy, situational homosexuality, and homosexuality as a "defense mechanism against contacts with the other sex blocked by fear" (121). His other texts from this period are also increasingly accepting of homosexuality (especially among women). In the article published in *The Mirror*, Lew-Starowicz (1987*b*, 12) noted that lesbians achieve orgasm more often than other women and that "lesbian relationships, like heterosexual ones, are diverse, subject to crises, and are characterized by specific stages of development." At the same time, in the next sentence, the author equates normality with marriage.

In the meantime, the recognition of homosexuality as nondisease behavior did not come easily to readers. The article entitled "Homosexuality among Youth," published in 1988, begins with a letter from a father who, as he claims, has managed to successfully convince his son to abandon his homosexual relations, in which he engaged twice after taking drugs: "He was always honest with us and he did not hide that he was attracted to homosexuality" (quoted in Lew-Starowicz 1988*b*, 23). As a result of the talks, "he changed his orientation and now he has a fiancée, in July they are getting married, they have successful sexual relations and he is not at all attracted to homosexuality." The letter's author agrees with the view that homosexuality is not a disease and that homosexuals deserve tolerance and understanding. However, this applies, in his opinion, to "adults, already fully developed persons. The case is different," he continues, "when it comes to the adolescent period, when the causes are different and when one can still turn around on this path" (23). The sexologist answered, "Homosexuality among youth is associated with many problems. I will mention the most significant: a sense of isolation from the typical heterosexual majority, mixing homosexual behavior with addiction to drugs or alcohol, mental health problems, suicidal tendencies, and prostitution. . . . Medical centers dealing with homosexuality among young people often report various sexually transmitted diseases, irritable bowel syndrome (among those engaging in anal contacts), AIDS and psychiatric problems" (23). Next he comes back to the issue of changing sexual orientation: "Research on youth homosexuality has shown that with proper therapeutic intervention or care on the part of the family (being in good mental contact with the child), many people are able to reorient their sexual development. This applies primarily to adolescents in early and mid-stage puberty, both girls and boys" (23).

An internally contradictory message about homosexuality returns in texts dating to even later periods. This is apparent in the book *Homosexuality*, on which Zbigniew Lew-Starowicz collaborated with his son and which came out after the removal of homosexuality from the list of WHO diseases.[15] In the introduction, we read that the work is aimed at fostering "attitudes of tolerance towards psychosexual otherness, such as homosexuality" and at overcoming "myths and stereotypes" (Lew-Starowicz and Lew-Starowicz 1999, 8). In what follows, the sexologist repeatedly sheds lights on the suffering, isolation, and discrimination that homosexuals face and cites numerous examples from Polish and world research, including his own therapeutic practice. He also discusses the issue of gay and lesbian rights (115) and refers to authors like Ken Plummer (37). Nevertheless, excerpts from the book typify the heteronormative mindset. When talking about homosexual women, the main author notes, "Among lesbians, sexual dysfunction is rather rare and at least in my practice, these were isolated cases. As a rule, lesbians do not have problems with sexual arousal or achieving orgasm" (188). The expert appears to positively recognize this type of relationship. However, in the part entitled, "Stereotypes about Homosexuality," he draws on French urologist Gerard Zwang in arguing against claims that "homosexuals are masters of the love art"—Zwang "writes that lesbians like to create an impression of enigmatic myth about the pleasure they supposedly give each other" (108). Then, the author explains, "In fact, what two women can do is quite limited. Lesbian erotic techniques are mainly limited to stimulating the clitoris. A minority of them uses artificial penises. Many lesbians remain virgins for the entirety of their lives and are not interested in either their own vagina or that of their partner. If a woman who had unsuccessful contacts with men, who tried to make her achieve orgasm during intercourse while ignoring her clitoris, has an orgasm with her female partner, she will have a hard time imagining that another, more affectionate man could give her similar pleasure" (Lew-Starowicz and Lew-Starowicz 1999, 109).

A few paragraphs further down, Lew-Starowicz makes generalizations about gay and lesbian sex in a way that makes it impossible to distinguish Zwang's views from his own: "People of the opposite sex possess a most significant virtue that is their difference. What reduces the erotic value of a man for another man and of a woman for another woman is that they do not turn out to be erotically different in bed. Sexually pleasing a person of the same sex is nothing particularly attractive. Sexually pleasing another person is of value when it concerns someone else, a person whose sexuality is fascinating because it is different, unpredictable, and somewhat mysterious" (Lew-Starowicz and Lew-Starowicz 1999, 109).

Although the elder Lew-Starowicz takes note of the fact that both the American Psychiatric Association and the WHO no longer consider homosexuality to be a disorder (Lew-Starowicz and Lew-Starowicz 1999, 80–81), the book also contains a chapter on the prevention of homosexuality. The author posits that part of the "homosexual population reveals early developmental and innate characteristics" (191). As far as this group is concerned, nothing can be done. However, "the matter is different when homosexuality develops as a result of certain mechanisms of intrafamily relations and seduction" (191). In this case, its further development can be counteracted: "Proper parenting, a good emotional bond with both parents, an equality-based relationship between the parents, clearly defined male and female roles between the parents, and harmonious cooperation between the parents in providing the child psychosexual direction may favor proper identification with their own gender and heterosexual orientation" (191).

In the part about therapy, Lew-Starowicz indicates that one of the methods of "treating" homosexuality is aimed at "reorientation" (1999, 196–199). Unfortunately, this fragment does not feature in the book as a curious fact from the history of medicine. Apart from iterating this type of information, the sexologist considers issues such as "conditions necessary for effective treatment" (198). References to Catholic publications are evident, and the bibliography includes the work of a controversial Dutch psychologist, Gerard J. M. van den Aardweg, who propagated the "treatment" of homosexuals.

Altogether, Lew-Starowicz's descriptions of homosexuality serve to reinforce the definition of good sex as reproductive and heterosexual. In his discussion of lesbians, the sexologist goes even further: although experience gained through his practice shows that lesbians do not experience sexual dysfunction, the options available to them in the area of sex are severely limited because real pleasure, as we learn, requires the fusion of two people of the opposite sex. At the same time, Lew-Starowicz explicitly demands acceptance of homosexuals and wrote about their life tragedies, trying to respond to the problems faced by his patients and readers. The opposite tendency—namely, pathologization—is also visible to some extent in his writing, as in the case of his answer to the father who managed to convince his son to reorient himself toward women.

In summary, a clear image of the sexual hierarchy emerges from sexological writing. Sexual intercourse between a woman and a man (wife and husband) who are both emotionally involved, mature, and open to parenthood by means of the classic missionary position is synonymous not only with normality, health, and behavior that is civilized and cultured but also with pleasure. Such is the picture painted by sexologists and their patients and readers. Accordingly, some disruptions are present: acceptance of clitoral stimulation (a negative attitude toward this issue might hamper marital harmony), acceptance of some forms of masturbation (that help women learn about their own bodies and that are not accompanied by inappropriate male fantasies), and even some acceptance of homosexuality. Nevertheless, these breakthroughs tend to be superficial—they often serve to strengthen the place of marital intercourse at the top of the sexual hierarchy.

Gender Relations

Appropriate gender roles, relations between the genders, and specific men's and women's agency constitute the foundation of good sex in the analyzed literature. I begin by examining how Michalina Wisłocka (1978) understood gender in her book, *The Art of Love*. This most famous Polish book about sex focuses primarily on women's sexual pleasure and on family-marital happiness, for which the wife is responsible. Andrzej Jaczewski, a sexologist and author of numerous books for adolescents, perfectly illustrates Wisłocka's chief intention in his preface to the book's first edition. He begins, noting Kinsey's research, by writing that lack of sexual pleasure is common among women (Jaczewski 1978). To remedy this problem, it is necessary to "change women's attitudes toward sexuality, because to experience sexual satisfaction, you need to approve of sex" (Jaczewski 1978, 6). This is exactly what Wisłocka accomplishes in her book, he notes. He continues: "Secondly, it is necessary to learn the technique of intercourse. Let us not delude ourselves: everyone must learn the technique of intercourse. 'Instinct' is not enough here" (6).

Wisłocka herself did not hide her woman-oriented perspective. As mentioned, the book relies heavily on conversations at the gynecologist's office and on letters from readers and patients. It is addressed to women because, according to the author, they are responsible for love in marriage (Wisłocka 1978, 10, 150).

How does the author understand gender roles? First, Wisłocka (1978) strongly emphasizes the fundamental differences between men and women. She departs from a critique of Kinsey's work, particularly his claims that men and women are basically the same when it comes to sex and hormonal functions. Wisłocka wrote of Kinsey's research, "Kinsey outlined . . . the curves of sexual tension in the life of men and women. He used a very large statistical sample in his research, treating the number of sexual intercourses carried out during the week as an exponent of tension" (26). Two inaccuracies are worth noting here. Kinsey did not talk about tension but something quite the opposite. What Wisłocka translated as "sexual tension," Kinsey referred to as "sexual outlet," or release (Kinsey et al. 1948, 1953). Furthermore, the unit of measure used by the American sexologist was the orgasm, no matter how obtained.[16]

Either way, Kinsey (Kinsey et al. 1948, 1953) showed that the tension or outlet curve for both sexes grows during adolescence (much less so among women than men), when it also reaches its peak. Among men, it then gradually decreases with age, whereas for women it remains at a similar level throughout their lives. Wisłocka saw it differently: "In my many years of practice in the field of gynecology, I noticed, just like other gynecologists, that sexual tension throughout a woman's life is not unchangeable, but rather that it undergoes very distinct fluctuations" (1978, 28). Wisłocka proposes a qualitative approach to the study of women's sexual tension: the number of intercourses is not enough, she argues— orgasms in dreams and those reached "by stimulation of the clitoris (masturbation) must also be studied" (29). She notes, "In addition, I took into account the degree of sexual initiative (on the part of men or women). I further differentiated the experiences of intercourse involving only clitoral, clitoral and vaginal orgasms and multiple orgasms during one intercourse" (29).

She divided tension into low, medium, high, and maximal. Regarding men, Wisłocka (1978, 29) claims that she uses the Kinsey method, supplanting it with nocturnal emissions and masturbation. But remember that she accused the American sexologist of having based his data only on counting sexual intercourses. Wisłocka's sample totaled 500 women and 170 men. If we take into account that Wisłocka misread the Kinsey method, the difference between her qualitative method and his quantitative approach is not very significant. Although Kinsey counted orgasms, no matter how they were obtained, Wisłocka added initiative and included multiple orgasms (this last notion did not exist in Kinsey's time; it was introduced to sexology by Masters and Johnson [1966]). To her considerations she added hormone-based research (Wisłocka 1978, 31).

Wisłocka (1978) proposes her own tension curves for both sexes. The female curve grows slowly to reach its zenith around age forty, whereas the male curve grows rapidly, reaching its peak when boys are in their teens, and then starts falling slowly. Wisłocka presents this curve using a chart diagram along with her commentary, which explains the basic assumptions of her understanding of gender and sexuality:

> The trajectories of these two curves are fundamentally different, they cross during adulthood, and they diverge significantly during young adulthood and in the pre-menopause period. The graph is divided into three distinct sections. The first, covering the period between twelve and twenty-five years of age, shows a huge discrepancy in tension. I called this the first phase of conflict. The period between twenty-five and forty years of age, when sexual tension among women and men reaches the maximum and high levels respectively, is a period of sexual harmony. The period after the age of forty when the male and female curves diverge, just as they do during young adulthood, I called the second phase of conflict. (31–32)

Wisłocka (1978) characterizes the subsequent phases as follows: during the first phase of conflict, boys are characterized by emotional underdevelopment and frequent masturbation; girls are more emotional and less focused on physical sensations. Next follows a period of emotional and sexual harmony; conflicts occur in other spheres, and both women and men reach the level of high and maximal tension. During the second phase of conflict, women reach maximum tension, whereas men's sexual tension decreases; this conflict ends in broken marriages. Women tend to look for young partners, and men look for young girls with limited needs (33).

The author discusses intergenerational relationships in great detail. Her considerations on this subject speak a lot about her understanding of gender and sexuality. She begins with a discussion of the problems associated with the first phase of conflict. As mentioned, in this period, boys experience maximal sexual tension, nocturnal emissions, and a need to masturbate: "These manifestations are accompanied by a vigorous search for a partner, often successful, as confirmed by statistical data, which shows that sexual initiation for a majority of boys occurs around the age of seventeen. Finding a partner among peers is not easy, thus contacts with mature women are not a rare occurrence" (Wisłocka 1978, 32). Despite the advantages of such an arrangement where boys can learn a lot and gain valuable experience, Wisłocka points to its faults, which include a lack of commitment on the part of women: "When people of the same age are in love they give it their best and treat each other seriously. A mature woman necessarily treats her younger lover a bit like a child, with condescension, never like an equal partner" (40).

During the first phase of conflict, girls function quite differently. A physiological "underdevelopment" occurs (Wisłocka 1978, 32), accompanied by the rapid development of emotions, which "manifests itself in the search for a boy 'to have'" (33). Girls masturbate less frequently (20%), they engage in intercourse under the influence of boys "and most often they do not achieve satisfaction" (33). Among boys, emotions begin to develop only between eighteen and twenty-five years of age. Women at this age start developing "sexual receptors," which leads to a gradual increase in their interest in sex.

Relationships between the genders during this period are reduced to girls loving boys, who in return expect girls to give them proof of their love. The author cites letters from a youth magazine that recount the stories of girls pressured by boys: "He said I should give myself to him. . . . He was telling me that he has to constantly hold back his drive when he's with me, and that he might get neurosis doing this all the time" (quoted in Wisłocka 1978, 37). When another girl refused to give proof of her love, she was told, "You are still only a child, so goodbye, this is the end" (38). Wisłocka also suggests another possible scenario: "If a girl gives in, it usually does not end with one-time proof of love, it is followed by more, and then pregnancy" (38). Boys have a different perspective: "If he manages to persuade a girl of his age to have intercourse with him, he soon realizes that a partner who is not sexually developed seems 'frigid.' He soon loses interest, cursing frigidity as if it were a disability, and then moves on in the search for easy prey" (39).

In following, Wisłocka (1978) once again discusses a particularly striking element in her reflections on gender: women's responsibility for men's lives, both sexual and otherwise. She notes, "If [a boy] has great sexual needs, but *does not meet a wise girl*, a form of physical and impoverished 'mini-love' perpetuates itself in his life. Not infrequently, he takes such habits to a mature age and embarks on the career of a playboy who 'collects' girls and is incapable of loving fully, not only physically, but also emotionally" (39; emphasis added). Wisłocka's definition of women's agency here is perplexing. Not only does married life lie on the shoulders of adult women, as we read in the introduction to her book, but teenage women are already charged with this responsibility. If a young boy does not meet anyone in this period of development who will induct him into emotional life, he will not be capable of starting a family in the future. The sort of girl he must meet should be his peer, for a mature woman will not take him seriously and will teach him only sex. But how is the teenage girl to know how to behave? In following Wisłocka, the young girl might learn a lot from an adult man. Accordingly, such a relationship is much more beneficial than that between a teenage boy and a mature woman. The downside, notes Wisłocka, is that the former has little chance of enduring because at some point when a woman in her thirties reaches maximum sexual tension, her much older partner will not be able to satisfy her needs.[17] Either way, a young girl who meets a much older man can benefit greatly and may be better equipped for the role of wife, responsible for managing family happiness: "A girl brought up by a mature boyfriend can *consciously sculpt* her future spouse to her liking in the field of sex, as she knows already what she can and should ask of him" (50; emphasis added).

Wisłocka (1978) discusses power relations in couples (although she does not call it that), or rather, as we shall see further, how power is exercised in relationships. Again, the gynecologist suggests that a teenage girl's relationship with an older man is of greater value than a teenage boy's relationship with a mature woman. "In the boy's situation," she explains, "he is led by and subject to a woman's orders" (50), of which the boy himself generally does not approve. The case is different when it comes to the second type of intergenerational relationship: "In the life of a woman, on the contrary, one of the most important moments to accompany love is the awakening of the imagination and admiration for her partner. He should impress, he should be a famous and popular actor, a scholar or a great athlete, so that the woman can admire him and be proud of him. A young boy does not always have specific life plans and is only a peer, who usually does not arouse admiration or respect. A mature man has these qualities by virtue of his position, financial situation and career" (51).

The vast majority of men in late socialist Poland married in their twenties, and the divorce rate was low (GUS 2016, 187–91). In effect, many of those who entered into relationships with much younger women were married and cheating on their wives. Putting aside the fact that not every mature man shines onstage or at the stadium, the type of knowledge these men could transmit about sharing life with another person seems problematic. The issues of agency and power are worth further consideration. Boys—and, later, adult men—do not like being ordered around. In contrast, women should live in admiration of a man, follow his advice, and depend on him (including financially, which is implicit in Wisłocka's writing about men's economic situations). At the same time, women are responsible for the couple's love life, for happiness in the family, and even for the emotional states of men. She is supposed to "sculpt him" or "raise him."[18] A contradiction is apparent here: the man is to be the woman's superior, but she is also to direct him and be responsible for him. Wisłocka thus proposes a type of behind-the-scenes power, in various places calling it "women's diplomacy" (1978, 76–77) or "women's action" (101). Wisłocka believes that in this way, a woman can attract and keep a man: "The old rule is simple and always invariable: a man asks, gains, reveals and charms, while a woman lets herself be seduced and charmed, but in words and in letters she should not be too straightforward in revealing her interest in him" (65).

Let us take a closer look at this strategy and its implications for women's agency. Flirting, for example, is an important element of male-female relations. In following Wisłocka (1978), women should know how to walk, sit, smile, or how and when to cry (6–77). They should know how to dress and how to look after the home's interior (81). Wisłocka calls these skills the love secrets of our grandmothers, who had no opportunities other than the aforementioned women's diplomacy. They thus developed the art of seduction, which mothers passed on to their daughters (76–77). Generally, flirting helps "on the difficult path of getting a man" (92). Wisłocka distinguishes the next stages of this process: admiration for the partner, encouraging him to talk about himself, and finally showing her female weakness and expressing her desire to be cared for. Yet women should remember never to discuss the mundane problems of daily life in bed or at the table. If the source of her worry is her beloved—his hygiene or health, for example—she should approach the matter with caution. How can she persuade a man to wash or to go to the dentist? "Under no circumstances should the boy's ambition be disturbed, women's resourcefulness must be put into action and the destination reached by an indirect path" Wisłocka notes (110). Women should not be direct in communicating their sexual needs, and they are advised to inhibit their partner's cravings (150). It must be mentioned that Wisłocka proposed this traditional relationship model in a country where the emancipation of women was the official gender policy. Effectively, she could not ignore the issue. Asserting that women should not initiate sex, because this could kill a relationship (150), the sexologist says, "You might shout with outrage: what about equal rights?" (151). She proposes arguments from both the world of science and common knowledge:

> In the domain of sex there is no, and there never will be, such a thing as two identical feelings. The basic differences as well as the psychosexual differences between men and women must be reconciled with, just the same as with the fact that men will never give birth to children. . . . Our grandmothers claimed that "man is a hunter and woman a bird he preys on." The more difficult to hunt, the more precious. Girls, don't take away from your boys the pleasure of hunting for a treasured prize. Look at the tremendously proud and delighted faces of men in magazines or television showing off with triumph the biiig fish they caught with their own hands. Their faces are a display of absolute happiness. He was the one to catch a fish that few can boast of. (151–52)

Elsewhere in the book, she characterizes gender roles as follows: "A man wants to be domineering, strong, and a caretaker, who is necessarily needed by his beloved and always worthy of her admiration. A woman wants to be caressed, she wants to arouse fascination, be cared for endearingly, especially in times when she is suffering and feeling helpless. Besides that, she also always wants to be wanted by her man" (90). Next she discusses in detail the theme of flirting, emancipation, and women being bound to the private sphere:

> As previous analysis shows, flirting is a powerful sexual-emotional mechanism that makes love endure. Initial play and word fencing from the period when feelings are just awakening is gradually transformed, as love ripens, into the rules of the game that almost come to determine its existence.

Contemporary women, excited by the opportunity of equality at work and in science, in their enthusiasm for making careers that were previously only available to men, throw the baby out with the bathwater, doing great harm to themselves.

You can be educated, you can work in science, you can be a professional, or you might be an activist, but at home and in love, a woman must be a woman and a man a man if they want to live a full life, avoiding disappointments and complexes. Love and the home are an inviolable asylum, and only the lifestyle and occupation of both spouses can be the subject of transformations or contracts of one sort or another. No emancipation can change the fact that a woman is a mother and gives birth to children, and that during motherhood and the nursing period she needs a man's care. Nothing will change in this area, unless they start breeding people in test-tubes and the family ceases to exist. (91)

Elsewhere, Wisłocka discusses femininity alongside motherhood (e.g., Wisłocka 1978, 42), to which, in her opinion, women always strive:

Pregnancy is a school of unselfish feeling that embraces the whole course of her life. Already then, a future mother can fully showcase what she is capable of. The child (in the mother's womb) is a beloved partner, for whom she goes out for a walk so it gets a lot of oxygen, for whom she finds special nourishment so that it is healthy and strong, for whom she controls herself and inhibits her bad moods so that it can be tranquil and serene. The child responds to its mother's care by growing and developing in a favorable and peaceful environment, or by deteriorating and wilting in an environment of stress, its mother's cries and anxieties. (17)

It is thanks to motherhood that women pass on the need for love to children. This makes for another aspect of women's responsibility: "The warmth and tenderness of a mother's feeling that fills the life of an infant is the foundation from which the instinct of love is born, the need for a bond and for intimate contact with another human being. We are convinced by a lot of research on the life of animals about how incredibly important is this period in a child's life towards the proper development of emotions in adulthood" (18).

In summary, for Wisłocka, gender roles are closely bound to sex. How do her considerations translate to a definition of good and bad sex? Good sex will, of course, be heterosexual: "The love between a man and a woman becomes the synthesis of all the forms experienced so far, the desire and realization of a physical and emotional union" (Wisłocka 1978, 22).[19] Some of its elements are related to gender. For example, Wisłocka positively assesses intergenerational relationships in which the appropriate gender roles are maintained, that is, when a woman is a woman and a man is a man—what is possible only in a teenage girl's relationship with a mature male partner. Consequently, transgression of the sexual hierarchy is only illusory. In marriage, proper gender roles are a precondition of harmony, successful sex, and, in effect, a happy family. Wisłocka sees women in the private sphere (she does not talk about women's autonomous functioning), and she burdens women with responsibility for the home and for teaching others how to love. She overamplifies women's agency and power in these domains, equating it with responsibility; however, women can exercise this agency and power in only in a very specific, indirect way, just as they should articulate their needs, including sexual needs. Accordingly, an emancipated woman, or a direct-mannered woman, who expects equality in the home sphere will not achieve success in love. Does it make sense to talk about agency in such a setting? Is it superficial here?[20] I return to these questions in the part 3, where I examine women's agency in the context of sexual violence.

How did Lew-Starowicz understand gender and relations between the genders in his publications from the 1970s and 1980s? *Sex on Equal Terms* (Lew-Starowicz 1983*f*) is another exceptionally popular Polish book about sex. Like Wisłocka's *The Art of Love*, it came about as the result of dialogue with readers and patients. This process legitimizes the knowledge presented in the book. As mentioned earlier, fragments were initially published in *Etc* in response to the letters that Lew-Starowicz received from readers. In the introduction, Lew-Starowicz notes, "My study of medicine and psychology, as well as my interest in culture-related issues made it substantially easier for me to gain a certain perspective on the problems of sex on equal terms, but I owe the most to my patients and to the readers who sent in letters to the magazines, with which I have been cooperating for a long time" (1983*f*, 5). What does sex on equal terms mean to Lew-Starowicz?[21]

> The idea of a relationship based on equal terms has been propagated for many years. This relationship is to be based on the principle of gender equality, the lack of dominance of any of the partners over the other, the division of duties, joint decision making, sexual cooperation, and the demand of a single morality (and not as before, a different morality for women and men). In the field of sex, a relationship based on equal terms is one in which there is sexual activity on the part of both partners, similar privileges and duties, equal treatment of gender (and not, for example, expecting virginity from the wife, while according the man the right to sexual freedom), shared responsibility for the course of sexual intercourse, birth control, and etc. A more practical vision of such a relationship based on equal terms assumes that both parties are active professionally, that they jointly run the household, raise children, there is egalitarianism between the partners, expression of their sexual needs and expectations, while the so-called sexual past is considered "meaningless." (205–6)

Lew-Starowicz wrote about relationships based on equal terms many times before. For example, in his 1970 article published in *Etc*, entitled "The Family," he explains, "The family transformation crisis is a fact, about which many observers of life are pessimistic. This is, however, a crisis of growth. A new opportunity is opening up for the family. That is a relationship based on equal terms, on interpersonal relations, and mutual love" (Lew-Starowicz 1970*m*, 14). The sexologist considers whether this opportunity is being seized. Some are not prepared for it, he suggests, because the social climate is not conducive, the home is treated like a hotel, and the depreciation of motherhood is underway along with the underdevelopment of fatherhood. He concludes that we are facing the effects of the lack of an ethical system.

Thus, we see a relationship model completely different from that described by Wisłocka. In *Sex on Equal Terms*, Lew-Starowicz (1983*f*) adds that although this model is gaining popularity by means of journalism and popular culture, it remains contrary to tradition and individual modes of upbringing. He also defines gender equality, which he believes denotes "a similar dignity and set of values, although there is no such thing as psycho-physical equality" (Lew-Starowicz 1983*f*, 206). Both sides often prefer activity on the man's part and passivity on the woman's. "The idea of a partnership based on equality in terms of dignity, rights, morality, and egalitarianism is correct," he resolves. But he goes on to add: "Daily life together requires a certain tactic and strategy that takes into account the specificity of gender differences and the partners' individual characteristics" (209). So being on equal terms also includes cultivating gender differences. The sexologist repeatedly wrote about cultivating femininity and masculinity, key issues in a good relationship. Lew-Starowicz understands these concepts in a manner similar to what Wisłocka (1978) described a few years earlier. This perspective is clearly evident in his analysis of successful and unsuccessful marriage. Conditions that determine the former include "strong male and female characteristics that give a sense of separate mental worlds complementing each other. Among women: intelligence, practicality, ability to self-control, ability to manage household affairs, to take care of herself (appearance, clothing), coquetry, grace, motherhood. Among men: reflexivity, stability, partnership, the ability to be independent, emotional warmth, having some constantly developing passion, strength of will and conviction" (Lew-Starowicz 1983*f*, 109). The characteristics of a failed marriage include "among women: features of strong domination, rivalry, frigidity and emotional dryness. Among men: lack of perseverance, excitability, suspicion, inability to behave, a boring personality, judging women based solely on sexual worth and their ability to be a housewife" (110). A certain contradiction is apparent here: sex on equal terms is possible if women are women and men are men in a stereotypical sense. Equal terms in sex do not mean equal terms in life.

Despite these limitations of equal terms, for readers—and perhaps primarily for women readers—Lew-Starowicz's writing implies progress. An example is provided by a young woman who signed her question to the sex expert as "Baby from Poznań," a big city in western Poland:

I am engaged to Andrzej, we will soon be married. I am concerned about one thing: Andrzej always tells me that in marriage, the man does the managing. He claims that this is in harmony with nature and historically proven. He tries to make me obey him even in our everyday decisions. We are students in the same class, we share common interests, I don't see any reason to give in to him, but I do anyway for peace of mind. I know well that at his house it was his father who decided about everything, and the same was at my house. But I can't agree with these "laws of nature." I love Andrzej and I want to go together through life with him. Maybe he'll read your article and come to the conclusion that it is the time of equality now. Could you please take a position on this in your article in *Etc.* (quoted in Lew-Starowicz 1970*h*, 14)

In his article responding to the letter, Lew-Starowicz notes that what the reader describes represents a problem for many married couples in Poland and is a result of a clash of relationship models. He notes, "Three models exist: the traditional (with patriarchal features, where man is the deciding party, and where the woman bears the burdens of family and household life), those based on equal terms (in which both sides are formally employed and share home activities, decisions are made together, women have much autonomy) and the modern-matriarchal, where woman is the leader" (14). He proceeds to give historical examples of various forms of, as he calls it, "patriarchy," after which he moves on to the current situation:

> Some men try to defend their dominant position. These attempts are, however, unsuccessful and inadvisable. Contemporary changes indicate that the model based on equal terms or that based on female domination are gaining strength and that patriarchy is becoming an anachronism. . . . A marriage based on equal terms is an expression of modernity. It no longer relies on the stereotypes of masculinity or femininity, or on the internalized models, but on the recognition of the equality and virtue of each gender. Everyone should pursue their interests, qualifications, take an active part in social life, and share the difficulties of family life or housework. Decisions and intentions should be of a collective character: they should be the sum of various opinions. Neither manhood nor womanhood should decide, but the authority of wisdom, and the good of mutual love and family. (14)

At the end, the expert turns to Baby from Poznań, encouraging her to express her own opinion: "Andrzej is guided by the traditional marriage model that now belongs to the past. Forcing obedience is a symptom of immaturity. References to the 'laws of nature,' or history are not justified, because these are determined by culture. I am concerned that the concessions you have been making might do more harm in the long run. One of women's tasks is to *sculpt* a real man, meaning help him acquire sensitivity, subtlety, responsibility, and especially in creating a collective WE" (14; original emphasis).

This piece of advice speaks a lot to how the sexologist understands masculinity and femininity. On the one hand, he promotes a model of masculinity open to the domestic sphere, which represents a certain departure from the "patriarchal model." On the other hand, like Wisłocka and in classical Polish sex counseling unchanged since the nineteenth century (see chap. 1), he places responsibility for the family on the shoulders of women.

This contradiction is also evident in Lew-Starowicz's critique of moral changes. He cites research finding that 29 percent of women fantasize about being raped. This may seem strange, says Lew-Starowicz, but he continues:

> After more in-depth analysis, it turned out that this type of erotic fantasy does not suggest masochistic cravings, but is rather an expression of an atavistic model of femininity, which implies the desire for being captured by a male predator. For many women, the idea of sex on equal terms, or mutual activity, the need for subtlety and sensitivity on the man's part, or his attention to the diverse love arts are

contrary to their needs. Living in the context of emancipation, where male and female roles are blurred, forced into various activities, domination, and burdened with duties, it is precisely "in bed" that they want to be conquered, in order to feel like women. For these women, their partner's subtlety or sensitivity is equated with his being effeminate. This interesting problem indicates that the processes of changes in morality are not unambiguous. (1983f, 76)

Is emancipation bad for sex? Lew-Starowicz touches on this problem in other places, for example, while reflecting on sex in the future: "Women are forwarding significantly greater demands and sexual expectations that indirectly result from emancipation and sex education. This phenomenon is currently one of the most frequent causes of sexual dysfunction among men" (334).

The emancipated woman as the source of sex problems appears in many other texts by Lew-Starowicz. In his 1975 article for *Etc*, based on his own observations, the sexologist tries to answer the question, "What personality traits attract the opposite sex?" One of the points touched on emancipation: "In our culture, women's visible domination, their independence and self-confidence lessens their attractiveness" (Lew-Starowicz 1975a, 20). As for men, "attractiveness . . . is more related to self-control, prudence, the ability to provide support and give a sense of security" (20). According to the expert, aggression is not recommended for either sex. Rivalry might also be a problem: "Attractiveness is greater when competitive tendencies do not dominate. Thus, relationships where the woman has a higher education or social position than the male partner are at greater jeopardy" (20).

A strong, modern woman can also negatively affect a man's sexual performance and, consequently, the overall quality of the couple's sex life. This perspective is already evident in Lew-Starowicz's early articles for *Etc*, such as "Male Sexual Neuroses" (Lew-Starowicz 1970e), in which he discusses the issue of premature ejaculation. In this article, he also aims to comfort young men upset after unsuccessful first attempts at intercourse (in his opinion, usually the problem passes on its own). The expert notes:

> For some patients the mechanism is even more complicated. Their partners are "contemporary" women experienced in love art who advance certain demands of the men. During sexual intercourse, they do not take on a passive and submissive attitude, but an active, inquisitive and challenging attitude. They become the "examiners" of a man's sexual performance. For the male partner, successful intercourse is not only a matter of sexual satisfaction, but of passing the "exam." He therefore commits to this trial all of his effort, skill and attention. Excessive concentration combined with anxiety paralyzes the ability to self-control at the point of climax and . . . symptoms of sexual neurosis emerge. (Lew-Starowicz 1970e, 14)

In another piece, Lew-Starowicz formulates this problem as follows: emancipation leads to neuroses, conflicts, and the blurring of boundaries between the genders. In effect, it fosters rivalry: "*Many modern women practically do not know what femininity is about. They do not know that it can be consciously shaped and molded.* In effect, these women take on the characteristics of male behavior, which often incites the resistance and reluctance of men. Others, in following the traditional concepts of femininity (submissiveness, passivity, and sentimentality) also face criticism and reluctance as increasingly more modern men value active women who cooperate in love art with a sense of reality" (Lew-Starowicz 1973h, 20; original emphasis).

In his 1988 text, "A Dominant Factor," Lew-Starowicz (1988a) considers why some women do not experience orgasm during intercourse except by stimulation of the clitoris. Among the reasons, according to the sexologist, are "male characteristics in the woman's psyche, dominance over the male partner, which implies that during intercourse the woman does not give herself fully and without restraint, she does not abandon herself" (23).

Strong femininity comes hand in hand with, as the sexologist defines it, a crisis of masculinity (see Lew-Starowicz 1983f, 15). In his article entitled, "The Twilight of Masculinity?" published in *The Mirror* magazine in 1979, Lew-Starowicz addresses the issue of the development of masculinity, in response to his readers. Based on research and observations, he asserts that in recent times, "the process of the formation of masculinity is disturbed, which leads to man lacking a clear picture as to his role" (Lew-Starowicz 1979, 26). For starters, the origins of this state of affairs should be sought in the strong position of the mother in the family and the feminization of education, through which boys lack "male authority figures." Also to blame are women's emancipation, women's increasing sexual experience, and the strong position of women in marriage: "Often . . . from the outset the woman becomes the dominant one. Once at the steer, she takes on the role of mother to her husband. The husband is like her first child" (26). The sexologist summarizes his considerations as follows:

> All these phenomena prompt the atrophy of masculinity, and its vague character. It is no wonder that this makes erotic fascination with men, their authority, and their position of an equal partner, difficult. In turn, women look not only to complement their psychological traits with characteristics from the masculine world, but also for the possibility of feeling like a woman and experiencing fascination. In result, a discrepancy ensues between seeing a partner as a man and as a husband. This last role can be accepted and highly appreciated: the husband helps at home, takes care of the house and the child, but fails in the role of erotic partner because he does not exhibit features that incite the fascination. (26)

At the end of the article, Lew-Starowicz places his reflections in the context of his female readers' experiences: "I might be accused of exaggerating the problem. After all, many letters and women's magazines give examples of the suffering of women who have 'manly' partners who are not much concerned with their feelings, who brutally enforce on them various 'marital duties,' who are focused on their own sexual pleasure, and who are out of tune with everyday family life. It seems to me that these women's protests are simply louder and their dramas more pronounced" (26).

Nevertheless, Lew-Starowicz gives a lot of space to noting what he considers positive changes that have taken place in male behavior: "Masculinity has been enriched with elements of creativity and made more sensitive to the individual needs and expectations of the female partner who now demands plasticity, maturity and responsibility in contact with another human being of a different gender" (1973g, 20). Furthermore, the sexologist links women's sexual problems with patriarchal culture. In his 1970 piece, "Women's Sexual Frigidity," he posits that men shoulder responsibility for the disorder. More precisely, men are at fault through their brutality and lack of skill, as well as the general conditions of life:

> Brutal behavior on the part of the male partner, pain, and fear of pregnancy are the most common causes of various types of frigidity. Other causes include obstacles to sex (shared housing, being in a rush, fear of being compromised or that an unwanted person will enter the room). Sometimes a woman is not in the mood for sex (exhaustion, irritability . . .) but a selfishly-minded partner might enforce her consent . . . at the cost of her developing neurosis. The stress of modern life, hasty shopping and anxiety at the workplace, all of this does not create the right aura for sexual relationships, which, taken up only as a marital obligation, can have sad consequences. (Lew-Starowicz 1970j, 14)

Although initially it may seem that Lew-Starowicz understands relationships and sex differently than Wisłocka, careful reading allows for finding many similarities between the two authors—most notably, placing women in the private sphere and linking emancipation with sex problems. Nevertheless, Lew-Starowicz is much more committed to responding to the social concerns articulated by his patients and readers, whereas Wisłocka trains her focus on a romantic vision of the relationship between the genders. In addition, Wisłocka concentrates on women's indirect expression and limits their agency to "women's diplomacy." Lew-Starowicz sees the genders in mutual collaboration during sex, whereas Wisłocka at once advances this type of cooperation and refuses women the right to initiate sex. How both Wisłocka and Lew-Starowicz approach femininity and women's agency is consistent with the understanding of gender that was prevalent in their times. An analysis of the women's press from 1974 (*Girlfriend* [*Przyjaciółka*], *Woman and Life* [*Kobieta i Życie*], *Filipinka*) conducted by Polish sociologists Mira Marody and Anna Giza-Poleszczuk (2000) revealed a similar interpretation of agency and power in relationships. Marody and Giza-Poleszczuk show that both readers' letters and magazine articles refer to women "raising" their husbands and encouraging men, in an indirect way, to change their behavior (161–62). In these descriptions, men seem inept and helpless; they are big children who cannot receive direct communication. The issue of indirect expression is also connected with another phenomenon, addressed by the cultural studies scholar Małgorzata Szpakowska (2003): conversation as a relationship method is a new occurrence. Juxtaposing diaries and letters from the 1960s and 1990s, Szpakowska argues that only texts from the later period suggest awareness that "lack of verbal communication is something bad and detrimental to cohesion in the relationship" (215).[22]

Responsibility for the family definitively lies on the shoulders of women, as also confirmed by Szpakowska's (2003, 38) research. The social historian Małgorzata

Fidelis (2009), who analyzed *Filipinka* magazine, noted that sexual restraint was encouraged among girls. In addition, girls were both warned against boys seeking closer contact and blamed for the sexuality of the latter (Fidelis 2009, 179).

Finally, regarding the issue of emancipation, Szpakowska correctly points out that after the postsocialist transformation in Poland, "the virtues of the post-war emancipation of women were repeatedly undermined" (2003, 110). Her exhaustive analysis of letters and diaries shows, however, that women's emancipation was a fact: "there was a development of the social personhood . . . of the wife-mother" that made the family a field of "negotiations" (108). This was forced to some extent by social and economic conditions that led to "occupational activation" (Marody and Giza-Poleszczuk 2000, 160), but women were proud of their successes at work and the fact that they managed despite often being in a difficult situation (Szpakowska 2003, 109). Nevertheless, the process of change in relations between the genders did not proceed without disruptions. Women continued to voice dissatisfaction concerning relations with their husbands and other issues like general exhaustion—a result of the need to handle both formal employment and housework. At the same time, men were not entirely enthusiastic about women's employment outside of the house on a massive scale (Szpakowska 2003, 54–63 passim).

Sex and the Double Burden

The work of sexologists could seem like the medicalization of stereotypes and the Catholic understanding of sex and marriage—that is, entrenching women in the home while situating men in the public sphere or identifying women with passivity and men with activity. Through this lens, transgressing the boundaries of predefined gender roles leads to an unsuccessful sex life. This interpretation has its limitations. Sexological works can be examined as a discourse transforming religious and common knowledge into science, as described by Thomas Laqueur (1990, 2003) and Michel Foucault (1978) using the example of Europe in the eighteenth through early twentieth centuries. However, this approach does not allow us to fully understand the processes that took place in state-socialist Poland or in the 1990s and after 2000. It might also be argued that sexology's antiemancipatory message was an element of socialist biopolitics—an expression of the official reaction to Stalinism, still on the agenda in the 1970s—that promoted the image of a woman-worker involved in the construction of socialism as a tractor driver or steel plant operator (about the Stalinist ideology of gender and the reaction to it, see Fidelis 2010).

Understanding sexological knowledge as dialogical allows for a different interpretation. Could the association of women with the private sphere—along with the criticism of their work outside the house and the general definition of good, as well as civilized and cultured, sex (the first element, of which, was knowledge about "gender psychology")—be an attempt to respond to the concerns of patients and readers relating to the existing gender politics? A 1970 article by Lew-Starowicz published in *Etc*, entitled "Emancipation and Eros," provides an example. As usual, the text takes the form of a reply to a letter and begins with its citation. K. L. from Warsaw wrote:

> In one of the articles you mentioned that the condition of successful sexual relationship is psychological comfort, meaning a state of rest, not being rushed, and of emotional balance. I think that for most married women that is utopia. First, I go to work, then I come back home and do housework, in the evening I am exhausted and I have only one desire—go to sleep, sleep as long as possible. Sex is a luxury for me. I desire it, but in fact sex is forced, I give it to my husband, but I take no satisfaction at all. Only during vacations and holidays I become more interested in it. A lot is being said about women's emancipation, but emancipation results in a double or even triple burden for women and a constant feeling of exhaustion, and when it comes to sex it brings frigidity. (quoted in Lew-Starowicz 1970b, 14)

In his response, Lew-Starowicz begins with a reference to sociological research (he does not give specific information) that "testifies to the existence of disharmony between the professional, the family and the erotic functions of women" (1970b, 14). He then argues that the level of emancipation has surpassed the expectations of those who fought for it, such as Narcyza Żmichowska, a nineteenth-century writer and women's rights activist whose struggle he reviews in the text. Next, he quotes Poland's foremost romantic poet, Adam Mickiewicz on gender equality and lists many positive effects of women's liberation. He notes, "The further course of emancipation allowed women air and movement for the body, legal protection for the child, the opportunity to develop their interests, and the right to vote." However, "Women's emancipation has also had negative effects: various forms of copying male behavior (smoking, drinking, sexual freedom). It has also brought about unhealthy competition between women and men, which appears in many households and workplaces" (14). This, he argues, makes women and men behave in new ways and take on new roles and has disastrous effects on sex and male-female relations. He explains, referring to the biblical Eve, "Warmongering Eve is deprived of grace, femininity, intuition, and goodness, or of all those qualities, thanks to which she can raise a real man. Meanwhile man, in encountering his 'doppelgänger' on the field of battle, usually bolts and descends into infantilism" (14).

The definition of gender roles proposed in this text is typical of Polish sex manuals. This sort of definition can be found in *The Art of Love*, in the nineteenth-century works referred to in chapter 1, and in the women's press of the 1960s and 1970s (see Fidelis 2009; Marody and Giza-Poleszczuk 2000), as well as in the already cited works by Lew-Starowicz (see, e.g., Lew-Starowicz 1970h, 14). In all these publications, the woman is responsible for the family and the husband. Such a perspective can be taken even further: the "upbringing" of real men was, after all, a fundamental patriotic duty and civic obligation of the traditionally idealized vision of the Polish woman, the *Matka-Polka* (Polish Mother; Matynia 2003; Ostrowska 2004).

Let us return to the sexologist's argumentation: "Rivalry has extended into the field of Eros. I have already discussed this as one of the causes of male sexual neuroses. Ideas of progress, women's liberation, women's passions are bandied about by proponents of female employment. Sociological research does not confirm this enthusiasm. Most women work because they have to" (Lew-Starowicz 1970b, 14). The sexologist confirms his argument with statistics. The higher the husband's earnings, the less frequent the wife's work. He discusses research, which shows that women are essentially interested in home affairs, and even if they are fascinated by work, they are aware of the fact that their household suffers in effect. Lew-Starowicz adds:

> It must be admitted that the modern woman who is employed outside the house, works double and sometimes triple time, as a result of which she is permanently tired and weary. Husbands are not helpful at all. Withdrawing from the battlefield, they do not give up their stereotypical thinking and leave the housework to women. Only 12 to 20 percent of husbands actually help out at home, the rest spend time in "manly ways" and have male sexual expectations. The above condition not only contradicts the principles of everyday psycho-hygiene, but also brings about the premature aging of women and secondary frigidity. (14)

The sexologist goes on to assert that he fully agrees with the author of the letter and proposes some utopian, as he contends, principles of psycho-hygiene:

1. Formal employment is good for women only if it stems from her interests.
2. Mothers of young children under three years of age should not work.
3. Women by nature need more sleep, especially during pregnancy and menstruation. As a rule, women need more sleep than men.
4. Women need daily relaxation, several times per day (lying down comfortably with the legs elevated) to regenerate the psyche and prevent the formation of varicose veins.
5. The ideal would be part-time work. (14)

The first five utopian principles of psycho-hygiene render woman a delicate creature in need of protection. The sixth principle is addressed to men: "Men's help in housework does not disturb his 'masculinity,' but rather helps to develop his involvement in household matters" (14). All of these principles are preconditions of good sex. According to the seventh and last principle, "Sex can become art only under conditions of psychological comfort" (14).

The problem of overworked women was intensely discussed in the period from which the letter is dated. Research on the subject was carried out by Hanna Malewska (1969), who could be called the Polish Kinsey. Along with her team, Malewska conducted a large-scale survey of women's approach to sexuality and reproduction in the mid-1960s, recruiting participants among gynecological patients. Her findings confirm that the author of the letter was not alone: "We have noticed a clear relationship between sexual satisfaction and the lack of fatigue. . . . Patients who answer that they never have time for themselves and that they do not have time for their own pleasures, have a much worse sex life . . . so we can conclude that a minimum of rest and mental comfort is necessary to enjoy sex" (Malewska 1969, 235–36). Malewska refers to the work of Magdalena Sokołowska, a medical sociologist, who examined the phenomenon of the double burden and its consequences in her 1963 book, *Working Woman: The Socio-Medical Specificity of Women's Work* (*Kobieta pracująca. Socjomedyczna charakerystyka pracy kobiet*): "According to the research cited, the average female inhabitant of a village or town spends 41 hours per week doing housework, and yet most women in the age group we are interested in also have full time jobs. Relieving women of excessive work at home is thus becoming a social problem that awaits urgent solution" (236).

The issue of exhaustion was also raised in earlier sexological studies. In *Sexual Life*, Imieliński wrote that man, "as a party active in the relationship" (1967f, 140), should strive not only to bring his wife pleasure but also to help out with housework: "The most necessary, however, may be assisting his wife in her work, her usually great effort, due to which she is overworked, physically exhausted, and has a hard time enjoying sexual pleasure" (140–41).

In this framework, sexological works iterate the voices of patients and readers who are confused by conflicting messages about gender roles and unable to cope with changes. These are the voices of women who spend forty-eight hours a week at work and another forty-one hours on cleaning and cooking at home.[23] These are the voices of men who do not know how to respond to the emancipation of women. The sexologists propose an answer: a return to traditional roles. Presenting these roles as a precondition of successful sex serves to naturalize them, thus the constantly recurring message of emancipated women as a threat to sex. At the same time, as we have seen, sexologists often explicitly appreciate moral changes and women's greater autonomy. They even encourage women to take on more active roles in sex (as in *Sex on Equal Terms* [Lew-Starowicz 1983f]) and openly criticize patriarchal culture, charging it with responsibility for women's sexual problems. In effect, their answer is just as contradictory as gender policy in state-socialist Poland.

The idea of reinstalling traditional gender roles (including the specific agency of women; i.e., her responsibility for family and sexuality, exercised from behind the scenes along with indirect expression) may have various sources. First to mind is the Catholic Church, the influence of which in the time of communism cannot be overlooked. But it is worth noting that the Catholic position on issues such as the gender division of labor at home did not necessarily have to be "traditional." For example, Szpakowska (2003, 56) mentions a debate that took place in 1961 in *The Catholic Weekly* (*Tygodnik Powszechny*) magazine and that began with an article by a priest, Stanisław Kluz, entitled "Raising Men." Szpakowska recounts that Kluz "argued that due to the fact that women, being responsible for the home and children, are usually more burdened than men, this state of affairs should not be considered right or worth maintaining" (2003, 56). Furthermore, Kluz called on husbands to help in raising children and to appreciate woman's work outside the house. He also wrote that it is important "to care for her sexual satisfaction"(56). Kluz's argumentation notwithstanding, many Catholics in Poland thought differently.

Other socialist countries, and primarily Soviet scholars, served as other sources of knowledge about gender in Poland. Interviewees for my research mentioned that during state socialism, scientific exchange between countries of the Eastern Bloc flourished, with sexologists taking active part and cooperating mainly with representatives from Czechoslovakia and the Soviet Union. Rivkin-Fish notes that in the 1970s in the latter country, strong and independent women were definitely considered a negative phenomenon: "Kul'turnost' or cultured-ness continued to be invoked as a scheme for proper behavior and etiquette in personal interactions, while women and men were now instructed that being a cultured, moral person required them to realize the dictates of their gendered 'nature.' While in Western Europe and North America the women's movement seized upon images of sexual equality, and egalitarian relations between men and women became popular among university educated groups, Soviet experts claimed the need to 'raise the culture of male-female interactions' by modifying girls' and women' s behavior" (1999, 804).

In the 1970s, Czechoslovak sexologists, who were proponents of gender equality in the 1950s, also hailed a return to traditional gender roles: happy marriage was imagined as being based on hierarchy (Lišková 2018). For ex-ample, one of the most popular Czechoslovak marriage manuals from this era reads, "The situation is easier for couples where the man has a higher intellect than the woman. These settings complement the patriarchal family system. It is truly a stumbling block if the situation is reversed" (quoted in Lišková 2016, 222).[24] In the Polish context, sexologists interacted with multiple thought col-lectives: they listened to the voices of their readers and patients, drew from dis-ciplines associated with the humanities and social studies (marked at the time by a male bias), and participated in scientific exchanges (e.g., with Czechoslova-kia and the Soviet Union; in the latter case, they probably obliged to draw on certain models). But did they come into contact with feminist thought, which could introduce a different perspective to this interactive process? Western feminism was not known in Poland, and the little information about it that reached the country was not taken seriously for political reasons.[25] In mention-ing the Hite report, for example, Lew-Starowicz signified his distance (see Lew-Starowicz 1983f, 154). While the League of Polish Women was indeed a dynamic and active organization (see, e.g., Grabowska 2018; Nowak 2009), in matters of sex, its main expert was Lew-Starowicz, who published regularly from 1977 to 1989 in the League's official weekly, *The Mirror*. The magazine previously pub-lished articles that touched only marginally on sex matters, such as conscious motherhood (there were also regular advertisements of spermicides, such as the suppository "Globulka Z" or the gel "Preventin"), abortion, and venereal dis-eases, and gave advice on matters of the "heart" (given by the novelist Zofia Bys-trzycka, who made sure that it included no references to sex).[26] The issue of sex education, or the lack of it, was discussed only as a social problem that should be solved. Issues related specifically to sex were never elaborated. Before 1977, Lew-Starowicz came up in *The Mirror* only once, as the hero of a short note in the column "Through Our Binoculars" (jot. 1971, 2). The note explains that the sexologist took part in a debate organized by the *Catholic Weekly* on women's formal employment and that he published a text entitled, "The Crooked Paths of

Women's Emancipation" (Lew-Starowicz 1971*d*). The author of the column, who signed their name "jot.," wrote, "It can be assumed, although he does not say it explicitly, that Lew-Starowicz favors the traditional family model" (jot. 1971, 2). According to jot., Lew-Starowicz presented women as lost, unable to cope in marriage, and in need of excessive comforts. The sexologist "expresses fear of the masculinization of the fair sex" and regrets the lack of marriage scenarios and positive models of motherhood. Jot. continues, "The author does not propose any new solutions. He talks about part time work, the development of services that would make housework and childcare less grueling, as well as . . . about the freedom to choose between having a job or doing housework only, or to combine one with the other. This only goes to show that there should be no ready-made *scenarios*. So what could make for a 'socially accepted' *model*? Or maybe three off the get-go? Unfortunately, the author does not write about this" (jot. 1971, 2; original emphasis).[27] This short note constitutes the only critical response on the part of the women's league to sexological antiemancipatory writings.[28] For example, Janina Pałęcka, a member of the editorial board of *The Mirror*, in her otherwise interesting interview with Wisłocka (1979) on *The Art of Love*, in no way problematized the book's traditional approach to gender during the conversation. In effect, the response of sexologists to their patients' concerns could not be different; at the time, women's groups were not a thought collective that could bring a critical perspective to the discussion about gender and sexuality. The social sciences and humanities, conducted from a male perspective, were likewise not capable of introducing sexologists to a critical perspective on gender. With time, however, the situation changed.

Notes

1. In Polish, the following terms are used: *kulturalność* and *kultura* for what Rivkin-Fish (1999) translated as *culturedness* (adjective: *kulturalny*). In this book, terms such as *civilized*, *cultured*, and *culturedness* are used to covey the complex meaning of *kulturalność*.

2. This is so, for example, when talking about the prevention of sexual dysfunction in women. According to the sexologist, treatment is effective, especially if both spouses participate. Most important, however, is prevention. This includes the following elements, similar to the elements of civilized or cultured sex, mentioned earlier: "1. The necessity of grounding proper awareness and upbringing at home in the atmosphere of a positive approach to sex matters, seeing in it a means of deepening the spiritual bond between spouses, as well as a source of maternal feelings, so primal to a woman. Linking sex with motherhood gives intercourse a completely different atmosphere. 2. Mutual love between partners, as well as mutual devotion and sacrifice. 3. Creating an appropriate atmosphere for intercourse (mental attitude, time, caressing and joint active participation). 4. A higher level of culturedness in sexual relations. 5. Eliminating the fear of pregnancy" (Lew-Starowicz 1970*j*, 14).

3. The sexologist uses the term *oral sex* for oral stimulation of the male genital organs only.

4. In following Masters and Johnson's findings, it is assumed in sexology that there is one type of orgasm, achieved by various means (e.g., by stimulating a woman's clitoris). Therefore, the proper term is *orgasm from clitoral stimulation*, but here I use the

shortened form, *clitoral orgasm*, which is also used by doctors in conversations and often appears in popular sexological literature.

5. The first important postwar Polish sexological publication on masturbation is Imieliński's (1963) work, *The Question of Self-Abuse in Light of the Outlook of Older Youth* (*Zagadnienie samogwałtu w świetle poglądów starszej młodzieży*). Imieliński conducted survey research among students (15) and showed the universality of one-on-one sex (he found that it was practiced by 93.6% of men and 46.8% of women; 39). He starts off his book with the following sentence: "The vast majority of researchers believe that self-abuse does not cause any serious diseases, but that it may bring about some changes in the psyche, such as feelings of guilt, a low sense of self-esteem, a weakness of the will, etc. But an excess of self-abuse, especially when sexual intercourse is an option, should be considered pathological and treated" (12). He points out, nevertheless, that fighting self-abuse by means of "intimidation" results in adverse psychological effects (13).

6. In the 1970s, both sexologists and their readers used the Polish term *samogwałt* to indicate masturbation. *Samogwałt* literally translates as *self-rape*, but here the old-fashioned term *self-abuse* is used.

7. In another article (Lew-Starowicz 1970k, 14), the expert critically refers to premarital petting, claiming that it is bad from the perspective of "shaping psychosexual maturity" because it "perpetuates self-abuse."

8. Imieliński shares a Freudian understanding of the "immaturity" of this type of orgasm. He wrote, "It is only at the end of puberty that the so-called 'psychological' transfer of sexual excitability from the clitoris to the vagina takes place. It is 'psychological' because although there are very few sensory nerve endings in the vagina, its stimulation still provokes very strong excitement" (Imieliński 1967f, 157).

9. In turn, in his 1981 article, Lew-Starowicz (1981b, 23) noted that many women attach greater value to the vaginal orgasm because of what he believes to be a result of certain morality.

10. This shows how much the discourse on pregnancy termination has changed since then; in mainstream discourse today, abortion is usually presented as fundamentally distinct from contraception (see also Graff 2001).

11. It is worth emphasizing that even today, medical researchers have not reached agreement about the effects of the contraceptive pill on women's health. This is related not only to worldview issues (on the conservative critique of contraception, see Kościańska 2013) but also to the strategies of pharmaceutical companies, which have manipulated results from the beginning. This has been evident since the first trials of the pill carried out by Gregory Pincus and his colleagues in the mid-1950s in Puerto Rico (contraception could not be tested in the United States at the time because of the conservative social climate; Oudshoorn 1994). Women who were recruited for the study through clinics run by the local Planned Parenthood organization often stopped taking the pill because of the numerous side effects. They were replaced with new volunteers. In presenting his results, Pincus analyzed the pill's effects on a sample number of menstrual cycles (1,279 in 1958 and 8,133 cycles a year later), which he converted to "woman-years." Careful reading of his articles shows that, on average, volunteers participated in the trials for less than a year (Oudshoorn 1994, chap. 6, esp. 132). In effect, when the US Food and Drug Administration approved the pill first in 1957 for menstrual disorders and then in 1960 as a contraceptive, its long-term effects on women's health were not known. Lew Starowicz's skepticism must thus be understood also in this context. Similarly today, even during official trainings, sexologists mention that pill manufacturers manipulate results by, for example, not warning patients that hormones can reduce libido.

12. Both *Etc* and *The Mirror* published a number of other articles by Lew-Starowicz on contraception (see, e.g., "The Pill" [Lew-Starowicz 1970*l*]). Here the author uses "ecological" arguments, whereby drugs interfere with nature and, as such, caution is advised. He also discusses the side effects of using the pill. In "Postcoital Contraception" (Lew-Starowicz 1986), he describes in detail the use of contraception after intercourse. In "The Temperature Method" (Lew-Starowicz 1972*b*), he examines the principles of using this method. In "The Condom" (Lew-Starowicz 1975*c*), he talks about the advantages, disadvantages, history, and use of condoms.

13. The sexological understanding of homosexuality and its changes deserve a separate discussion, going beyond the scope of this book (see Bojarska 2010; Kościańska 2017, 2020). I draw attention only to the heteronormative dimension of these publications and point to the fact that they contribute to the larger definition of good sex.

14. Sometimes Lew-Starowicz even makes appeals for tolerance (1975*b*) and provides information about the development of the gay and lesbian rights movement in the West (1970*d*).

15. The introduction reads, "Michał Lew-Starowicz's contribution to this work consisted of the translation and analysis of foreign literature" (Lew-Starowicz and Lew-Starowicz 1999, 8).

16. Kinsey took into account all forms of sexual activity, even contacts with animals (see chap. 1).

17. Wisłocka puts it this way: "A girl . . . seamlessly introduced into the world of sex by an experienced partner develops quickly and her expectations begin to grow. When she attains the height of her sexual abilities at the age of thirty, her partner basically ends his active life in this field, reaching the age of sixty" (1978, 50).

18. Raising men is also an issue taken up by Lew-Starowicz. I discuss this in later sections.

19. Wisłocka hardly wrote about homosexuality, making only brief mentions of the topic sporadically. In *The Art of Love: Twenty Years Later* (*Sztuka kochania: W dwadzieścia lat później*), for example, we read, "The struggle for women's rights started off very interesting and constituted progress after the era of the 'female house slave.' It brought happiness to women and the family. As it started gaining momentum, it began serving its own interests, with lesbian perversion as its final outcome" (Wisłocka 1988, 30).

20. During her lecture as part of the Religionswissenschaftliches Seminar Sigi Feigel Gastprofessur fur Judische Studien at the Universitat Zurich (June 6–7, 2013), Israeli anthropologist Tamar El Or pointed to the limitations of feminist research, which focuses on the agency of women in every situation. Although on many occasions she has written about the agency of orthodox Jewish women, a group usually regarded as deprived thereof, she warns against going too far in the search for agency and proposes the term of *fake agency*.

21. Lew-Starowicz's numerous articles in the press focused on the issue of sex on equal terms (on stereotypes that prevent sex on equal terms, see Lew-Starowicz 1974*a*, 1981*c*, 1987*a*; on encouraging the mutual activity of both partners and women's greater involvement in sex, see Lew-Starowicz 1983*a*).

22. This is evident in, for example, Lew-Starowicz's articles from the late 1980s (see Lew-Starowicz 1987*h*, 1989*c*).

23. At the time, the working week lasted six days, from Monday to Saturday.

24. Such an approach was not a rule in socialist countries. In Bulgaria and the German Democratic Republic (GDR; Ghodsee 2017; Harsch 2009; Sharp 2004), insistence on equality was much more apparent. The situation of the GDR was specific in that attempts

were constantly made to show contrasts with West Germany and to cut off the Nazi past (Herzog 2005; on sex and sexuality in the Third Reich, see Mosse 1985, chap. 8; see also Meier 2007), so a comparison is difficult. Interestingly, in his article "Marriage of the Future," Lew-Starowicz (1973f) refers to the study of an East German sexologist who determined that well-educated, working women are "better sex partners." He did not try to transfer these findings to the Polish context. Regarding Bulgaria, Kristen Ghodsee's research has shown that progressive gender policy was due to the thriving women's league there. Bulgarian women, similar to Polish women, struggled with the double burden and the lack of time for pleasure (including sex); however, the league ordered scientific research and referred to it widely and thus influenced experts to promote other solutions, such as the socialization of housework and childcare (Ghodsee 2012b). As a thought collective, the Bulgarian league participated in the process of creating expert knowledge.

25. The only brief references appear in the press, for example, reviews of works such as *Against Our Will* by Susan Brownmiller (1975; see J.B. 1976; "Gwałt . . . [Rape, American style]," 1983). A more extensive presentation of the achievements of Western feminism became available with the volume edited by Teresa Hołówka (1982).

26. Spermicide ads appeared also in other women's magazines (see Ignaciuk 2014, 514).

27. The article seems strikingly conservative in comparison to the text written ten years earlier by the priest Kluz (Szpakowska 2003).

28. It is worth noting that jot. (1971) is too overtly critical of Lew-Starowicz (1971d), who, in the article discussed, raises the problem of women working two or even—as he writes—three full-time jobs.

5 | Gender and Pleasure in Expert Discourse Today

The Problem of Sources

In examining the 1970s and 1980s, we can easily point in retrospect to what constituted the main trend of expert discourse on sexuality. The matter is not so evident when analyzing the present, especially as I try to describe both the mainstream of expert thought and alternative approaches. In determining what ideas were important in the 1970s and 1980s, I considered the popularity of a given publication (there is no doubt that *The Art of Love* is the most important Polish publication on sex, given the high print run and subsequent editions), and the publications that my interview partners designated as significant. I also examined older publications written by well-known contemporary sexologists.

I applied a similar method to the present. With respect to mainstream sexology, as I described in detail in the section on research in the introduction, during the participant observation I chose people (lecturers or other experts) I wanted to interview or read their publications. As for alternative approaches to sexology, I looked for people who were critical of the dominant discourse. These were not only physicians and psychologists. Expert knowledge has undergone significant democratization and become heterogeneous since the 1970s (Clarke, Shim, et al. 2010*b*, 54, 72–75), allowing people without a medical or psychological education and without certificates (e.g., activists) to become specialists in the field and to challenge established experts. Participant observation served as the starting point from which I expanded my field of research using the snowball method.

Sexological Education

In Poland, two educational paths lead to the sexological profession. A physician who is already a specialist in internal medicine, obstetrics and gynecology, psychiatry, adolescent and child psychiatry, or neurology can specialize in sexology (CMKP 2000, 1). Candidates must attend a list of courses (including introduction to sexology, clinical sexology, forensic sexology, social sexology, and oncological problems in sexology); complete internships at a sexological, urological, gynecological, and psychiatric clinic; take active part in conferences; acquaint themselves with recommended reading materials; and publish an article in a sexological journal.[1] Specialization can be attained in two years and ends with an examination, preceded by regular testing of the acquired knowledge and skills by the program coordinator (CMKP 2000).

A psychologist can also become a sexologist. To specialize in sexology, a psychologist must obtain a clinical sexology certificate issued by the Polish Sexological Society.[2] According to the regulations adopted in May 2011 and effective since January 2012, the candidate must have therapeutic experience in the field of sexology, obtain a certificate from one of the Polish psychological societies, complete the required number of hours of personal therapy and supervision, participate in workshops and conferences (and present a paper), complete an internship (at a marriage clinic and a psychiatric clinic or at a psychiatric ward), conduct sex education classes (for children or adolescents), and have publications.[3] These activities translate into educational credits. For example, an hour of clinical supervision receives three credits (in total, three hundred credits must be collected in this category), one hour of workshop participation receives one credit (one hundred credits for workshops in total), presentation at a national conference receives forty credits, and sixty-five credits are awarded for presenting at an international conference. Credits can also be earned by defending a doctoral dissertation and completing a postdoctoral degree (habilitation), with four hundred and a thousand credits, respectively, provided that Polish Sexological Society clinical supervisors were among the review committee) or obtaining a sex educator certificate (150 credits). In total, a candidate must collect 1,500 credits and pass the final exam.

My participant observation and interviews show that training sessions and conferences, for both doctors and psychologists, are held in accordance with the interdisciplinary and holistic model developed by Imieliński. The psychological perspective is always emphasized, even during trainings addressed to physicians. In addition, frequent references are made to nonmedical and nonpsychological knowledge. Students are encouraged to look for information on their own, not only in specialist publications. Because sexuality is approached holistically, it is important that—as I heard many times during my participant observation—a sexologist be familiar with literature, film, theater, art, and cultural diversity. Papers that went beyond the medical or psychological perspectives were presented during conferences.[4] Nevertheless, the list of reading material for exams (e.g., *Homosexuality* by Lew-Starowicz and Lew-Starowicz [1999]) institutionalizes a specific message, including the sexual hierarchy.

Some interview partners who were Imieliński's students and who represent the senior generation of sexologists (mainly but not only psychologists) acknowledge that medicine is increasingly important in the world of Polish sexology. Psychology, along with the social sciences and humanities, is becoming less important. They link this occurrence with political changes (the development of neoliberal capitalism) and the impact of pharmaceutical companies (I described these processes in chap. 1). The pharmaceutical industry has become a chief donor for sexology, as corporations sponsor research, conferences, and doctors' trips to congresses abroad. This trend is also demonstrated by the establishment of a sexological association open to physicians only (i.e., the Polish Society of Sexual Medicine) and does not accept psychologists as members. Is this a dominant trend? Is the Polish interdisciplinary and holistic sexological tradition passing into oblivion?

A key issue is how knowledge is legitimized in the training program. During lectures, slides presenting the findings of medical research carried out with large samples are often displayed. But the lecturer usually does not discuss them in detail, instead using the time to study the case of a particular patient and considering the multifaceted nature of sex. In addition, the lecturer might encourage students to read an interesting novel about the subject. Although it may seem that medical-scientific research is coming to the fore, a closer look at the process of knowledge transfer suggests that other elements are still important.

The dominance of the medical perspective is hampered by structural matters. Although the data that Polish lecturers present during sexological trainings has often been produced by international clinical trials, such research is rarely conducted in Poland. In effect, sexologists see patients with various problems, sexual and other (sexologists are also often gynecologists, psychiatrists, etc.); they do not enclose themselves in the laboratory with a selected group of "research subjects." Some sexologists with whom I spoke complained about this state of affairs, but such an approach honors the patient-oriented tradition of Polish sexology and gives physicians a holistic perspective on the human being. One of the doyens of Polish sexology, when asked about the sources of his knowledge, indicated the development of scientific research and the "life of patients" as being on par.

Consequently, even doctors who directly collaborate with industry and who are convinced of the importance of inventions such as Viagra see the limits of pharmacotherapy. They link some of their patients' problems (including erectile dysfunction, for which a variety of effective drugs exist) with psychological, cultural, social, and economic factors. This issue came up on many occasions during the trainings and conferences in which I participated and during the interviews I conducted. As a result of these conditions, sexology in Poland is much more comprehensive and directed at the social sciences than in Western Europe and the United States (see Åsberg and Johnson 2009; Fishman 2012; E. Johnson 2008; Tiefer 2000). This approach also positions the field differently on issues such as feminism.

Education Outside the Mainstream

Despite its various merits, many people who seek sexological training disapprove of the official sexological program. Like some psychologists of the older generation, they condemn the overt prominence of the medical perspective. They point to sexism and heteronormativity in the knowledge transmitted. Both problems lead these people to look for other ways of acquiring knowledge and of organizing themselves outside the official structures.

Before discussing alternative forms of education and organization, I want to describe how the feminist sexological milieu approaches the official program. My feminist interview partners noted that jokes were an issue. Interlocutors who tried to collect credits for a certificate were repeatedly outraged at the sexist jokes that came up during courses and conferences. I heard them myself on many occasions. They were often accompanied by various allusions, gestures, and charged glances to strengthen the message. For example, when a lecture on the sexuality of women in the menopausal period was announced at a conference, a member of the audience—a doctor of the older generation—exclaimed with relief, "Luckily there are no such women here." During another lecture, jokes were made about the sexuality of feminists—while ordinary women often enjoy their partner's pleasure, a man's orgasm arouses aggression in a feminist, who immediately wants to "stick it to him." During the November 2011 debate on the findings of Zbigniew Izdebski's research on the sexuality of Poles, the professor-speakers did not shy from making jokes about "loose vaginas," despite the presence of several hundred people and numerous journalists in the room. This did not last long, however, as Maria Beisert—the only woman among the panelists and a member of the Polish Sexological Society executive committee—turned out to be a champion of the quick retort and countered that perhaps a "small penis syndrome" was at fault. This was probably the only time I witnessed someone so resolutely protest this kind of behavior. A young student who is hoping to pass an exam held by such a professor-lecturer may be afraid to openly voice her (or his) criticism. Another means of opposing sexism, which happens quite rarely, is asking questions from the audience. On several occasions in response to a sexist comment, I observed someone asking, "But how do you know this to be true?" (nonetheless, it is hard to undermine a joke this way). These people were usually associated with the feminist milieu.

Most students listen to these lectures and comments in silence. They also do not complain about their teachers consistently being late for class or answering their phones during lecture. From my observations and conversations, this approach appears to be a kind of conformist survival strategy; course participants just want to get their certificates, and they prefer not to risk that, since the lecturers are also the examiners. One of the interviewees, a self-declared feminist, had an interesting approach to the jokes. She called them "professional jokes," recognizing that they should not be taken seriously, as sexologists encounter various, strange sexual problems every day and jokes are a form of release.

In addition to jokes and harassment, the interviewees drew attention to outdated data presented during official courses, inconsistent with WHO standards, and unscientific and stereotypical information on gender and relationships. Non-heterosexual orientation, for instance, was frequently discussed using stereotypes. As mentioned, the book *Homosexuality* (Lew-Starowicz and Lew Starowicz-1999) is among the required reading, in which the authors discuss treatments aimed at changing homosexuals' orientation. During a course in which I participated, I heard hypotheses that the latest scientific discoveries could cure homosexuality and transsexuality at the prenatal stage. One of my interview partners summarized the official sexological program as "sexism and fable-writing instead of solid research." Interlocutors who described themselves as feminists were, paradoxically, most critical of the discussion of specific case studies, considering it unscientific. At the same time, most feminists, like many psychologists of the older generation, disapproved of medicalization. A contradiction is evident here: as I noted earlier, medicalization is counteracted by references to patients' experiences and other "unscientific" sources that, as I intend to show later, open dialogue between sexologists and feminists and that distinguish the

Polish and North American situations (see also chap. 1). It is worth keeping in mind that stereotypical conceptualizations presented by scientists like Wisłocka and Lew-Starowicz are rooted in their patients' experiences. Feminists use the same strategy that Kinsey did (see chap. 1; Irvine 2005). As a new form of knowledge, feminism needs a scientific, objective, and preferably Western (Owczarzak 2009b) source of legitimacy to gain impact. This outlook contradicts the feminist approach to sexuality, in which the subjective experiences of women are placed at the center, as in the Hite (1976) report. Polish feminist sexologists often seek a middle ground: they call on the authority of the WHO; use Western research conducted from a feminist perspective; and refer to patients, clients, the practices of different groups of women with whom they work, and even their own experience.

Feminists who want to specialize in sexology look for nonofficial forms of education. Because news spreads quickly, some people do not even attempt to start the official program, having heard from their friends about the stereotypes, sexist jokes, and pathologizing approach to homosexuality. Others drop the course. When I asked one of my interview partners if she had already obtained the Polish Sexological Society certificate, she replied:

> No, I rebelled, I did not want to . . . due to the . . . content . . . although I was close and I had gathered basically all the credits needed to get the certificate, I consciously decided not to do the certificate, because I was not sure if I wanted to . . . represent their logo with my name, because not all the solutions and not all content . . . that are necessary for the exam for this certificate . . . I do not feel that it reflects my view of sexuality, so I decided not to do the certificate.

Another interlocutor said that she was disgusted by the comments that some people from the Polish Sexological Society executive committee had made. She also disliked rendering homosexuality a form of pathology and the gender stereotypes rampant in the recommended reading. In effect, these women made the decision to conduct sex therapy without a certificate. They do this legally because they have completed all the necessary requirements to perform psychotherapy. The same applies to counseling, running workshops, and sex education classes. Those who want to work in this field and who have a degree in education or psychology do not need to complete specialized courses or postgraduate studies.

Representatives of the feminist and queer milieus look for other forms of education given their critical assessment of the official sexological program. One option is to study abroad. The progressive Institute for the Advanced Study of Human Sexuality in San Francisco (closed in 2014), for example, offered courses in the field of human sexuality at the master's and doctoral levels and specialist courses to obtain certificates such as the sex coach certificate or the sexological instructor/advisor of AIDS/STI prevention certificate.

The most common form of learning in the field is self-education. In reconstructing their intellectual paths, my interview partners indicated that they had gained the most through independent reading (also during international fellowships). They had mainly read contemporary Western publications on sexuality, often written from the perspective of feminism or queer theory. One of the interlocutors, an important figure of feminist sexology, described her background as "mostly self-education, because in these formal education systems, the issues I was interested in were not touched upon or only touched upon a little, or they were touched upon through an angle that I was skeptical of, so basically . . . the main resource of my sexological education is the knowledge I gained myself; I brought over books, publications, read, traveled, and talked."

Interlocutors also pointed out that they benefited from gender studies, attending antidiscrimination workshops or courses on counteracting violence or participating in feminist and queer conferences and seminars. In addition, various (more or less formal) groups invite renowned specialists from home and abroad, including sexologists, to conduct special trainings addressed to their members.[5] Some people associated with feminist and queer sexology have significant academic achievements and hold positions at universities. Participation in their classes is an important part of education in this community, as is the exchange of knowledge in general. As a young sex educator and therapist told me, "Everything that I have learned, and that I'm learning, comes from women who are wiser than myself . . . and from . . . the literature that they suggest . . . we simply pass on such knowledge to each other, we discuss it and most things among ourselves, the perspective that I have, I either learned at home, . . . I was weaned on it, I come from a feminist home, and from women wiser and older than myself."

Some interviewees would like to see the community "formalize," as one of them put it, by forming an expert group outside the Polish Sexological Society structures. They claim that the Polish Sexological Society is closed to people who are critical of mainstream sexology.

In Poland, as in the United States, it is difficult to talk about one feminist community or a single, cohesive feminist approach to sexuality. By feminist sexology, I mean therapists and educators for whom identification with feminism is important. To some extent, this group often intermixes with activists from LGBTQ circles, which is why I often write about "feminist and queer sexology." The milieu functions partly outside the mainstream, and thus information about its activities must be sought on specialized portals,[6] during the workshops and events they organize (e.g., Pussy Days, V-day), at some sex shops for women, or at feminist organizations (e.g., Ponton, a group of educators affiliated with the Federation for Women and Family Planning, a major Polish feminist organization). Sometimes, however, their ideas permeate mainstream culture, for example, by means of the series of interviews that feminist sexologist Alicja Długołęcka gave to *High Heels* (*Wysokie Obcasy*), a women's magazine published weekly with *Gazeta Wyborcza*, a major Central European liberal daily newspaper (Długołęcka and Reiter 2011).

Interactions

Some interviewees were extremely critical of mainstream sexology. One of them, when asked about the classics of Polish sexology, simply exclaimed "Burn them!"

Nonetheless, the feminist milieu and mainstream sexology do not represent two separate camps, or thought collectives, between which there is no dialogue and that do not affect one another. Some feminists appreciate the holistic orientation of the Polish school of sexology. One of the interviewees, when asked about the books and the people that shaped her thinking about sexuality, mentioned Foucault's (1978) *History of Sexuality*, and then added, "Imieliński, not in content but in the approach. That his approach to the topic was so wide, this I liked very much." When asked about Wisłocka, she appreciated her feminine perspective and compared her with the much more progressive writer and reproductive rights activists from the interwar period, Irena Krzywicka, pointing to the historical roots of Polish feminist sexology.[7]

It is worth asking: Does feminism have an impact on sexology? The interviews suggest that even in the 1980s and 1990s, the emerging feminist community addressed issues related to sexuality and tried to establish a dialogue with sexologists. As a leader of the time remembers, "We tried to persuade professionals into cooperating with us, we tried to persuade them to look at things through a more feminist lens, like Dr. Sierzpowska, who did not have this feminist eye but had a lot of knowledge about medicine, at times also in the social context, but always through the male norm, while we wanted to see wider, to introduce a different perspective."

The sexologist Anna Sierzpowska, an important figure in the Polish Sexological Society at the time (she died in 1997), took part in one of the first Polish feminist conferences organized by the Polish Feminist Association in Mądralin near Warsaw in spring 1993. In the paper, "Woman's Sexuality," Sierzpowska (1993) presented a sexological approach to gender and sexuality, highlighting the cultural components that define gender (the typical, holistic sexological approach). In her presentation, Sierzpowska (1993, 8) also discussed the findings of American feminist research on sexuality, which showed that equality serves the verbalization of sexual needs. Sierzpowska came to accept feminist ideas and propagated them among sexologists, which is remembered today.[8] Another example of interaction between feminists and sexologists in that period is the support provided by the Polish Planned Parenthood Association (PPPA; until 1991, the association was the only sexological organization in Poland) for activism focused on the right to abortion in the early 1990s; new post-Communist leaders wanted to completely ban abortion, which was accessible on demand under socialism (Zielińska 2000).[9] One of the interlocutors, a sexologist, mentioned with pride in an interview that the PPPA allowed feminists (including members of the Polish Feminist Association) to use its headquarters and supported the establishment of the Federation for Women and Family Planning, now the main Polish feminist organization, which the PPPA joined and continues to be a member. The interlocutor also expressed appreciation for the intellectual achievements of feminism. Meanwhile, Wisłocka (2000) gave an interview to feminists Agnieszka Grzybek and Barbara Limanowska, which appeared in the *OŚKA Bulletin*, a major feminist magazine in the 1990s, where she spoke strongly against the antiabortion law and withdrew some of her earlier statements. In the interview, she said, for example, that homosexuality is not a "perversion" and that oral sex is a full-fledged form of intercourse (Wisłocka 2000, 5).

Contacts between feminists and sexologists had, and continue to have, a personal character. Often under informal conditions, an exchange of ideas takes place that ends with the incorporation of feminist ideas into sexological knowledge. During classes it happens that the lecturer refers to the opinion of a feminist friend or her publication and notes the ideas with esteem. As mentioned, feminists are also among future sexuality experts and take sexology classes. Furthermore, while collecting materials for this book in the years 2008–2012, I saw how some sexologists changed their views on gender issues as a result of conversations with feminist friends. Feminists are also invited as experts to sexological events, such as the 4th National Debate on Sexual Health in November 2011, which was focused on the results of Zbigniew Izdebski's large-scale survey on sexuality in Poland. Among the panelists invited to participate in the debate were Kazimiera Szczuka (invited as a feminist) and Monika Płatek (invited as a lawyer but who does not hide her feminist perspective). Consequently, feminism permeates sexology in various ways.

Another example of dialogue is the postgraduate program in social sexology opened in 2013 at the Center for Social Research on Sexuality at the Institute of Applied Social Sciences at the University of Warsaw. Jacek Kochanowski, a foremost specialist in queer theory and the social study of sexuality (see, e.g., Kochanowski 2004, 2009, 2013), leads the center and lecturers include well-known sexologist Andrzej Depko and icons of Polish feminism Magdalena Środa and Małgorzata Fuszara. The description of the program of study directly references the Polish sexological tradition: "The aim of the program is to provide access to knowledge, competences and skills in the field of social sexology understood in accordance with the concept of K. Imieliński as a social science of the cultural determinants of human sexual behavior" (Center for Social Research on Sexuality 2013, 1).

Furthermore, some persons identifying themselves with feminism and the LGBTQ movement lecture in the official program, and their articles appear in mainstream publications (Bojarska and Kowalczyk 2010). In turn, sexologists participate in conferences and other feminist events (e.g., during the jubilee of the Federation for Women and Family Planning in October 2010 or in the Feminoteka Foundation's presentation of its report on sexual violence on November 29, 2011).

A constant exchange of ideas exists among these milieus, or thought collectives, despite some mutual animosity. As I argue below, the feminist approach to sexuality has an impact on mainstream sexology. In chapter 1, I show that in the United States, some feminist ideas were largely incorporated into the mainstream pharmacological current (more directly speaking, they were appropriated by that current; see, e.g., the activities of the Berman sisters [Fishman 2004]). Meanwhile, there is no place for dialogue between "independent" feminist therapists and pharmacological sexology (see, for example, chap. 1, n. 22). The next sections show continuity and change in Polish sexology. I argue that because of different historical experiences, the fate of feminism and sexology took another path in Poland. Here, feminism and sexology draw knowledge from the experience of actual women (and men).

Gender and Pleasure in Mainstream Knowledge: Continuity

The emancipation of women, an issue widely discussed in the context of sexuality in the 1970s and 1980s, is still considered a problem. Emancipation continues to be credited as a source of sexual difficulties. This is evident in Lew-Starowicz's recent publications. In his trilogy, *About Woman* (2011a), *About Man* (2012b), and *About Love* (2012c), focused primarily on gender and relationships, hardly anything is left of the technical advice that was so important in *Sex on Equal Terms* (1983f). Referring to the experiences of patients and, to a much lesser extent, contemporary quantitative research on sexuality, the sexologist wrote profusely about the difficulties associated with the emancipation of women, which are greater currently than during state socialism. In the past, women worked to supplement the husband's earnings, whereas today they build real careers (Lew-Starowicz 2011a, 29). Men, in turn, are immature, lazy, and mentally weak, a consequence of too much mothering (mothers overcompensate for their lack of time for their sons by being too caring), the absence of male rites of passage like the military, and the lack of male authority figures, which is associated with the feminization of education.[10] Moreover, the sexologist posits, because women do everything, men feel relieved of all responsibility (see Lew-Starowicz 2011a, 201–207; 2012b, 9). Emancipated and domineering women face countless problems in their emotional lives. Many remain single by choice, although the sexologist claims that they often want to enter into relationships but are incapable of doing so because they are too independent (Lew-Starowicz 2011a, 9–15). They are unable to "raise men" (a theme discussed widely in his previous works, e.g. Lew-Starowicz 1970b, 14; chap. 4). At the same time, these women are not attractive to potential partners, for whom physical appeal is most important: "An education, a career—these features can complement the perception of a woman, a partner. But the fact that she is a high-class manager or an outstanding intellectual is not an aphrodisiac. Men basically want an attractive, loyal, and resourceful woman, who can start a home for them where everything will be fine" (Lew-Starowicz 2011a, 75).

Women do not like fools; an intelligent woman's partner would have to make an effort all the time (Lew-Starowicz 2011a, 76). Problems also arise when the wife suddenly begins to be successful in her professional life, spurring discontent on both sides: he does not like her to be superior to him, and she in turn loses interest in him (see Lew-Starowicz 2012b, 163; Lew-Starowicz 2011a, 76). The author also claims that inappropriate roles and gender characteristics make relationships unsuccessful (Lew-Starowicz 2012b, 190), repeating what he wrote almost thirty years earlier in *Sex on Equal Terms* (1983f). Another theme present in earlier writing is the issue of women being overburdened (Lew-Starowicz 1970b). Independent women building their careers would also like to pursue their sexual lives, but they simply do not have enough energy left to do so (Lew-Starowicz 2011a, 29).

I asked about new gender roles in the interviews. A psychologist from the older generation, when asked about relationships in which the woman earns more than the man, responded:

This evokes [among men] a sense of inferiority, guilt, low self-esteem, that a woman is more educated, that she has a good position at work, that she earns more, that she is not dependent on a man, because once she was dependent, she sat at home, she raised children, and now she is independent and that causes . . . a lack of self-confidence among men. . . . If women are attractive and nicely dressed, men are afraid sometimes, . . . they are afraid to have sex, because . . . they think that they are not worthy of such a woman who is so sexually attractive.

This interview partner associated moral change with the invention of the pill: "Woman was liberated, she can have sex with whomever she wants and when she wants, I'm simplifying the matter a little, that she is independent, that she does not have to avoid sex, she does not have to live in fear of getting pregnant."

As for the therapeutic response to male fears, for the interviewee the matter was different than for doctors, who in such cases often write out a pharmaceutical prescription:

Viagra . . . and Viagra-like drugs . . . I have such a very cautious attitude toward this. Viagra, of course, can help a very small percentage of men, sometimes when a man is insecure, afraid, well, once he tries Viagra, then maybe he'll be able to do it without Viagra, but if he gets addicted he's only able to with Viagra, well, that's worse, because later, it's somehow not possible without it. Viagra heals symptoms, not causes. As I said, I deal with the causes, so you have to look for why a given man, if he is healthy, his hormone levels are in normal range, why can't he have intercourse with that woman.

Another interlocutor, a doctor of the older generation, approaches the issue of new gender roles more generally, referring to evolution:

Actually it's like this: . . . we still have archetypes from the times of the cavemen. That is, he hunts, delivers the animal . . . to the cave doorstep, while she sits in the cave, takes care of the children and gossips with her girlfriends providing each other mutual support, and thanks to this, the woman can see the color red better, because if fire burns in the cave next door, it can be a lifesaver. Men have a better spatial imagination, because he had to chase that antelope, but that more or less, that remains, but times are changing.

Then he analyzes the contemporary situation:

An example: there is a couple who decides to have a child, but it turns out that if she takes care of the child, then they will lose a lot of money, because she got a promotion, earns a lot, and so on. So the couple comes to the conclusion that the husband will take care of the child, he will change the diapers and so on, he will take care of it for some time, and now she is making a career and earning money. A relationship based on equal terms, a common sense decision, very sensible, indeed, she makes more money, okay. A very good choice, but the archetypes begin to bite, he's stuck sitting on eggs inside the chicken coop, he feels as if he's being castrated and he becomes irritated because he's so pitiful, . . . and she . . . his authority falls in her eyes, her husband has turned into a hen, and she meets active men at work . . . who have something to say, archetypes gnaw here, that is, the roles have changed clearly and it is this contradiction between the archetypes and roles that can make the relationship fall apart. Well, that's why it's not a simple thing, yes, there are people, there are relationships, where the reversal of roles suits them, meaning all configurations are possible, but I am negatively inclined toward social theories that speak of a complete inversion of roles, that it's good no matter how you look at it and so on.

Yet another interview partner, a sexologist and gynecologist, while discussing the subject of sexual dysfunction among men, asserted that such dysfunctions may have "psychological and sociological causes"—namely, they may be a consequence of the appearance of "alpha females." He pointed out that this applies to young, athletic men from big cities who experience "erectile dysfunction not necessarily associated with vascular problems." He summarized his considerations in this way: "These are healthy, athletic guys who spent time at the gym, ride a bike a bit . . . and lead a healthy lifestyle, they have erectile dysfunction, because it's as if they just can't cope with the domination of women, which is increasingly more common." The interlocutor immediately proposes a psychological and medical solution:

> Not all gentlemen feel good with a dominant female partner. . . . I am talking about big cities, on the one hand we have girls who have sex with guys, who really do not know why they have intercourse, and on the other hand we have girls who know very well why they have sex, they know very well why on this day they went out to dinner with this or that guy, and actually they do not intend to go out with him again . . . but they know very well what they want from him, but he is not always able to meet these expectations and in these situations. . . . Applying a phosphodiesterase inhibitor [e.g., Viagra], even if temporarily, to increase their self-confidence, can sometimes bring results.

The issue of new gender roles was also discussed during classes for future sex experts. A woman I interviewed mentioned that during her course for sex educators at the public university, she attended a seminar where she was told that "the worst thing that a family can do to an adolescent son is if the father helps his mother out in her daily duties, for example, he cooks, or cleans together with her, because this can disrupt the son's gender roles and lead to various problems with his gender identity." It was also mentioned that "feminism is . . . the cause, at the moment, of the increase in pedophile behaviors among men, because . . . men are unable to cope with emancipated women, which is why they go for weaker, more vulnerable people, that is, for children."

During a class for future sexologists in which I participated, a new disorder was discussed: premature female orgasm, a female counterpart to premature ejaculation. This concept is rooted in ideas presented during this class. Within this framework, "normal women" need even twenty-four hours of arousal to achieve orgasm, after which they want to cuddle with their partner. In contrast, there is a group of dominant, working, well-educated, and highly paid women who quickly achieve orgasm and then immediately return to work. They behave like men, which is why Polish sexologists often call this phenomenon a "male-type orgasm." The lecturer who cited this example warned that although this problem may seem insignificant, more and more patients come to see him about it.

During another class, it was argued that in relationships where fathers take parental leave, men may experience erectile dysfunction; by doing women's work, they may experience "a deficiency of masculinity." On a few occasions, the question of evolution was raised. For example, it was alleged that the best aphrodisiac is a fat wallet, along with power and intelligence (as a way of acquiring the wallet in the first place). Furthermore, the lecturer referenced a study that showed intelligence among women is of little importance—what counts is physical appeal. "We may disagree," she commented, "like the feminists, but evolution wants the best genes to meet." From this perspective, a successful sexual relationship is a hierarchical one that maintains traditional gender roles.

When it comes to other issues, a certain degree of continuity with the 1970s and 1980s is also evident. The approach to masturbation reiterates previous takes to some extent. In *Sex According to Him and Her* (*Ona i on o seksie*), Lew-Starowicz (2007, 219) notes that the WHO recognizes autostimulation as healthy behavior to which everyone should have the right. He has reservations, some of which arise from his concern for patients (e.g., behaviors that pose a danger to life and health, such as electric shock or compulsive behaviors). His other concerns, however, buttress the hierarchy of good and bad sex, putting traditional attitudes at the top. Masturbation associated with pornography is dangerous because real-life sex may become less attractive. Sadomasochistic pictures and films are especially risky: "This may lead to deviant behaviors" (220). Masturbation is also risky because it "diverges from the physiology of sexual relations" and "can lead to conditions that hinder sexual intercourse in the future, like stimulating oneself using the water stream" (220). One lecturer spoke in a similar vein during a class at a postgraduate medical center. She argued that women who want to get to know their bodies should avoid vibrators because these tools will make it difficult for women to have sex with their partners in real life.

Feminist Sexology

Feminism introduces new perspective to the discussion of sexuality. As I argued in chapter 1, in the US context, feminist sexologists like Hite (1976, 2006) or Tiefer (2001, 2004) represent women's perspectives on sex. They see female sexuality as autonomous (i.e., not viewed through the lens of male pleasure), they stress the link between emancipation and openness to sexuality (i.e., they see hierarchy and traditional gender roles, including women's passivity, as obstacles to achieving sexual satisfaction), they deconstruct the central position of penetration and intercourse, they emphasize that good sex is possible outside the traditional relationship (e.g., polyamory), and they see sex holistically by pointing to its various aspects. Furthermore, they oppose the pharmacologization of sexuality and the technical approach to sex through the lens proposed by Masters and Johnson (1966). According to the feminists, their research leads to identifying pleasure with orgasm and the pathologization of women who do not climax (they also propose acceptance of asexuality; for more on asexuality, see, e.g., Kim 2010). Consequently, they propose the deconstruction of the traditional sexual hierarchy and the introduction of alternative rules (see chap. 1; see also Barker 2013, chap. 4).

How does this perspective translate to the Polish context? When it comes to a holistic view of sexuality, the Polish school of sexology is unquestionably closer to feminist ideals than North American mainstream sexology and includes a critical approach to pharmacotherapy. The Polish tradition has long contextualized the problem of orgasm. As early as in 1985, for example, Lew-Starowicz (1985f) published an article in the magazine *The Mirror*, entitled "Tyranny of the Orgasm." This term was used almost twenty years later by the icon of North American feminist sexology Leonore Tiefer (2001). Lew-Starowicz wrote in *The Mirror*:

> Interest in the phenomenon of orgasm and the development of sexology has enabled many women to enter a world of experiences hitherto unknown to them. There is also the other side of the coin, however: the dissemination of popular sexology, publications devoted to the phenomenon of orgasm, and the propaganda of successful sex have brought about the tyranny of the orgasm. For many women, the capacity to orgasm is a measure of their self-esteem as women. They focus on the necessity of experiencing orgasm. Of their partners they expect skillful arousal as well as development in the range of erotic sensations. (1985f, 12)

The sexologist approaches the issue holistically and points to the consequences of this state of affairs for women, men, and relationships:

> Life in many relationships has become a nightmare for this reason. The partner thinks about whether he can make the woman orgasm, he treats it as a task and a test of his own masculinity. The woman, on the other hand, treats orgasm as the goal of intercourse, a confirmation of her own appeal. She raises the bar of requirements and expectations for her partner. The tyranny of the orgasm has made life difficult for many people, it has imposed specific expectations and changed the meaning of the sexual bond (from the creative to an orgasm-focused bond). . . . Women who felt content in their relationships and satisfied with their sex lives despite the lack of orgasm, began to doubt the normality of this situation and lost their sense of happiness. (12)

Although Tiefer (2001, 82–85; see also chap. 1) uses this term in a slightly different context, she argues that feminism should pay attention to various forms of women's pleasure. In her opinion, the central position of orgasm in the common perception is due to the popularity of Masters and Johnson's studies, which showed female and male sexuality as equivalent. Lew-Starowicz, in turn, wrote about popular sexology, and in *The Art of Love*, Wisłocka (1978) presented in detail the achievements of this pair of American researchers.

Other North American feminists assert that the lack of orgasm does not necessarily denote dysfunction (Canner 2009). Similarly, in the current Polish feminist approach to sex, orgasm is subject to contextualization. Alicja Długołęcka, perhaps the most well-known contemporary Polish sexologist who self-identifies with feminism, notes that in the 1970s, we were told that a woman has the right to orgasm, but now "we are moving away from this to the belief that successful sex is not necessarily sex, which always ends in orgasm. It should simply be pleasant" (Długołęcka and Reiter 2011, 196). Długołęcka also pays close attention to the sociocultural determinants of orgasm (199).

Other issues important to American feminist sexology have counterparts in Poland. A critique of the definition of sex as penetration is one of the main elements of feminist sexology in Poland. As one of the interviewees argued: "When you see the sexual act as penetration, it turns out that lesbians do not have sex. Androcentrism is the approach, in which the penis constitutes the crown of creation, with male orgasm through penetration as the crown jewel. There is no place for diversity."[11]

Długołęcka proposes an interesting deconstruction of sex as penetration in the book, *Sex on High Heels* (*Seks na wysokich obcasach*; Długołęcka and Reiter 2011), a collection of interviews given to Paulina Reiter and published in the "women's" supplement to the liberal daily *Gazeta Wyborcza*, entitled *High Heels*. As befits a student of Lew-Starowicz and the Polish school of sexology (Andrzej Jaczewski, who wrote the introduction to *The Art of Love*, was her PhD supervisor; see Jaczewski 2009, 152), which she links in an interesting way with feminism and queer theory, Długołęcka begins with her patients' experiences, although these are people who speak from a marginal position: "In my work, I deal with men with severe injuries of the nervous system who have significant, persistent erectile dysfunction and ejaculation problems. . . . For me, the opportunity to listen to men who, being in this situation, rediscover their sexuality, is an important experience. This radically changed my way of thinking about male sexuality in general" (Długołęcka and Reiter 2011, 128).[12] How do these experiences translate to understanding sexuality?

> It happens that I accompany them in reconciling with this situation and I support them in building relationships with women. What turns out? Their sexual partners, although they use the help of certain auxiliary methods, do not assess the quality of their sex lives as lower. The problem they report instead is their partners' excessive concentration on their sexual performance. If the men in this group are active and do not focus excessively on having intercourse, they become open to other forms of giving pleasure. Sex of this sort can be even better than before an injury or illness. Men who manage to adapt to this situation reach the same conclusions. (128)

At the end, Długołęcka makes more general observations:

> Healthy men do not accept this, because they are not forced to do so by circumstance. For this reason, probably no woman will ever be able to convince any man that if he has erectile dysfunction and problems with ejaculating, that it's okay and that they can do other fun things together. I will repeat, however: women's perspective is such that this is not particularly important . . . men who let go of their frustration, open up to women despite this type of dysfunction, they talk about it themselves, that they discover something new and beautiful in sex, and they are not ashamed to admit to this "feminine element." (129)

Długołęcka notes that women are not usually bothered by their partners' erection problems (Długołęcka and Reiter 2011, 120). She draws from the experience of other groups with which she works, such as lesbians (she is the author of one of the first Polish works on nonheterosexual women's sexuality; Długołęcka 2005) and women with spinal cord injuries (see, e.g., Długołęcka 2011a, 2011b). These women's experiences go beyond penetration and even, in the case of spinal cord injuries, beyond clitoral stimulation. Długołęcka uses these marginal perspectives to redefine sex and pleasure.

In *Sex on High Heels* (Długołęcka and Reiter 2011), we find many other elements typical of feminist sexology. Długołęcka encourages her readers to visit a women's sex shop (173). She writes of fantasies and female pornography (55), rouses her readers' imaginations with a discussion of the "orgasmic platform" (48), and concludes that girls need strong female role models (261). Furthermore, Długołęcka reiterates in her publications that sexology was established as an androcentric discipline, looking at sex from the male perspective (Długołęcka 2008).

Other feminists who deal with sexuality also call attention to this fact, linking it with the question of how to reach orgasm. One of my interview partners summed up the knowledge taught by traditional sexological works as follows: "The best way to orgasm is penetration. But in reality: yes, penetration is the surest way to orgasm, but for men, not for women. To prescribe this thinking, female authors began to write about what they call the pathologizing of female sexuality, as a concept. Because while penetration is the surest way to orgasm, it would turn out very often for women that something was not right . . . or that women were frigid because they did not have a vaginal orgasm." The interlocutor also extends this to men: "They too have a problem, . . . because the message is that sex positions and intercourse: that's what makes sex. The rest is just frills." For the domination of this framework, my interview partner blames homegrown specialists. As I have tried to show, however, mainstream sexologists like Lew-Starowicz or Imieliński depathologized rather than pathologized the issue of reaching orgasm by stimulation of the clitoris, as a result of their openness to the needs of patients and readers.

Another issue raised by feminists concerns gender roles. In the mainstream, as we have seen, a strong tendency exists to talk about traditional gender roles, linking their maintenance with sexual pleasure. Alternatively, feminism proposes renegotiation as a way to successful sex. As a therapist who identifies with feminism and draws from queer theory told me in an interview:

> People continue to have quite strong socialization messages related to . . . traditional gender socialization, which they take away from the family home and bring to their beds, to their bedrooms and later this turns into dysfunctions that come out at some point, for example as a double standard, or an internalization of the belief that a woman must be passive or that a woman's role in sex is passive, while the man takes over all activities including taking 150 percent responsibility for the woman's orgasm, so that the woman basically lies motionless in bed smelling nice, passively of course, while the guy not only has to show how good he is in bed, he also has to have an erection from the beginning to the end leading the sexual performance to its culmination, meaning he has to achieve orgasm without making a fool of himself by failing in his male role, further he has to make the woman orgasm and not just once, because that's for amateurs, but she has to have multiple orgasms and with so-called "female ejaculation," because that has recently suddenly become . . . the goal and people just internalize these sorts of things.

The interlocutor illustrates this with an example from her own therapeutic practice:

> I remember one client who came to me and said that the trouble is that her partner has a much smaller sex drive than she does and that she has already tried to do everything she can, that basically when she comes back from work she puts on sexy clothes and waits until he comes back from work, and once he comes back from work, she waits for him looking sexy and she's looking sexy and waiting, and waiting and looking sexy until he finally proposes something, so again she waits there looking sexy and behaving all flirtatious and she waits, and then he does nothing. So I asked her, but why do you wait . . . why don't you just propose to your partner that the two of you do something together, and she says: "You know, that didn't even occur to me," and these types of things happen.

The interview partner also partly blames mainstream sexology for this state of affairs: "This sort of model is not only present in older publications, but it is reproduced in today's sexological education," from which many people draw their knowledge about sex.

Długołęcka, meanwhile, combines a feminist approach with the Polish sexological tradition. In her writing, she reiterates the arguments that Lew-Starowicz (1983f) posited in *Sex on Equal Terms*, whereby building one's own femininity and masculinity constitutes the key to a satisfying sex life. According to Długołęcka, for a relationship to be successful, "we need to build strong, positive images of ourselves as women and men" (Długołęcka and Reiter 2011, 126–27). Yet femininity means something a bit different to Długołęcka than to her former teacher and current colleague at the same university.[13] Nonetheless, in line with the classics of Polish sexology, she repeats certain reservations about intimacy and sincerity: "Unfortunately, excessive closeness is deadly for sex. As a woman I say this with regret, but sex doesn't like you to be pals. Sex likes separateness, individuality. This is what they write about in guidebooks: be a secret to your man, be unpredictable, because predictability is wonderful in friendship, but it kills sex" (16). Her conviction on this subject has been criticized by other feminist sexologists, who contend that honesty is particularly important in sexual relations.

Another issue raised by feminists is the importance of contraception for women. Thanks to birth control methods, women can decide for themselves and their sex lives, and they can separate sex from reproduction or love. One prominent feminist sexologist recognizes with regret that this change is only superficial:

> This is the first generation of women who can consciously decide what they do in this sphere, they can experiment with this sphere. I don't assume that experimenting is a value in itself, but they can do as they want, so this is a radical change. They don't have to be scared of pregnancy, they don't have to be afraid of being socially ostracized because that's also changing, you can be with as many guys as you want. These models are changing, something that would once condemn a girl . . . obviously this only applies to young girls, because when a girl decides to marry and to have a child, these stereotypes return, even if she was, so to speak, "a modern woman," whatever we mean by that, nonetheless she begins to feel the social pressure then, especially as to the role of mother and wife.

Feminist sexologists note, however, that women frequently take advantage of the new opportunities that open up with inventions like contraception or because of social change in general.

The feminist response to women's sex-related problems is often what one of the interlocutors called "gender work": women must learn to think about themselves and what their capable of in a different way, and they must stop taking on passive roles. This gender work also comes up in the therapeutic context. Accordingly, psychological intervention might concern gender roles rather than sex itself. This may involve, for example, encouraging women to be active (as in the case cited above about the client who did not even consider suggesting sex to her husband) or getting to know their own genitals (masturbation) and sources of pleasure.

Interlocutors also drew attention to forms of relationships and sexuality that standard sexology is either silent about or that it pathologizes. These were mainly polyamory (the warm reception in 2012 of the Polish edition of *The Ethical Slut: A Practical Guide to Polyamory, Open Relationships and Other Adventures*, by Easton and Hardy [1997] testifies to the considerable interest in the subject matter), asexuality (usually not treated seriously in the official sexological training program), or BDSM (a practice still considered pathological).[14] For my interview partners, these behaviors deserve full rights. Masturbation is accepted as obvious and healthy. It is also worth noting that in their world, homo- and bisexuality and various forms of transgenderism are perceived as completely normal.

Feminists are thus reformulating the traditional sexual hierarchy and undermining the central role of married, procreative intercourse associated with specific gender roles. They emphasize the importance of women's independence by proposing new gender roles and means to pleasure other than penetration. Does their thought style affect mainstream sexology?

Gender and Pleasure in
Mainstream Knowledge: Change

To what extent have feminist or queer ideas influenced today's mainstream sexology? The material presented thus far may suggest that no flow of information occurs. But no single, homogeneous, mainstream sexological message exists, and what sexology tells us is often contradictory: it retains some "traditional" content while integrating the feminist thought style. In *About Woman* (2011*a*) and in *About Love* (2012*c*), for example, Lew-Starowicz recommends one of the most important feminist works on female sexuality, *The Vagina Monologues* by Eve Ensler (1998; Polish edition 2003), and encourages readers to watch feminism-inspired pornography for women (Lew-Starowicz 2012*c*, 151, 159–60; 2011*a*, 31–32). Furthermore, Lew-Starowicz raises the issue of myths and stereotypes associated with sex in *About Woman* (2011*a*) and in an earlier work entitled *Sex According to Him and Her* (2007), in which he cites and analyzes patient cases. One such myth is man's responsibility for woman's orgasm: "It is not known when this myth originated; fortunately, it is beginning to be less and less popular. Nevertheless, in some relationships, partners still try hard to adapt their sexual practice to this end. In such cases, it ceases to bring pleasure and becomes a task to accomplish" (Lew-Starowicz 2007, 208).

Lew-Starowicz (2007, 210) argues that this belief possibly derives from the book *Ideal Marriage: Its Physiology and Technique*, by Theodoor Hendrik Van de Velde (1926), written in an era when the female orgasm was a taboo subject. But Lew-Starowicz contends that times have changed. Women today gain sexual experience before marriage, so the issue of women's activity should also change: "Both men and women, not only men, bear responsibility for the quality of sex in their relationship" (Lew-Starowicz 2007, 210). Nonetheless, the sexologist continues to receive male patients who blame themselves for not being able to please women (see also Lew-Starowicz 2012*c*, 114).

Another myth being toppled is that women are unable to experience pleasure without love (Lew-Starowicz 2007, 217). Furthermore, as part of a discussion of Viagra in *About Man* (Lew-Starowicz 2012*b*), the sexologist explains to male readers that if a woman experiences orgasm only through stimulation of the clitoris, then they should just accept it; extending sexual contact in time will not help in this matter (130).

Finally, Lew-Starowicz presents a slightly different concept of the relationship based on equality than before. His work once again shows how the process of knowledge formation is interactive and patient-oriented. In the chapter entitled, "Changes in Relations between Partners" in his book, *Sex According to Him and Her*, Lew-Starowicz notes, "Couples' psychotherapy often reveals conflicts that result from discrepancies between the declared model based on equal terms and the archetypical and universal expectations of both sexes, as well as stereotypes about gender roles" (2007, 49). The sexologist defines three spaces of reference. First is "the equality-based model: the principle of equal rights and responsibilities, friendship, cooperation, respect for autonomy and difference, tolerance, common problem solving" (49). The second space comprises the following:

> Universal sex differences and expectations (according to D. Buss):
> Men expect of women: physical attractiveness, younger age, fidelity . . . , resourcefulness.
> Women expect of men: psychological maturity, education, intelligence, ambition, entrepreneurship, slightly older age, affluence, being settled. (49)

Third:

> Stereotypes on gender roles
> Masculinity: dominant, independent, competitive, focused on success, possessing clout, able to quickly make decisions, good physical condition, rough but with a sense of humor, self-confident, self-sufficient, comfort-loving, doesn't show his feelings, open to the world, open to experimenting in sex.
> Femininity: empathetic, caring, nurturing, engaging in others' problems, gentle, flirtatious, concerned with her appearance, resourceful, emotional, irritable, sentimental, capable of sacrifice, reflective, delicate, shy, naïve. (49–50)

A successful relationship based on equal terms depends on balance between the three spaces. This approach differs from that forwarded in the 1980s, when equal terms were defined as the full internalization of gender roles (Lew-Starowicz 1983f; see also chap. 4).

Lew-Starowicz (2007) follows this introduction with detailed examples from the lives of patients: an unemployed husband, once a resourceful and outgoing entrepreneur, now spends his time sitting at home and watching TV. Even when he eventually returns to work, he is not his old self, which makes him less attractive to his wife. Only after seeing the sexologist does he become ambitious and sociable again, and the wife regains her desire to have sex. In another case, the wife gets promoted, she starts earning a lot of money and spending a lot of time at work, the husband is not satisfied with this turn of events, the couple does not have sex, the man decides to get a divorce, and soon after, he starts a new relationship with someone else while she ends up alone (51). Although these stories reiterate the stereotypical approach to gender so common in the work of Lew-Starowicz, he make an exception: "Many readers might know relationships that are doing well where one of the partners achieved success or survived a failure. The dominance of relations based on equal terms, on love and friendship, allows for making it through the crisis and for maintaining balance" (62).

The interviews were also grounds for observing the continuous interplay between the older discourse and the influence of feminism and other alternative thought styles. This could be seen, for instance, in reflections on the emancipation of women. Many interlocutors who identified with the mainstream discussed the relationship between women's emancipation and sex. Some respondents did not pathologize these changes, although they asserted that such changes constituted a challenge for some of their patients. The sexologist and gynecologist cited earlier noted, "Today for some girls it is easy to orgasm, I say this, because their approach to sex is really like the guys', she meets a guy to use him, she does not care what this guy feels, she has to have an orgasm, period and bye-bye. . . . But let's not forget about tradition, because we have two things, women's problems that go in completely different directions, at least that's what I've noticed."

The experts discuss female agency and gender roles in a completely different manner than Wisłocka. A female sexologist and gynecologist in her midthirties argued that women, mainly well-educated women from the big cities, are increasingly open when it comes to issues of sexuality. These women use lubricants and sex toys. And thanks to contraception and financial independence, they are not on the prowl for a man who will support them financially—they look for a "good sex partner" instead. Yet independence comes with a certain risk: "those who are too dominant are usually alone." As for how women function sexually, the interlocutor does not see any problems. She notes that today she sees women who experience anorgasmia, or delayed orgasm, less frequently. They "gain . . . the ability . . . to derive sexual satisfaction much more quickly" than ever before. In their fast lifestyle, "quick booty calls become very natural . . . they learn through their lifestyles." This affects relationships: "If we cannot make time for two hours, it turns out that these fifteen minutes can also be very good, successful sex. Worse if later on we find a male partner who needs those two hours. Just as relationships change, so do the sexual needs of men. Perhaps man will soon be the one who will have to get a box of chocolates to be persuaded to have sex. Not all men accept a woman who says directly: I want it now and I want to do it in the toilet for fifteen minutes."

The interlocutor notes that changes in sexual behavior patterns can be observed on a more general scale "because of this attraction and the need for fast sex, not the normal, traditional sex in the bedroom, with the lights turned down low. That sort of relationship is becoming quite unpopular among adults." During the classes for future sexologists, these types of convictions were placed in the context of the "partner norm." If both partners accept a given behavior, then it must be considered normal; no objections of the sort articulated in *Sex on Equal Terms* are present (see also chap. 4).

Another sexologist, reflecting on changes in gender roles, explained in an interview that men just have to catch up with women:

> I think, yes, . . . it is obvious that we have a crisis of masculinity. From the late nineteenth and early twentieth century . . . women began to demand their rights. We are talking about a relationship model based on equal terms, this is a new model and now a question, now I will call on Długołęcka for support, women have done a great job in the sense that they are able to make use of man's repertoire. But when it comes to these men, I feel that they are lost in the context of identity. Because for them being a woman is a form of degradation, having certain qualities that were stereotypically associated with femininity, is a certain form of degradation. When we talk about this patriarchal model, boys don't cry and that's what we should continue to tell them. Man should be a sexual leader, that still functions and now the

question, okay, if a woman starts to initiate that sexual contact, then what am I there for, right? Does that mean that I am, the argument falls, reduced to the role of impregnator?

When it comes to therapy, some psychologists who represent the mainstream talk about a concept known from the feminist context: "gender work" (they do not call it that), meaning that intervention is to help the patient accept their new gender role. Among interlocutors who identify with mainstream sexology, there were also voices critical of the lack of equality in older publications.

The mainstream is thus a site of conflicting messages. Fundamental changes in comparison to the 1970s and 1980s are also evident.[15] Feminists take part in interactions that shape discourse. For them, the answer to women shouldering the double burden or to relationship troubles resulting from their professional careers is not a return to traditional roles but a total reconstruction of the gender system. Increasingly, doctors and therapists consider the emancipatory perspective. In the sexological program, the *f* word—feminism—is a frequent reference point.

In the context of the 1970s and 1980s, I described how homosexual behaviors were pathologized; the situation has changed in this regard. As a result of the activities of the gay and lesbian rights movements most notably, homosexuality is no longer considered a disease (Bayer 1981; Rubin 1984, 280). In Polish sexology, homosexuality is increasingly understood as "normative," although my feminist-queer interlocutors would hardly agree. Indeed, as I mentioned, books are still on the list of obligatory reading for the "sexologist exam" that present homosexuality as deviant. Yet during the 2011 course, lecturers talked about "partners," suggesting that this could be a person of a different or of the same sex. Furthermore, affirmative therapy was recommended for homosexual patients who had trouble with self-acceptance or coming out. An activist from the Campaign Against Homophobia, a major LGBTQ rights nongovernmental organization in Poland, was invited to speak. During the aforementioned debate on the results of Izdebski's research on sexuality in Poland, which showed that Poles want homosexuals to receive treatment, Lew-Starowicz decisively cut off all discussion of this subject, asserting that homosexuality is not a disease. The Polish Sexological Society also issued a statement affirming that homosexuality is not a disease, nor is it associated with pedophilia. But again, action on the part of the LGBTQ movement was necessary. The statement in question cannot be found on the Polish Sexological Society websites; it was published only on the Campaign against Homophobia website, from which it found its way to Wikipedia.[16] After intervention by a progressive sexologist of the younger generation, who belongs to the sexological mainstream but also collaborates with LGBTQ NGOs, the Polish Sexological Society issued a few more statements stressing the normative character not only of homosexual orientation but also of same-sex parenting and published them on the Society's website (Polish Sexological Society 2016, 2017). The active engagement of the LGBTQ movement led to at least a partial depathologization of homosexuality.

The same applies to the issue of women's emancipation. Whereas earlier sexologists (as a thought collective) followed their patients (representing multiple thought collectives) in the belief that emancipation is bad for sex, doctors today consider, at least partially, a new voice or a new thought collective: the feminist. Feminists demand the redefinition of gender roles and fight for the appreciation of various forms of feminine pleasure and ways of reaching it, breaking down the sexual hierarchy in the process. The feminist voice is something more than a form of Foucauldian reverse discourse; it introduces new values, such as women's sexual autonomy. Feminists and psychologists are equally wary of the medicalization of sexuality. But aren't feminist sexologists in danger of being co-opted, as in the United States (Clarke, Shim, et al. 2010*b*)? Across the Atlantic, certain feminist ideas, like those regarding women's right to pleasure and sexual activity, or the idea of sexual health, have been appropriated by the pharmaceutical industry (see chap. 1). In Poland, the holistic and interdisciplinary tradition serves to counteract this process. If it is possible to develop an approach to sexuality that draws from the various thought styles of different disciplines and cultural influences, then feminism can likewise be included on equal terms. In the end, sexology, as a science and form of therapy, and feminism, as a movement and critical theory of culture and society, have many common goals, which include advocating for sex education and women's sexual pleasure.

Notes

1. Recommended readings include Imieliński 1990; Kratochvíl 2002, Lew-Starowicz 1997; 2000; Lew-Starowicz and Lew-Starowicz 1999; and *Polish Sexology (Seksuologia Polska)* journal.

2. Details are available at http://pts-seksuologia.pl/images/ckeditor_photos /regulamin_uzyskiwania_certyfikatu_seksuologa_klinicznego.pdf_____51bac7bf061cc .pdf.

3. In the past, it was easier to get a certificate. The requirements included the same activities, but fewer hours/credits were necessary.

4. For example, the three-day congress of the Polish Sexological Society in October 2011 was characterized (1) by the fact that many psychologists were in attendance and (2) that papers presented during two plenary sessions went beyond medicine and psychology. The first was on the history of sexology, and the second focused on social sexology. During the second, the sociocultural conditions of sexuality were discussed, and there was even room for my paper on the feminist perspective in sex therapy in the United States. In addition, the speakers, both doctors and psychologists, considered social, cultural, and economic aspects in their analyses of sexual problems. For example, Marek Blajer (2011), in his paper, "Change in Sex Life Quality among Perimenopausal Women," presented during the session on clinical sexology, accentuated the impact of people's life situations (professional career, family life, material conditions) on sex during menopause.

5. Ponton, a peer sex education group, is one organization, which trains sex educators in this way. Later feminist therapists often emerge from its ranks (see, e.g., Ponton 2020). As the interviewees recall, one of the first such workshops was organized in the late 1990s by one of the feminist organizations, and it was entitled, "You Hold the Reigns over Your Orgasm."

6. Examples of specialized portals include Seksualność Kobiet.pl (http://seksualnosc
-kobiet.pl), Barbarella.pl (http://barbarella.pl/), Instytut Pozytywnej Seksualności/Sex
Positive Institute (http://sexpositiveinstitute.pl/), and MoreLove.eu (https://www
.facebook.com/MoreLoveeu-e-magazyn-o-%C5%9Bwiadomym-seksie-e-magazine
-about-conscious-sex-315779818473002/).

7. Frequent references are made to the community that formed in the early 1930s
around *Literary News*, consisting of writers, physicians, and sexual and reproductive
activists, with Irena Krzywicka and Tadeusz Boy-Żeleński as leading figures (Gawin
2009). For example, the organizer of the Pussy Days was a group of activists (some with
a sexological education) who called themselves *Boyówki Feministyczne* (Boy-Żeleński's
Feminist Squads—untranslatable phrase: in Polish, *bojówki*, or squads, when written
with a capital *B* and a *y* instead of a *j* refers to Boy-Żeleński himself).

8. This matter was discussed, for example, during the conference, "Polish Sexology:
20 Years of the Polish Sexological Society" in October 2011.

9. Even Wisłocka (1993*c*), who was generally an opponent of abortion, argued
repeatedly that a woman should have the right to decide.

10. This was already mentioned in *Sex of Equal Terms* (Lew-Starowicz 1983*f*, 15).

11. Within what I call Polish feminist and queer sexology, there are numerous communities representing different approaches. This diversity is blurred in my text because
I want to protect the anonymity of my interview partners in this group (in case they decide to get their sexological certificates through the Polish Sexological Society). I cannot
disclose all the details, as that would reveal their identities.

12. Długołęcka studied men who have spinal cord injuries as a result of an accident.

13. Both Lew-Starowicz and Długołęcka teach at Józef Piłsudski University of
Physical Education in Warsaw.

14. The interlocutors also often talked about sexuality among people with disabilities.
Although this topic goes beyond the scope of this book, it is worth noting that mainstream sexology has engaged this topic for a long time.

15. The issue of civilized and cultured sex, for example, no longer comes up at all.

16. Wikipedia, s.v. "Homoseksualizm" (http://pl.wikipedia.org/wiki
/Homoseksualizm#cite_note-55, accessed October 21, 2013). The entry has since been
modified and does not include the statement at the moment.

Part 3
Violence: Expert Discourse of Rape

6 | Rape: Definitions, Legal Understanding, and Statistics

Introduction

Then there was that conversation with the prosecutor. . . . It felt like she was interrogating me, as if I was somehow guilty, that I had provoked it.

Rape survivor

In the 1970s, when experts were increasingly forthright in speaking out about sex, sexologists, educators, journalists, and lawyers also engaged in discussion about rape. Media coverage of judicial proceedings, popular at the time, often took up this matter, presenting drastic events in great detail.[1] These media reports were unsparing in condemning degenerate perpetrators: in cases of gang rape, they were referred to as "cavemen" (e.g., Kąkol 1966; Szymańska 1972; Rymuszko 1972). Frequently, however, journalists would also conclude that the victims had contributed to the crime with their "reckless" behavior (see also Kościańska 2012d). Experts discussed various aspects of this phenomenon. The press reported that the number of rapes increased as a coefficient of wider moral decline and society's general sex craze (e.g., Bereżnicki 1972; see also Perkowski 2011, 291). In 1951, 218 adults and forty minors were convicted of rape in Poland. The numbers remained steady throughout the 1950s and began to grow in the early 1960s; for example, in 1961, 454 adults and forty-eight minors were convicted of the crime, whereas in 1965, 597 and 118 were convicted, respectively (Leszczyński 1973, 187–88). By the end of the 1960s, more than a thousand adult perpetrators were convicted of rape per year in Poland (1,133 in 1967, 1,169 in 1969, and 1,341 in 1971). As for the number of rapes reported and recognized by law enforcement to meet the legal requirements of the definition of rape, there were 1,462 in 1965 and 2,280 in 1971. Since then, the official number of rape crimes committed per year in Poland has not changed significantly.

The experts' thesis that the number of rapes increased suddenly in the 1960s and 1970s is difficult to accept. More likely is that with growing interest in the sphere of sexuality, greater numbers of people began to talk about rape and victims more often reported rape to the police, called the "citizens' militia" in state-socialist Poland (see Perkowski 2011). Knowledge turned out to be performative but not in the sense that rapes took place with greater incidence. Rather, certain acts were named, lawyers and law enforcement officers began to notice them, and victims were more likely to talk about what happened.

Since the 1970s, sexual violence has maintained a presence in the press and in discussions among specialists, whereas the statistics, as noted, have remained stable. However, the language used to describe rape has changed; as I will show, this change was associated in part with the emergence of a new group of experts. This new group, composed of women who work at organizations established to provide legal aid for survivors of sexual violence and feminists, acted intentionally to bring about this change. Assuming that expert knowledge constitutes a central element of power that constructs both individual subjects and population biopolitics, the language shift also prompted transformation in judicial and law enforcement practices. How did expert discourse of sexual violence change? How did definitions of gender (primarily of women's agency) change within its framework? What led to the shift in knowledge, and what made specialists see the issue differently?

In this part, I analyze various sources: popular sexological publications like *The Art of Love* (Wisłocka 1978), law books, interviews with experts whose work deals with sexual violence, notes from participant observation during training sessions and conferences, and court files.[2] I focus on how victims are construed by expert knowledge and the extent to which stereotypes play a role—mainly, the stereotype of provocation.

Two approaches to rape survivors emerge from these materials. One approach views rape is a bestial act that brings about great suffering and that requires immediate intervention, meaning severe punishment of the perpetrators. The other approach views rape as provoked by the victim, making her at least partially responsible.[3] These two takes on rape tend to interlink, with individual experts often expressing both simultaneously. In writing about female sexuality, anthropologist Carole Vance (1984, 3–4; see also Vance 2011) has argued that in patriarchal culture, only women who fit into the binding gender model deserve protection. All transgressions, like excessive interest in sex and relations that fall at the bottom of the sexual hierarchy—notably, sex for money, nonreproductive sex, nonnormative sexuality, nonstandard gender roles, or independence (Rubin 1984; Miller 2000)—result in the loss of protection from the state and society (Vance 2000; Miller and Vance 2004). In Poland, this also applies to rape survivors. Effectively, despite the progressive law on rape, many women who fall victim to sexual violence cannot count on just treatment by institutions established for their protection (for a discussion of this issue in a global context, see, e.g., Miller 2000). Sadly, stereotypes about rape and the unfair treatment of rape survivors are not specific to Poland. Research conducted in various parts of the world points to the universal prevalence of this problem. In response, many feminist organizations operate both locally and globally to change this situation by running information campaigns and providing aid for survivors (see, e.g., Brownmiller 1975; Bourke 2007; J. E. Johnson 2009; Merry 2009).

Transferring responsibility for rape to survivors implies a very peculiar understanding of women's agency. I have noted already that since the nineteenth century, manuals on sexual and family life have typically been addressed to women. Michalina Wisłocka (1978), author of the most popular manual on sex in Poland, for instance, argued explicitly that women are responsible for these spheres of life. Wisłocka notably encouraged her female readers to work on a beloved man by efficiently but indirectly managing his feelings and desires, as well as of other aspects of his existence. Wisłocka argued that women should take action to fit into a certain model of femininity. In effect, she claimed that women would be able to secure happiness and sexual satisfaction for themselves and their partners, which would not be possible without that behind-the-scenes effort. Texts like Wisłocka's construct women's agency as responsibility, assuming it even when individuals have no control over the situation because of sociocultural conditions. Paul Farmer (1996) has called this "structural violence." In this approach, as a result of factors like social status (notably, gender) or dominant ideas (e.g., sexism), an individual cannot affect his or her fate and, at the same time, is blamed for the position in which they find themselves. Farmer has argued that many politicians, doctors, and specialists in HIV prevention believe that seropositive people must have engaged in risky behavior and thus share responsibility for their infection. Experts are often unable to understand the structural conditions that lead to the lack of choice or to a limited set of options in a given situation. Farmer's observations might be applied to advice books like Wisłocka's *The Art of Love* (1978), which fail to consider the sociocultural conditions that potentially limit the scope of women's actions and that equate agency with responsibility and blame. How are survivors of sexual violence treated when such an understanding of agency dominates?

Rape: Definition

Today's legal understanding of rape in Poland is based on regulations passed in 1932, that is, the provisions of the first penal code ratified after Poland regained its independence in 1918.[4] Legislators of the time defined rape regardless of gender and the relation between perpetrator and victim. Accordingly, it was possible to convict someone for raping a man, a wife, or a prostitute, and women could be tried as perpetrators (Płatek 2010).[5] Furthermore, rape was understood broadly and was not limited to sexual intercourse.[6] These regulations were remarkably progressive, especially compared with those in other countries. Progressive Sweden, for example, recognized rape in marriage in 1975 (Płatek 2014). Today in the United Kingdom, only men can be tried for rape because the crime itself requires penetration of the vagina, mouth, or anus by the penis.[7] Nevertheless, the Polish penal code of 1932 stipulated that rape be prosecuted on the victim's motion. Lawyers argued that this provision served the victim's interest. They reasoned that given the socially stigmatizing nature of this crime, disclosure followed by legal trial could cause great injury to the victim. Logically, this principle assumed that it was the victim, and not the perpetrator, who was to feel shame as a result of rape.[8] This approach reflects an understanding of women's agency already noted: it accords women the right to choose (to report or not to report) while imposing great responsibility on them. My research shows that rape survivors are often pressured by the perpetrators along with their family and friends, and by their own relatives, not to press charges. This legal construction implies that the rape survivor must come to the conviction that she has been wronged and deserves protection despite what people around her think—and, as we shall see, against the stereotypical thinking about rape strongly rooted in both Polish culture and in Polish expert discourse. In other serious crimes that violate individual freedom and bodily integrity, that decision belongs to the state. Monika Płatek, a feminist criminal law expert, analyzed the commentary to the 1932 penal code and observed that the article on rape was written from a male perspective, by men and for men: "Despite its modern framework, in the doctrine, rape crime was treated as a potential threat to the interests of men, hence the emphasis placed on treating victims with special caution. Diametrical differences in experience led to a kind of ambivalence; here the modern framework of the rape crime collided with the misogynist prejudices inherent to a biased doctrine that identified with the representatives of its own sex, while the voice of the opposite sex remained inaudible" (2010, 362).

As an example, Płatek (2010) uses commentary on the penal code, written by the leading legal scholar of the interwar period, Leon Peiper. Płatek notes that Peiper "does not hide his reluctance and suspicion in relation to allegations of rape" (362). He believes that sexual crimes "are a field where hard evidence and the control of witness testimony are difficult. The judge's decision is based on the testimony of people . . . who very often have a personal interest in convicting the accused, like hatred, revenge, jealousy, or a desire for profit (blackmail). In general, low incentives are the order of the day here. Thus, lascivious crimes make for a gigantic cemetery of the judiciary's undisclosed errors in punishment" (quoted in Płatek 2010, 362–63).

After 1932, new penal codes were ratified twice in Poland, in 1969 and 1997.[9] Provisions concerning the prosecution of rape regardless of gender or relations between offender and victim as well as on the victim's motion remained unchanged. Only in 2013, after fierce discussion and partly under pressure from the Council of Europe, the law on prosecution was amended and ex officio prosecution was introduced, entering into force on January 27, 2014. In addition, with the exception of special circumstances, the new provisions allow victims to testify only once and outside the courtroom; they are no longer forced to participate in the legal process or to attend meetings with perpetrators (Grabowska and Grzybek 2017). As I will show, legal experts nevertheless continue to regard victims with suspicion.

Changes to the twentieth-century penal codes cover only three issues. Rape was transferred from the chapter on lasciviousness (1932 penal code) to the section involving offenses against liberty (1969 penal code) and, finally, to the section on crimes against sexual liberty and decency (1997 penal code). In addition, whereas the 1932 and 1969 codes contain the enigmatic term "lascivious act," the concept was replaced in the 1997 code by the more precise "sexual act" (*obcowanie płciowe*) and "other sexual activity" (*inna czynność seksualna*). Nonetheless, the exact significance of these terms and other aspects of Article 197 of the 1997 penal code are the subjects of debate among experts. By "sexual act," most contemporary judges and legal scholars understand vaginal, anal, and oral (fellatio) hetero- or homosexual relations. When it comes to oral sex during which the female genitals are stimulated, opinions are divided. For instance, in an article published in the journal *Prosecution and the Law* (*Prokuratura i Prawo*), legal scholar Bolesław Kurzępa notes, ""Sexual act' is certainly a broader concept than 'copulation,' which should be understood as the sexual intercourse (coitus internus) between people of different sexes, but also including the homosexual and thus lesbian act (coitus analis cum viro or cunnilingus). The scope of the term 'sexual act' includes, in addition to the already mentioned copulation, sex without full penetration and all other forms or methods that constitute ancillary sexual practices, including those that do not make use of the genital organs (e.g. inter femora or in axilla), and even if ejaculation does not take place (emissio seminis)" (2005, 62).

Another legal scholar, Marek Bielski (2008), considers cunnilingus a typical "other sexual activity." When it comes to vaginal and anal penetration, most scholars agree that the penis does not have to be involved for it to be recognized as a sexual act. A bottle or a vibrator might be used to penetrate instead.[10] The case is different if the mouth is concerned:

> The anus (coitus in anum) and the mouth (coitus in ore in the form of fellatio) must be considered surrogates of the female genital organs since they can serve a similar function during sexual contact as the female genital organs because of their physical characteristics. Undoubtedly, the use of body parts other than the male genital organs or the use of objects towards vaginal or anal penetration makes for a sexual act. On the other hand, behaviors that consist of inserting objects or parts of the body other than the male genital organs into the mouth are not of an objectively sexual character. The mouth can therefore be considered a surrogate of the female genital organs only in the case of oral sex in the form of fellatio. (Bielski 2008)

According to some lawyers, not much has to actually happen in order to call it rape. For example, a sentence passed by a court of appeals says, "In order to recognize the crime of rape, it is indispensable that the perpetrator commences (initiates) the sexual act; the situation, where the perpetrator lays on the naked victim and is unable to fully execute his intention because of the lack of an erection bears no meaning upon the admission of the qualifications stipulated in paragraph 3 of article 197 of the penal code."[11] Similarly, in gang rape, some judges and legal scholars share the opinion that a defendant who contributed to forcing the victim to have sex, although he did not take part in it directly, can also be tried for rape: "The essence of a rape carried out in tandem with another person is not that everyone present engages in sexual intercourse with the victim. Suffice it that even one of those involved satisfies his sex drive in contact with the victim's body for the others to have been involved in bringing this person to engage in a sexual act using one of the forms of behavior provided for in paragraph 1 of article 197 of the penal code."[12] Other judges, however, argue differently: "He who does not personally carry out the rape crime, but only facilitates in the stage preceding the execution of the crime, is not an accomplice, but a helper."[13]

The issue of the sexual nature of rape is also incoherent. Some judges of Poland's Supreme Court and courts of appeals believe that the motives for rape do not have to be sexual. Rape may serve, for instance, to humiliate the victim.[14] Others, on the contrary, think that sex drive represents the keystone: "If the perpetrator is steered by aims other than sexual satisfaction (arousal), it cannot be assumed that he is guilty of the crime described in paragraph 2 of article 197 of the penal code."[15] At times, a distinction is also made between "objective" and "subjective" sexuality:

> To fulfill the conditions of the crime described in paragraph 2 of article 197 of the penal code it is enough that objectively in the context of the case, the acts . . . to which the victim was brought or to perform which he or she was forced, were of a sexual nature, and therefore sexual. In terms of paragraph 2 of article 197, it is not important whether the perpetrators associated their behavior with the sexual sphere of their lives and the forms of sex in which they engage, but whether the actions taken against the victim or those which the victim was made to perform were objectively related to the sphere of sexuality.[16]

Lawyers also define consent and resistance differently. According to some interpretations, resistance must be physical, whereas for others, verbal refusal is enough. Some lawyers consider that consent to sex covers all of its forms, whereas others consider consent to be given only to a specific act. In the following chapters, I discuss this matter in detail, analyzing court cases and professional literature.

Other aspects of the crime of rape are likewise subject to diverging interpretations. Although the Polish legal system is not a common law system, judges call upon decisions of the Supreme Court and the appellate courts and on commentary on the penal code for guidance.[17] As already shown, a dissonant approach to the crime of rape emerges from the legal commentary, leaving much room for interpretation. In accordance with Article 7 of the code of criminal procedure, interpretation should rely on the assessment of evidence "with due consideration given to the principles of sound reasoning and life experience" (Adamczyk 2014, 15) and to the principles or indications of knowledge. Sexological knowledge thus enters the courtroom in two ways, as indications of knowledge and as life experiences. If we adopt a constructivist understanding of sexuality, scientific knowledge also shapes the life experience and common knowledge of judges and other lawyers.

Rape: Statistics

How should rape in Poland be quantified? For an accurate estimate, it must be considered that not only Article 204 of the 1932 penal code, Article 168 of the 1969 penal code, and Article 197 of the 1997 penal code refer to acts that can be called rape. Other acts like incest, taking advantage of a dependent relationship, taking advantage of various forms of vulnerability, and sex with a minor can also be forced and thus constitute a form of rape (Płatek 2011). These acts are defined in separate articles of the penal code, making it difficult to determine the scale of the phenomenon.[18] Officially, between 1,600 and 2,600 rapes occur each year in Poland (see Filar 2010, 351); however, the actual number has not been determined. One reason for this state of affairs is the classification of certain forms of forced sex as other crimes.

The principal reason that establishing the actual number of rapes is problematic is that survivors do not report to the police. Among those who do report, not all file motion for prosecution. Organizations that aid women who experience sexual violence estimate that only 8–10 percent of these crimes ever come out (see Borkowska and Płatek 2011, 12).[19] In a recent survey of the prevalence of sexual violence in Poland, designed by feminist researchers Magdalena Grabowska and Marta Rawłuszko (2016, 15–16), 22 percent of women reported being raped and 23 percent experienced attempted rape. The survivors keep silent, frequently blaming themselves and feeling ashamed of what happened. Often, they are afraid of revenge on the part of the perpetrators and their relatives or simply do not believe in the efficacy of law enforcement agencies and do not want to take part in a court trial that will last many years (which was necessary until 2014). Before rape became prosecuted ex officio in 2014, it also happened that police discouraged victims who tried to file a motion for prosecution. A psychologist from an organization that helps survivors of violence noted in an interview that "police officers, if they see that they can talk to the victim, they carry out so-called preliminary talks, that is, before filing the motion for prosecution, they try to discourage it. . . . If there are no witnesses and there is no forensic examination, it's already the norm to suggest that you cannot file a motion for prosecution at all. If someone insists on it, they will file it, but there is this sort of tendency to discourage it."

If a victim decides to press charges against a perpetrator, how effective are law enforcement agencies? In 2005, for example, 1,987 rapes officially occurred, and the detection rate was 83.7% (official police data, quoted in Borkowska and Płatek 2011, 13). In legal trials, according to the Ministry of Justice, the average sentence for rapes committed in that same year was 27 months of imprisonment (33.3 months for sentences without suspension and 18.2 months for suspended penalties) for crimes defined in paragraph 1 of Article 197 (rape) and an average of 41.7 months of imprisonment (46 without suspension, 21 with suspension) in the case of crimes defined in paragraph 3 of Article 197 (cruel and gang rape) (Polish Ministry of Justice 2007a, 14).[20] The statistics do not include acquittals.

In the 1990s, when the courts tended to give somewhat higher sentences for rape, legal scholar Andrzej Siemaszko (2011) noted that the actual terms of imprisonment were usually shorter:

Out of 378 persons convicted of rape, who completed their sentences in 1999, almost one third (31%) served the entire term of their sentence. 262 persons (69%), meanwhile, were granted a parole. The courts had decided on prison terms that ranged from 6 months to 12 years. The average sentence was 40 months (3 years and 4 months), while the average time served in prison was 32 months, or 2 years and

8 months. . . . Of the 145 defendants who were convicted of gang rape, particularly cruel rape, and raping a minor, who completed their sentences in 1999, only one in four (26%) served their sentence in full. The average sentence was 50 months (the shortest sentence was 8 months and the longest 13 years), or slightly more than 4 years, while the actual sentence was 41 months, or 3 years and 5 months. The actual time served in prison accounted for 80% of the sentence imposed.

The vast majority of those convicted and sentenced are men. For instance, among 2,278 people found guilty of rape and serving time in prison (pars. 1 and 3 of Article 197 and pars. 1 and 2 of Article 168 of the 1969 penal code) or suspected of having committed the crime of rape and temporarily detained at the end of 2005, only seven were women, all facing charges for gang rape (Polish Ministry of Justice 2007b, 276–277).

Attitudes of Police and Doctors toward Rape Survivors

What happens when a woman decides to report rape? What must the survivor go through in order for the crime to be noted in any official statistics? Does progressive law guarantee that rape survivors are treated with decency? To begin, the survivor must go to the police station, where she will be interrogated. If the rape took place directly before the report, the police will usually take her to see an on-call gynecologist at the emergency room for medical examination. The procedure can take many hours. From the moment of rape to the time of the forensic examination, the victim should not wash herself.[21] Police officers, and sometimes doctors complete training programs that focus on the specificity of rape crime. As part of the program, they learn about various stereotypes about the subject and how to proceed in the situation: how to talk to women, how not to aggravate their injuries, and how to secure evidence.[22] Many doctors prescribe postcoital contraception and drugs to reduce the risk of contracting a sexually transmitted disease, including HIV. Some Catholic doctors, however, refuse to prescribe the morning-after pill. They either do not propose it or outright refuse to issue a prescription. In some cases, everything runs smoothly: certain police stations work with psychologists or always have a policewoman on duty, guided by the belief that the survivor will have an easier time confiding in another woman.[23] Nonetheless, many critical matters tend to be neglected at this stage in terms of both securing evidence and treating women with due care.

One of my interview partners, a female police psychologist who deals with the problem of sexual violence, gave the example of a policeman who sent a raped woman home: "The lady will go home, wash, and get some rest," he told her. With good intentions in mind, he did not want her to spend all night at the police station, but the evidence in this case was irretrievably lost. Another interlocutor, a female psychologist and an activist with an organization that supports women who experience violence, including sexual violence, said, "It all depends on if you happen to get a good police officer and a decent prosecutor. That basically determines everything. And that is just so terrible. Because one of them might be really great, but most police officers say that the victim must convince them." Asked for an example, the interlocutor continued, "There was this one guy, who took off the rape victim's clothes and checked if she had actually been raped because he didn't want her to trick him. . . . He checked if her underwear was torn or if she had any wounds." She drew attention to the lack of standard procedures, which results in survivors being treated in different ways depending on whether they are judged to be decent or indecent women:

> And it's so terrible that we have such flimsy procedural tools, that it depends on who happens to be assigned to your case. . . . Police officers tend to wake up and see the light if they have daughters the same age as the victim. It all depends on whether he'll recognize the victim as someone from his own group. And then they would really apply themselves. But if a girl came, you know with a low-cut shirt or something, talking street language, then she was totally off the radar and they would do nothing at all. And they can just do that. Because I'm not interested in whether someone is a Catholic, if they have kids or not, if they understand that guys can be sexually aggressive or if they don't understand that. I think that there have to be procedures in place that obligate this person to keep their beliefs and personal opinions to themselves. But domestic and sexual violence is the sort of thing where everyone is an expert. They'll tell you how it is and how it's not, how the victim had tricked them, because later on she got back together with the perpetrator. And, in general, [it's] this sort of yakking that makes for the reality of the legal process for someone who's in crisis and that's the worst.

Such situations take place despite the fact that police are trained in this field. According to the female police psychologist who conducts courses organized by regional police headquarters, the officers "are told that regardless of your personal beliefs . . . the type of duties you're on, it does not matter. . . . There is a list of these sorts of stereotypes, that the victim is guilty herself, that a man sometimes can't control his sexuality." During these courses, participants also discuss the psychological state in which rape survivors often find themselves.

The interview partner from the victim assistance center called attention to the low level of knowledge among police officers that came up in the monitoring project conducted by her organization:

> When we were doing our research, we prepared the entire interview really well. First, we would ask if he knew what the legislation was and how the law should be applied in the area of sexual violence. And there was not a policeman who didn't say that he knew it all, and perfectly well at that. And there was not a prosecutor who didn't say that either. When we asked what the law actually says, it was from pillar to post . . . starting with the sentencing, to what conditions must be met in order to meet the criteria of rape, the conditions when the police can drop charges, whether it's prosecuted on the victim's motion or ex officio by the state—it was just hodge-podge in their heads.

Furthermore, she spoke about the police approach to survivors and how they place victims into categories:

I met a policeman who claimed that if the victim grinds her fingers, she's lying. Or that, for example, the conviction that . . . because the basic police methodology is the division into *real victims and pseudovictims* [emphasis added]. And he, the policeman must first make this distinction. Is he dealing with a pseudovictim, a liar who for some reason wants to frame a decent guy, or a person who, for example, and this comes up very often, that for example, she was having an affair with some guy, the husband found out and now she has to explain it somehow.

Based on in-depth interviews with women who experienced rape and with police officers, feminist researchers Agnieszka Grzybek and Barbara Błońska examined changes in the position of rape survivors as a result of the recent amendment to the law, according to which rape is prosecuted ex officio and the victim is supposed to testify only once, outside the courtroom:

> The material collected illustrates that in the opinion of police officers, the change in the rape prosecution procedure, which was introduced in 2014, did not bring expected results. The majority of police officers evaluate this change negatively, indicating the lack of implementation "in the field." Police officers argued in particular that the new procedure of single examination of the victim (by the court) does not work in practice (difficulty in scheduling hearings immediately, inability to get additional statements from the woman), and that there is a lack of satisfactory collaboration between the police and other institutions, including prosecution and the courts (inability to contact the prosecutor outside of office hours, superficial hearings in the courts). (2016, 52)

In addition, as Grzybek and Błońska write, "Due to persisting stereotypes, social and cultural prejudice that is still very much alive among police officers (for instance, the belief about the motivations of women who report cases of sexual violence), and the lack of options for providing practical assistance to women who experience violence, a large number of rape cases remain unresolved, even if the rape was reported to the police" (2016, 52).

Research conducted in 2011 by the leading feminist foundation, Feminoteka, shows that the health-care system is likewise not prepared to comprehensively support rape survivors. Emergency rooms do not have adequate space, and doctors lack proper training (e.g., psychological; some also do not know how to secure evidence, which stands out in my analysis of court files). Nevertheless, many health-care workers put a lot of effort into helping survivors as best they can. Nevertheless, some approach survivors in a stereotypical manner, downplaying the situation or even turning it into a joke.[24] For many women, the gynecological examination after rape is a particularly trying experience (Grabowska 2011).

The physicians with whom I spoke as part of my research pointed out that despite good intentions, sometimes it is very difficult for them to care for survivors. Sometimes when police bring in a rape victim, a few births are taking place in the ward at the same time and fully absorbing the doctors' attention. This problem could be solved by establishing centers that specialize in carrying out forensic examinations, equipped for this purpose, and by employing properly trained staff. Institutions of this sort operate in some Polish cities, but they are usually open from 8:00 a.m. to 4:00 p.m., whereas many, if not most, of these crimes take place in the evening hours.

Since the mid-1990s, steps have been taken to improve official procedures associated with rape. This task was primarily taken up by nongovernmental organizations. In 2005, for example, the Women's Rights Center and the PPPA, supported by the police, lobbied for the introduction of rape kits, which were to include tools for securing evidence (e.g., the perpetrator's pubic hair) and free postcoital contraception, a supply of which the PPPA was able to gather, thanks to private donors. But handing out contraception turned out to be too controversial. Other initiatives were similarly torpedoed (Turkowicz 2005, Marianek 2003). Changes seemed to work only on a local scale. For instance, at one point in one of Warsaw's districts, a rule took effect whereby rape victims were interrogated only once, by a specialized female prosecutor, while the police offered postcoital contraception (Grabowska-Woźniak 2001). In another big city, a victim-support organization tried unsuccessfully to make health-care providers and law enforcement cooperate. As the interview partner, a psychologist from such an organization, recalled:

> Well, we initially managed to get them to cooperate, but it didn't work out. The medical director was positively inclined to it. A system was set up, but it was created by . . . two . . . policemen, they went to a conference in the United States and brought back this sort of system of interinstitutional cooperation, a type of kit. That there was, for example, a piece of foil . . . because it's often this sort of thing, for example, a comb to brush out an attacker's pubic hair. These are very simple procedures, it's a kit, spatulas, things are organized a certain way inside, when you have a kit like that with instructions, you just take it and get things going, it's really simple. . . . We estimated this kit would cost fifteen zlotys [about four US dollars], really simple things. . . . And everything was in place, but it just fell apart. The police commander general said it was jumping ahead of the crowd, that we have to wait. . . . I think he was mainly afraid that those two police officers would want to take advantage of their own professional success, that they would go to other police stations, to the headquarters, and that they would become stars.

Finally, in 2010, the office of the Government Plenipotentiary for Equal Treatment announced a procedure of conduct for police and medical facilities in dealing with survivors of sexual violence. That procedure has still not been implemented and, furthermore, needs to be amended. Notably, it does not provide specific instructions on the issue of postcoital contraception or matters related to sexually transmitted diseases (Nawrocka 2011, 52–53).

After interrogation and medical examination, the rape survivor is allowed to go home, but even this can prove problematic. The survivor who reports to the police station must hand over her clothing as evidence. If none of her family or friends brings her a change of clothes, she must return home in clothing provided by the police, which is usually a "prison jumpsuit," as one of the interview partners called it. "And then that woman who had reported to them, returned home on the tram in a prison jumpsuit," she concluded.

Once rape is reported, the police and the prosecutor's office establish the course of the incident, interrogate witnesses, often order the arrest of suspects, and appoint experts. In the end, the prosecutor files the indictment, and so begins the court process that usually takes years.

Notes

1. Much was written on sexual violence in *Law and Life*, a widely read magazine published by the Association of Polish Lawyers that featured reports on rape, mainly gang rape, and rape trials (see, e.g., Popkowicz-Tajchert 1971; Rymuszko 1972; a series of articles by Marek Rymuszko [1976] entitled, "The Incident"; Górski 1983). A lot of media coverage focused on the trial of Zdzisław Marchwicki, convicted of rape and murder, who became known as "The Vampire from Bytom" (Osiadacz 1975a, 1975b; for an analysis of the press's portrayal of Marchwicki and his family, see Tomasik 2012, 50–58). The press also reported on the rape trial and conviction of Ireneusz Iredyński (see Kąkol 1966), a famous Polish novelist, poet, and playwright of whom the Communist Party disapproved for promoting a libertine lifestyle. Although the writer's trial had a political undertone, his defenders' speeches are striking in their assumption of his absolute innocence and in how they downplayed any manifestation of sexual aggression on his part (see, e.g., Siedlecka 2005). Similar arguments were forwarded for years in the context of another well-known Polish artist of the same generation, Roman Polański (for an analysis of how Polański's case was presented in the Polish media, see, e.g., Kaim 2011, 82–83). Journalists, experts, and readers vividly discussed various aspects of the crime of rape, entering into polemics with one another (which I discuss in the following sections of this chapter and in in chap. 7). For example, the progressive lawyer Michał Bereżnicki (1977) reacted sharply in *Law and Life* to Jerzy Urban's 1977 text published in *Politics* (no. 18). Urban, a journalist at the time who would later become the spokesperson for the government of the Polish People's Republic (1981–89), proposed to draw legal boundaries between rapes "proper" (unexpected, brutal attacks on victims who tried to defend themselves) and other situations where "the limits of consent in sexual contact are crossed" (quoted in Bereżnicki 1977, 5). For Urban, in turn, the pretext for presenting his views on the subject was a report published in *Law and Life*, entitled, "A Girl and a Mercedes" (Osiadacz 1977), which told the story of a young woman who wanted to engage in rather innocent play with a man she had just met but did not want to have sex with him. She clearly told him no. Readers also expressed their opinions on the situation, for example, in letters published in *Law and Life* no. 20, 1977. (In chap. 7, I discuss in detail the readers' critique of Lew-Starowicz's articles, which appeared in *Law and Life*).

2. Representatives of state institutions call on expert publications (e.g., *The Art of Love*) when working with rape survivors (see Grabowska 2011, 145).

3. By far, women are the most frequent victims of this type of crime, and I center my focus on them in this book.

4. In the 1932 penal code, rape is defined in Article 204: Sec. 1. Whoever by violence, illegal threat, or artifices, shall cause another person to submit to a lascivious act, or to perform such an act, is punishable by imprisonment up to 10 years. Sec. 2. The prosecution shall take place on motion of the injured person (Lemkin and McDermontt 1939, 65).

5. Monika Płatek (2010, 362n44) points out that the legal scholar Juliusz Makarewicz, who coauthored the 1932 penal code, wrote in commentary that a woman can, for example, tie down a man to be raped by another man. In other crimes, such action, notes Płatek, would be considered aiding and abetting, not actually committing the crime.

6. In a sentence from 1933, the Polish Supreme Court defined the lascivious act broadly, including in the concept the "act of copulation" and "any act that aimed to satisfy the sexual drive or incite sexual arousal" (quoted in Leszczyński 1973, 40).

7. Such is the legal definition of rape in the United Kingdom according to the 2003 Sexual Offenses Act. Earlier, only forced heterosexual vaginal penetration was considered rape (for more on the legal understanding of rape and rape trials in the United Kingdom, see Smith 2018). This definition is a good example of how rape was understood in Western Europe in the twentieth century.

8. Over the years, changes to this provision have been proposed repeatedly (see, e.g., Bereżnicki 1972; for a discussion of this issue, see Płatek 2010), with the argument that prosecution of the victim's motion does not serve to protect the victim but rather burdens the victim with additional responsibility and exposes them to attacks and pressure on the part of perpetrators and their relatives.

9. In the penal code of 1969, the crime of rape was defined as follows: Chapter 22, entitled "Offences against liberty," Article 168: Paragraph "1. Whoever by violence, illegal threat, or artifices, subjects another person to a lascivious act, or forces another person to perform a lascivious act, is punishable by imprisonment for between one year and 10 years." Paragraph 2. "If the offender acts with particular cruelty, or commits rape acting in unison with other persons, he or she is liable to the penalty of imprisonment of a time not shorter than 3 years". Paragraph 3. "Prosecution shall take place on motion of the injured party." In turn, the 1997 penal code places rape in chapter 25, entitled "Offences against Sexual Liberty and Decency," and states: "Art. 197. Rape. § 1. Anyone who, by force, illegal threat or deceit, subjects another person to sexual intercourse (Polish: *obcowanie płciowe*) is liable to imprisonment for between two and 12 years. § 2. If the offender forces another person to submit to another sexual act, or to perform such an act in the manner specified in § 1, he or she is liable to imprisonment for between six months and eight years. § 3. If the offender commits a rape 1) in concert with another person, 2) towards a minor under the age of 15, 3) towards a descendent, ascendant, adopter, adoptee, brother or sister, he or she is liable to imprisonment for at least three years. § 4. If the offender commits the rape specified in §§ 1–3, with particular cruelty, he or she is liable to the penalty of imprisonment for at least five years" (Faulkner 2012, 153). It is also important to add that the Polish term *obcowanie płciowe*, translated by Nicholas Faulkner for the bilingual (Polish and English) edition of the 1997 Polish penal code (published by the specialized legal press C. H. Beck) as "sexual intercourse," is a broad term covering all sorts of sexual acts, not only the situation in which the penis penetrates the vagina. This broad understanding is confirmed by legal scholars' commentaries to the penal code, discussed later in this section.

10. II AKa 328/06, court of appeals decision, November 16, 2006, Katowice, KZS 2007/5/68; II AKa 40/07, court of appeals decision, April 19, 2007, Katowice, LEX no. 331806.

11. II AKa 308/00, court of appeals decision, November 30, 2000, Katowice, OSA 2001/5/29.

12. WA 19/00, Supreme Court decision, July 13, 2000, LEX No. 550495.

13. II AKa 186/98, court of appeals decision, January 20, 1999, Lublin.

14. For example, II AKa 147/08, court of appeals decision, June 19, 2008, Katowice, KZS 2008/9/53.

15. II AKa 209/06, court of appeals decision, February 14, 2007, Krakow, KZS 2007/3/29.

16. II AKa 286/07, court of appeals decision, December 12, 2007, Lublin, LEX no. 357225.

17. A detailed, historical analysis of legal commentary and jurisprudence goes beyond the scope of this book (see, e.g., Leszczyński 1973; Płatek 2010).

18. According to Article 198: "Anyone who takes advantage of the vulnerability of another person, or their inability to recognize the significance of the act or ability to control their conduct, as a result of a mental disability or disorder in order to subject such a person to sexual intercourse, or to force him or her to submit to another sexual act or to perform such an act is liable to imprisonment for between six months and eight years" (Faulkner 2012, 153). Article 199 concerns the abuse of "a relationship of dependency or manipulating a critical situation" (155) for the above-mentioned purpose (penalty of up to 3 years imprisonment), also when the victim is a minor (from 3 months to 5 years imprisonment). Furthermore, Articles 200 and 201 relate to incest and sex with a minor that are not forced by violence, threat, or deception. In such cases, consent can be problematic: does a child possess the capability of expressing informed consent to engage in sex with an adult? In other words, with some exceptions, these articles include specific forms of rape.

19. This issue was already pointed out in the 1970s. For analysis of the discussion around the so-called gray number of rapes, see Perkowski 2011.

20. Statistics kept by the Ministry of Justice also include sentences decreed in the two previous years due to data reported from appeals.

21. It happens that women do not report immediately after the event. This is interpreted to their detriment.

22. The content of training programs often depends on the instructors. Although participants in some sessions discuss stereotypes about rape, the content transmitted can actually perpetuate them. For example, Zofia Nawrocka (2011, 59) points out that training materials published by the General Police Headquarters of Poland present rape as a crime that takes place in a dark alley; sexual violence in relationships is not mentioned.

23. As I learned from one of my interview partners, in a big city in the 2000s, police psychologists were summoned to a given police station when a rape survivor came to report. Later, however, according to orders passed by Poland's Police General Commander, police psychologists were to look after police officers only.

24. For example, women's rights activist Barbara Limanowska once mentioned a joke she had heard from a doctor: "Well, they didn't use a condom, so we can expect a baby" (quoted in Synowiecka 1999).

7. | The Provocative Victim and the Male Limits of Self-Restraint: Stereotypes in Expert Literature

Analysis of press discourse shows that the most prevalent stereotype about rape is provocation.[1] According to this narrative, the victim behaves provocatively and recklessly, which drives the perpetrator beyond his limits. From this perspective, at some point, a man is no longer able to hold himself back.[2]

In 2002, a major Polish public opinion research agency confirmed the vitality of the provocation stereotype in a survey of a representative random sample (1,017 respondents aged fifteen and older). Respondents were asked how perpetrators should be punished for rape. According to 72 percent, the penalty should be prison time without suspension, whereas 20 percent opted for life behind bars. The next question concerned rape "preceded by the woman's provocative behavior." The fact that the questionnaire reiterated the stereotype testified to its ubiquity. Meanwhile, when the same study asked about punishment for other crimes like assault or theft, the victim's prior behavior was not important from the point of view of the study's authors. The survey did not include questions about robbing rich people who had been flaunting their money or about whether the victim of a beating had been aggressive or provoked his fate. The respondents' answers serve to further confirm the strength of the provocation stereotype: 8 percent marked that no punishment was necessary, 6 percent proposed a settlement (in the case of rape without provocation, no one had been in favor of these solutions), 4 percent opted for a fine (compared with 2 percent if there were no provocation), and 14 percent chose a suspended penalty (2 percent if there were no provocation). Of those surveyed, 48 percent were in favor of prison terms without suspension, while 7 percent marked life in prison (TNS OBOP 2002, 9–10).

Rape occupies an important place in expert discourse of sexuality. In the following sections, I examine the role of stereotypes about provocation and the message about gender contained within them. I analyze statements made to the press by various experts: sexologists and psychologists, as well as lawyers, who often refer to knowledge from the field of sexology. I study popular sex books through this lens, and I examine the training process of future court experts and other people who work with rape survivors. Finally, I focus on selected legal publications. When it comes to sex crimes, experts from the field of law, sexology, and, more generally, forensic medicine, psychology, and psychiatry work closely together. In effect, the thought styles typical to each discipline intertwine.

Popular Sexological Literature

What do sexologists write about rape? We begin with *The Art of Love* (Wisłocka 1978), the most popular Polish book on sex, discussed in detail previously. As I have shown, in Wisłocka's view, young men (and sometimes older men) experience unrestrained sexual desire due to hormonal and developmental processes. Consequently, they constantly strive to release this desire. In contrast, girls and women are driven by feelings. In chapter 2, entitled "Youthful Love," the author describes how "almost from the period of puberty, boys reach the maximum intensity of sexual tension in their lives in a short period of time, which goes hand in hand with the ability to engage in physical sexual contacts" (36).

This certainly differs from what young women experience: "Girls, at low sexual tension, begin to exhibit the desire for emotional love much earlier and start seeking a boy 'of their own,' without the instinctive need for physical contact" (36). Consequently:

> Boys, who are basically bursting with an excess of excitability in this period of life, look for the company of girls with the curiosity and inquisitiveness of a puppy (as one of my younger patients described it). To touch, see, try . . . these are the projects and plans that fill their imagination. In this period boys experience uninterrupted yearning for intercourse and unloading tension, while emotions are only at the threshold of development. They avoid any responsibilities or ties, because girls are for them at this time of life only objects of discovery. Yes, the more intelligent and smarter, the more skillful at creating the appearances of love. Realizing quickly that wanting to achieve the desired effect, it is necessary to play on the imagination of girls, they talk about love, and blackmail girls that they will leave them, if they do not give "proof of love" . . . etc. (Wisłocka 1978, 37)

Wisłocka then describes various situations and experiences of youth of both sexes (their mutual relations are described as the first phase of conflict, which I discuss in detail in chap. 4). She discusses the various ways in which boys satisfy their physical needs and girls their emotional needs in turn (e.g., boys' relationships with older women or girls' relations with older men). She does not mention masturbation in this chapter.

A consequence of this first phase of conflict is, as the author calls it, "dangerous and sometimes criminal forms of releasing excess sexual tension" (Wisłocka 1978, 41). She explains, "I am thinking here of teen gang attacks on girls and mature women in order to see them and even rape them. The driving force behind these actions is, among others, very high sexual tension, and the fact that psychological brakes among boys from the less civilized backgrounds do not work properly" (41). In considering these situations, Wisłocka takes up issues of gender responsibility and roles: "While watching film accounts of gang rape, I was wondering if in many cases 'victims' of individual or gang rape are not in the same way guilty of what happened as the rapists, and in the end only more hurt? Maybe even the word 'guilty' in regards to girls is not right, rather it should be applied to parents and educators" (41). The author associates this with generational changes:

> During the times of our mothers and grandmothers it was unthinkable for a young girl to go out with a man she had only recently met for a walk, to a restaurant or to a desolate place. The notorious chaperones of the old times . . . were meant to prevent unexpected physical aggression on the man's part. Today we laugh at this. Girls go out with boys they do not really know, they let themselves be picked up on the street by unknown men, they agree to go with them to their apartments or to the forest. They think that these are signs of progress and modernity, and not of shameful recklessness. Parents, unfortunately, also often do not realize the danger of such behavior and do not warn girls about the possible consequences of these actions. (41)

Wisłocka explains that this comes about, as I mentioned, as the result of natural excitability: "The boy cannot control his level of sexual arousal, but the girl should know that every situation mentioned above is for him an explicit invitation to 'rape,' and if she does not want to be raped, she should not allow for the opportunity. . . . Unfortunately, in analyzing court files and press reports on this subject, in the great majority of cases it is clear that the girl agreed to going to the apartment, to the forest or to a secluded place with a boy she had just met" (41–42). The sexologist emphasizes that women are responsible not only for themselves but also for men, once again defining the agency of women as responsibility: "The ordinary recklessness of girls puts boys, carried away by sexual arousal . . . at risk of being compromised, subject to legal punishment and frequent derailment from the path of proper development already in their early years" (42). The author asserts that these words do not apply to random women who were simply attacked and did not show a lack of foresight (42), thus outlining the distinction between the two types of victims: those deserving of protection on the part of the state and those undeserving.

Wisłocka (1978) draws attention to the importance of knowledge: only its universalization can be as effective as the chaperones of days past. She explains, "I think that the broad popularization of knowledge about the physiological processes that take place during the adolescent period in the bodies of boys and girls should bring about girls' more careful use of their hard-won equality. . . . In the field of sex, progress and equality between the rights of girls and boys has surpassed knowledge of the immovable laws governing physiological and mental changes in the adolescent body, leaving girls defenseless in some sense, and vulnerable to sexual aggression" (42). Young women who accompany men to desolate places are guided by a certain feeling, argues Wisłocka, "among girls of this age (and throughout their lives) the dominant feeling is a subconscious maternal instinct" (42). She explains that these feelings and instinct underlie women's relationships with men. Women are not aware that boys and men have different intentions.

If we espouse the biological point of view, as does Wisłocka (1978), would it not be better to scold young men for their lack of self-control than to absolve them of their brutality and shift responsibility to women, civilizational change, the family, or society? Or perhaps young men should be encouraged to masturbate instead, as postulated by some, such as activist and writer Artur "Caesar" Krasicki, author of *The Masturbation Manifesto* (*Manifest Onanistyczny*; for a discussion, see Kościańska 2012*b*, 2017). Also striking in these fragments is the extremely stereotypical portrayal of women and how they are associated with the private sphere. If women find themselves outside of it, they are considered reckless and provocative. Recklessness and provocation, as I will show later, play key roles in court discourse. Another feature of the approach to rape that Wisłocka represents is its location in a purely sexual context: the young man is unable to control himself because of high sexual arousal. Nonsexual motives for rape are not mentioned—for example, the desire to dominate or punish someone who does not fit into accepted gender models or the dynamics between peers, especially men (so important in the context of gang rape)—and this silence is also typical to this approach to rape (Wołosik and Majewska 2011, 7–12, 58–66). Furthermore, although sexual violence among young people makes for the starting point of Wisłocka's reflections on rape, the tone of her arguments suggests that the author writes about rape in general. In chapter 4, I discussed Wisłocka's belief that women should not communicate their needs directly. Accordingly, if women want to seduce and then keep a man, they should use deception, hints, and indirect language.[3] As we will see later, a subject of frequent debate regarding rape is the survivor's behavior: what she said, how she said it, and whether the perpetrator understood that she was expressing refusal. In this context, the method of communication that Wisłocka proposes leads to the fact that "no" could mean "yes."

Worth adding here is that Wisłocka edited *The Art of Love* before its subsequent editions were published, notably updating the part on contraception. Still, the fragments on rape she kept unchanged.[4] They are to be found even in the latest edition, available for sale as I write.[5] The only change made in some of the later versions applied to the passage beginning with the words, "In the field of sex, progress and equality," which were put in boldface type.

How do other popular sexologists approach the issue of rape? Lew-Starowicz addressed this problem on many occasions, showing that his perspectives on rape varied. In an article from 1970, for example, he does not say anything about provocation, and although he generally links rape with the sex drive, he presents it as a wider problem. He indicates that this issue is socially conditioned and suggests that rape may have something to do with criminal subculture: "There are strict rules here, the leader's despotism, the desire to become like the leader, and rivalry in showing ruthlessness, toughness, and brutality. Rape is then a test of these inhumane abilities, and for a new member of the gang, a test to fit in as a real 'knight'" (Lew-Starowicz 1970*c*, 14). Another root cause of rape might also be "broken or conflicted family environments. Hotbeds for criminal behavior are the homes of alcoholics, quarrel-ridden, full of mutual hatred, and the extreme self-interest of the spouses" (14). But, as Lew-Starowicz notes, rape is not limited to this social group: "It might seem paradoxical that some young rapists come from very 'noble,' well-established homes. The reason for going down the path of crime is, according to the parents, a bad environment, at school for example. In fact, the reason is the lack of proper upbringing at home, in which the 'miraculous' child was showered with money, presents, protected from criticism and responsibility for the deeds it had committed" (14). The sexologist also raises the issue of models of masculinity, for which rape may be, "in some juvenile circles," a type of trial: "This is generally related to how primitive these individuals are who adhere to the myth of manhood. Masculinity is for them the epitome of brutality, arrogance, humiliation of women, and sporting exploits in intercourse. Rape serves here for a specific symbol of male maturity" (14). Another article, published in 1972 in *Etc* magazine and entitled "Gang Rapes," is written in a similar vein. The author also draws attention here to the fact that perpetrators do not see how their victims suffer (Lew-Starowicz 1972*a*).

In a 1973 article entitled "Mystifications," Lew-Starowicz (1973*h*) presents a completely different take on the issue. He notes that an example of the title mystifications may be the situation in which a woman agrees to sex but later claims that it was rape. He quotes from Ovid: "Though you call it force: it's force that pleases girls: what delights is often to have given what they wanted, against their will" (14).[6] Readers were outraged by this text. They sent comments to the editorial staff of *Law and Life* magazine, where lively exchanges on the problem of sexual crime took place. One reader, Wł. Marcinkowski, a physician from Krakow, claimed that Lew-Starowicz's article "called for vengeance to heaven" (1973, 5). He characterized the text as follows: "The author has scientifically 'explained' to young people that girls generally want to be raped." The reference to Ovid also raised this reader's objections: "Evidently, the scholar takes the poet's playful, frivolous verse for scientific truth." He argued further:

> As a doctor and a human being, I am forced to protest against such definition and explanation of rape, because it offends our sense of dignity, because it offends our girls and women. . . . This type of "information" is in my opinion unacceptable. . . . The author does not realize that his pseudoscientific information can, and does, encourage to rape in real life, also gang rape. He does not realize that it might be an argument of defense for some disreputable "attorneys" with no conscience and who serve as counsel in the legal trials of rapists. Or, that it might even be the very means of defense taken up by the accused in court, and in calling upon the greatness of sexological medical knowledge. (Marcinkowski 1973, 5)

At the end of his letter, Marcinkowski accuses Lew-Starowicz of what is usually said of rape survivors: "Astounding is the recklessness and irresponsibility of the doctor, who like some visitor from another planet, has not heard about the growing epidemic of mass, bestial rapes of often underage victims" (Marcinkowski 1973, 5). Finally, he states his own position clearly: "I direct my humanism . . . toward murdered and raped youth, and therefore children, and not toward cruel, beast-like criminals" (5). Three weeks later, a forty-five-year-old reader, who signed her comment with the initials Z.B., also sent in a letter of protest against "the claim that girls in general want to be raped": "I have NEVER met such a girl or woman in all of my already rather long and active life. . . . In the name of girls and women, I shout—no! We do not want to be raped. This is a crime equal to murder! I am afraid that articles like that by Mr. Lew-Starowicz have already done a lot of damage to the psyche of young readers" (1973, 5).

The angered reader Marcinkowski stipulated that Lew-Starowicz probably received a lot of letters of protest. Perhaps this was the case. The sexologist's next article about rape for *Etc* magazine came out in 1978. In "Playing with Fire" (Lew-Starowicz 1978a), he again raised the question of provocation. A reader who signed her name Jadwiga described in a letter how she was raped by her husband's friend. In the opening, she wrote that only because of her good will did she not report to the police. Then she presented herself as follows: "I am an attractive woman, quite flirtatious, men like me and I like to flirt with them, but always to a certain limit" (quoted in Lew-Starowicz 1978a, 30). Next, Jadwiga described what happened to her. She was at a party at a friend's house, the guests left, and she was waiting for her husband to pick her up. She found herself alone with the party host: "We began to talk, watch his 'porn collection,' we kissed, but innocently, suddenly he turned into an animal and he practically raped me. . . . I have to admit that I have already seen a man change suddenly into a wild beast. Does this mean that you have to keep a distance from a man when you only like him?" (30). In response, Lew-Starowicz explains the mechanisms that lead to rape: "Specialists in sexual violence (victimologists) have repeatedly emphasized that some rapes occur because women cross the 'threshold of sensibility and male self-restraint' [and that these] men were . . . provoked, unawares" (30). Lew-Starowicz finds the root causes of this state of affairs, like Wisłocka, in the lack of knowledge: "A poor understanding of the specifics of psychosexual difference between the sexes is evident here. Thus, the frequent misunderstandings, which sometimes end with someone getting hurt" (30). His next sentence leaves no doubt as to who bears responsibility: "Women's behaviors can vividly resemble playing with fire" (30). Behavior of this sort leads to unforeseen developments. Interestingly, the author adds that women can also react differently to sexual situations, but he does not develop this theme.

In the next part of the article, Lew-Starowicz (Lew-Starowicz 1978a) examines the question of "the threshold of erotic sensibility." He notes that it depends on individual (temperament) and situational circumstances. He answers the reader's letter as follows: "In the letter cited, many things favored the development of such a situation: the party atmosphere, alcohol, watching pornography together, being alone, touching, and flirtatious female behavior" (30). He reflects on the issue of consent:

> Revealing the boundaries of what is allowed may not be taken seriously. Everyone knows that very often, "no" means "yes," as this is the language of flirtation. The fact that we have a certain threshold of sensibility and a limit to flirting does not mean that the other person is on the same level of feeling. In rapes that happened as a result of this type of situation, the following behaviors on the part of women most commonly preceded the incident (clearly, the problem concerns only certain rapes):
>
> • driving the man to a "borderline" situation and then suddenly announcing refusal to continue the "harmless play,"

- playing the role of a sexually experienced woman endowed with a great temperament, which aroused the imagination and made certain hopes develop,
- kissing and petting, or partial love art,
- flirting combined with promises "for the future." The dimensions of this "future" can be judged differently in terms of time by both parties. (30)

The sexologist then wonders why women behave like this: "Conscious and subconscious erotic provocation has various possible causes: the need to confirm her attractiveness or sensuality, treating sex as a form of play, the need to reveal her 'sexiness' (which is very popular at the moment). I also know of cases where erotic provocation concealed aggressive tendencies towards the other sex; you can then 'play' watching and seeing the reactions of the person being provoked. There are also people endowed with erotic 'grace' and natural sex appeal. In such cases, their completely unintentional sexy behavior can, in favorable conditions, unleash great sexual arousal" (30). At the same time, the author underscores that rape cannot be justified: "This does not mean that provocative or unconsciously provocative behavior entitles the other person to force intercourse." Immediately, however, he adds, "But we are, nevertheless, co-responsible for driving the other person to a borderline situation, and therefore we must control our behavior and be aware of how other people perceive us" (30).

Lew-Starowicz develops the question of provocation in several articles from the first half of the 1980s, published mainly in *The Mirror*. In "Provoking Fate," Lew-Starowicz argues that the belief that "'perverts' are out there taking advantage of those 'poor' women" makes women "provoke their fate by trusting too much in men's pleasant external appearances, so incompatible, in the general understanding, with the stereotypical criminal" (1983e, 12). In an article published a few weeks later, entitled "The Price of Being Naïve," Lew-Starowicz advises women and girls how to "protect themselves from misfortune" (1983b, 12). He embarks on an analysis of rape scenarios, starting with examples of women's reckless behavior: "Here is a young, 17-year-old girl, who after leaving the movie theatre in the evening, accepts an invitation to listen to vinyl records at the apartment of a young man she just met. Another young girl agrees to go for a nighttime walk on the beach with a stranger. Yet another girl goes to a party and voluntarily drinks all the alcohol that was poured into her glass." The expert notes, "In their behavior, the women were guided by the sexual need to have fun, end their boredom, spend time with a charming, newly met man, but they allowed the men to do the directing; they left the initiative in the men's hands" (12). These women did not realize the effect they had on the men or that they might be provoking them: "All of this comes about because of the lack of elementary knowledge about the nature of psychosexual differences between the sexes, about dissimilarities in attitudes towards sex and intercourse, about the most common mechanisms of behavior." In effect, "at least a third of rapes were unknowingly provoked by the women themselves" (12). Some perpetrators might be deceitful or suffer from sexual disorders, but many were just provoked. Either way, according to Lew-Starowicz, women should behave rationally and have adequate knowledge of male sexuality.

He spells this out even more clearly in an article published a year earlier, entitled "The Provocation of Rape." Here, Lew-Starowicz argues that women's behavior drives *"their partners* past their limits" (Lew-Starowicz 1982*b*, 12; emphasis added). Thus, "some rapes are not actually rapes, because they were provoked as a hidden need of the female psyche." He calls on statistics: "I do not intend to question rape being a brutal act of violence, but I am convinced that about 30% of rapes are provoked in some way" (12).

In an article from 1985 published in *Etc*, Lew-Starowicz starts off with rapists and their character traits: "Forcing intercourse, as research has shown, is most often exhibited by people who have problems with their own masculinity, are full of complexes, who fear women and love, and who also have personality disorders" (Lew-Starowicz 1985*c*, 22). But, he continues, "Nowadays, increasing importance is attributed to the victim's conscious or unconscious provocation of rape, as well as to her gross recklessness (like setting up a date late at night at the guy's house, nighttime walks in the park, drinking alcohol, and so on)." In effect, "Rape prevention first and foremost draws attention to avoiding situations that might provoke it" (22). Women who have already found themselves in these situations are advised to engage the rapist in a conversation, call him by name, show interest in him, and tell him about themselves.

Not all of Lew-Starowicz's texts from the early 1980s focus on women's improper behavior. His 1984 article, "The Consequences of Rape," is written in a completely different tone. Here, the sexologist observes that rape "will always be a brutal and painful act" (Lew-Starowicz 1984*b*, 12) and examines in detail the disorders that survivors may experience in the aftermath. In another piece, Lew-Starowicz goes beyond the sexual dimension of rape to examine the psychosocial conditions that create sex offenders. His analysis is based on his experience as an expert witness in cases of rape, pedophilia, incest, and exhibitionism. Among the psychosocial conditions, he includes "the domination of mothers and other women in the upbringing of sons and boys in general" (Lew-Starowicz 1981*d*, 14), the lack of ties within peer groups, and the lack of sex education. In other articles he discusses taboo topics like rape in marriage (Lew-Starowicz 1988*c*) or postcoital contraception in case of rape (Lew-Starowicz 1986). In one of his most important books, *Sex on Equal Terms*, he criticizes the stereotype of provocation (Lew-Starowicz 1983*f*, 30; for other examples, see Kościańska 2012*d*).

Such inconsistency is also evident when Lew-Starowicz discusses survivor behavior in one of his academic publications. His book *Forensic Sexology* (*Seksuologia sądowa*; Lew-Starowicz 1988*e*) contains a subchapter entitled "Rapes." The author reports the results of both Polish and international research on sexual violence. He discusses works that focus on victim behavior. During a symposium on atypical sexual behaviors held in Jabłonna (a conference center in the Warsaw area) in 1976, "It was stressed that steadfast resistance may prevent rape" (80). The types of rape survivors were also analyzed: "Victims of rape include:

accidental women (resisting aggression is important here), the unconsciously provocative group (make friends easily, show off their alleged sexual experience, and are later surprised by how the situation developed), and the group of deliberately provocative women who most often provoke, and later try to draw back at the last moment, which proves ineffective" (80–81). Lew-Starowicz then presents Polish research on rape survivors: "After examining 23 cases of gang rape in the Warsaw area, Jabłońska . . . notes that in 18 cases, the women had behaved recklessly while in 7 cases they were sexually provocative. In 17 cases, the perpetrators had no prior intention of committing the crime, which eventually took place in conducive circumstances. 75% of the rapes occurred between 8 p.m. and 10 p.m., and 10 of victims were at the perpetrator's house. The majority of rapists were strangers to the victims" (81).[7] The next paragraph also relates to this problem: "In discussing gang rape, Szczybr . . . writes that the initial stage of demoralization was specific to the victims, moreover, that they exhibited 'culpable' behavior: recklessness, provocation, and naïveté. Victims did not make use of the means of defense available to them, they also did not press charges. Some of the victims did not seem to feel hurt and later they maintained contacts with the perpetrators" (81).[8]

Lew-Starowicz does not, in principle, take a stand on this matter. Perhaps he could be compared with Kinsey, who regularly avoided expressing his opinion. The only exception is a short commentary that can be inferred to represent Lew-Starowicz's own ideas. A few pages later in the same text, he refers to the types of consent distinguished by other researchers, one of them being "passive consent, when a woman does not desire sex, but does not resist, what is understood as consent" (Lew-Starowicz 1988e, 83). The author observes, "This . . . type of consent raises the most doubt during court hearings. Another problem is the issue of consent in acts of gang rape, when the victim consented to sex with one partner, but did not agree to sex with the others" (83). It should be noted, however, that in the subchapter on rape, the doctor also presents research that points to how much rape survivors suffer and the personality disorders typical of perpetrators. He also makes reference to scholars who call for taking marital rape seriously.

In 2000, a revised edition of *Forensic Sexology* was published. New content was added in the section on rape. The author refers to multiple theories on the causes of rape, listing the victimological concepts (rape is the result of reckless behavior and alcohol consumption), the psychiatric, the feminist (aggression has to do with the male gender role), and the social (Lew-Starowicz 2000, 287). He also mentions the classification outlined by less known sexologist Julian Godlewski, in which types of rape are distinguished as sexual and nonsexual. He does not, however, reveal his stance on the matter. Causes include the situational (rape occurs because of a misunderstanding of the victim's reaction; e.g., the perpetrator perceives resistance as flirt), the instrumental (e.g., rape is linked with pedophilia), and the sadistic (Lew-Starowicz 2000, 290–92; see also Godlewski 1987).[9] In addition, Lew-Starowicz lists the myths associated with rape, among them the belief that when a woman says no, she is really thinking yes (Lew-Starowicz 2000, 303). The new edition includes a fragment on the personality traits of rape survivors. We learn here that survivors are often passive and patient and exhibit masochistic tendencies (302).

The two-track approach is also evident in Lew-Starowicz's (1992) nonacademic book *Sexual Violence* (*Przemoc seksualna*), in which he examines sexual violence against minors and the problem of rape in detail. He cites examples from various parts of the world suggesting that law enforcement agencies do not treat rape with due seriousness, which he attributes to stereotypes, including the stereotype of provocation (135–36). He also emphasizes that although some women fantasize about rape, this does not mean that they actually want to be raped (139). He outlines the nonsexual motives for rape (148) and deconstructs various other stereotypes, for example, that a prostitute cannot be raped (154–58). He discusses in detail the problem of marital rapes and violence against women in the family, calling on psychologists to pay more attention to the issue (110–21). Finally, he illustrates his analysis using often tragic examples from his medical and court practice. *Sexual Violence* breaks with many stereotypes by centering on the suffering of rape survivors and putting the social, cultural, psychological, and familial contexts of rape on display. This book, in my opinion, is one of Lew-Starowicz's most interesting works. Nonetheless, here too, the topics of provocation and womanly recklessness appear. The author posits that one of the causes of rape may be "instances of unconscious provocation on the part of women": "Studies reveal that many women act recklessly, I would say foolishly, while others flirt and provoke erotically with no intention of engaging in sexual contact. Still others provoke aggressive behavior in men by playing on their male ambitions, etc." (141).

How can discrepancies in approaches to violence be explained? Is it not again that only certain types of (decent) women deserve to be protected by the state and the law? Lew-Starowicz presents a somewhat altered take on this issue in his latest works, which I discuss in chapter 9.

Discussions among Experts:
Interviews and Participant Observation

My ethnographic research focused on contemporary expert discourse of sexual violence. I took part in training sessions for expert witnesses, but this issue was also discussed during other courses and conferences I attended.[10] I asked about sexual violence in interviews. Most professionals with whom I spoke served as expert witnesses or were in regular contact with survivors of sexual violence as part of their work.[11]

Distinction between survivors who deserve and who do not deserve protection, as made by Lew-Starowicz and Wisłocka and by the police, also comes up in the materials I collected during my participant observation. The problem of rape was discussed at two three-day training sessions in forensic sexology organized by a state educational center. The training session was mainly attended by psychologists and doctors, but police officers were also among the participants. Classes were conducted by the center's staff and invited guests—expert witnesses with many years of experience.

During both sessions, the training on sexual violence began with what the lecturers called the abolition of rape myths. They explained that our understanding of rape is strongly marked by stereotypes. The stereotype of provocation was referred to as a form of "social atavism." One lecturer told the class that "we [doctors] very often succumb to myths." She added that the same applies to the police and is the effect of our cultural settings and upbringing.[12] Drawing on scholarly literature, the lecturer outlined these myths and refuted them one by one. She problematized the belief that a woman was always able to escape. She discussed the prevalent conviction that the lack of marks on the survivor's body implies consent to sex on her part. It turns out, the lecturer told the class, that less than 20 percent of survivors have any traces left on their bodies; most women are afraid they will be killed, so they decide not to resist. At this point, the female police psychologist interjected that the goal of many rapes is to dominate the victim. Another popular myth, the lecturer added, is that women survivors cry after rape. In her opinion, this is not always the case because women react differently. In discussing this aspect, the lecturer pointed out that it also happens that women want to "frame" someone with rape. Finally, she argued that it is a myth that women provoke aggressors with their dress and behavior. Doctors and policemen, said the lecturer, often act as if they believed in this fable. This is a "men's approach" to the problem, chimed in the female police psychologist, "but we are teaching them," she resolved. "There should be more discussion about rape," commented the lecturer. Next, the lecturer and the active participant joined in the conclusion that when a rape survivor reports to the police station or to the hospital, there is usually no one designated to take care of her. We need procedures and the famous "kits," they concluded. Another myth discussed during the session concerned men: it is not true, the participants learned, that men are unable to control their sexual drives. Rape is usually not a crime of passion. Later, the lecturer referred to research carried out by the Center for Women's Rights, according to which 83 percent of survivors know their rapists—often they are husbands or lovers—and rapes tend to occur at home and at work, not in dark alleys. At the end, the lecturer discussed the myths that derive from psychoanalysis, according to which women have masochistic tendencies and dream of rape. "Our fantasies have nothing to do with reality," she concluded.

The lecturer drew attention to the fact that women often do not reveal what happened because they are afraid of revenge and blame themselves. Other reasons include the fear of being stigmatized because of sexism and because, to this day, many people believe in the provocation myth. She also cited the rape classification proposed by Godlewski (1987; see also n9) and stressed that in addition to sexually motivated rape, violence of this sort may have nonsexual motives—for example, revenge, domination, or humiliation. She presented other classifications and analyzed various situations (date rape, the date rape pill, marital rape, incestuous rape, and homosexual rape) and pointed to the suffering of rape survivors and their ill-treatment on the part of state institutions.

During her discussion of rape, the lecturer confessed that she was "a bit of a feminist," arguing that when it comes to rape, feminists are right on many issues.

She often referred to feminist analyses, which she knew of mainly from personal conversations with feminists. These conversations, she explained, had influenced her perception of the issue. But, she added, "woman is of a submissive nature." Evolution formed her so that she would nurture and provide care, and "regardless of what feminists would say, there is some truth to evolution." When I attended a training session organized by the same institution and run by the same lecturer three years earlier, the course was very similar. But the feminist themes were absent then, although feminist organizations that support survivors were mentioned. This shows that personal contacts with people who represent a feminist approach to rape had changed the training session.

The next part of the training session focused on the consequences of rape. Psychological problems were discussed, such as eating disorders and rape trauma syndrome. Participants learned about organizations like the Polish Nationwide Emergency Service for Victims of Domestic Violence "Blue Line" and the Center for Women's Rights. Some attention was also paid to the psychological and social factors that shape rapists' behavior.[13]

Still, during this training session and in others, some lecturers discussed rape with irony. During the 2009 course, for example, which focused in part on pedophilia, a lecturer argued that female therapists were reluctant to work with pedophiles but much more eager if the client were a handsome rapist. Interestingly, no one in the room expressed indignation, and everyone seemed to find this "joke" funny. The so-called joke was accompanied by the lecturer's suggestive smile and deep eye contact with one of the female participants. This type of "professional" humor rears its head on other occasions, such as conferences. On several occasions, numerous people told me a supposedly witty story about how "female gynecologists" were asked if they would rather be raped or murdered first. In general, during training sessions for sexologists, various kinds of understatements or ironic comments would come up implying something completely different than the official narrative forwarded in the lectures, as the ones described above. It is often said, for example, that women in relationships with "effeminate" men, meaning those who participate in childcare and housework, want to be raped because, according to sociobiology, they need a real (i.e., "masculine") man. These stories are told with smiles, suggestive looks, and gestures; the audience accepts them without protest. Cases of the alleged "framing" of husbands into various types of sexual offenses by wives who want to divorce favorably are also discussed in detail. Thus, the official narrative, which clearly defines rape as a brutal act and condemns it, is contradicted by a jocular narrative that also appears in the realm of nonverbal communication. What is unspoken and what is ridiculed gives context to words and can be a way of questioning the official version (Herzfeld 1997, 22).

Another frequent problem is the lack of reflection on the social, cultural, and economic determinants of gender. During the training session described above, this issue was only mentioned. Sexism was referred to on several occasions. Male socialization was discussed rather briefly as a factor responsible for the greater tendency among men to commit sexual crime. It was only noted that according to the norm in our society, boys are required to demonstrate their sexual capacity. The same was the case at other training sessions. One of the interview partners, a psychologist from an organization that provides support for survivors and who had completed a course at a prestigious forensic center that trains expert witnesses, said that "gender thinking, which analyzes the structure of the stereotypes about the victim" did not come up in that course at all. This time, however, the audience did not remain passive. Along with another activist who attended that course, the interlocutor called out the stereotypes in the knowledge transmitted: "They thought we were freaks," she said. She pointed out that expert opinions that present stereotypical content should not be considered only in the context of lack of knowledge: "We asked about it, when we pressed them against the wall, it had to come out, and the boss of that [prestigious forensic center] said that she believes that expert opinions should also be consistent with the level at which the court functions, so it should not be something that will pose a big problem for the court to understand and should also be in line with social norms. Because the court is also a place where verdicts are made, which is a signal for the community, and society has customary norms that expert analyses should express."

The interview partner mentioned that literature on the subject often describes women as "provocative." Everything is presented in scholarly language, for example: "the strong flow of adrenaline makes you cope better for example . . . it's quite complicated, maybe I can't explain it, but many victims of rape, to their own complete confusion, say that they experienced very intense strong sexual sensations, of the physiological type. You know that, in short, in the physiological sense, it was very intense and in some sense pleasant. This confuses them even more. This simple fact lies at the core of that stereotype, that when a woman says 'no,' she thinks 'yes.'" The interlocutor also invokes the idea of "pseudo-rape" and "real rape," forwarded by leading victimologist, Ewa Bieńkowska. In pseudo-rape, "women commence a ritual of behaviors that men must read conversely to what they are saying. Men must use violence to cope with this coquettish distance while in the state of deep desire." I examine Bieńkowska's work in the next section.

My interviews, observations, and court research suggest that expert witness opinions can change the course of a given trial and that the experts themselves are usually aware of their responsibility. Many judges have a stereotypical understanding of rape. One of the interlocutors, a psychologist and a sexologist of the younger generation who serves as an expert witness, sees it this way: "The court calls to ask, and in this informal contact you get a sense of the judge's preconceived notions and stereotypes, for example, he might say: 'I don't understand: she says she was raped, but she didn't cry for help!' The judge will never say this at the hearing, he will not refer explicitly to these stereotypes, because they try to control themselves, but in informal conversations the judge says: 'I think she's lying, this needs to be assessed, she's lying, something is wrong with her.'" Only after having read the expert opinion, which explains the mechanism of rape (e.g., that because of the structure of her psyche, the survivor did not defend herself or shout because this was her reaction to stress), does the court look at the matter differently. But expert opinions often only serve to reinforce stereotypes.

Another interlocutor who works as a member of a forensic expert team that is asked to evaluate cases after appeal does not have a good opinion of the quality of the expert witnesses' work: "They are weak, very superficial, you can see that the less knowledge someone has, the more they make up for it with common knowledge, stereotypical thinking, they appeal to the way society thinks, not knowledge based on research." This interview partner encountered, for example, an expert witness who argued that a prostitute could not be raped: "We were reading the court files and the expert said he does not see rape here, because whatever happened, this lady is a prostitute, period." In his perspective, rape was "a natural consequence of her work, which [the victim] has to take into account," added a second interlocutor. The expert team took a different position: "We thought that you can be a prostitute, but that does not mean that you consent to all behaviors. You can still be in control, giving consent or not to what is happening . . . he'll be choking you, burning you, cutting you, there has to be consent to this behavior."

During the training sessions, in which I participated, lecturers also drew attention to the weak points of many expert opinions. For example, diagnostic errors appeared in some, and in others the experts failed to notice omissions in existing medical documentation, which used names of disorders not listed in the current classification of the World Health Organization (*International Classification of Diseases, Tenth Revision*). Some expert witnesses suggest treatment instead of giving an opinion. Furthermore, expert witnesses are often unaware of the specific settings in a given social group or sexual culture of which the examined person is a member.[14]

Provocation, Recklessness, and Gender in the Legal Literature of the 1970s and 1980s

The problem of sexual crime was discussed vividly in the 1970s. Lawyers also took part in this debate. Publications discussed the specificity of rape, along with its causes and effects. Perpetrators and victims were characterized, commentary on Article 168 (the rape article) of the penal code was released, and there was debate about whether the crime should be prosecuted on the victim's motion or ex officio. Various aspects of rape were considered. What constitutes force, illegal threat, or deceit? How should consent and resistance be defined? Frequent references were made to sexology, while doctors and lawyers worked together and raised similar issues. As a result of this interaction, their thought styles and thought collectives strongly affected one another.

Lawyers took note of the social significance of the problem. Juliusz Leszczyński, author of the book *The Crime of Rape in Poland* (*Przestępstwo zgwałcenia w Polsce*)—one of the most important works on the subject—wrote that the crime of rape violates not only sexual personal freedom but also the public interest. He asserted that the protection of the freedom of "sexual disposition" (the freedom to use one's sexuality according to one's will) is necessary "so that society can live and develop normally" (Leszczyński 1973, 80–81). Experts of the time also linked rape to the excessive presence of sex in contemporary culture.

How were allegations of provocation and recklessness perceived in this debate? Did the right to sexual freedom that Leszczyński wrote about really refer to everyone, and was it always in the public interest?

Law and Life gave a considerable amount of space to deliberations on the problem of rape. This magazine, published by the Polish Lawyers Association (*Zrzeszenie Prawników Polskich*), features both court and court-related reportage (see chap. 6, n. 1). These pieces often discuss gang rape and include statements made by experts, predominantly lawyers, on such issues as legal solutions and prevention, with frequent reference to sexological literature. The October 1, 1972, issue of *Law and Life* focused largely on the problem of gang rape. The journal's front page featured a fragment of a text by the lawyer Janusz Eksner, entitled "Ex Officio Prosecution or on the Victim's Motion?" that was originally published in a popular daily newspaper, *Warsaw Life* (*Życie Warszawy*), on September 13, 1972. Eksner firmly advocated for change of the existing regulations, linking it with progress: "Prosecution of rape on the victim's motion is not an achievement of the (communist) people's legislation. It is simply a copy of the prewar penal code. . . . Prosecution on the victim's motion of a terrible crime is a relic of the past and collides with the social sense of justice" (1972, 1). The same issue also includes a record of the debate held by the Social and Legal Commentators Club, during which the experts also discussed the prosecution procedure. Some agreed with Eksner, whereas others held that not all women want to disclose the case and that rape is a subjective matter (according to one of the judges, some women might enjoy brutal sex that looks forced from the outside). Interestingly, journalists and educators spoke in favor of changing the prosecution procedure, and mostly lawyers were against. The nonsexual aspects of gang rape were also examined (Pinkwart 1972).

An article by the lawyer Michał Bereżnicki (1972) also begins on the issue's front page. The text opens with the argument that rape should be understood in the context of "certain phenomena and processes of a more general nature" (1), after which the author cites "the well-known sexologist K. Imieliński." In the fragment quoted from his book *Sexual Life*, Imieliński (1967f) draws attention to certain features of today's world: "Contemporary civilization creates many opportunities for the artificial excitement of the imagination when it comes to sexual matters, despite the obvious pedagogical and psychological contraindications. This leads to satisfying the sex drive in a variety of ways. Artificial stimuli, like the visual (pictures, photos, photographs and erotic videos) are very widespread. Artificial excitement of the imagination does not always go hand in hand with the ability to satisfy one's sex drive in the proper way, with a partner, especially among young people" (quoted in Bereżnicki 1972, 1). In effect, Imieliński continues in the passage quoted by Bereżnicki, "due to the impact of artificial excitement, the forms of satisfying one's sex drive also become artificial and increasingly diverse in their artificiality. As civilization progresses the number of sexual perverts also grows. Arousal of the sex drive at a too early age in the absence of established psychological brakes leads to . . . the supremacy of the sex drive over a youth's personality. Regaining control over the sex drive becomes almost impossible and man is, in effect, helpless" (1).

Bereżnicki (1972) transposes what Imieliński wrote about to the problem of rape (the sexologist himself did not go so far). He quotes journalist Jacek Moskwa, who wrote in his article for the Catholic magazine *Common Word* (*Słowo Powszechne*) that "the epidemic of gang rape is yet another alarm signal to testify to the current state of morality" (1). Bereżnicki adds that a ban on "erotic content" would not help much, especially because it would only "prove our powerlessness and helplessness in inciting among young people *rational* attitudes toward sex and gender" (1; original emphasis). Bereżnicki locates the problem of rape in the context of "a weakening traditional (in our conditions, anachronistic) sexual morality, and on the other hand, a lack of consistency in implementing *new* values into social practice" (1; original emphasis). The author next addresses the issue of prevention. He argues that strict punishment of perpetrators might only be "auxiliary." However, it is necessary to improve the prosecution and justice system, which, from his perspective, should start prosecuting rape ex officio. Bereżnicki notes that this change was proposed in 1956 by another legal scholar, W. Daszkiewicz in an article for the legal journal *State and Law* (*Państwo i Prawo*). Bereżnicki reiterates arguments posited previously by the lawyer A. Rowiński, according to whom the requirement of pressing charges means that the perpetrators of these crimes usually go unpunished.

Bereżnicki, Rowiński, and other proponents of changing the mode of prosecution typically face the same criticism. Bereżnicki cites an article by M. Kulczycki published in *Warsaw Life* in 1972: "In the name of humanism, the people's legislator allows for refraining from imposing punishment on the perpetrator of a crime, if this were to occur at the expense of the victim's interest" (quoted in Bereżnicki 1972, 2). It is worth noting that this argument, already prevalent in the 1930s (Płatek 2010), continues to be the subject of discussion among experts today. Bereżnicki again quotes Moskwa, who wrote for *Common Word*: "Every rape is a tragedy for the victim who must not be forced to disclose her misfortune in the public forum—to act in the role of witness in court, to answer often drastic questions. She must not be exposed to the suggestive comments of neighbors, acquaintances, and even the people closest to her. Public opinion can often be cruel and unjust. The law cannot arbitrarily interfere in such an intimate sphere of personal life" (quoted in Bereżnicki 1972, 2).

The experts fail to mention that changing the law and their own discourse on rape could serve to improve the situation of rape survivors. Bereżnicki (1972) engages in polemics with supporters of prosecution on the victim's motion in a completely different manner. He notes that victims' reasons for not pressing charges are diverse. Victims usually fear revenge and doubt that they will win their case in court, especially if they have no witnesses. Furthermore, Bereżnicki wrote, "Victims tend to convince themselves that they had behaved without caution and foresight" and they fear that their reputation will be "compromised" (2). To complicate matters even further, perpetrators often ask victims not to press charges—"in particular," Bereżnicki adds, "when they recognize the harm . . . to have been remedied, by, for example, marriage [whenever the victim became pregnant]." Finally, victims sometimes simply accept that they have been harmed (the author notes that this also applies to other offenses prosecuted on the victim's motion). Bereżnicki proposes what he calls a middle-ground solution: law enforcement agencies would have the right to prosecute ex officio if the victim feared vengeance. He concludes with deliberations on how to improve the situation of the victims, calling on police and prosecutors to maintain discretion and proposing "confidential" trials closed to the public (2).

Bereżnicki (1972) also draws attention to how victims are treated by the defense, a problem that clearly stands out in the court materials and that I analyze in the next chapter. He proposes "to advance rape trial proceedings": "First of all, it is necessary that 1) strict and resolute disciplinary action be taken against those lawyers, who regardless of the nature of the evidence in the case, seek to prove that 'the victim generated the circumstances that encouraged the defendant to commit the criminal act' (genuine!, one lawyer wrote in his appeal), and 2) a method of interrogating victims in criminal proceedings be developed, which allows for obtaining evidence, while at the same time eliminating the possibility of the unnecessary (and for the victim, very nasty) probing of the intimate *details* of a given criminal act" (2; original emphasis). In addition, Bereżnicki proposes to limit the possibility of parole and to work toward more effective prosecution of pornography, which, in his opinion, spawns "circumstances conducive to rape." Moreover, he suggests that "judicial *reporting* and journalism should be modified. . . . Instead of focusing on a detailed description of the crime's circumstances, . . . its context, the defendant, the specificity of his social environment, and the plaintiff should be analyzed first and foremost" (2; original emphasis). It is worth noting that he does not develop the latter idea further, which is problematic from the feminist point of view.

Ideas like Bereżnicki's (see also 1973, 1977) were rarely forwarded, and his appeals have only recently and only partially been implemented. Most experts who speak publicly on this topic take up the issue of provocation and partly blame the victim for what happened. A good example is Leszczyński's (1972) text, "Prevention and Repression in Cases of Gang Rape," written in response to Bereżnicki and also published in *Law and Life*. Leszczyński agrees with Bereżnicki's diagnosis of the causes of rape but rejects most of his appeals. He notes that demanding discretion for such trials is unnecessary because they take place behind closed doors anyway. Moreover, he argues, the sentences that the courts were handing out in the early 1970s were severe. Next, he considers the question of the trial's uncivilized character and the disciplinary action against the defense:

> M. Bereżnicki's claim that the approach of lawyers who argue that "the victim generated the circumstances that encouraged the defendant to commit the criminal act" renders the criminal process uncivilized is far too biased and unfair. Everyone, even litigators who are hardly involved in this type of proceeding, knows that in light of previous decisions of the Supreme Court, the victim's morale does not exonerate

the defendant, and severe sentences for rape of even notorious prostitutes are not uncommon. On the other hand, there is no reason to take insult at claims made by the defense, let alone take disciplinary action against lawyers only for the fact that they present to the court the defendant's arguments aimed at proving the victim's reprehensible or at least ambiguous behavior in order to question this person's *truthfulness*. In cases of gang rape this circumstance is particularly important, since the only people who can actually explain things to the court are the accused and the victim. (5; original emphasis)

Next, Leszczyński (1972) centers on one of the most frequent themes in the debate on sexual crimes: provocation. He states, "It should also be taken into account that with their behavior, many victims often either consciously or unconsciously *provoke* young people to engage in acts that would have never occurred, were they not prompted by this kind of behavior in the first place. This problem is dealt with by arguably the newest branch of criminology called *victimology*, and its research confirms the above thesis" (5; original emphasis). The expert contends, "Even in the most drastic gang rape trials, the role of the victims is quite often unclear. Victims can be quite rightly accused of gross recklessness in the least and an excess of loose morality, almost the proverbial 'playing with fire'" (5). Leszczyński then examines the issue of the victim's dignity and how to ask her questions: "Methods of interrogating victims in criminal proceedings have already, in my opinion, improved to such an extent that it is rare in practice that law enforcement institutions engage in the 'unnecessary probing of the intimate *details* of a given criminal act.' Of course, the very nature of these types of proceedings usually does not allow for the omission of drastic details that have considerable procedural significance, but nothing can be done about this" (5).

Perhaps the beginning of the 1970s made for an exceptional period; however, as we will see in chapter 8 in the materials that I collected dating from the 1980s onward, the undue probing of details remains standard judicial practice. One victim's testimony drastically illustrates this problem. She recounted that only in court did she learn about anal and oral sex and about what these types of sex are called.

Leszczyński (1972) takes issue with Bereżnicki's argument that pornography contributes to increases in the number of rapes and looks for explanation elsewhere: "In my opinion, rape prevention should be carried out by combating *alcoholism, sadism* and *hooliganism,* the *three fundamental etiological factors in rape*" (5; original emphasis). In the spirit of socialist propaganda, he suggests making youth who are not studying work, because "an excess of free time and the parasitic lifestyle of young hooligans serves to direct their interests in a wrong, and socially undesirable, direction causing them to derail and get into crime, not only of the sexual type" (5).

Although Leszczyński (1972) is critical of many of Bereżnicki's progressive arguments and develops the issue of provocation, he takes a firm stance against the mode of prosecution on the victim's motion: "I claim that paragraph 3 of Article 168 of the penal code has become obsolete and should be repealed as soon as possible" (5). He encourages readers to acquaint themselves with the results of his research, which supports this argument.

In his 1973 book, *The Crime of Rape in Poland*, Leszczyński indicates the importance of the victim's behavior for the case, though in a more subdued way: "The victims' ability to make casual acquaintances too easily and too effortlessly, their excessively careless behavior, their naiveté, their lack of the sense of danger, as well as exaggerated flirtation and sometimes unconscious provocation ('revealing fashion') are often the cause of rape. This creates a convenient situation for the perpetrators or an incentive to commit crime" (249). Elsewhere, he elaborates on this argument, making reference to national and world literature on the subject: "In rape, conscious or unconscious provocation on the victims' part may play a key role.[15] As a matter of course, 'an erotically dissatisfied individual, sees . . . invitation, provocation and flirtation in the polite and even indifferent behavior of those around,' but 'women revealing themselves . . . provokes the other sex to instigate assault and rape.'[16] It is not only exaggerated flirtation and revealing clothing that can spur criminal acts; a more serious problem is the victims' gross recklessness" (170).

As a rule, Leszczyński associates rape with sexuality. He is a proponent of targeting prevention at young people by steering their interests to other tracks, for example, encouraging them to play sports (Leszczyński 1973, 294). Yet he points out that "as far as gang rape is concerned, it is not an expression of the sex drive, but rather it stands for the boycott of social and moral norms" (164). He also outlines in detail the various types of damage that survivors incur (147–152).

Leszczyński (1973) refers in his work to sexologists, including Imieliński and van de Velde. He considers whether the sex drive can be controlled. He examines hormonal issues and the influence of cultural settings. He highlights differences between the sexes: "Due to anatomical and physical aspects, and partly also the mental, man's sexual drive is aggressive in character, while woman's is passive. Sexual aggression among men is one of the most specific features. . . . The sex drive in women is more emotional, while in men the physical elements are dominant" (113).

He reflects on the issue of consent. He assumes that it must be informed, in the context of "the normal functioning of . . . one's will" (Leszczyński 1973, 91) and that it can be expressed in various ways. This may lead to some uncertainty because "it is difficult to require a woman to explicitly and unambiguously consent to a sexual act every single time. This would contradict the principles of modesty and flirtation" (91). In effect, we have so-called implicit consent. Perpetrators often claim implicit consent was given, saying that they thought the woman had agreed (Leszczyński uses the term "partner" in this context). Still, Leszczyński posits that consent should relate to a specific situation and a specific act, which in turn contradicts his previous assertion that giving consent each time anew is incompatible with the principles of modesty and flirtation. He then turns to the issue of resistance, departing from the guidelines set out by the Supreme Court (in its rulings from 1926 and 1934). Accordingly, resistance must be "real (not superficial), continuous (uninterrupted) and not simulated . . .

The perpetrator must know that resistance is real. Resistance cannot be superficial, or put up because of shyness or *in the aim of making the attacking party more excited* [emphasis added]. . . . If the victim puts up resistance and then voluntarily resigns from it, she cannot consider herself to have been raped" (91–92). He adds right after that victims can defend themselves by any means necessary and recounts the story of girls who severely injured their would-be rapist with a knife. In Leszczyński's opinion, even though in 1965 the Supreme Court ruled that the victim does not have to use all possible forms of resistance, resistance should be obvious so that the perpetrator is left with no doubt:[17]

> One might, however, have reservations as to whether it is unnecessary to exhaust all the available means of defense, because then the boundary would be blurred between implicit consent and resignation from putting up resistance by the person being forced to do something. It cannot be expected of the victim to resort to some extraordinary means of resistance, but depending on the situation, she should exhaust the means available to her, manifest the lack of implicit consent and deprive the perpetrator of any illusions as to her voluntary resignation from putting up further resistance. For the purpose of proper assessment, the court should take into account the reasons for low intensity resistance, so as to separate real from superficial resistance. (92)

Leszczyński finds himself in agreement with the Supreme Court's 1926 decision, according to which "the intensity of resistance is of great importance" (quoted in Leszczyński 1973, 93).[18] "It is difficult not to share this position," he resolves (93).

Based on data he collected from court records for the city of Łódź and the wider Łódź Voivodeship, Leszczyński (1973) delineates the social context of rape in Poland. Notably, he examines the survivors (243–49). Other experts refer extensively to his data. One of them is the legal scholar Marian Filar (1974), author of an important and widely cited legal analysis of the crime of rape. According to Filar, Leszczyński's research showed that many victims are uneducated and unemployed and that in spite of their young age, rape was not their first sexual contact. Leszczyński noted that victims are also often school students, and in expressing fatherly concern for this group, he argues that it is necessary to "provide special care for this category of people, because their naiveté and carelessness often serve to create the right circumstances for perpetrators" (1973, 246). Filar, in turn, concludes, "Refraining . . . as much as possible from generalizing the problem, it should be noted, as it has already been outlined in the literature, that in many cases, future victims behave in extremely reckless ways, which significantly facilitates the perpetrators' actions. Often the victims agree to certain sexual activities with their partners, but they do not agree to going further" (1974, 28).

In referring again to Leszczyński, and to other literature on the subject, Filar (1974) discusses examples of recklessness, such as drinking alcohol with the perpetrator. He suggests that victims often come from communities where liberal customs are the norm. He points to numerous sexual stimuli that we encounter regularly in the contemporary world, linking rape with sexual arousal (43). Nonetheless, he too positions himself in favor of ex officio prosecution (179). Unlike Leszczyński, Filar considers that resistance must be clearly expressed, but its form is irrelevant (94–95), although he does note that in our culture, women might oppose even when they actually agree.

Another important voice in the debate on sexual violence was articulated in the book *Rapes* (*Zgwałcenia*; 1976) by Tadeusz Hanausek (long-time head of the Forensic Department of the Jagiellonian University), Zdzisław Marek (at the time, head of the Department of Forensic Medicine at the Medical Academy in Krakow), and Jan Widacki (at the time, a faculty member of the Forensic Department at the Jagiellonian University). The authors based their argument on an analysis of statistics from Krakow (published in the *Statistical Yearbook* and in official police statistics) and on research conducted at the Department of Forensic Medicine of the Medical Academy in Krakow. The scientists proposed a detailed analysis of the problem of provocation: "We understand the term *provocation* broadly. Mostly, we refer to situations, in which the victim purposefully induces in the offenders the impression that she agrees to have intercourse. An example of such culpable and active provocation might be the situation, in which the victim agrees to go to the perpetrator's house, where he lives alone, in the evening, and actively participates in far-reaching love game" (Hanausek, Marek, and Widacki 1976, 64; original emphasis). The concept of provocation is connected with the issue of resistance: "It should be stressed that even culpable and conscious provocation does not deprive the victim of the right to resist and does not remove responsibility from the perpetrator. It does, however, constitute a factor that must be taken into account in the analysis of the crime and must affect the assessment of the perpetrator's mental attitude. It must be kept in mind that the crime of rape is a deliberate crime, and therefore demanding of the will to break someone's resistance. The perpetrator must thus have prior knowledge of the existence of this resistance" (65).

According to the experts, in order to recognize that the act was forced, palpable resistance is necessary: "This resistance, as an expression of the will of the victim, must be understood by the perpetrator; otherwise it is impossible to speak of deliberate coercion" (Hanausek, Marek, and Widacki 1976, 64). The whole matter, in the experts' opinion, is complicated by the status of resistance in erotic play and in various, as we would say today, sexual cultures. Young women, they argue, end the love game decisively, whereas older, traditionally raised women often treat resistance as an additional form of arousal. This prompts misunderstandings because real resistance is taken to be superficial. The experts conclude that differences "result from discrepancies in attitude toward the act and the assessment of this attitude by both *partners* [emphasis added]" (67).

The experts conducted a study of thirty-five rape survivors at the Department of Forensic Medicine at the Medical Academy in Krakow. Based on this study, in the chapter entitled "Victims of Rape," they distinguish three types, giving expression to the idea of certain survivors being worthy and others being unworthy of the state's protection (Hanausek, Marek, and Widacki 1976). The first group includes women who just happened to be in the wrong place at the wrong time; they did not provoke and they defended themselves fiercely. This group counted the fewest cases. The second category comprises girls under the age of eighteen who have no sexual experience but whose behavior "may have given the idea that they were 'easy'" (19). As such, their behavior allegedly facilitated the crime. They might have paid visits to men in the evening hours, "walked in desolate places," "accepted alcoholic beverages from men," or boasted about their alleged experiences. In the third group are women with a rich history of sexual contacts. They behaved provocatively, allowed for petting, knew the perpetrators, often had sexual intercourse with them, and had a reputation of being "easy." A significant percentage of these women, noted the experts, came from broken families. "Some of the women studied, despite their young age, had considerable sexual experience" (19), they wrote. Next, the experts listed examples of this sexual "experience": relations with a father or stepfather (both concerned 14-year-old girls), prostitution, and sex with their peers. Although in one instance, the experts referred to a fourteen-year-old girl, as the victim of "incestuous relations with her father," they usually write: "she began her sex life with her father at the age of 13." Or, "The 14-year old victim of gang rape initiated her sex life far before the event in question, with her mother's boyfriend" (19). They make no mention of the fact that sex with a minor under fifteen years of age is a crime. They do note, however, that many of the victims are demoralized and that it is often difficult to distinguish women from groups two and three.

Sexual experience and early initiation represent key elements, in the experts' opinion:

> It is worth highlighting that the sexual experience of girls is an important factor facilitating and even favoring the choice of victim. It constitutes a symptom of a certain moral attitude and the girl's personality. Perpetrators, especially juveniles, often justify their actions with the girl's behavior. They are convinced that they have done nothing wrong. In their understanding, forcing such a girl to have sexual intercourse is not a crime. The victim's reputation sometimes gains primary rank and becomes the basic cause of her predestination. Therefore, as our research and not only our research shows, girls with early sexual experiences face a greater chance of finding themselves in situations where rape can take place. The analysis of victims' character, demeanor, and behavior might bring important insight to the evaluation of the phenomenon of rape as a whole. Such analysis is also of forensic importance. It allows for the more effective prosecution of perpetrators, in using the well-trodden path, known from classical criminology, that leads from the victim to the perpetrator. (Hanausek, Marek, and Widacki 1976, 25)

The experts draw conclusions from their research and instruct forensic physicians on how to examine rape victims. Accordingly, victims should be questioned about the details of their sexual lives: whether they had previous sexual relations (with how many partners and when) and whether they had been raped in the past. Critical, the experts argue, are the circumstances that accompanied the incident: whether the perpetrator used a condom; whether the victim incurred injuries; whether she knew the perpetrator; whether she met him before the incident and in what context; whether he used violence, made threats, or stripped her; and finally, how she was dressed before the incident (Hanausek, Marek, and Widacki 1976, 104).

A major specialist in victimology, Ewa Bieńkowska (1984), also focuses on the victim's role in rape in her book *The Impact of the Victim's Behavior on Court Rulings in Rape Cases* (*Wpływ zachowania ofiary na rozstrzygnięcie sprawy o zgwałcenie*). Bieńkowska conducted impressive research: she analyzed 464 court cases and 168 cases that did not end up going to trial (Bieńkowska 1984, 61). These cases came from almost all the Voivodeships (provinces) and heard final judgment in the second half of 1976. Bieńkowska fundamentally disagreed with the ruling of the Supreme Court's Criminal and Military Chamber of 1972, according to which "reckless behavior on the part of the victim immediately prior to rape, when it results from young age and inexperience, is not relevant to assessing the perpetrator's fault and thus to imposing penalty" (Bieńkowska 1984, 6). Bieńkowska contends that the relationship between the victim and the perpetrator is not always based on active/passive opposition (6). She makes abundant reference to literature on this subject (including the book *Rapes* [Hanausek, Marek, and Widacki 1976]) and asserts that only a small minority of experts disagree with this thesis (one of the three cited, Michał Bereżnicki, is quoted above): "Since the victim's behavior sometimes determines the rise and execution of criminal intent, then it should accordingly bear specific meaning for the assessment of the degree of menace that the crime of rape poses for society" (Bieńkowska 1984, 9).

Bieńkowska considers the victim's role in what she calls the "genesis" of rape. She replaces the words "provocation" and "fault" with what she believes to be a more neutral concept—"contribution": "This is a situation that involves the occurrence of a dynamic and mutual relationship between the victim and the perpetrator, during which the victim actively co-shapes the development of the victimogenic and criminogenic situation with her behavior and thus, to a lesser or greater degree, influences the processes that give rise to the intention to commit a crime and conceivably also the manner and possibility of the crime's execution" (1984, 68). The victim's contribution to the crime of rape can be of an "inspirational," "enabling," or "facilitating" nature. It involves the conscious (explicitly sexual) or unconscious (implicitly sexual, like accepting proposals to spend time together) behavior (145), perceived as the pursuit of intimate contact. Bieńkowska writes in a similar tone as the sexologists quoted earlier: "Sexual behaviors, in contrast to many other behaviors, are impulsive. For the perpetrator to control them, in a situation where the victim also exhibits such behavior, can prove impossible or at least very difficult" (70).

Bieńkowska draws distinctions among various types of rape depending on how the victim carried herself, for example, "interactive rape with the conscious contribution of the victim" (1984, 85). Her research shows that among "possible rapes," or those in which the legal proceedings were dismissed before the case could go to trial, half of the cases involved conscious contribution (145). As for "actual rapes"—those in which, following her definition of crime, the court handed a guilty sentence—a quarter of the cases involved "contribution," usually of the unconscious sort (146). Bieńkowska notes that prosecutors and judges take into account the victim's demeanor by, for example, dropping cases involving "conscious contribution." In cases involving "unconscious contribution," lower sentences are given, although Bieńkowska notes that this seems to happen quite randomly and is not usually mentioned in the court's justification of its decision (145–47). In one instance, Bieńkowska posits that sentences should be higher when perpetrators cynically make use of a very young victim's reckless actions (148), but the overtone of her work is unmistakable: woman's behavior is a key factor leading to crime. She proposes the introduction of a "legal provision that will require the victim's contribution to be taken into account during sentencing" (154). This aspect must be analyzed and the courts must be aware of it (152). She also claims that consideration of the victim's behavior might help develop better "general prevention" strategies (151). The lack of analysis of the victim's role in rape leads to her being left out of rape prophylactic activities. These should be aimed at "people who are particularly vulnerable, because of their behavior, to become entangled in victimogenic and criminogenic situations" (152). In her opinion law enforcement should fight false accusations, which in Bieńkowska's opinion likewise stem from the lack of analysis of the victims' contributions (147). To reduce the number of false accusations, she proposes (quite rightly at that; see Płatek 2011) to allow youth aged fifteen to eighteen years to file motions for prosecution on their own because parents refuse to acknowledge that their child had consented to sex (Bieńkowska 1984, 153).[19]

I agree with Bieńkowska that relations between subjects in social interactions are never without any ambiguities (Kościańska 2009a, 2009b). I argue, however, that like Hanausek, Marek, and Widacki (1976) and sexologists such as Wisłocka (1978), she is mistaken in her understanding of individual agency, which is not free from the power relations and the sociocultural conditions that shape interactions between victims and their oppressors. Her perspective leads to blaming the survivors and justifying the perpetrators (for a critical analysis of such a take on agency in the sexual context, see Farmer 1996). Furthermore, this perspective is just another version of the approach that categorizes survivors as deserving or undeserving of the state's protection. The underserving category clearly comprises women who are interested in sex, independent, and not tied down to the home sphere. These sorts of women allegedly inspire or facilitate men's violence.

In conclusion, with a few exceptions (e.g., the 1972 Supreme Court ruling), lawyers in the 1970s and 1980s focused on the sexual nature of rape and the behavior of victims. In effect, an understanding emerges from this debate in which rape is a cruel and serious crime that intensifies in tandem with cultural changes and that requires decisive moves on the part of law enforcement agencies and the judiciary. But at times, quite often even—according to this understanding—it turns out that this heinous act might never have come to fruition were it was not triggered by the way the victim had carried herself. Both legal and sexological discourses point the spotlight at a group of women who presumably do not deserve full protection and the right to say no. These women are independent, interested in sex, and engage (sometimes by force) in sexual acts that fall at the bottom of the sexual hierarchy, thus transgressing the boundaries of gender. Agency on the part of survivors of sexual violence is seen here as unconstrained by sociocultural conditions. How does this debate affect what happens in court or the thought styles of attorneys and judges? Does the conviction of lawyers and doctors about the survivor's coresponsibility for the crime manifest in court practices?

Notes

1. By stereotype, I understand here a generalizing portrayal of a given group (in this case, female rape survivors and male perpetrators), rooted in the social imagination (for a discussion of the history of the term and its use, see, e.g., Gilman 1985, 15–35).

2. This is confirmed in my analysis of Polish press clippings collected in the Central Archive of Modern Records (for a detailed discussion, see Kościańska 2012d) and a query of the magazines *Etc*, *The Mirror*, and *Law and Life*. Other studies have shown the same thing (see, e.g., Kaim 2010/2011, 2011).

3. Mira Marody and Anna Giza-Poleszczuk (2000) argue that this way of communicating also applied to other spheres of life in the 1970s.

4. I examined all editions in this respect.

5. The new 2016 edition also contains the passages on rape in an unchanged form (although some changes were made to the book; notably, the chapter on contraception was updated). The new foreword to the book, written by well-known sex researcher and educator Zbigniew Izdebski (2016), likewise does not include any commentary on the matter. Voices critical of the book were published only in the left-wing press, whereas *Gazeta Wyborcza* (the main liberal newspaper in Poland), whose publisher was also the coproducer of the biographical film about Wisłocka, did not print any critical reviews. The newspaper's online edition initially included a link to an interview that I gave to one of *Gazeta Wyborcza's* leading journalists in 2014 (Kościańska 2014a), when the Polish version of my book came out, and in which I pointed to the hurtful gender stereotypes in Wisłocka's *The Art of Love*. The interview also included the passages about rape discussed here. However, the link to the interview was quickly removed. The interview was also not recalled in any way during the debate that accompanied the premiere of the film.

6. The quote from Ovid was translated by A. S. Kline.

7. Lew-Starowicz cites the article, "Analysis of the Behavior of Victims of Gang Rape for Criminological Prevention" ("Analiza zachowania ofiar zgwałcenia zbiorowego w aspekcie profilaktyki kryminologicznej") in *Criminological, Forensic and Penitentiary Studies* (*Studia Kryminologiczne, Kryminalistyczne i Penitencjarne*), 1977, vol. 7.

8. Lew-Starowicz cites the article, "Victimological Aspects of Gang Rape" ("Aspekty wiktymologiczne zgwałceń zbiorowych") in *Criminological, Forensic and Penitentiary Studies*, 1979, vol. 10.

9. Departing from multiple studies of the subject, Godlewski categorizes rapes based on motives: the mainly nonsexual (power-driven, anger-driven, or repressive), the sexually nonspecific or combined (psychopathic or sociopathic), and the sexual (situational, related to other deviations, or sadistic). From the perspective of my research, his definition of situational rapes is worth mentioning: these occur "due to an erroneous assessment of the *female partner*'s intentions or attitude, often while in the state of arousal, in attaining which the *female partner* actively took part. The *female partner*'s resistance

might be misinterpreted as flirtation, or that resistance might ultimately be understood in the right sense, but *strong arousal limits the ability* or readiness *to modify (cease) the activity*" (Godlewski 1987, 298; emphasis added). Godlewski refers not only to survivors and perpetrators as partners, in the footsteps of other scholars, but he also introduces to the definition of rape the concept that sexuality cannot be controlled. Many experts use Godlewski's classification system (see, e.g., Kowalczyk, 2012; Eichstaedt, Gałecki, and Depko, 2012.

10. In the Polish court system, expert witnesses are called by a judge, not by parties to the criminal proceedings.

11. The information presented here comes from field notes and interviews.

12. It is worth noting here that another lecturer, a sexologist of the older generation, pointed out during the same session that expert witnesses are likewise not free of stereotypical thinking.

13. Field notes, November 7, 2011.

14. Field notes, November 7–9, 2011. Guidelines for writing expert opinions in cases of sexual offense are outlined in textbooks recommended during the training sessions and conferences (i.e., Lew-Starowicz 1988e, 2000; Eichstaedt, Gałecki, and Depko 2012). I also discuss this matter in chap. 8.

15. Here, Leszczyński refers to P. Crespy, "The Sociological Aspects of Gang Rape" ("Socjologiczne aspekty gwałtu zbiorowego"), *Problemy Kryminalistyki* (Criminological Problems) 1966, no. 60: 308.

16. Leszczyński quotes W. Witwicki, *Psychologia* (*Psychology*), Warszawa 1962, 1, no. 35: 230.

17. OSNKW 1965, No. 7–8: 133.

18. ZO SN 1926, item 158/26.

19. Sex with persons younger than fifteen years of age is prosecuted ex officio, both at the time and currently.

8 | In the Courtroom

Court Research

After examining expert discourse on sexual violence, I decided that checking how this knowledge translates into social practice was not only a matter of anthropological diligence but also my responsibility. To what extent do gender stereotypes and victim blaming, pervasive throughout expert statements, affect the perception of rape and the situation of survivors? I was certain that the court would best demonstrate the scope of potential impact. Initially, I wanted to carry out participant observation of the court's legal proceedings under the rape article. However, because these cases are not public, obtaining permission from the president of the court and from all parties involved in the trial, which derives from research ethics, turned out to be highly complicated, although not unrealistic. In the end, I abandoned this path because of something else: like other trials in Poland, rape trials last a very long time. In the course of one year, during which I wanted to complete this stage of research, I would not be able to participate in a rape trial from its beginning to the end. Together with the appeals, a rape trial can take eight to ten years.

I decided to study court files. In accordance with Article 27 of the Act on Personal Data Protection (in force while I was conducting my research), scholars who conduct research with the aim of obtaining academic degrees figure into a small group of people who are allowed to access and process sensitive data, such as information about sexual life, health, and criminal records. A precondition is that the material must be presented in a way that makes it impossible to identify the persons whose data were accessed. Accordingly, as I mentioned in the introduction, I do not even specify the location of the district court from which I collected the data, and I have changed some details.

My court research consisted of two stages: analysis of registries, which enabled me to select cases for analysis, followed by study of the case files. In Poland, the registries are large-format books in which all cases that take place in a given branch of the court are recorded. They list basic information: the defendant's data, the article and paragraph under which the case was prosecuted, the decisions, appeals, the further fate of the offenders, and the case reference number. First, given the availability of the registries, I had to modify the scope of my research. Initially, I wanted to analyze cases from the 1970s to the present, but it turned out that registries were not kept in the 1970s. At the end of the 1960s, the court records system was modernized, and cases were chronicled on perforated cards; however, this system was flawed and the cards were lost. Some court employees claim that the perforated cards can be found in a certain state archive, but they are not listed in its catalog. I decided to focus on the period from 1981—that is, from the moment when the registries were restored—to 2009.

Study of the registries allowed me to single out cases that were of interest to me, and it gave me a glimpse of the mechanisms associated with how the justice system functions. Many cases that go to trial never come to an end. They are adjourned until the following year, the defendants leave the country, and the hearing never takes place. Others drag on for years; as I mentioned, along with the appeals, they can last up to ten years. Finally, I selected sixty cases for closer examination to select thirty for analysis (ten for each decade). I chose cases in which rape was the main crime. I scrapped cases of incestuous and homosexual rape (among the sixty that I examined, there were three cases of rape in a prison cell and one outside the prison, although still closely related). I avoided (although not completely) cases in which rape was accompanied by other crimes. I chose cases with different courses—some ended with a conviction and some ended in an acquittal, some with appeals and others with a final judgment immediately after trial.

From 1981 to 2009, the court division in which I conducted my research heard on average just over 425 cases per year, with the smallest case load of 235 in 1988[1] and the heaviest of 613 in 1995. As a district court (formerly a Voivodship-level court), it dealt with serious crimes. In the case of rape, these were gang rapes and rapes that involved particular cruelty. Such cases were not numerous: in the examined period, the court heard 275 of these cases in total—an average of 9.5 cases per year, with the most, twenty-five, recorded in 1984 and the least, one case per year, in 2004 and 2008. I quickly realized that these cases take a long time, and I chose not to consider those registered in 2010–2012 because, as a rule, they would not end anytime soon.

Court files in rape cases usually have two to eight volumes. They contain everything: the motion for prosecution, testimony, evidence collected by the police, notes made by officers, photos from the crime scene and showing the victim's torn clothing, a list of the victim's injuries, the expert opinions of doctors and psychologists, indictments, arrest decisions, reports from hearings, appeals, correspondence, and various types of certificates from the hospital, school, the psychological clinic, the alcohol recovery center (the drunk tank), and even the parish. In effect, the files contain the entire history of the plaintiff and the defendants. In particular, the psychological or sexological opinions list detailed information about them, their families, and their social environment.[2] For example, a sexological interview (a basic examination performed by an expert sexologist) covers general data (age, education, marital status, place of work), hobbies, and worldview. In addition, it includes information about successive stages of development (childhood, adolescence, adulthood) and sexual and romantic life. The interviewer asks about relations with parents and peers, feelings, forms of play, favorite reading, relations of domination and of love, relations based on equal terms, and sex, including sex education, masturbation, initiation, satisfaction, and fantasies, ending in a general assessment (Lew-Starowicz 1988e, 122–26; for a slightly modified version, see Eichstaedt, Gałecki, and Depko 2012, 237–39; Lew-Starowicz 2000).[3] Psychologists and psychiatrists ask about similar issues (usually excluding sexual matters; see, e.g., Eichstaedt, Gałecki, and Depko 2012, 203). Textbooks recommend that expert witnesses recount the collected information in detail in their reports to the court (Eichstaedt, Gałecki, and Depko 2012, Lew-Starowicz 1988e, 2000). During trial, the families, acquaintances, neighbors, and teachers also often tell the survivor's and defendants' life stories.

The files provide descriptions of what happened. Both parties and sometimes the witnesses describe the crime and, in due course, express their views on issues like consent to sex. Defense lawyers and prosecutors present their expert understanding of the case—in the indictment, in the appeals, and in questions asked in the courtroom. Finally, after handing the verdict, the judges write a justification of their decision that summarizes what has been said and written, reproduces the course of events, and evaluates the people involved according to the "factual" version of the case. The justification also presents the judges' interpretations.[4]

Expert language comes up in the files at all stages of the legal process—in the expert opinions, the indictments, and the testimonies, which are often preceded by consultations with lawyers, and in the appeals and justifications. To what extent do the stereotypes established in this expert knowledge affect what happens during trial? Is the distinction between victims who are worthy or unworthy of protection salient in court? Do courtroom statements reflect the expert definition of agency that holds women responsible for men's actions? In this chapter, I discuss four cases, two from the 1980s and two from the 2000s. This analysis is not representative; rather, I aim to draw attention to certain features of expert discourse that arise in the context of rape cases and the role of that discourse in court practices. However, in almost all cases I studied, the victim's credibility was challenged in a similar manner (for an analysis of court rape trials in the Anglo-Saxon context, see Cuklanz 1996; Matoesian 1993; Smith 2018).

Expert Discourse in the Courtroom

Case 1

The incident occurred at the beginning of April 1983 in a suburb of a big city. The case has four defendants, three born in 1965 (called W., S., and R.) and one born in 1966 (F.). They had no prior convictions. All are childless and unmarried. According to the file, the ringleader W. neither goes to school nor works; he comes from a good family, and his parents are well educated. The other defendants grew up in farming or working-class families and were studying at technical or vocational schools. All but the one minor (seventeen-year old F.) were held in custody pending trial.

The plaintiff (called A.) is a seventeen-year-old student at a renowned high school in a big city and also from a good family. Her parents are divorced, and she lives with her mother and her mother's new partner. The father is an important figure in an ethnic minority community.[5]

The indictment, dated to 1983, reads, "After having forced A., with the use of violence, to take a seat in the car and then threatening her, they made her repeatedly submit to lascivious acts." The prosecutor explains:

In the course of the investigation, the following facts were ascertained. . . . They [the defendants] rode in a "Fiat 125p" driven by S. to the town of X. in order to find a girl with whom all of them could have sexual intercourse.[6] Their arrival . . . was preceded by proposals to have intercourse directed at their acquaintances, their refusal, and a subsequent search for girls in cafes. . . . W. noticed A., who was familiar to him, on the street. He got out of the car and during the conversation tried to persuade her to meet him. A. refused and turned to go home. They caught up to her in the car and W. again began insisting that she get into the car. He pressured her with a series of threats, and in response to A.'s refusal and her attempt to get away, he squeezed her hand and ordered her to get into the car. At the same time, he asked F. to help him force the victim to get into the car. Fearing that the threats will be fulfilled, A. conceded to his order. She found herself in the back seat between R. and F.

W. kept telling A. that they were going to a party; however, they drove toward the forest. The prosecutor continues:

W. revealed to A. the true intentions of all four attackers. He also made gestures that simultaneously testified as to his purpose like raising her skirt and grasping her knees. A. firmly refused to submit to these lascivious acts, but in view of the circumstances, she did not undertake an active defense fearing being beaten. In the forest, W. ordered her to undress. Because of her refusal, using violence, he removed her clothes, and then using physical force he made her engage in a perverted lascivious act.[7] W. got dressed and let the next perpetrator know. The second person who raped A. was R. He pulled off the skirt that she had used to cover herself and her panties. Then he had sexual intercourse with her without encountering active resistance at this point. Not seeing a way out of the situation, and at the same time fearing violence and beating, A. did not defend herself, and only told the other perpetrators that she did not want to have sexual intercourse. After R. it was F. and then S. who committed rape. W. presided over the course of the incident. . . . After S. finished the deed, the perpetrators allowed the victim to get dressed and drove her back to X. During interrogation as suspects, S. and F. admitted to the crime, although in his explanations F. did not indicate the circumstances confirming his guilt. W. pleaded not guilty to the act he was accused of. In his explanations he confirmed having directed threats at A., although in his opinion these were only jokes. R. initially denied that he had had intercourse with the victim, but in the course of the investigation, he admitted to having had intercourse. Independently of the above, it must be noted that the investigation revealed that the parents of S., R., and F. attempted to persuade A. to change her testimony, but this did not bring any result.

We learn from the case file that A. claimed that this was not the first time W. had forced her to have sex. A. told the prosecutor that in November 1982, W. and others had brutally raped her. For that reason, she did not want to talk to him and was afraid of him. After the first rape, she did not return home for a week. Once she did come back, she confided to her neighbor, who advised the fifteen-year-old girl to report to the police; however, the mother and stepfather were against reporting. A. described the incident to an expert witness psychologist. The expert's opinion, contained in the files, reads that in November, A. met a boy who invited her for tea to his parents' house but instead led her to W.'s apartment, where she was forced to engage in brutal sex; the girl cried out, calling for help in vain. After this event, she was afraid to return home, especially fearing her stepfather. Fifteen-year-old A. wandered about for a week, and during this time she experienced violence on several occasions. She was exhausted, as she told the psychologist. She went back, first to her father's and then home. After the injuries and humiliations she suffered, she had a hard time at school, but she did her best. Everything fell apart when she again met W. in April of the following year.

A. seems to be a girl who breaks established gender roles: she reads a lot and does not like housework, as we learn from her mother. A. tells other experts herself that she was interested in sex, her body's sexual reactions, and masturbation. These issues, as readers might remember from the previous chapter, are considered part of boys' domain. Girls are usually interested in the "home nest," which was not an interest of A.'s.

What else do we know about the victim? According to the opinion of the expert witness psychologist, she had problems at school and a tense situation at home. A. was in constant conflict with her stepfather, who beat her. She calls him a "primitive jerk." A. is close with her well-educated father. The girl tells the psychologist, "My father thinks that this rape is my fault, that the case should not be in court, that I should forgive them. I hold that against him." In the psychologist's opinion, the mother's anxiety makes it difficult to live at home. Once she started high school, A. began going out to clubs in the ninth grade, which was when she first began experimenting with boys. The parents did not approve of this. Looking back, A. tells the psychologist that they were right.

Because of her problems at school, A. attended educational and vocational counseling. Counseling centers of the sort that she attended (since 1993, called pedagogical and psychological counseling centers) offer the assistance of educators, psychologists, and speech therapists. They provide support for dyslexic children and help students who have learning difficulties. They are not psychiatric or even strictly psychological counseling centers. In the aftermath of the rape, from this counseling center A. was sent to a psychological clinic and from there to a psychiatric facility, where she spent a month.

The trial began in August 1983. W. was the first to testify. He explained they were sitting in the car and waiting for S. When he came, "he got in the car and asked if we knew a girl that we could all have sex with." W. replied that he knew a few, so they went to the café but did not find any there. "In the meantime, we agreed that we would take the girl to the forest," he said. They could not find a girl for a while. Finally, W. said, "I remembered that I know one girl. I meant the plaintiff. . . . I know her because once I had voluntary group intercourse with her. I knew she did these things. . . . She had the reputation of being easy. It's not true that in November 1982 anybody behaved rudely towards the plaintiff or threatened her. Everything happened in a nice atmosphere. The plaintiff even danced naked in front of us. We had group intercourse with her then." They did not know her address, but in the end they found her walking down the street. She did not want to talk to them. "It's not true that she refused to meet and told me to leave her alone. She walked away." They caught up with her. And then, according to W.:

> She said she loves me very much and wants me to be her boyfriend. I already have a girlfriend, so I said I have to think about it. I asked her to go with me to Y. [name of a town] to a party. I told her that I was the only one without a girl. At one point I joked and said, "Come on or I'll take you by the legs and put you in the trunk." Then A. got into the car. . . . She didn't know yet at that point that we were going to the forest. It's not true that I used threats and violence against A. We had a very polite conversation. . . . If she was scared, she would have asked someone for help. . . . At some point in the car, I put my hands on A.'s knees and told her that we were going to the forest. She said she's disappointed that we're not going to a party. When I put my hands on her knees, she told me not to be so fast, but she did not move my hands away.

When they reached the forest, W. and A. stayed alone in the car. According to W., A. began reminiscing about the group sex they had in November. W. told the court, "After that incident, she would come to me and tell me how much she liked it with me. Once she came to me and said she had financial problems, and she asked me if I knew someone who would have sex with her for money"; he replied that he did not. When asked what happened that April evening in the forest, he said she started kissing him. She asked him to help her take off her skirt and blouse. He did not resort to violence because he did not want to have sex with her: "I only took her there because my friends asked me to." She undressed, embraced him, kissed him, and asked him to have intercourse with her. He did not have a shirt on because it was hot in the car, as he said (it all took place around 11:00 p.m. in the early spring, which means it was rather cold outside). Finally, W. agreed to oral sex. He explained that he did not want to have intercourse because he was tired. He told A. that his friends would be happy to take advantage of the opportunity. "She asked to bring around that one in the black jacket . . . she called them one by one, she was smiling, when they would come back, she was satisfied, she laughed."

The minutes from the hearing read that while testifying, the defendant used extensive notes, which may suggest that he had been carefully prepared by his attorney on how to testify. Therefore, W.'s account of the rape can be understood as a manifestation of expert discourse.

A. was next on the stand. She told the court that she neither wanted to talk to W. nor to get into the car. She recounted: "So W. began threatening me. I knew him and I knew what he was capable of." The girl became very distressed in the courtroom and could not continue giving her testimony. The court ordered a break. After the hearing was resumed, the girl's mother was asked to speak.

She talked about A.'s psychological problems, about the fact that A. had anxiety attacks after the rape and was under psychological supervision and that later she was treated at a psychiatric facility.

During the investigation, A. was interrogated in the presence of her mother, her father, and a psychologist. Her father wanted her to refuse to testify. During trial, the prosecutor asked that the girl be questioned in the presence of a female psychologist. The court asked for documentation from all three care centers where A. had been treated. The next hearing was scheduled for September, and the court called the expert witness psychologist to testify.

The expert, however, did not appear. The September hearing was limited to reading a note written by W. to F. that had been intercepted by the prison guard. In the note W. tells F. that he must say what W. tells him (e.g., as can be inferred, he must lie) or they will be convicted:

> Start off the way it really was. . . . Later one of you suggested that I get you a girl. *But you don't remember who. Remember that!* . . . I absolutely did not threaten her, you fucking piece of shit.[8] I will only say that I threatened her in this way, "come on or I'll take you by the legs and put you in the trunk." The point is, that was just talk. . . . There was polite conversation in the car. . . . I didn't threaten her at all. . . . Remember that! You stood around 50–80 m from the car, no less. That's important! . . . Later I got out and told R. that she wants to fuck him. . . . Remember! When you got into the car, she was lying undressed on the seat—that's important! You sat next to her and didn't do anything because you didn't know how. She told you literally "Come on love, let's start." She unbuttoned your pants and pulled you on top of her.[9] During intercourse, she kissed you on the shoulders. . . . She took active part in the intercourse, because she liked it, she wanted it herself, do you understand? This is very important F. (that no one came up to the car when you were fucking . . .) No one insulted or threatened her, only me. I threatened her in this way, say it literally: She told me she loved me and wanted me to be her boyfriend, etc. I was laughing at that a lot and I told her that for me she's just a whore, that I won't go out with her and that I'll tell all her friends that we all fucked her. . . . She said that I'm a jerk and she got mad at me. . . . That's all very important! You have to testify just as I wrote you—word for word. . . . Then we'll for sure get out of this mess and get our beloved freedom. I beg you. (original emphasis)

At a subsequent hearing, the expert witness psychologist appeared, along with a child psychiatrist who had treated A. during her stay at the psychiatric facility. According to the expert witness psychologist's opinion in the case files, she finds A. to have an emotional disorder and draws attention to problems in the family: "In the particular family circumstances, the girl could not develop a normal personality capable of repelling attacks from the outside world." Significantly, she discusses the issue of resistance: "Not every personality reacts with aggressive resistance. Some of the girl's personality traits can explain this passive form. . . . It is impossible to predict the reaction of a human being in response to certain stress." The girl's abnormal personality also leads her to engage in risky and uncontrolled behavior.

The child psychiatrist testified in court that A. came to see her of her own initiative and had been a patient in the psychiatric ward from June to July. A. remains under the psychiatrist's care because she suffers from anxiety. The girl's testimony is not biased, the psychiatrist told the court. A. had come to see her because "she was afraid of being punished for having reported the incident to the police, she was afraid of being beaten. . . . She was also afraid that she would not be able to say anything in court." The psychiatrist described the victim's personality: "A. has a passive-dependent personality. She cannot react with aggression. When she feels threatened, her form of self-defense is crying and withdrawal . . . resignation is a form of defense. The victim's behavior was a form of passive resistance."

The case files also contain the results of A.'s examination at the psychiatric facility, where the doctors found that A. exhibits "a slightly reduced, in relation to the average for her age group, ability to understand the proper behaviors and social-moral norms." Someone later underlined this fragment in the files.

After this testimony, a guilty sentence was passed. W. was sentenced to five years in prison, S. to three and a half years, and R. to three years. F., the minor, was sentenced to probation in addition to community service.

In the justification of the verdict, the judge wrote that the facts were consistent with A.'s testimony. "The victim refused [sex] recoiling herself to the corner of the car," while W. maintained control over the whole incident. The court ruled that A.'s testimony was "definitely consistent, clear, and logical." The court did not give faith to the defendants' explanations: "They are all consistent with each other, but unnaturally so. Their testimony in court conflicts with what the defendants said during the investigation. Above all, however, they are not in agreement with the plaintiff's testimony." In the justification, the judge focuses on the evolution of the defendants' testimonies. It is noted that the defendants first claimed that W. threatened A. but then withdrew from this claim. W. changed his testimony regarding oral sex. Initially, he maintained that A. yielded to him and stopped putting up any resistance, whereas later he alleged that it was all her initiative. The court also took into account the intercepted note. The court was not convinced by the arguments of the defense that sex was voluntary or that the earlier group sex in which A. and W. took part had occurred with A.'s consent. The court took into account the expert opinions, which argued that she did not report to the police because of her stepfather and her father. After the first rape, she wanted to change her life around, so she went to the educational and vocational counseling center to get help with school: "These attempts were interrupted by the incident that is the subject of this proceeding." The court put stress on the girl's passive personality and the lack of a tendency to make things up. The court linked A.'s early sexual initiation and her interest in sex with an inappropriate "mode of upbringing," implying the parents' divorce. The girl's verbal resistance was noted as well as recoiling her body. Although there may have been opportunities to escape (emphasized by the defense), the victim was unable to make use of them because of her personality. The defendants knew that they were acting against her will. The opinions of the two (female) expert witnesses turned out to be decisive. They shed light on a psychological mechanism that led to a certain type of behavior during rape. The court recognized this behavior as a form of resistance and did not credit the explanations inspired by the lawyers in which the girl had basically been the one to initiate sex.

The defense lawyers appealed to the Supreme Court, placing the survivor at the center of their arguments.[10] One of the lawyers took up the issue of victim's resistance, making reference to a legal interpretation on which he wrote: "If the victim puts up initial resistance, then voluntarily, and not in being defeated by violence, resigns from that resistance, the victim cannot be considered to have been raped (thesis 4, p. 392 Commentary to the penal code).[11] Meanwhile, W. knew A. as someone extremely easy to have sexual intercourse with . . . he was deeply convinced that she had a significant need for sex." Furthermore, the defense lawyer argued that the court had required "the defendants to have knowledge of the law, psychology, and psychiatry in such contacts with girls." The lawyer added that A. did not suffer any injuries, which in his opinion means that she did not resist. He tried to portray her as a sexually active person, with much experience in this domain: "she was quick enough to tilt her head so that . . . semen would not squirt on her face." He focused particularly on intercourse with the minor, F.: "After all, what A. had done with F., who had never had intercourse before in his life, testifies to the lack of any verbal resistance. The alleged victim helped F. in having intercourse as he could not find her vagina. Despite this fact, the boy was found guilty of the crime defined in Article 168, paragraph 2 of the penal code, which is some sort of a legal misunderstanding." The lawyer also pointed out that the victim could have called for help, as other girls had rejected the defendants' proposals that day. He underscored that A. ran away from home on numerous occasions and argued that the importance of the intercepted note had been blown out of proportion. The defense lawyer representing another defendant wrote in the appeal that A. had an "intense sex life" and indicated that resistance must be judged from the perspective of the defendants' level of cognizance. The third lawyer contended that A. had participated in orgies. Only the defense lawyer representing the juvenile F. focused on the severity of the punishment, arguing that his client is a student who enjoys a good reputation.

In April 1984, the appeal hearing was held. The Supreme Court overturned the verdict. The defense lawyers' arguments were profusely cited in the justification, which stressed that resistance must be permanent so that the perpetrator is able to recognize that the victim is defending herself. The judges also argued that the role of the intercepted note was not sufficiently explained in the first trial.

Furthermore, the Supreme Court justification claimed that not enough attention was paid to the fact that the victim was under psychiatric care. The appointment of new expert witnesses was ordered: psychiatrists and a sexologist. It is worth noting that the Supreme Court judges completely disregarded the fact that A. sought psychiatric treatment as a consequence of the rape being tried.

The case returned to the district court. It was again written onto the roster in 1987. The defendants hired new attorneys, including one superstar of the Polish bar. In accordance with the Supreme Court's suggestion, new expert witnesses were appointed. What did the new experts find?

The expert sexologist wrote an opinion based on an interview and on other sexological examinations. He acquainted himself with the available medical documentation, including documents from the period following the rape, in which physicians first suspected A. to be suffering from paranoia and then, in subsequent years, diagnosed her with manic-depressive psychosis and schizoaffective psychosis. The sexologist noticed that A.'s release form from one of the psychiatric establishments mentions a disorder of the sexual drive. In writing his expert opinion, he focused on the fact that the Supreme Court ruled that A. must be examined "due to the fact that the victim was observed to have a thinking disorder characterized by a disorder of logical thinking, in addition to sex drive disorders, difficulties in controlling impulsive acts, and suspected paranoia." According to the sexologist, A.'s sex life began in 1982, at the age of sixteen. She learned about sex at the age of fifteen through reading. She reached sexual maturity at the age of eleven. She began masturbating at the age of twelve by stimulating the clitoris with her hand. "She got excited very quickly and achieved orgasm," wrote the sexologist. The expert opinion reads: "The initiation of masturbation was autonomous. It was accompanied by imagination of being caressed by a man; she felt psychological satisfaction." In the period when the examination was carried out, A. was on medication and did not masturbate. When she did masturbate, however, she did not feel guilty about it. She had sex with many partners, she switched them because she wanted to achieve orgasm during intercourse, but she managed to do so only by stimulating the clitoris: "In the period of interest to the case, the frequency of masturbation was at several times during the day. She felt very excited and always had big sexual needs."

Sexual initiation occurred when A. was sixteen years old, with an older partner. It was the effect of curiosity: "She would get excited quickly and liked sex." The sexologist ruled out what he referred to as "deviant contacts," meaning homosexual, anal, or incestuous. The opinion notes that the victim does not remember many details of the rape; she does not remember because she tried to forget, notes the sexologist. She felt defiled and humiliated: "She is worried about the current state of the case, about the fact that the perpetrators are no longer in prison and are taking part in the case as free individuals."

In his examination, the sexologist applied the scale of sexual stimuli. This method was developed at the end of the 1960s by Lew-Starowicz: "It consists of giving the examined person 30 pieces of paper with sexual slogans and asking them to arrange a hierarchy of stimuli from the most positive to the least positive and from the most negative to the least negative" (1988e, 136). Regarding A., the results came back as follows: "The subject evaluates oral sex and ejaculation outside of the vagina negatively. As the most accepted forms of sexual contact, she chose caresses, stimulation of the clitoris, intercourse, mutual activity of the partners, and various positions."

Next, the expert applied the scale of sexual pathology among women. This test is also a method developed by Lew-Starowicz and includes questions about issues such as the effect of alcohol on intercourse, achieving orgasm, and pain during intercourse (see, e.g., Lew-Starowicz 1988e, 73–74). The expert describes A. as follows: "The examined subject reports that alcohol is good for her sexual experience. She orgasms rarely because 'she is afraid to say that her orgasms arise by stimulating the clitoris.' Intercourse itself is painless in her case, and it gives her a positive feeling. Starting from sexual initiation, she always wanted to experience orgasm during intercourse, but she was only able to do so twice and she considers this type of orgasm 'better.'"

The case file includes the results of an examination conducted based on projective psychological tests. Using the Rosenzweig frustration test, the sexologist challenged the findings of A.'s psychological examination from the first trial and the investigation: "In frustrating situations, the examined subject employs various forms of defense including direct and verbal aggression. . . . The subject was not, however, found to exhibit passive behavior and withdrawal." Next, the sexologist applied a Rorschach test: "The subject's reserved commentary makes interpretation difficult. The subject reveals the predominance of emotionality, poor rational steering, and traits of regression, while she associated the sexual inkblots with a sense of threat and fear, which suggests problems in this field."

Somatic testing was next in order: A. "reveals a high level of sexual reactivity, correct construction of the genitals, and the existence of a sensory center in Gräfenberg's space. No defensive attitudes. The erotic imagination develops very quickly, spontaneously." In following, the doctor discussed A.'s behavior during the examination. He wrote that he had full contact with the victim and that she did not exhibit symptoms of psychosis. He indicated that her defensive attitudes relate to the memory of the events, which are the subject of the court's proceeding.

Based on the tests and the available documentation, the sexologist formulated the following conclusions:

> In the period of interest to the case, the subject was experiencing hyperlibidemia, and difficulty in controlling her behavior.[12] . . . The level of libido was at the time, and continues to be, very high, which is evident in her rapid arousal and sexual reactivity, her erotic imagination, and considerable sexual needs. The complex she developed as a result of experiencing orgasm by stimulating the clitoris and not during intercourse has favored her establishing many sexual contacts and changing partners. In considering the subject's psychological state and psychiatric diagnosis it must be asserted that the hyperlibidemia is strictly related. The subject's psychological state was conducive to the difficulties she faced in managing her conduct, also in her sexual life. The above-mentioned diagnoses may have been responsible for the subject's lack of a demonstrated attitude of resistance and defense in sexual situations.

A team of psychiatrists from one of the leading psychiatric institutions in the country also wrote an expert opinion. In keeping with the rules that apply to writing expert opinions, as did the sexologist, they started off with an outline of the contents of the case file. They wrote that an expert psychologist had diagnosed the subject with emotional immaturity but that she did not display any tendency to fabricate information. Their expert opinion reads: "During the hearing on August 30, 1983, information was obtained that A. had been psychiatrically treated for a long time, and she herself appeared exceptionally anxious while testifying." Of note, my analysis of the file, including the medical records, suggests something completely different. A. was treated psychiatrically only after the rape. Earlier, as I mentioned, she received educational and vocational advice at a center that provides learning help but does not deal with mental disorders. Returning to the opinion, the medical records show, wrote the experts, that A. has been under continuous psychiatric care since the event and currently (meaning in 1987) is treated with lithium. The experts concluded that A. suffers from cyclic schizophrenia, which began at the age of twelve to fifteen. In their opinion, she was repeatedly hospitalized at the time. During the incident she was experiencing manic disturbances from which ensued a lack of control. The opinion further reads: "Clinical practice has shown that inhibitions in the sphere of emotions . . . usually result in increased sexual desire and the absolute need to satisfy that desire."

After the presentation of expert opinions, the case ends in an acquittal. Let us examine the judges' justification of their decision and the role of the new expert opinions. The judges concentrated on the victim. They highlighted her emotional dysfunctions and the fact that during the investigation, it was not known that she was being treated psychiatrically (which is only logical since she was not). They wrote that her assessment of the situation was inadequate: "She exaggerated aspects that were supposedly threats or violence, which would not have been perceived as such by someone else." They focused on the fact that A. told F. "something like 'let's get started' and helped him put his penis into her vagina." They also placed emphasis on the fact that W. testified that he had been joking when he said that he would beat her if she refused to get into the car and that he knew that she had engaged in intercourse with many partners (A. called this rape, but the judges made no mention of this). Another defendant testified that A. did not agree at first but that later she did not say anything. In the justification, the judges resolved that the victim had been passive and her resistance verbal only.

The expert opinions were of particular significance to the sentence: A. "suffered from a mental illness in the form of schizophrenic psychosis, she was repeatedly hospitalized and during the incident she was in a state of manic disturbance, which brought about a lack of control over her actions. As a result of this state, she experienced increased sexual desire and an absolute need to satisfy it (p. 323, 324 in the court files).[13] This diagnosis corresponds with her behavior from before the incident, as she described it herself. It is also consistent with the sexologist's expert opinion who found that because of the recognized hyperlibidemia, she had difficulty in directing her sexual drive."

The question of resistance was also discussed in the justification. For a crime to be recognized as rape, it is necessary that "violence, illegal threat, or artifices on the part of the perpetrators and resistance on the part of the victim" be present. The court did not find these aspects to be present in this case. Putting aside all the other issues, the defendants had unanimously testified that after pulling A. into the car, they told her that they were going to a party. Being driven out to the forest and having sex with four men certainly goes far beyond the definition of a social event. Most important in the justification, however, seemed to be that the survivor represented an unacceptable model of sexuality placed at the bottom of sexual hierarchy; she was interested in sexual issues and did not consider it to be anything bad. The sexologist found that she did not feel shame about masturbation; accordingly, he placed her at the bottom of the sexual hierarchy. The ultimate argument was the girl's active sex drive. "Being easy," rechristened in the language of the experts as "hyperlibidemia," excluded the possibility of rape in the eyes of the court.

Case 2

The first case is worth comparing with another legal proceeding that is more recent but similar in many respects. Considering the two cases will highlight the role of experts in court.

In November 1985, a group of young people were hanging out at a café in the suburbs of a big city. One of the girls, a sixteen-year-old student at a vocational school (called U.) was waiting there with her girlfriends for the train home. At some point, a group of boys acquainted with U.'s friends became interested in her. After leaving the café, one of the girls struck U. and asked her if she was a prude, and then, without waiting for an answer, added "either way nothing can save you now." Then the defendants, the acquaintances of U.'s girlfriends, approached. U. told them to leave her alone, but no one from the group of young people standing there made any move to help her.

U. claimed, and the court believed her, that she was afraid of being raped and beaten. The attackers, three young men under age sixteen, had much more leverage, thus U. was passive. The boys dragged her down to a basement, but they were uncomfortable there, so they went into the bushes and, as the files note, they forced U. to have vaginal and oral sex. Then they wanted to make plans to meet up with her the next day. U. went home crying, but she did not tell her mother about what happened right away.

The defense strategy of the perpetrators was similar to that used by W. and his friends. U. maintained that they held her hands down, whereas the defendants alleged that it was she who had held onto them. The defendants claimed that U. had sex voluntarily, that maybe their behavior was a bit rough or arrogant but that they did not force her to do anything. One of the defendants posited that U. had "caught him by the fly," and that "she took his penis into her mouth by herself." The files note, "Of her own accord, she unbuttoned his pants, took out his penis and put it into her mouth. After a moment he pushed her away and zipped up his pants." The defendants claimed that the girl had undressed herself. They were particularly proud of having accompanied the survivor to the train station, as was W. and his friends of having given A. a ride home. The defense also tried to make use of the fact that U. initially did not tell her mother about the incident.

The court ordered a psychiatric examination of the accused. Psychiatric experts found one to be immature and a second to suffer from motor hyperactivity. They found all the defendants to be demoralized, to possess poor ability to internalize social norms, and to exhibit a tendency to adopt subcultural norms. The court also asked for an opinion of the survivor. A female expert psychologist examined U. She found that the girl was not fabricating information and that her development was appropriate for her age. The expert pointed to the survivor's passive-dependent personality. These conditions determined her behavior during the incident. Because fear weakens the ability to act, she chose the lesser evil.

After the first hearing, the court acquitted one of the defendants, and the other two received suspended sentences. Clearly, the defense strategy based on the argument that the victim had actively participated in the incident turned out to be effective. But the prosecutor's office filed for appeal, as a result of which the Supreme Court referred the case for reconsideration. During the next trial, the court found the defendants' explanations unconvincing. In 1988, the perpetrators were sentenced to prison terms of three years and six months. The court also ruled that they pay one hundred thousand zlotys (the equivalent of two average monthly salaries) to the survivor in compensation. The judges' justification of the verdict emphasizes the opinion of the expert psychologist. It explains, "The impact of emotions, which emerge in a state of danger in someone like the victim, made her behavior such that it might have been perceived as voluntary, but only by an outside observer and not by the accused, whom she repeatedly asked to leave her alone. Thus, having given obvious expression of her will, she did not want to engage in sexual relations with them." This reasoning allowed the judges to locate the incident within the context of one of the legal interpretations of resistance:

> It must be noted here that according to prior Supreme Court decisions, any action aimed at physically overcoming resistance is considered violence. If the intensity of resistance is small, then a small intensity of violence suffices. To recognize the criminal act described in Article 168 of the penal code it is not necessary that the victim exhaust all available means of defense. Resistance on the part of the victim does not have to take active forms, but it must be real, and not "superficial," it must manifest at least verbally, by means of protests, shouting, pleading, or refusal to submit to the lascivious act. It does not, however, have to manifest actively, by for example wrestling away, beating or kicking the rapist, protecting oneself from having the clothes pulled off, running away, and etc. The victim's ability to resist three young men was limited and even negligible due to her age, physical development, and due to the abovementioned passive-dependent personality.... Her state of hopelessness ... brought on by threats ... effectively paralyzed her will.

Recklessness came up in the justification. It was used to explain why the victim did not immediately tell her mother about what happened (she was also guided by shame). Recklessness was understood here in accordance with the guidelines set out by the Supreme Court from the early 1970s (that victims' reckless behavior should not be taken into consideration while ruling in rape cases),

against which Bieńkowska and other legal scholars had argued. The concept was interpreted in a manner completely different from any other legal procedure that I have analyzed: "Even if it were established that the plaintiff's behavior had been reckless before the rape, this cannot be of any relevance to the assessment of the defendants' guilt, or to the penalty, because that recklessness was due to her young age and inexperience." Yet the mere consideration of recklessness (the girl was raped while coming home from school) is the effect of a gender order, which demands great caution from women in moving about outside of the home area. This belief is reinforced by expert knowledge, both medical and legal.

After the defense attorneys' appeal in 1989, the Supreme Court slightly eased the sentence but did not question the verdict. Expert knowledge again proved decisive: the expert psychologist's assessment of the survivor's particular mode of reaction to danger convinced the judges to lean toward a specific definition of resistance. In addition, in contrast to the first case, the survivor was not sexually experienced. The last issue seems to be of crucial importance because U., unlike A., could not be placed at the bottom of the sexual hierarchy.

Case 3

Resistance put up by the survivor, her behavior, and her sexuality continued to play a leading role in more recent legal proceedings. This case involves an incident from early September 2002. Sixteen-year-old D., who was in Child Protective Services at the time, was drinking alcohol with two young men, one of whom lived in an orphanage. The event ended in brutal sex that the victim did not want and from which she defended herself.

In the opinion of female expert psychologists, written on the basis of available documentation, interviews, and participation in the interrogation, the girl did not exhibit a tendency to fabricate information and the alcohol did not inhibit her assessment of the situation. Furthermore, her development was normal, but like other victims (notably, A. from the first case), she did not adhere to social norms and was sexually active. One expert opinion contends that she allegedly provided sexual services. The rape brought on strong trauma. The account notes that when she talks about it, she cries. "Currently, she remains under the impact of trying experiences associated with the violence committed against her, which may in the future cause long-term psychological trauma," wrote one of the experts. The victim also cries when her father is mentioned. In the period between the rape and the trial, the father was sentenced for having raped his daughter.

The prosecutor's office asked for an assessment of the mental health of one of the defendants. Expert psychiatrists found that he did not suffer from any disorder. The second defendant suffered from epilepsy, but this did not reduce his culpability.

The incident was reported to the police by a tenant who had been awoken by shouting in the stairwell and who came to help the girl. The tenant testified that the victim had sperm, blood, and feces on her body. In the indictment, we read that one of the rapists refused to testify. The second testified that there was intercourse but with the plaintiff's consent. He hit her only once because she bit his penis. The prosecutor's office found this to be inconsistent with the evidence.

The trial began in January 2003 and the defendants were acquitted in March. In the justification, we read that the girl had behavioral problems. Moreover, although the experts testified that the victim was credible, the court did not give her faith: she was drunk (the police who were called to the scene, after completing "procedures," took the victim to the "drunk tank," or the alcohol recovery center).[14] This was confirmed by the doctor who arrived on the scene of the incident. Conversely, the defendants' state of intoxication did not reduce their credibility in the eyes of the court. The same doctor also declared that drunken offenders leave more distinct marks on their victims' bodies. The court ignored the doctor's lack of competence in the matter of rape, such as the fact that he failed to examine the victim's anus (this issue proved of particular importance in the next instances of this case).[15]

As explained in the justification of the verdict, the expert's opinion of the victim's partial consent worked in the defendants' favor: "According to the expert witness, it cannot be ruled out that D. may have consented to certain of the defendants' actions. Some of the defendants' behaviors, as presented in the plaintiff's testimony, were rejected by her and in effect, in the end, she perceived the whole event to have occurred against her will." The justification suggests that perhaps—to put colloquially—because she was drunk, she wanted it at first and then changed her mind.

The survivor's mother was put on the stand, and her testimony was taken into account in the verdict. The mother claimed that her daughter had falsely accused her father of sexual harassment, and when the court found the man to be innocent, she ran away from home. As already mentioned, in subsequent stages of the case, we learn that the father had raped his daughter and was ultimately convicted. In addition, the court questioned the survivor's credibility because she did not tell her mother about the rape (a mother, who according to the files, for years did not notice that her husband was sexually assaulting her daughter).

In June 2003, the court received the prosecution's appeal, which called attention to the mistakes made in determining the facts. After all, two experts had found the victim to be credible, whereas the court considered their opinions only selectively, using the quote about partial consent cited above. Interestingly, the appeal does not mention that a woman can consent to certain types of sex and refuse to engage in others (e.g., anal sex) or that this in itself constitutes assault on her sexual autonomy.[16] The prosecutor's office attempts to undermine this piece of the expert opinion, arguing that the psychologist only suggests this and it is not her general conclusion. Thus, despite good intentions, the author of the appeal (a female prosecutor) does not go beyond the stereotypical understanding of rape. She also tries to break down the alcohol argument, again, in a rather stereotypical way. Instead of pointing to the defendants' state of intoxication, she notes only that it is easier to break resistance when the victim is drunk.

In October 2003, the appellate court agreed with the prosecutor's appeal and overturned the verdict. The case was referred back to the district court for reconsideration. The prosecutor's arguments, although stereotypical (or maybe because of this), proved effective.

The case was put on the court's roster in March 2005, but neither the defendants nor the plaintiff showed up to several hearings. It came to light that one of the accused was homeless and could not be officially summoned.

Again, everything revolved around the victim. D.'s counselor at Child Protective Services was asked to testify. She told the court that the girl was there because she claimed that she was being sexually abused by her father. Later, according to the counselor, D. withdrew this accusation under pressure from her parents. The woman testified that D. did not avoid contact with men, although after the rape she stopped running away, which she had often done before. The counselor had the impression that D. was afraid of something. Nevertheless, after the incident, the victim behaved provocatively toward men. This last theme also appeared in the testimony of other witnesses, and I will return to it in a moment.

Meanwhile, the survivor did not attend subsequent hearings. The court set a penalty for her absence in the amount of one thousand zlotys, almost half of the average month salary at the time.

D.'s mother was again asked to testify. She told the court that her daughter did not want to talk about what happened. "She didn't really suffer any severe experiences because of the rape," she said. The mother added that she did not trust her daughter because she ran away from home. She wanted to go to Child Protective Services herself. She claimed that D.'s father kept her on a short leash, that he beat her when she ran away from home and for having boys, so D. accused him of rape and earlier of harassment.

Finally, D. was again put on the stand. The court consented to her request that the defendants leave the courtroom. D. testified that she did not remember details (more than three years had passed since the incident). She remembered only that they had held her down and that she felt in danger. She was in psychotherapy after the rape. She also told the court about her father: he took her to the basement and touched her private parts. Then he raped her. He did not admit to this in court, but he was convicted and was currently serving a prison term.

Then questions about the incident began. One might get the impression that this part of the hearing was based on a script written more than twenty years earlier by Hanausek, Marek, and Widacki (1976), even though they had addressed their text to forensic experts and not to lawyers. D. was considered sexually experienced, like some other victims that the three authors had studied—after all, she had intercourse with her father. Effectively, the court saw it necessary to question her about the incident. The judge asked if she had considered the possibility that she would have sex with the defendants. D. replied that had she considered it, she would not have gone with them. Then the defense drilled her about her previous sexual experiences, suggesting that because she knew about sex of a certain type, she must have engaged in it herself. Did she have oral and anal sex in the past? D. responded, "The fact that I was talking about different types of sex is not because I had this type of sex before, I only found out about it during the court trials." Next D. was forced to deny: it was not true that she worked as a private escort or that she starred in porn films. Questions about these issues were posed during the hearing and addressed to a still-teenaged girl who, as the victim of various forms of sexual violence, was undergoing therapy. Finally, D. confessed that she wanted to forget about everything.

The court appointed another expert psychologist who was to check whether the victim was lying. The opinion is straightforward: the fact that the victim does not remember is brought on by trauma and a mechanism of denial. The girl is definitely not lying. The psychologist also drew attention to the girl's difficult life experiences and the fact that she grew up in a dysfunctional family.

At the next hearing, the court summoned D.'s father from prison. He was sentenced to eight years for abusing his daughter, for "another sexual act" (Article 200, par. 1) and for raping her (Article 197, par. 1).[17] The father testified that his daughter had not told him anything about the rape. He threatened to kick her out of the house if she did not tell him. He testified that D. did not want to live with him, and so she went to the Child Protective Services center. He did not believe that his daughter was raped. He laid out his argument as follows: the fact that she had previously had contacts with men means that she was not raped. He said, "She already had sex with men before, and she was 15 when she was raped. I think the mere fact that she had sex before proves that she was not raped." Besides, he added, she reacted nervously to the question about rape, she bit her fingernails. He further developed the theme of D.'s sexual life. "My daughter does not carry herself well," he said. She accused him of touching her, "supposedly by grabbing her breasts and her butt."

Then another expert witness, a gynecologist, presented his opinion. He questioned the gynecological expertise from the previous trial. In his opinion, each case is different, and the injuries suffered by the victim may corroborate her version of the incident. He asserted firmly, "Defining rape depends on the victim's disapproval, regardless of her social and moral status, her usual behavior and her state of sobriety."

After this speech, the court ordered another opinion from a group of experts from a prestigious forensic center. The question posed to the experts was this: Is the plaintiff's version credible if we consider the injuries she incurred? The experts responded, "The victim's injuries do not clearly indicate significant active resistance on her part. It should be noted, however, that her skin abrasions and bruising on the left forearm may have been caused by forced immobilization, such as when holding down the forearm. Skin abrasions on both knees could have arisen as a result of contact with a hard surface while kneeling," which may indicate anal sex. "Referring to the victim's account of the event, we conclude unanimously that the defendants' actions did not have to lead to other injuries."

During the next hearing, one of the defense attorneys returned again to the infamous passage from the first expert opinion. He asked the experts, "Could D. have rejected the defendants' behavior, meaning the amount and type of sexual intercourse they had because of, for example, some reflection she had or situational post-incident evaluation, which made her in the final result (effect) interpret the entirety of the incident as having occurred against her actual will at the moment of the incident?" When the experts did not confirm the possibility of such a course of events, the defense tried to undermine their opinion.

The next hearing took place only in 2007 because neither the witnesses nor the defendants showed up to previous hearings. The expert witness also did not come when summoned. This time, however, instead of a fine, the court ordered the defendant who notoriously ignored his summons to be temporarily arrested. Finally, the expert psychologist answered the defense lawyer's question regarding the survivor's interpretation of the incident. Because the victim refused to take part in another examination, the answer could be only hypothetical. The expert purported that if it was like the attorney suggested, the psychologist would have noticed it before. It happens that victims change their minds about consent to sex, but they do so in order to, for example, have an abortion or to extort compensation—in such cases, they are steered by "hard motives."[18]

In June 2007, both rapists were sentenced to three years in prison. In its justification, the court relied primarily on expert opinions that corroborated D.'s version.

One of the defense lawyers filed an appeal. He claimed that according to the defendants' account of the incident, the victim's parents, and the opinion of the expert witnesses, D. had consented to sex. The lawyer analyzed the issue of consent, citing verdict justifications from other cases: "Rape did not occur if the victim, even if reluctantly, allows for sexual intimacy, and especially if through her earlier behavior, she gives a man the impression that she will consent."[19] Furthermore, he argued, "The crime defined in Article 168 of the penal code requires not only that the acts described in this regulation take place. Also necessary is the subjective feeling of the act by the person against whom it was committed, as an act that occurred against this person's actual will at the time that it took place, and not after later reflection or situational assessment."[20]

In calling upon these justifications, the lawyer again tried to make use of the suggestion of one of the expert witnesses during the first trial—namely, that the victim had consented to some acts but not to others. In addition, he centered his case on the victim. He described her behavior as reckless and argued that the alcohol had an effect "not only on the presumed, but also on the actual consent." In the appeal, the victim appeared to be overly or even obsessively interested in sex. She is described as sexually mature, maintaining relations with men despite her bad experiences of harassment, and she is vulgar. Rape did not make a lasting impression on her because she has been laughing and partying. The appeal cited a witness who said that "she was demonstratively provocative toward the boys." These issues were discussed earlier in the case. When asked about this, the expert explained during one of the hearings that these are typical reactions to sexual violence. Consequently, to sustain his argument, the lawyer had to challenge the opinion of this expert psychologist along with the opinion of the experts from the prestigious forensic medicine center, who found the victim's version to be credible because it was confirmed by the evidence on her body.

In February 2008, the appellate hearing took place, during which the judges ruled that certain information was lacking. In effect, they decided to summon the expert psychologist and the victim, but neither turned up for the hearing. Ultimately, the expert came to the hearing scheduled for October 2008 and testified that the victim came from a "demoralized" milieu and was reluctant to cooperate with law enforcement agencies, thus he was unable to gain more information.

After this testimony, the appellate court overturned the verdict. The justification reads that during the first trial, the expert witness found that "the victim could have consented to some acts, and not to others." The appeals court commented on this finding as follows: "At what point did she express her disapproval and was it clearly legible for the defendants?" Furthermore, the judges argued that the experts did not note any signs of active resistance: "The [district] court did not analyze and did not rule out the possibility of intimate contact taken up voluntarily by the plaintiff with the defendants, or the possibility of that consent being withdrawn in the course of the incident, in a way imperceptible to the other two participants." Significantly, the justification makes reference to so-called life experience and expert knowledge about sexuality: "Life experience, which also features in the personal repertoire of those who make judgments in similar cases, along with the indications of knowledge, outright oblige us to take extreme caution in assessing gestures expressed or words spoken during intimate contact" (read: especially when there are no traces of resistance). The judges omitted the fact that the expert opinions diverged in this matter. Clear reference to expert literature can be made out here, according to which misunderstanding can easily occur in intimate situations. The survivor's young age; her abundant alcohol consumption, as purported by the judges; and her risky behavior (i.e., hanging out in the stairwell) worked to the detriment of her credibility. According to the appellate court, the district court did not determine whether "the intention of the defendants was to make another person engage in sexual intercourse by force, illegal threat or deceit. . . . Of course, it is impossible to exclude that both of the defendants, in the least, made illegal threats or used force to commit against D. the statutory features of the crime described in Article 197, paragraph 3."

D.'s bad reputation withstood all factual evidence, emplaced in the context of the belief propagated by expert publications about the importance of the survivor's earlier sexual experiences: "It is impossible to omit that the victim herself, despite her young age, had some experience in the field of intimate contact. . . . The above circumstance should induce the District Court to pay more attention to D.'s behavior, which indisputably comes up in her testimony and shows that it was her choice to spend time together with the defendants." Therefore, the judges ask, why question the defendants' version, since the plaintiff voluntarily went to the stairwell at 1:00 a.m.? How then did she express her lack of consent? The defendants might not have noticed her withdrawal of consent; she could have been shy about it or afraid of being ostracized in the group, or perhaps her resistance was only symbolic. Finally, the survivor's absence at the appeal hearing ultimately undermined her credibility.

Interestingly, the justifications of the verdict and the appeal contain the same inaccuracy: the expert witness's name is misspelled, although it is written correctly in all the other case files. Did the appeals court not study the case files and make its decision based only on what the defense lawyer wrote in his appeal?

In December 2008, the prosecutor's office filed for cassation (i.e., annulment) to the Supreme Court, pointing out that the appeals court had not fully considered the case. The prosecutor argued that it was likely that what happened could be defined as rape. The cassation procedure was suspended for almost a year because, again, the court could not locate one of the accused. Finally, in November 2009, the Supreme Court overturned the verdict and remanded the case to the appellate court for reconsideration. The Supreme Court judges wrote that the victim was not guided in her actions by the will to make a false accusation. Furthermore, they posited that the appellate court did take into account the overall circumstances but focused only on undermining evidence unfavorable to the defendants. The Supreme Court asked how D. could scream when they had forced her mouth shut.

In December 2009, the appellate court considered the 2007 guilty verdict for the second time and upheld it on the grounds that D.'s testimony did not suggest that she had consented to any sexual behavior at all. The defense filed for cassation, but in July 2010 their motion was dismissed by the Supreme Court. Finally, after eight years of discussing D.'s sex life, the court found the rapists guilty.

Case 4

Another case in which the survivor's "recklessness" played an important role related to events of June 2000. A woman came to the police with her minor daughter (born in 1985; in Poland, the age of consent is fifteen). She reported the theft of a telephone but finally said, "These men raped my underage daughter." An expert psychologist took part in the interrogation and found that the daughter (called G.) was not inclined to fabricate information. What happened? G. met the perpetrators on the street. There were three of them, but two were involved in the incident under investigation. Together with a girlfriend, G. was returning in the early evening from a trip to the center of a big city where they had gone for ice cream to celebrate the end of the school year. G. had just graduated from the eighth grade. Her girlfriend went home. The young men proposed to G. that they would walk her home. On the way, they raped her, both orally and vaginally, ejaculating their sperm into her mouth at the end. They also took her phone. They threatened her, and she did not break away. She told her parents immediately about the theft and that she had been held down by force. Once she went to the police station with her mother, she revealed that she had been raped.

In the psychological expert opinion, we read that G. "is immature and unable to predict the effects of her actions" (G. was not even fifteen years old, it took another expert to assert that her development was in the norm) and that she has been suffering from sleep disorders since the incident. The police quickly found the perpetrators because they used the survivor's phone. They were arrested.

Genetic and biological tests were carried out and showed a lack of sperm in the vagina and the presence of semen on the victim's clothes, which was in agreement with G.'s testimony. One of the accused refused to testify, and the other claimed that he had bought the phone at the market.

The trial began in February 2001, and a sentence was passed in April of the same year. The court acquitted the defendants of the charge of rape but sentenced them to four years of probation for having stolen the phone. The court found that indeed they had intercourse with a person under the age of fifteen, but she looked older than that and had consented to sex.

In the justification, the judges argued that while the issue of sex was indisputable, it was necessary to consider whether it took place voluntarily: "Attention must be paid to the fact that upon returning home, the juvenile did not tell her mother about the incident, but only informed her about the stolen mobile phone. Only after some time from the incident in the park, wanting to explain the lost phone and her late arrival at home, she interpreted the whole incident as rape." In addition, the judges determined that "before the moment of the incident, the victim had already begun her sex life, thus it can be assumed that she already had some awareness in this regard. In displaying such recklessness that evening, she allowed for the course of events to take place." The court considered G.'s testimony to be unreliable; therefore, it did not share the expert witness's opinion on this matter. The girl's behavior was read as consent to sex: "In the court's opinion, G. agreed to have sexual intercourse. This is confirmed by her behavior. She admits herself that she voluntarily entered the park with the men she had frivolously met on the same evening. While in the park, she had the option of withdrawing, but she remained in the company of [the defendants]—thus allowing them to become sexually intimate."

The court found the defendants' testimonies coherent. They stressed that they did not use violence: "From G.'s behavior the defendants inferred that she expected events to unfold as such that evening, thus intimate contact occurred by mutual consent." The court accepted their account that they did not realize that she was not even fifteen because she was tall and sexually developed. Although her ID was in the bag they took from her, it was dark in the park, so they could not check. Earlier they asked her friend how old she was. The friend was older than G., but G. said nothing about her own age: "with her passive attitude she confirmed her companion's words."

One of the judges was of a different opinion. In her evaluation, the fact that G. did not immediately inform her mother did not mean that she gave false testimony. Moreover, this judge shared the opinion of the expert witness who contended that it was usual to rape that the victim was afraid and did what she was told to do. The judge found the expert's argument that the victim was not emotionally mature important. She also decided that the claim that the men were innocent was based on "a shallow conviction that entering the park at night with strange men means that the woman agrees to have sexual intercourse with them (stereotype: why did she go with them, she knew what they were going in there for, etc.)."

In June 2001, the prosecutor's office filed an appeal, arguing that going to the park does not imply consent to sex and that reckless behavior is typical of the victim's age. This time, the fact that G. did not tell her mother did not render her testimony dubious. The prosecutor employed classical feminist arguments and referred to "life experience": "The prosecution considers the court's contention that a fourteen-year-old child consented to having sexual intercourse at least 3 times with 2 men as contrary to the principles of logic and life experience. The fact that the victim had already embarked upon her sex life is irrelevant in the prosecution's opinion."

The appellate hearing took place in November 2001. The court upheld the verdict as to the phone theft but ordered the rape case to be reconsidered. The trial started again in April 2003. As usual, due to numerous absences, everything was prolonged. In 2006, the psychologist wrote and presented his opinion of the victim to the court. He called attention to the fact that G. had undergone eighteen months of therapy. She was particularly stressed about having to testify again, since she had already told the story of what happened four times in court. "At the moment, she is upset about having to testify. . . . She has nightmares in which she is testifying in court in the presence of many people. She wants the defendants to leave the courtroom when she testifies." The psychologist argued that the defendants should leave for the benefit of the victim. In addition, he said that the girl had depressive states and, most likely as a result of the rape, still had an unstable personal life. He also noted that risky behavior is characteristic of adolescence.

In July 2007, the defendants were convicted and received a sentence of two years in prison for raping a minor. In the justification, the judges wrote that it is difficult to consider the defendants' allegation to be logical that after they took her phone, she agreed to sex. The court also considered the fact that the girl did not immediately inform her mother about what happened (and did not tell her father at all): "It was not only the fear that they would not understand the situation in which she found herself, undoubtedly in part due to her own recklessness, which she was aware of, but also because of embarrassment and shame in reporting the circumstances of this incident."

The victim's version was additionally corroborated by her behavior after the incident. As her mother testified, the girl "scrubbed her face and teeth." The following commentary was written in the justification of the verdict: "Undoubtedly, this type of reaction is not the reaction of someone who had consented to intercourse."

The court also took into account the psychological consequences of rape and the fact that G. had undergone therapy. This interpretation contrasts with the first case described, in which psychiatric treatment was used to the survivor's detriment.

Importantly, the justification highlights that the girl's reckless behavior did not lessen the responsibility of the perpetrators: "Acceptance that the plaintiff's behavior can be judged in terms of recklessness does not constitute a circumstance that affects the defendants' degree of guilt." The question of her age was also discussed in the justification: the accused were not interested in how old G. was—she had her school identification card in the bag, which they searched looking for valuables.

Finally, the court presented its position on the issue of violence and resistance, so often of critical importance in rape cases: "An assessment of the extent of the force used is of no relevance here, because every action, including holding down someone's hands, aimed at physically overcoming their resistance falls into the category of force described in Article 197 of the penal code. The same goes for the magnitude and effectiveness of the plaintiff's resistance in the context of being trapped by the perpetrators and fearing that resistance will only increase their aggression."

In following this decision, the defense lawyers appealed in turn, pointing once again to the victim's recklessness (equating it with consent), the fact that the perpetrators did not know how old she was, and the claim that the girl looked older in reality. The court upheld the verdict but changed the classification of the act, acquiescing to the defense's argument that the perpetrators did not realize that G. was not yet fifteen years old.

Conclusion: Who is the "Real" Victim?

In the cases described, and in others I studied in the course of my research, the opinions of experts proved to be decisive for the course of the trial. This was particularly evident in the first case, during which the examination conducted by a new group of experts brought about a diametrically opposed interpretation of events. Expert knowledge also manifests in the courtroom in the argumentation of attorneys, prosecutors and judges. An important theme that comes up throughout rape case files is the allegedly provocative and reckless behavior attributed to the survivor, along with her previous sexual experience. Both tend to be understood by some as (implied) consent. Another running theme is women who violate gender norms, their sexual experience, and their sexual activity that falls at the lower end of the sexual hierarchy. Simultaneously, the undertone of some lawyers' and experts' arguments suggests the image of a man unable to restrain himself and to whom refusal is a form of coquetry. Such an image stands out especially in the expert literature discussed earlier. It implies that women and girls should know not to "play with fire" or "provoke" if they do not want to be raped. Experts charge them with coresponsibility, defining women's agency in a manner detached from gendered social, cultural, and psychological constraints but in agreement with ideas about women's agency presented in the expert literature. Accordingly, women are fully responsible for family and sexual life but are not supposed to express their needs or concerns directly. As such, women should always say no to sex, as a form of flirtation. Some experts and lawyers try to deconstruct this model by highlighting the diverse reactions that survivors might have to rape (i.e., even if a woman does not scream or try to get away, in a given context, it is still clear to the perpetrator that she is not consenting to sex). Another approach tries to prove that a woman's sexual history does not imply that she can be forced to have sex. Nevertheless, such arguments must operate in relation to a certain model of rape present in the literature on the subject.

Within the dominant discourse, what should the rape survivor be like? How should she carry herself so as not to raise a shadow of doubt that she did not want to have sex and that she tried to resist? Another case from the 1980s answers these questions. The incident occurred in autumn 1982. A forty-seven-year-old woman was attacked by a drunken twenty-four-year-old man who had previously made two suicide attempts and who, as the files indicate, never had any prior sexual intercourse with the woman. The expert psychiatrists who examined him found that he "exhibits . . . the characteristics of an abnormal schizophrenia-type personality" and can be declared insane.

What happened? The assailant knocked his victim to the ground, started beating her, and shouting, "You whore, I will rape you." But the woman began to defend herself. She hit the man and called for help. Her son ran out of the house, overpowered the would-be rapist, and called the police. In effect, the attacker was hospitalized with severe injuries. The court sentenced him for attempted rape with particular cruelty to two years and six months in prison. He also lost his civil rights for this time and was ordered to pay twenty thousand zlotys (almost two average monthly salaries) in compensation. In contrast to the teenager who drank alcohol in the company of future rapists, the survivor's status as a stable mother and wife who had nothing to do with the attacker made for a condition that left no doubt in this case.

Notes

1. When I note that a case is from a given year, I mean that it was recorded in the registry in a given year (it usually went to trial that same year) and was given a reference number.

2. In such cases, psychological opinions are more prevalent than the sexological.

3. This approach to sexuality is an effect of the interdisciplinary tradition of Polish sexology, which I described earlier.

4. There is no jury in the Polish court system. Professional judges and lay assessors decide about a defendant's guilt: "In cases tried by a first-instance court under a regular procedure, the court usually sits in a panel composed of one professional judge and two lay assessors. . . . The court may decide to hear a complex case in a panel of three professional judges" (Murzynowski 2005, 387).

5. I examined the ethnic dimension of this case previously (Kościańska 2012c).

6. The file even contains photos of the car.

7. The "lascivious act" here was oral sex.

8. F. testified earlier that W. had threatened A.

9. One of the perpetrators testified that A. helped F. enter his penis into her vagina. A. claimed that she helped the boy have intercourse because she wanted it to end as soon as possible.

10. In the 1980s, appellate courts did not exist in Poland. A verdict could be appealed by submitting a revision to the Supreme Court.

11. This understanding of resistance derives from a 1926 decision of the Supreme Court. Among its proponents is, for example, Leszczyński (1973, 92; see chap. 7).

12. Lew-Starowicz defines hyperlibidemia as follows: "Hyperlibidemia is a disorder, which involves a pathological increase in sexual needs and behaviors . . . sexual activity becomes the basic life goal, frequent changes of partners dominate, [patients exhibit] an inability to form long-lasting relationships" (1988*e*, 28).

13. This is a reference to the opinion of an expert sexologist.

14. The breathalyzer test at the drunk tank where the victim was transported showed that D. had 0.084 percent alcohol in her breath; for a woman weighing 55 kilograms (121 pounds) at four hours after drinking, this indicates, on average, two large beers with 5% alcohol (http://www.kazdypromil.pl/alkomat/, accessed December 12, 2012).

15. This case shows the extent to which there is a dire need for specialized medical examination centers and detailed instructions for doctors.

16. The Supreme Court's more recent verdicts (II KK 504/04, decision of the Supreme Court, September 8, 2005) consider such a possibility, which will be discussed in chap. 9 on changes in the courtroom.

17. According to the case file, D. ran away from home because her father beat her with his hands, his belt, and a cable and kicked her. Her mother saw this but did not intervene because she was afraid of being beaten herself and had to take care of the younger children. A school nurse saw the injuries on the girl's body. Along with the school counselor, the nurse paid a visit to the family home. The father also had "educational talks" with the daughter, during which he shouted and beat her. From 2000, the father became interested in his daughter's sexuality. He pulled up her blouse and kissed her and when she struggled, he threatened her, beat her, and held her down. He put his penis on her stomach and ejaculated. He came to the girl at night. D. did not tell her mother because she was afraid she would not believe her, but she told the nurse. As a result, the case went to family court, which sent D. to Child Protective Services. When D. returned, at first everything went well, but then the father began to touch her again, put his penis on her belly, and threaten that he would kick her out of the house if she refused. He told her that he loved her like his girlfriend, not like his daughter. When he touched her, "D. did not scream, but she asked the defendant not to do anything to her, she tried to break away." In total, he raped her seven times; he did not use violence, only threatened to throw her out of the house. Once he took her to a tent and tried to force her to have sex again. This time she refused, he threw her out, she went to a friend's house, and the friend called the police. In court, the father confessed only to corporal punishment. The father thought that his daughter was making things up when she said that she was gang raped. The file reads, "He did not know the course of this incident, but he was sorry that these men were in custody, and by means of continuous 'educational talks' he tried to make his daughter admit that it was her fault and persuade her to change her testimony." He testified that he had called her to the tent because he wanted her to tell him about the rape, that he was drunk, and that he hit her in the face and threw her out of the house.

According to the case files, both of D.'s parents were alcoholics. D. explained that she had testified against her father because she was afraid that he would do the same thing to her younger sister, who was also in therapy. The expert opinions note that during the father's trial, the girl was persistently under pressure to change her testimony. She was pressured by her mother, her uncle, and by the defendant himself, who sent her a message from prison: "The defendant told her that because she already had sex, it did not matter who she was going to do it with." A school counselor who was summoned as a witness testified that D's mother did not support her daughter and accepted her husband's version. The experts' opinions played an important role in D.'s father's trial. The court, in following an expert psychologist, pointed out that some witnesses expressed stereotypical opinions about raped women—for example, they said that she could not have been raped because she was partying a lot afterward. Initially, the victim had been a good student. The expert told the court that the victim's change of behavior from a good student to a girl who focused mostly on her social life and who had sex was typical and that, professionally, this is called child sexual harassment syndrome and post-traumatic stress disorder. The experts asserted that sexualization was typical in such cases. One of the experts told the court that "in her 35 years of professional practice she did not encounter a single case in which sexual abuse would lead to better grades at school."

The experts were also asked to evaluate the perpetrator. A psychiatric observation showed that his behavior was within the norm and that he suffered from alcoholism. An expert sexologist asserted a heterosexual orientation and did not find the defendant to be a pedophile (according to the sexological definition, a pedophile is someone who is attracted to children or to people who have not yet developed secondary sexual characteristics), while his libido was in the norm for his age. The expert concluded that the father's "occasional incestuous behavior was associated with the desire to satisfy his sexual needs."

18. In Poland, pregnancy that is the result of crime constitutes grounds for legal abortion.

19. 1994.02.23, Court of Appeals decision II Act 11/94, KZS 1994/4/16.

20. 1980.07.18, Supreme Court decision III KR 149/80, LEX nr 21875, 1979.02.12, SN III KR 241/78.

9 | Feminism: Changes in Expert Discourse and in the Courtroom

Expert discourse is not stable, and change can be perceived in the cases presented. My analysis of the press shows that since the early 1990s, a new type of discourse on rape has appeared that relies heavily on the feminist perspective (Kościańska 2012d). This is associated in part with the rise of a new group of experts, including female experts, involved in survivor support. These female doctors, therapists, lawyers, or simply activists in organizations that deal with sexual violence have often been interested in feminism. One of the interview partners from this group described herself as an activist psychologist, which I believe makes for a good reflection of this group's approach.[1]

New Experts

Starting in the early 1990s, the new experts started speaking in public about sexual violence. Their professional knowledge, their ability to refer to research conducted in the country and abroad, and the fact that they describe the experiences of survivors—a group that was largely omitted in the past—make them strong advocates. The press printed telephone numbers of helplines run by newly established organizations, such as the Federation for Women and Family Planning and the Center for Women's Rights. Sexual violence was also taken up by the Polish Feminist Association and the National Women's Information Center (OŚKA), which were both very active in the 1990s. The latter organization wrote an open letter to Hanna Suchocka, the minister of justice at the time, arguing that judges were not prepared to rule in rape cases because they tended to be guided by the way the victim looked in their assessments of the situation. In 1995, the National Emergency Service for Victims of Domestic Violence, known generally as the "Blue Line," was launched. In 2001, the Feminoteka Foundation, which focuses to a great extent on the problem of violence against women, was established. In 2006, the association Toward Girls was founded to counteract sexual harassment at school. Women affiliated with these organizations aim to overcome stereotypes and to represent the survivors' perspectives by trying to give them a voice. For example, in the Feminoteka Foundation's report, entitled *End the Silence: Sexual Violence against Women and the Problem of Rape in Poland* (*Dość milczenia. Przemoc seksualna wobec kobiet i problem gwałtu w Polsce*; Piotrowska and Synakiewicz 2011), the survivors are the experts. The publication ends with a record of a survivors' discussion, during which they analyze subsequent chapters and present their positions on the issues discussed therein.

Organizations that work to support women survivors of violence publish information pamphlets and conduct research that is later reported in the mainstream press (see, e.g., Musiał 2000). These experts appear in the media and talk about how difficult the experience of violence is for women.[2] They publicize abuses on the part of institutions that are supposed to help victims. Furthermore, they can be credited for having forwarded the argument that the vast majority of rapists are not random men attacking in dark alleys but rather husbands, lovers, and friends with whom the survivor is usually well acquainted.

Feminists involved in survivor support define rape completely differently than sexologists and lawyers. Above all, they understand it in the context of patriarchy; rape is not about sex but about power. In this approach, sexual violence against women serves male domination. Such an interpretation of rape is widespread in feminist organizations, both in Poland and in the United States. It was first formulated by Susan Brownmiller (1975) in her book, *Against Our Will: Men, Women and Rape*. In this work's most famous passage, Brownmiller argues, "From prehistoric times to the present, I believe, rape has played a critical function. It is nothing more or less than a conscious process of intimidation by which *all men* keep *all women* in a state of fear" (5; original emphasis). In her understanding, it is the fear of violence that limits women's activity and serves to co-organize their lives (Kelly 1996, 192). In the sphere of North American feminism, theorists like Robin Morgan (1980) and Catharine MacKinnon, just like some Polish legal scholars of the 1970s, have linked rape to sex, for example, seeing its sources in pornography (MacKinnon 1996, 59; for a discussion of this issue, see Bourke 2007, 13, 140–46). This last position is not common in Polish feminism, although some activists see pornography as an element that functions to promote sexual violence (see Czapczyńska 2011, 98, Nawrocka 2011, 65).

Among Polish activists, the approach to rape in the context of violence and control is predominant. These matters were addressed in the interviews. As a thirty-five-year-old lawyer explained, "Sexual violence is a part of violence." Accordingly, "if there is violence in the family, violence in the family understood broadly, in the relationship, then usually one of its elements is also sexual violence." There is no doubt that rape can occur in marriage or on a date. Feminists are opposed to understanding agency as responsibility, as was the case in older legal and sexological literature. Rape is a limitation of women's agency. Another interview partner, a fifty-year-old woman who conducts workshops on sexual violence against young women, puts this thought in the framework of the provocation stereotype:

> If we stick to this example, that girls provoke, that they hold part of the responsibility for male sexuality, then it is assumed here that violence in general or contacts that go beyond the norm, or the manner of behavior, has its source in erotic arousal meaning there is no awareness . . . that there are other sources of this behavior— power relations, again derived from gender stereotypes, which attribute higher rank to what is male, and men feel higher in the hierarchy, and one way of showing this superiority is sexual violence. This never comes up and it is difficult to accept, because the medical conviction that erotic arousal is associated with puberty is so strong that it explains everything.

My interview partner also points out that during training sessions, which she conducts, she often encounters a failure to notice violence. She hears, for instance, "that's a form of flirting that just lacks subtlety, he was just hitting on her, or, it was a game." Like other feminists, she understands the problem to be systemic, as part of a culture that sets certain roles for women and others for men—their transgression can lead to violence: "Harassment is a way to defend gender boundaries, whoever crosses them is punished, whether it be a sensitive boy, and sensitive means a momma's boy, a fag, for not being the right type of boy or the man he should be. And girls, if they transgress their gender role, if they're not passive, . . . if they take up men's space, . . . this sexual aspect serves to remind them that they are nothing more."

In the book *Sexual Harassment: Stupid Game or Serious Problem* (*Napastowanie seksualne. Głupia zabawa czy poważna sprawa*), authors Anna Wołosik, from the association Toward Girls, and academic Ewa Majewska (2011) review North American literature on the subject. They argue that the fact that attackers often chose defiant or assertive girls confirms that violence serves to perpetuate the status quo between the sexes, as these girls threaten male identity and domination (58). Based on her many years of experience in conducting workshops on this issue, the previously cited interview partner agreed that these observations are also valid in the Polish context.

Such understanding of sexual violence stands in stark contrast to Godlewski's (1987) definition, propagated among sexologists. Every rape is nonsexual but rather "power-driven." The feminist interviewees place rape in the context of violence in general. For this reason, some of them posit that rape should be defined as a crime against liberty, as in the 1969 penal code.

Feminists negate the conviction evident in sexological literature, notably in Lew-Starowicz's writing, that after crossing a certain boundary, men can no longer hold themselves back. Feminists also challenge women's alleged responsibility for rape. As one of the interlocutors argued:

> We particularly fought against the concept of the limits of male self-restraint; sexologists often argued that there is a certain border and after crossing it nothing could be done. This thinking is very dangerous for women. And the concept of provocation that translates into women's responsibility in the field of sexuality. We tried to explain how dangerous this thinking is. A lot of us had the experience of a situation which was sexually extreme when suddenly the parents come home. In such a situation, there isn't any border of self-restraint, the lover just hides in the closet. I'm joking of course, but this border was justifying rape, it was dumping responsibility for rape and men's sexual behavior in general on women.

The feminist approach refutes the understanding of women's agency, according to which it is women who control the way men act during sex (and more generally in the family). Furthermore, it contests identifying some survivors as worthy and others as unworthy of protection, as described in sexological works such as *The Art of Love* (Wisłocka 1978). This perspective is perfectly illustrated in the Feminoteka Foundation's "10 Tips on How to Prevent Rape"—all of which are addressed to men (Piotrowska and Synakiewicz 2011, cover).

Interviewees who were involved in rape prevention efforts argued that women have the right to withdraw from an erotic situation at any time or to consent to one sexual behavior but not to another. What is more, *no* cannot be interpreted to mean *yes,* they argue. One of the interlocutors notes that this makes for a serious problem in the courtroom: "So there are also these very deep evaluations of consent—what constitutes consent. Is it a set of behaviors, nonverbal communication, elements of the outfit, or maybe is it the context that allows someone to think that a woman is consenting to sex? In these situations, you have to work hard to prove that it was rape." At the same time, for these activists, organizing against violence is accompanied by the affirmation of female sexuality expressed through the slogan "Yes means yes!" borrowed from North American feminists (Friedman and Valenti 2008). This translates to an understanding of rape as an attack on the sexual autonomy of the subject (Płatek 2010, 368). As the feminist expert in criminal law, Monika Płatek, notes, "Autonomy requires that three conditions be simultaneously fulfilled: the internal possibility to make responsible, mature, and rational choices, the external freedom from pressure and restriction, and finally, the bodily integrity of an individual. To approach rape in terms of sexual autonomy allows for seeing that it is a crime, in which sexual behavior is used to impose one's power upon another person" (2010, 368n63; see also Płatek 2005). From this perspective, rape occurs not only when the victim resists but also when she does not give her informed consent. This perspective is based on an understanding of agency as limited by social and cultural conditions (see also Cowan 2007).

Another feature of the feminist perspective on sexual violence, as presented by the interlocutors, calls attention to the survivors and their suffering. It aims to give them voice, as in the report published by the Feminoteka Foundation (Piotrowska and Synakiewicz 2011). An interview partner discussed the damage that women experience as a result of rape and how health-care services, law enforcement, and the justice system exacerbate that damage. I have already discussed examples described by my interview partners in which the police or doctors proved particularly incompetent and harmful. The feminist experts also point to the difficult situation that survivors face in court. As noted by a lawyer from an organization that assists survivors of violence:

> If we are talking about emotions, corporality, about sexuality, the more we go into intimacy, the more difficult it is to express it all, at that point the [judicial process] is already very, very brutal; it requires a lot of determination. I personally think that without psychological support it is virtually impossible to go through. . . . That psychological support does not always have to come from a professional psychologist, it can be the family that stands solidly beside the victim . . . and in those moments of doubt it supports her, but if that family is not there, then it's really hard.

Survivors who are emotionally unstable find the reality of the courtroom difficult: "These women say that they have the impression that the court is judging them, whether they deserve it or not, whether they did something that might have given permission to it," continued the interlocutor. She pointed to an issue that was also evident in the cases presented: "Provocation, or as I said, the assumption that she might have provoked it with the way she was dressed . . . in rape cases it happens that suddenly the trial takes an unexpected turn, meaning we start to focus on where she went, with whom she went there, how she went there, how she was dressed. . . . This might also be the role of the defense, to lead the court astray to matters, which theoretically should not have any meaning." She added, "Most of the judges, I think, are inclined to consider such questions that maybe in fact she did something that incited this aggression. There's often that innocent question, like for example: 'And what, in your opinion ma'am, might have made him react like this?' An innocent question, it cannot be said that it's taken out of context, or that the judge offended her, or violated something."

For the new experts, the legal process is also important from a therapeutic point of view. As one of the psychologists said, "My conviction is that if you do not start legal action in parallel, which takes the social form of reconstructing the rape as a crime, then the victim gets so caught up in guilt and in searching for her own agency by blaming herself that she is practically unable to go through therapy." For this reason, the new experts I spoke with encourage women to file motion to prosecute offenders. Some activists even believe that "therapy is a sort of cultural fraud" because it excludes the social dimension and privatizes rape. As an expert said in an interview:

> Women do not want to go to the police or reveal it. Therapy is very difficult in these cases because as a matter of fact it's hard for me to analyze early childhood relations with victims of rape. Because I think it's not like her relationship with her mother, father or brother led in the long run to her being raped . . . I also worked in a psychiatric hospital, I did different things in my life, so I know that it's not that I suck at being a therapist in this sense, because I know there are people I can work with. And with victims of rape, whether it is the specificity of the relationship that I develop with these women, whether it is the specificity of my ambivalence, whether it's them, I just can't, you know.

Even though as feminists they advocate the prosecution of perpetrators, knowing how difficult the entire police-judicial procedure is for the survivor, the female activists were not certain whether they themselves would decide to press charges in case of rape. One interview participant recalled, "Once five of us did a project together. Sharp witted, we were all used to talking back, each one of us was well educated, for years in all those women's organizations, so for us it was full speed ahead. It turned out later when we got to talking that two of us had been raped in that five-person group. . . . So we asked ourselves, would we press charges today if something like that happened to us, and all of us said 'no.'" Another interviewee, a therapist and a feminist, put it this way:

I think it's impossible to heal if you don't file for prosecution. I mean that it's just such a nasty kind of trauma, so complicated, recurring, strong and chronic, that simply for therapeutic reasons it's necessary to go through the whole ordeal. On the other hand, when you see what we saw going around to the police stations, when you see how harsh it all is in reality; when you drive out to say [a suburb of a big city], when you see the police station there, the sergeant with a mustache . . . it's just so dramatic to confront it all that I understand people who just don't want to go ahead with it. I understand them.

These statements again raise the question of individual agency and challenge understanding it as full responsibility or control. To contend that therapy is a "cultural fraud" implies a refusal to equate agency with guilt and responsibility for male sexuality. Therapy without trial puts the burden on the victim: she was raped and now she must heal. Meanwhile, in the approach proposed by these new experts, it is not she who needs to be repaired but the culture and community responsible for the violence, which is structural (Farmer 1996).

Some organizations that provide aid for rape survivors run court watch programs. A representative of such an institution accompanies the survivor during trial. One of the interviewees, a lawyer, talked about the case of a sixteen-year-old girl who was repeatedly gang raped by her male friends. In her case, the issue of provocation came up. The prosecutor in charge of the case told her, "You were drinking with them, so . . . if you went out with the likes of them, then you were asking for it." Nonetheless, the perpetrators were charged, arrested, and then convicted. The interview partner noted how the survivor had perceived the trial:

She said that she was very afraid, that she did not know where or how it would happen, that they would laugh at her and we went to court with her for the first time then, that was a few years ago already. I went to court with her, we found the room where it would be, we waited for another trial to end, I asked if we could stay for a while and told them what this was about, no problem, I said: see here the judge will sit here, you will be here, you'll come in, here is your place, here's the prosecutor's, here is the podium, if you stand at a certain angle, you won't even see them. . . . She was afraid because she had never been in this situation before.

In short, women involved in survivor support understand rape as an act of violence bolstered by patriarchal culture. They believe that women have the right to sexual autonomy, that is, to say "no," regardless of the situation. They question the claim that men are unable to control their lust. They do not divide survivors up into those who are worthy or unworthy of protection. They call attention to their suffering during and after rape, and try to give survivors a voice. They do not define agency in terms of guilt and responsibility.

Although Polish feminism of the early 1990s is associated mainly with the fight for abortion—and, indeed, it was this struggle that drew people to activism at the time—violence was already an issue that activists were taking up in this period. One of the first feminist publications, for instance, Urszula Masny-Sokołowska's (1993) text entitled "Cases of Rape in Poland," was featured in the volume published after a conference organized by the newly funded Polish Feminist Association in spring 1993 in Mądralin, not far from Warsaw.[3]

At the beginning of the 1990s, Masny-Sokołowska, a Polish sociologist of law who worked in the United States, conducted interviews with judges, observed court cases, and analyzed files. The materials she gathered show clearly that despite progressive law, the situation of rape victims in court is deplorable. Although the penal code of 1969, in force at the time, defined the crime of rape as a crime against liberty, some judges interviewed by Masny-Sokołowska saw it differently:

> To my question, how is rape defined in Polish law, one judge responded to my surprise, I quote: "it is a crime, the act of releasing sexual tension, sexual pressure [accumulated] in the attacker." I wanted to make sure that in his opinion, the Polish criminal code defined rape in this way. He said yes. I asked if the Polish penal code defines rape as a sexual crime. He replied yes. Then I pulled out the code and showed him the definition of rape. He was a judge of the regional court with ten years of service under his belt. He was surprised that rape was defined as a crime against liberty, and that there was nothing in the code about the release of sexual pressure that accumulates in a man. As he told me earlier, men are very easily sexually aroused and from time to time, they have to find an outlet for their emotions. (1993, 37)

The same was true during the court trials that Masny-Sokołowska observed, where men were treated as sexually hyperactive and easily provoked by women: "One judge allowed the defense to ask a question about the victim's past sexual life: was she a virgin? He also allowed a question about how she was dressed. I asked him later why. 'We live in a certain environment,' he said, 'and it is obvious that if a woman acts a certain way, then it is assumed in our society that she wants it at this moment'" (37).

In the interviews that Masny-Sokołowska conducted, just as in the cases that I examined, rape appears as a strictly sexual act: "Several judges claimed that rape is a specific type of sexual act that does not bring women satisfaction, which is why women who want to punish men report the matter to court. This claim was posited by judges of both sexes. One female judge told me that rape cases are very strange cases, they're about sex after all, while feelings should be treated differently" (Masny-Sokołowska 1993, 38).

Masny-Sokołowska called attention to what also stands out in the publications and cases subject to analysis in this book—in the eyes of lawyers, only certain types of survivors deserve protection:

> A woman has a certain role to play, she is bound by certain social norms, transgression of this role, violation of these norms justifies carrying out a crime on her. If a woman was drinking alcohol with a rapist, she was at his house, she had on a "skimpy" outfit: all this is taken into account not in establishing guilt, but in the punishment. . . . Generally, the best type of rape victim would be a virgin who goes somewhere, preferably to see her sick grandmother, she's bringing her food, of

course, preferably during the day (because the evening raises doubts), she must pass through the park and some pervert drags her into the bushes and rapes her. Then it is clear that it was rape. In other circumstances the case is very unclear. (1993, 37–38)

References to her research can be found in the press. For example, *The Krakow Gazette* (*Gazeta Krakowska*) describes the story of a thirteen-year-old girl raped by three young men aged fifteen and sixteen: "Her mother reported the case to the prosecutor's office. The thirteen-year-old rape victim was the subject of observation and psychological examination. It was found that the rape occurred as a result of the girl's provocation. The boys' reactions were described as normal" (Cwynar 1993). The author of the article refers to Masny-Sokołowska: "In cases of rape, the court takes into account such elements as: the way the woman was dressed, if she previously had sexual relations with other men, or if the situation in which she found herself, could have provoked the man in some way" (Cwynar 1993).

The fact that the media wrote about Masny-Sokołowska's report was no coincidence. From the beginning, institutions and associations that worked toward supporting survivors tried to establish cooperation with other experts and to promote the feminist perspective (also in the media). They organized trainings, invited people from outside the feminist circle to their conferences (including sexologists), and tried to share their reflections with personal contacts. Such exchanges took place during the Mądralin conference. As mentioned, among the participants at that conference was Anna Sierzpowska, who served at the time as a liaison between these milieus. Sexologists continue to be invited to conferences organized by feminist organizations. Often they take active part in discussions during such meetings, although this participation does not mean that they fully embrace the feminist perspective.[4] Feminists, in turn, attend sexological events, also in the role of discussion panelists (see chap. 5). I have already described the feminist influence on courses in forensic sexology. In the interviews, many sexologists spoke about feminist theories with appreciation, although critical voices were equally frequent. Either way, there is cooperation and dialogue between these thought collectives. The aim that the feminist interview partners mentioned has at least partially been achieved. Furthermore, the new experts have begun to make more frequent media appearances (see Kościańska 2012*d*). In effect, feminists contributed to the change in discourse about rape.

Starting in the 1990s, experts more frequently zeroed in on the issue of harmful stereotypes in the press. They turned the problem into a public issue and rebuked ideas about women's coresponsibility for rape. They spoke out about victims being held responsible by police and judges for allegedly provoking rape and about how victims were questioned regarding their sex lives (see, e.g., Miklaszewska 1999). Psychologists and sexologists began to make a stand in the feminist spirit. For example, Agnieszka Widera-Wysoczańska (2000), a psychologist and forensic expert, contended, "In the case of rape, the victim is always without guilt. Women can dress as they want, go where they want. . . . For the rapist, the woman's appearance makes no difference." Maria Bik-Matuszczyk, a sexologist, noted that she keeps hearing that women want to be taken by force, but this, in her opinion, is not true, as no one gains pleasure from being the victim of crime (Berezowski 1997). In turn, Sierzpowska called into question another stereotype by explaining that wives are also raped by husbands who are decent and well-educated citizens (Nowacka 1996).

Zbigniew Izdebski (2005), a well-known sex researcher and educator, also took a firm stand. He argued that "we are slaves to stereotypes":

> Every woman has the right to dress and act the way she wants. Of course, a man can interpret certain behaviors as consent to sexual relations. But when a woman says "no," that means "no." . . . There is no justification for rape. Of course, such behavior [the question concerned agreeing to a ride home from a man she just met] can be considered risky, but certainly we cannot say that the woman was guilty. She was perhaps imprudent, naïve, or too trusting. But on the other hand, it is not advisable to treat every new person like a rapist.

Izdebski linked the fact that 80 percent of rape victims do not report to the police with widespread stereotypes.

Sexologists also speak out more frequently about the consequences. For example, Alicja Długołęcka argued that "date rape often takes place at parties where there is alcohol and drugs. The girl is in love, in the romantic phase, and is forced to have sex by her boyfriend. How can she admit to it? Because she did want something, but not that. These stories often come out later, when working with adult women who only years later are able to admit to themselves what had really happened and cure their trauma" (quoted in Podgórska 2008).

Even experts who previously reiterated stereotypes about provocation now turn their attention to survivors. Lew-Starowicz discusses in detail the consequences of rape and how survivors should be treated in the aftermath. He points out that common beliefs clearly increase their suffering: "One of the reasons why the consequences of rape are so hard to get rid of are the widespread stereotypes about rape, for example: 'if the woman does not want it, she will not be raped,' or 'women provoke rape' and etc. It is not surprising then that many women feel complicit or encounter distrust on the part of people in their immediate surroundings" (Lew-Starowicz 1995).

In an extended interview in 2011, Barbara Kasprzycka asked Lew-Starowicz, "When a man says 'no,' does he always have 'no' in mind?" The sexologist replied, "Yes, that is just obvious obviousness." Then she asked, "But it is assumed that when a woman says 'no,' she means 'maybe.'" Lew-Starowicz replied:

> True, at a certain stage of the sexual game, men do not take women's words directly. Meanwhile, just like the feminists, I think that a woman has the right to say "no" on any level of her sexual contact with a man. Many men still think that after crossing a certain boundary, she loses that right. Men can no longer hold themselves back. What's more, they know that women often say "no" because they feel guilty.

Meaning she takes it to a bed situation, then begins to withdraw, subconsciously hoping that her resistance will be broken. After this type of sex, she will feel that she is not guilty, that she was forced. And with such conviction she will feel better. There are women who tell their partners with a smile on their face: "But you raped me, you had your way with me." And men in general understand perfectly how this game works. (Lew-Starowicz 2011a, 56–57)

An evolution in the perspective of the most important Polish sexologist is discernable here. Not only does he explicitly refer to feminist thought, but he now considers the concept of the male limits of self-restraint, which he once promoted himself, somewhat outdated.

In the interview for the *The Krakow Gazette* conducted in the mid-1990s, Hanausek likewise talks about rape a little differently than he did in the book *Rapes*. He notes that an important factor is "the conviction, common among many men, that they have unbelievably good looks, which no woman can resist. . . . I would not go so far as to talk about the complicity of the women who are raped. But in many cases the victim undoubtedly contributes to rape in some way. Often unconsciously" (quoted in Lubaś-Harny 1995).

In previous decades, the press often published advice for women on how to avoid rape. This usually boiled down to not going out after dark (e.g., Mierzejewska 1984). With the advent of a new discourse, female readers can now learn about their rights in case of rape (Pol 2002). Experts and the journalists who talk about them continuously criticize the courts for heeding stereotypes. They point out that women tend to become victims all over again during the investigation proceedings and the trial: "Have you ever worn shorts? Did you have on leather underwear? You weren't wearing a bra? Did you have too much alcohol to drink? Were you dancing seductively at the night club? Were you seeing a therapist? You didn't pass to the next grade? Did you use contraception? If the answer is yes, and you were raped, each of these things can be used against you in court" (*Marie Claire*'s editorial staff 2004). Feminist Joanna Piotrowska encourages women to be forthright about what they want and to refuse decisively when they do not want something (Podgórska 2008). Finally, as I already mentioned, in the Feminoteka Foundation's report, prepared by Piotrowska, advice is addressed to men, thus redefining agency and removing responsibility from women:

1. If a woman says "no," then that means "no." 2. Don't put drugs in women's drinks. 3. When you see a woman walking alone, leave her alone. 4. The fact that you helped someone repair a car does not give you the right to have sex in return. 5. Don't try to explain your aggression toward others by saying that they were the ones who provoked you. 6. The elevator is not a boxing ring, don't attack in it. 7. REMEMBER! You cannot have sex with someone who's sleeping or unconscious. That's not sex—it's rape! 8. Sex that a woman does not consent to is rape. 9. Treat other women the way you would like your male friends to treat your loved ones: your girlfriend, sister or mother. 10. Don't rape. Don't be the one who does it. (Piotrowska and Synakiewicz 2011, cover)

Changes in the Courtroom

A change in discourse has also taken place in the courtroom. The cases presented already suggest this change to some extent. Notably, in the fourth case described, the prosecution argued that the plaintiff's previous sexual experiences had nothing to do with the rape, thereby negating the categorization of survivors as worthy and unworthy of protection. There was also a consensus as to the fact that the survivor's undergoing therapy made her version credible. The same shift is evident in other cases that I analyzed and in the jurisprudence of the courts of appeals and the Supreme Court. A 2003 trial involving an incident from 1993 (the perpetrator was at large for ten years) is a good example. Five men drove up to the bus stop in a car and offered two young women, one of whom was the girlfriend of one of the guys, a lift. Instead of going home, however, they took them to the forest and gang raped them. Three of the men were charged based on Article 168. Two were sentenced to three years in prison. The third went into hiding. When he was finally brought to trial after ten years, he was convicted. In this case, the court interpreted the survivors' psychological disorders and their emotions in the courtroom totally differently than in the first case I described in chapter 8. The judges no longer questioned the survivors' credibility. The verdict justification for this case reads: "Crimes of rape are crimes of exceptional gravity, among others due to the enormous psychological burden that the victims are left with and the fact that they find it extremely difficult not only to wipe such incidents from memory, but also to gain distance from them. Rape leaves a mark on the psyche, which usually constitutes a burden for the rest of the victim's life. The victim's tear-filled reaction . . . in the course of testifying ten years after the incident was only an external, but how significant an expression of this burden."

The issue of resistance is also approached differently. In the justification of a 2000 conviction, the judge wrote that typically in cases of gang rape, "not all the accomplices must encounter the victim's resistance directly. This does not imply her consent to the perpetrators' actions, but only that her resistance was broken earlier . . . [Another accomplice], in satisfying his sex drive, does not encounter the victim's resistance (OSNPG 1972, No. 8, item 128)." The court wrote further, "Even if her resistance declined at times, this was as the effect of an assessment of the situation, in accordance with which, afraid of further beating, as she stated directly, she ceased to resist actively." This argumentation definitively contrasts with that forwarded in the first case I described.

Importantly, courts are increasingly assessing the reality of what happened from the survivor's perspective. As noted in the justification of a 2008 verdict that called on the Supreme Court's decisions, a victim does not know what intentions the perpetrator has—for example, she does not know whether or not he intends to carry out his threats.[5] Jurisprudence established in the appellate courts also suggests that the victim's resistance can be understood in various ways: "In order to consider that rape crime took place, any visible resistance on the victim's part indicative of her lack of will to engage in intercourse is sufficient."[6] This comment denotes a broader understanding of resistance than, for example, Leszczyński's (1973, 91–92) interpretation presented in his influential book.[7] According to another verdict of the appellate court in Katowice, violence does not necessarily lead to physical wounds. This verdict simultaneously brings to light the matter of sexual freedom:

> The criminal act defined in Article 197 of the penal code constitutes an assault on a victim's sexual liberty and does not have to bring about bodily injuries in the event of rape. So long as the victim's lack of consent was externalized, rationally in proportion to the force used against her, then the act fulfills the definition of this crime. The victim's resistance does not have to involve physical opposition to the means of force used by the perpetrator. Depending on the situation, the externalization of that resistance, perceivable to the perpetrator, may be reduced to other forms such as crying, verbal statements, jerking away or attempts to call for help. If the accused were aware that they were dealing with a helpless and a very young person, whom they physically dominated, then in keeping that in mind along with the fact that the place was alien to the victim, it must be asserted that they did not have to use excessive force to overcome her resistance to have sex with them, which she manifested in a way available to her.[8]

The Supreme Court also decided in a similar vein:

> The evidence collected indicates that the defendant forcibly spread the victim's legs apart, simultaneously put his hands under her skirt and touched her pubic area through her underwear, then unzipped his pants, and finally, undressed himself naked. Regarding the second victim, he pulled her towards him, sat her on his knees, unbuttoned her blouse, touched her breasts (through her underwear), touched her buttocks (through her skirt), and embraced her. The court's argumentation that "these incidents did not take on a serious form, and that their occurrence did not bring about highly negative effects (both in the psychological and physical sphere) for the victims themselves" and that "the defendant did not see the victims naked" or that "none of the victims suffered even the slightest physical injury," are not arguments that allow for accepting that his behavior toward the women he assaulted was of negligible social harm.[9]

The courts tend to understand rape as a strictly sexual offense, which Masny-Sokołowska's research showed so succinctly and that can be observed in almost all of the cases I analyzed in my own research. To some extent, this definition was strengthened by the 1997 penal code, in which rape was categorized in the section on crimes against sexual liberty and decency (in the 1969 code, rape was located in the section concerning crimes against liberty). Nonetheless, conceptualizations of rape do exist that go beyond the satisfaction of the sexual needs of rapists. For example, in the 2008 verdict justification of one of the cases I examined, there are considerations about complicity. According to the court, to be guilty of the crime, a perpetrator does not even have to engage in intercourse with the victim: "The essence of gang rape does not boil down to all those involved engaging in sexual intercourse with the victim." It suffices that, for example, one had intercourse while the rest of them held the victim down.[10]

It is worth noting that judges' considerations of the victims' perspectives often refer to Supreme Court decisions from the 1970s. Perhaps earlier there was a lack of a discursive context, or a thought collective, that would strengthen such interpretations. The same justification cites the verdict passed by the appellate court in Katowice, which found that the perpetrator is not only whoever engages in or intends to engage in intercourse but also whoever "uses force to bring, or tries to bring the victim to submit to sexual intercourse, even involving another perpetrator. It is the very assault on the *victim's sexual liberty*, carried out using means such as force, that defines the crime of rape, and not the perpetrator's pursuit to satisfy his own sex drive" (emphasis added).[11] In the context of the case in which the court passed the above verdict, this meant that even the victim's "girlfriends" who handed her over to the rapists (which they justified by explaining that they wanted the victim to have a bad reputation) were complicit in her rape. Such reasoning reveals a new interpretation of the crime of rape, which has evolved independently of penal code reform. Masny-Sokołowska showed that although in the early 1990s rape was defined as an assault on liberty, judges understood it in a strictly sexual context. The same was striking in the cases from the 1980s presented in chapter 8. The approach to the matter is completely different in the verdict justification cited above. The 1997 reformed penal code speaks explicitly about the sexual aspect of rape (a crime against sexual liberty and decency), but the judges focus rather on the aspect of autonomy.[12]

A verdict passed by the appellate court in Katowice on June 19, 2008, also points to the nonsexual motives for rape and centers on the victim's sexual freedom:

> The concept of the crime of rape, to which the provision mentioned before refers as an assault on the victim's sexual liberty, includes the sexual activities referred to in paragraph 1 and 2 of Article 197 of the penal code. At least two perpetrators must cooperate to commit this crime. They do not have to be motivated by the desire to satisfy their sex drives, instead their crime may be associated with their desire to humiliate the victim. The perpetrator of the act referred to in paragraphs 1 and 3 of Article 197 of the penal code may also be anyone who uses force, illegal threat, or deceit directed at the victim to force her to submit to a sex act in the presence of the aggressors, even though they might not have physical contact with the victim themselves. This behavior constitutes "subjecting another person to sexual intercourse," steering in this way the victims to take part in acts against their will.[13]

The Supreme Court further develops the concept of the victim's sexual freedom:

> The perpetrator's pursuit to satisfy his sex drive does not constitute the crime of rape (Article 168 of the 1969 penal code, respectively: Article 197 of the [1997] penal code). To recognize that in his deed, the perpetrator exhausted the definition of this crime, important is not the aim in which the perpetrator acted, but whether or not his actions, in accordance with the statutory description, constituted an assault on the victim's sexual liberty. Assault on sexual liberty occurs not only when the

victim does not consent to sexual intercourse, but also when her lack of consent refers to the manner in which the perpetrator executes this act.[14]

The courts of appeals also pay attention to how survivors behave after rape. In the third case discussed in chapter 8, an argument used against the victim was that she was partying after the incident, as one witness testified. Only the expert opinions, which explained that this behavior may be typical in reaction to violence, managed to convince the judges. The appellate court in Katowice ruled in a similar vein on October 30, 2008:

> It is difficult to qualify the behavior of a rape victim, especially of a minor, that has a personal context and is different each time. An incident of this sort may lead one to shut themselves up to the world, or on the contrary, to make attempts at turning the unpleasant memories into something insignificant and pushing them aside into the background. As mentioned above, the issues under discussion are individual, fully dependent on the degree of emotional development and on the victim's personality predispositions, as well as on the social environment from which the victim derives. Bearing in mind the above considerations, it was necessary to accept that the attitude taken on by the victim was her defensive reaction, mistakenly assessed by her girlfriends as a form of acceptance or approval of the whole event.[15]

Clearly, the formal and informal efforts of feminists to modify expert thought style and change the understanding and way of talking about rape—to take into account the experiences of women, to stop dividing victims into those worthy and unworthy of protection, to not equate agency with guilt, and to give voice to survivors—have proven successful at least in part. Although the authors of the Feminoteka Foundation's report (Piotrowska and Synakiewicz 2011) argue that the situation of rape survivors is very difficult, a comparison of more recent cases, jurisprudence, and expert discourse to the judicial practices of the 1980s and the work of lawyers and sexologists from the 1970s and 1980s highlights the positive changes that have taken place. These changes were possible thanks to the dialogical nature of Polish socialist sexology and to the work of women's organizations. This work has included a focus on matters such as defining agency, understanding resistance, drawing distinctions among victims based on their sexual experiences, positioning them in the sexual hierarchy, understanding the importance of suffering, and addressing the question of the sexual or other character of rape. This last issue has evolved somewhat independently of legal provisions: the 1969 code defined rape as a crime against liberty, but in legal practice, it was treated as strictly sexual. Although the 1997 regulations directly associate rape with sex, the aspect of liberty is emphasized and the nonsexual elements tend to be articulated in accordance with the feminist perspective.

Notes

1. Other sources of this change can also be identified: the influence of pop culture, "Western" scientific theories, and human rights discourse. Still, even here, feminism

played an important role. In particular, I mean Western feminisms, mainly American, and their impact on science, popular culture, and antidiscrimination activism in Western Europe and the United States. It was also through these channels that the feminist message about sexual violence reached Poland (on feminist knowledge transfer, see, e.g., Bustelo, Ferguson, and Maxime 2016).

2. An example is Urszula Nowakowska from the Center for Women's Rights Center (Nowacka 1996).

3. A report on the subject of rape was published at the same time by Beata Fiszer of the Polish Feminist Association for the Federation for Women and Family Planning.

4. For example, during a press conference promoting the Feminoteka Foundation's report, sexologists accused the authors of methodological errors, discrediting the qualitative approach (Warsaw, November 29, 2011).

5. 17.04.97, II KKN 171/96, and 26/02/1973, III KR 284/72.

6. II AKa 305/08, court of appeals decision of October 30, 2008, Katowice, LEX No. 477649.

7. The 2001 Supreme Court decision gives an example of an indirect form of resistance (V KKN 95/99, Supreme Court decision of July 26, 2001, LEX No. 51671): "When the perpetrator of the crime of rape uses 'force,' the form of externalizing disagreement should be a certain, related to the proportion of strength on both sides, degree of resistance on the part of the victim, although resistance does not have to solely involve physical opposition to the means of force used by the perpetrator (for example: loud calling for help, screaming, crying, etc. is enough). The externalization of resistance by the victim in a manner clearly perceivable to the perpetrator and unequivocal in its meaning, is of particular importance in situations where the perpetrator may assume that the resistance is unreal and constitutes, for example, a form of love game."

8. II AKa 72/09, court of appeals decision of April 8, 2009, Katowice, KZS 2009/9/65. See also II KK 97/08; Supreme Court decision, November 13, 2008, LEX No. 485013: "The lack of gynecological injuries does not indicate that rape did not take place."

9. WA 28/07, Supreme Court decision, July 18, 2007, OSNwSK 2007/1/1683.

10. Reference was made here to the Supreme Court's decisions of November 6, 1970, III KR 170/70, OSNPG 1971, No. 2, item 35, and from February 11, 1971, I KR 220/70, OSNKW 1971, No. 7–8, item 112.

11. II Aka 61/02, KZS 2002/11/28.

12. It is worth noting that Makarewicz, the author of 1932 penal code, wrote about the fact that a woman can rape another woman by "giving her" to a man, but his interpretation did not consider the issue of sexual autonomy (see chap. 6, n. 4).

13. II AKa 147/08 court of appeals decision June 19, 2008, Katowice, KZS 2008/9/53.

14. II KKN 349/98, Supreme Court decision April 9, 2001, OSNKW 2001/78/53.

15. II AKa 305/08, court of appeals decision October 30, 2008, in Katowice, Biul. SAKa 2008/4/8.

Conclusions

In her search for an answer as to why women have better sex under socialism, Kristen Ghodsee (2017) argued that economic independence, access to knowledge in the field of sex education, and access to birth control are conducive to women's sexual satisfaction:

> Although gender wage disparities and labor segregation persisted, and although the Communists never fully reformed domestic patriarchy, Communist women enjoyed a degree of self-sufficiency that few Western women could have imagined. Eastern bloc women did not need to marry, or have sex, for money. The socialist state met their basic needs and countries such as Bulgaria, Poland, Hungary, Czechoslovakia and East Germany committed extra resources to support single mothers, divorcées and widows. With the noted exceptions of Romania, Albania and Stalin's Soviet Union, most Eastern European countries guaranteed access to sex education and abortion. This reduced the social costs of accidental pregnancy and lowered the opportunity costs of becoming a mother.

As already mentioned, her article—reprinted in many languages—incited global outrage, especially in the United States. Commentators outdid themselves in ridiculing Ghodsee's arguments, completely ignoring North American experts on sexual pleasure like Tiefer, who generally agree that for women, birth control, knowledge, and economic independence from men favor greater pleasure.

My research shows that a specific model of the development of sexology (which constitutes the basis of not only therapy but also sex education) could be observed in state-socialist Poland: one that was open to the needs of patients, holistic, and rooted in the humanities. Such an approach to the matter raises doubts among those who think about socialism through a totalitarian lens. For example, the achievements of socialism are not valued by some feminists in the West. As Ghodsee (2017) observed, "Some liberal feminists in the West . . . were critical of the achievements of state socialism because they did not emerge from independent women's movements, but represented a type of emancipation from above. Many academic feminists today celebrate choice but also embrace a cultural relativism dictated by the imperatives of intersectionality. Any top-down political program that seeks to impose a universalist set of values like equal rights for women is seriously out of fashion."

Doubts are also voiced in Poland, but they concern the heritage of state socialism—namely, sexuality in the country today. During the Fourth National Debate on Sexual Health in November 2011, Zbigniew Izdebski, a researcher of sexuality who specializes in the quantitative approach, presented another set of findings on sexuality in the country. The results were surprising. The vast majority of respondents gave an extraordinarily positive assessment of their sex lives. For example, only 7 percent of women said that they have problems achieving orgasm, whereas North American studies point to 30–40 percent of women having this dysfunction.[1] During the debate that accompanied the research presentation, the invited guests—who included doctors, sociologists, and feminists—received the results with disbelief and drew attention to the still very low aspirations of Poles in this regard. One of the panelists, leading Polish feminist Kazimiera Szczuka, called it a "sexual Soplicowo."[2] Yet if we assume, in following Michel Foucault, that expert discourse construes sexuality and creates a framework in which we experience pleasure, then research on the history of sexology might suggest a somewhat different interpretation. Thanks to the fact that discourse on sexuality formed for many years outside the influence of the market—away from erotica, pornography, and the "pursuit of orgasm" so omnipresent today and instead with emphasis on relationships and sociocultural conditions—subsequent generations of Poles became immune to the currently dominant physiological, biomedicalized, and commodified (Clarke, Shim, at al. 2010a; Fishman 2004) models of sexuality. These generations located pleasure not in the reactions of the body but in the nonmeasurable experiences of a different kind, such as the emotional—confused by Izdebski's respondents with orgasm.

Beginning in the 1970s, Poles read the works of experts who described sexuality in a holistic and interdisciplinary fashion. These texts were often written in response to readers' own concerns expressed in letters and included advice not only on sex but on life in general. This discourse engendered specific assessments of sexual life that proved so surprising to commentators.

As I have shown, this dialogic, contextual, and interdisciplinary nature, drawn from interactions with multiple thought collectives, distinguished Polish from mainstream North American sexology and had its own brighter and darker sides. It cannot be unambiguously described as progressive or conservative. Its development was neither unilinear nor organized in "pockets" of gender equality and sexual liberation (on similar dynamics in Czechoslovakia, see Lišková 2018). In the 1970s and 1980s, sexology made it possible to understand sexuality under specific cultural, social, relational, and psychological conditions; this is what feminist sexologists are currently calling for in the United States. Expert works articulated the concerns of patients and provided answers. They assured readers that sex is "healthy" and "normal" behavior that plays an important role in building relationships and ensuring happiness, both personal and in the family. Nevertheless, Polish sexologists advocated procreative intercourse within marriage based on traditional gender roles, seeing it as the essence of good sex. They highlighted its pivotal location in the sexual hierarchy, pointing to various limitations of other forms of intimate life. At the same time, they convinced readers and patients who experienced orgasm by stimulating the clitoris and who were afraid that their sensations deviated from the norm that this type of orgasm was nothing to worry about. They took up social issues widely and, above all, tried to find answers to contradictory messages related to the socialist emancipation of women. On the one hand, women were encouraged to work; on the other hand, equal sharing of household duties between the genders was not promoted. This situation brought on the double burden for women, an effect of which was their chronic exhaustion. Patients and readers claimed that too many duties and too little time made women lose interest in sex. Therefore, doctors tried to solve their problems. Accordingly, they proposed a return to the so-called traditional gender roles. As I have shown, it was difficult to come up with a different answer: Polish expert discourse on sexuality of that time did not have a feminist perspective. Even though women's organizations were active, they usually did not address issues of sexuality, and even if they did, gender emancipation was not linked with sexual liberation.

The structure of the Polish school of sexology, or sexological thought style, proved resilient to biomedicalization. It did not lose its identity with the end of the Cold War, even though it did integrate some elements of North American biomedical sexology and even as doctors use Viagra and other drugs for sexual problems with success in their therapy. Psychology still plays an important role and codefines the mainstream of sexology in Poland. Sexologists also try to place the sexual problems of their patients in the context of neoliberal reality, which demands even more of women (and men) than socialism did. Now, however, the social solutions they propose are more complex. The interdisciplinary nature of sexology also implies openness to feminist and queer theory. It connotes dialogue with activist communities, which have been trying to influence sexology in both formal and informal ways since the second half of the 1980s. This alternative expert discourse is increasingly gaining importance. As I have attempted to show, because of the humanist tradition of mainstream sexology, the alternative expert discourse is less exposed to the process of biomedicalization and the threat of being co-opted by medical discourse (in comparison with the United States; Clarke, Shim, et al. 2010a). It also stands a real chance of actually transforming the mainstream approach.

But let us not idealize Polish sexology of the socialist era, as did the producers of the biographical film about Wisłocka. There is no simple interpretation of the relationship between sexuality and socialism. Methods applied by sexologists in their work, which spoke to the strength of this discipline in Poland, also brought unintended consequences. In effect, Polish sexology is rampant with stereotypes, especially of gender (even though sexologists considered themselves the progressive opponents of all stereotypes). Answers to the concerns of patients and readers were sought in culture, which further reinforced stereotypical thinking (e.g., the proposed return to traditional gender roles as a solution to the problem of women's double burden). Perhaps a Masters and Johnson–style laboratory experiment was missing that could suggest new solutions.[3] In a society that limited the freedom of speech and prohibited self-organization, critical voices were lacking. Particularly tragic consequences are, for example, the reiteration of false beliefs about rape by doctors. Worse perhaps is that these ideas were formalized as scientific concepts, as in the case of Wisłocka, who set out to prove that young men cannot stop themselves because of their hormones and high level of sexual tension.

Once a new voice and a new narrative emerged in the form of feminism, sexologists began to gradually incorporate it into the elements of a holistic understanding of sexuality, according to the principles grounded in the 1970s and 1980s. This new voice demands the reconstruction of the sexual hierarchy and the redefinition of the gender order, including the understanding of women's agency within the conceptualization of both pleasure and violence. These changes, as I have shown, are now taking place within expert discourse on sexuality, and the methodology of the Polish school of sexology facilitates that process. But the transformation of gender and sexuality will not happen overnight. The fact that they are socially constructed does not mean that they do not generate lasting identities and models (Vance 1989). The fate of these changes depends on alliances among various communities, including feminism with sexology. Such cooperation should not be too difficult: both feminism and sexology strive for women and men to enjoy successful sex lives. The different approaches to human sexuality espoused by these two communities can only enrich the spheres of knowledge and practice. A testament to their shared interest is the positive attitude of both circles to the declaration of sexual rights enacted by the World Sexological Congress. As mentioned (chap. 1), Polish readers can access this document on the websites of Polish feminist organizations , as translated into the Polish by the most important figure of national sexology, Professor Zbigniew Lew-Starowicz (2002*a*).

Notes

1. Field notes, November 23, 2011. For a discussion of American research, see, e.g., Laumann, Paik, and Rosen (1999) and resources of the Kinsey Institute (https://kinseyinstitute.org/research/faq.php, accessed May 17, 2020). For Polish research, see Izdebski (2012).

2. Soplicowo is the setting in one of the most important Polish romantic works, an epic poem by Adam Mickiewicz. In Polish culture, Soplicowo symbolizes unrealistic optimism.

3. This does not imply that sexology based on clinical trials is free of stereotypical content (see, e.g., Jordan-Young 2010, chap. 6).

WORKS CITED

Adamczyk, Joanna, trans. 2014. *The Code of Criminal Procedure*. Bilingual ed. Warszawa: Wydawnictwo C. H. Beck.

Altman, Dennis. 2001. *Global Sex*. Chicago: University of Chicago Press.

A.P. 1965. "Pornografia w filmie włoskim." *Itd*, no. 15.

APA (American Psychiatric Association). 2013. *Highlights of Changes from DSM-IV-TR to DSM-5*. Washington, DC: American Psychiatric Association.

Åsberg, Cecilia, and Ericka Johnson. 2009. "Viagra Selfhood: Pharmaceutical Advertising and the Visual Formation of Swedish Masculinity." *Health Care Analysis* 17 (2): 144–57. https://doi.org/10.1007/s10728-009-0112-5.

Attwood, Feona. 2005. "What Do People Do with Porn? Qualitative Research into the Consumption, Use, and Experience of Pornography and Other Sexually Explicit Media." *Sexuality and Culture* 9 (2): 65–86. https://doi.org/10.1007/s12119-005-1008-7.

Barker, Meg. 2012. "What Is (Normal) Sex?" Paper presented at the Sexual Culture, Theory, Practice, and Research Conference, April 20–22, Brunel University, London.

———. 2013. *Rewriting the Rules: An Integrative Guide to Love, Sex, and Relationships*. London: Routledge.

Bauer, Heike, ed. 2015. *Sexology and Translation: Cultural and Scientific Encounters across the Modern World*. Philadelphia: Temple University Press.

Bauer, Heike. 2017. *The Hirschfeld Archives: Violence, Death, and Modern Queer Culture*. Philadelphia: Temple University Press.

Bayer, Ronald. 1981. *Homosexuality and American Psychiatry: The Politics of Diagnosis*. Princeton, NJ: Princeton University Press.

Beccalossi, Chiara. 2018. "Latin Eugenics and Sexual Knowledge in Italy, Spain, and Argentina: International Networks across the Atlantic." In: *A Global History of Sexual Science, 1880–1960*, edited by Veronika Fuechtner, Douglas E. Haynes, and Ryan M. Jones, 305–330. Oakland: University of California.

Bereżnicki, Michał. 1972. "Gwałt zbiorowy." *Prawo i Życie*, no. 20.

———. 1973. "Przestępczość seksualna." *Prawo i Życie*, no. 6.

———. 1977. "W roli kryminologa." *Prawo i Życie*, no. 23.

Berezowski, Kajetan. 1997. "Gwałt co 40 minut." *Gazeta Robotnicza*, August 22.

Bernstein, Frances Lee. 2007. *The Dictatorship of Sex: Lifestyle Advice for the Soviet Masses*. DeKalb: Northen Illinois University Press.

Bielski, Marek. 2008. "Wykładnia znamion 'obcowanie płciowe' i 'inna czynność seksualna' w doktrynie i orzecznictwie sądowym." *Czasopismo Prawa Karnego i Nauk Penalnych* 12 (1): 211–230.

Bieńkowska, Ewa. 1984. *Wpływ zachowania ofiary na rozstrzygnięcie sprawy o zgwałcenie*. Wrocław: Zakład Narodowy im. Ossolińskich.

Blajer, Marek. 2011. "Zmiana jakości życia seksualnego u kobiet w okresie okołomenopauzalnym." Paper presented at the meeting of the Polish Sexological Society, October 21–23, Warsaw.

Bland, Lucy, Laura Doan, eds. 1998a. *Sexology in Culture: Labelling Bodies and Desires*. Chicago: Chicago University Press.

———. 1998b. *Sexology Uncensored: The Documents of Sexual Science*. Chicago: Chicago University Press.

Bojarska, Katarzyna. 2010. "Analiza merytoryczna wybranych pozycji piśmiennictwa poświęconego problematyce homoseksualności, wydanego w języku polskim w latach 1970–2008." In *Raport o homo-, biseksualności i transpłciowości w polskich podręcznikach akademickich*, edited by Agata Loewe, 15–63. Warszawa: Kampania Przeciw Homofobii.

Bojarska, Katarzyna, and Robert Kowalczyk. 2010. "Homoseksualność i społeczeństwo." In *Podstawy seksuologii*, edited by Zbigniew Lew-Starowicz and Violetta Skrzypulec, 34–61. Warszawa: Wydawnictwo Lekarskie PZWL.

Borkowska, Olga, and Monika Płatek. 2011. "Skala przestępstwa zgwałcenia w Polsce" In *Dość milczenia. Przemoc seksualna wobec kobiet i problem gwałtu w Polsce*, edited by Joanna Piotrowska and Alina Synakiewicz, 10–22. Warszawa: Fundacja Feminoteka. https://pl.boell.org/sites/default/files/dosc_milczenia._przemoc _seksualna_wobec_kobiet_1.pdf.

Boston Women's Health Book Collective. 1971. *Our Bodies, Ourselves*. Boston: Boston Women's Health Book Collective.

Bourke, Joanna. 2007. *Rape: Sex, Violence, History*. Berkeley, CA: Shoemaker & Hoard.

Boy-Żeleński, Tadeusz. 1930. *Piekło kobiet*. Warszawa: Wydawnictwo Alfa.

Brownmiller, Susan. 1975. *Against Our Will: Men, Women and Rape*. Harmondsworth: Penguin.

Brundtland, Gro Harlem. 2001. "Mental Health: New Understanding, New Hope." *JAMA* 286 (19): 2391. https://doi.org/10.1001/jama.286.19.2391.

Buchowski, Michał. 2006. "The Specter of Orientalism in Europe: From Exotic Other to Stigmatized Brother." *Anthropological Quarterly* 79 (3): 463–82. https://doi.org /10.1353/anq.2006.0032.

Buchowski, Michal, and Hana Cervinkova. 2015. "On Rethiniking Ethnography in Central Europe: Toward Cosmopolitan Anthropologies in the 'Peripheries.'" In *Rethinking Ethnography in Central Europe,* edited by Hana Cervinkova, Michal Buchowski, and Zdenek Uherek, 1–20. New York: Palgrave Macmillan.

Bullough, Vern L. 1994. *Science in the Bedroom*. New York: Basic.

Burszta, Jędrzej. 2019. "'Do czego się było przyznawać, jak nie istniał homoseksualizm?' Różowy język w narracjach pamięci o męskiej homoseksualności w PRL." *Inter Alia* 14: 7–27. https://interalia.queerstudies.pl/wp-content/uploads/2020/03 /burszta.pdf.

Bustelo, María, Lucy Ferguson, and Maxime Forest, eds. 2016. *The Politics of Feminist Knowledge Transfer: Gender Training and Gender Expertise*. Cham: Palgrave.

Butler, Judith. 1991. "Imitation and Gender Insubordination." In *Inside/Out: Lesbian Theories, Gay Theories*, edited by Diane Fuss, 13–31. New York: Routledge.

Canner, Liz, dir. 2009. *Orgasm Inc.* [film]. West Groton, MA: Astreamedia.

Center for Social Research on Sexuality (Ośrodek Badań Społecznych nad Seksualnością). 2013. *Seksuologia społeczna*. Warszawa: Uniwersytet Warszawski.

Chalker, Rebbeca. 2011. "The Unrecognized Post-1960s Feminist Pleasure Revolution That Transformed Sexuality for Women." Paper presented at the Western Region Annual Meeting of the Society for the Scientific Study of Sexuality, April 14–17, 2011, San Francisco.

Chałupnik, Agata. 2008. "Świadome macierzyństwo: jak skończyć z piekłem kobiet." In *Obyczaje polskiej*, edited by Małgorzata Szpakowska. Warszawa: W.A.B.

Chauchard, Paul. 1972. *Życie seksualne*, translated by Krystyna Wróblewska. Warszawa: PAX.

Chauncey, George. 1982/1983. "From Sexual Inversion to Homosexuality: Medicine and the Changing Conceptualization of Female Deviance." *Salmagundi* 58/59:114–46.

Chełstowska, Agata, Małgorzata Druciarek, Jacek Kucharczyk, and Aleksandra Niżyńska. 2013. *Relacje Państwo-Kościół w III RP*. Warszawa: Instytut Spraw Publicznych.

Clarke, Adele. 2010. "Thoughts on Biomedicalization in Its Transnational Travels." In *Biomedicalization. Technoscience, Health, and Illness in the US*, edited by Adele Clarke, Laura Mamo, Jennifer R. Fosket, Jennifer R. Fishman, and Janet K. Shim, 380–406. Durham, NC: Duke University Press.

Clarke, Adele, Laura Mamo, Jennifer R. Fosket, Jennifer R. Fishman, and Janet K. Shim, eds. 2010. *Biomedicalization. Technoscience, Health, and Illness in the US*. Durham, NC: Duke University Press.

Clarke, Adele, Janet K. Shim, Laura Mamo, Jennifer R. Fosket, and Jennifer R. Fishman. 2010*a*. "A Theoretical and Substantive Introduction." In *Biomedicalization. Thechnoscience, Health, and Illness in the U.S.*, edited by Adele Clarke, Laura Mamo, Jennifer R. Fosket, Jennifer R. Fishman, and Janet K. Shim, 1–46. Durham, NC: Duke University Press.

Clarke, Adele, Janet K. Shim, Laura Mamo, Jennifer R. Fosket, and Jennifer R. Fishman. 2010*b*. "Biomedicalization. Technoscientific Transformation of Health, Illness, and US Biomedicine." In *Biomedicalization. Technoscience, Health, and Illness in the US*, edited by Adele Clarke, Laura Mamo, Jennifer R. Fosket, Jennifer R. Fishman, Janet K. Shim, 47–87. Durham, NC: Duke University Press.

CMKP (Centrum Medyczne Kształcenia Podyplomowego; Center of Postgraduate Medical Education). 2000. *Program specjalizacji w seksuologii*. Warszawa: CMKP. www.cmkp.edu.pl/wp-content/uploads/2013/07/SeksuoProgPodst1999.pdf.

Coates, Patricia Walsh. 2008. *Margaret Sanger and the Origin of the Birth Control Movement, 1910–1930: The Concept of Women's Sexual Autonomy*. Lewiston: Edwin Mellen Press.

Cocks, H. G., and Matt Houlbrook. 2006. "Introduction." In *The Modern History of Sexuality*, edited by H. G. Cocks and Matt Houlbrrok. New York: Palgrave.

Conrad, Peter. 1979. "Types of Medical Social Control." *Sociology of Health and Illness* 1 (1): 1–11.

———. 1992. "Medicalization and Social Control." *Annual Review of Sociology* 18: 209–32.

Cowan, Sharon. 2007. "'Freedom and Capacity to Make a Choice': A Feminist Analysis of Consent in the Criminal Law of Rape." In *Sexuality and the Law: Feminist Engagements*, edited by Vanessa E. Munro and Carl F. Stychin. Abingdon: Routledge-Cavendish.

Cuklanz, Lisa M. 1996. *Rape on Trial: How the Mass Media Construct Legal Reform and Social Change*. Philadelphia: University of Pennsylvania Press.

Cwynar, Karolina. 1993. "Gwałt." *Gazeta Krakowska*, June 25.

Cybulski, Aloizy. 1973. "Wszystkie dzieci są równe." *Itd*, no. 22.

Czapczyńska, Agnieszka. 2011. "Chcę o tym zapomnieć—psychologiczne konsekwencje gwałtu." In *Dość milczenia. Przemoc seksualna wobec kobiet i problem gwałtu w Polsce*, edited by Joanna Piotrowska and Alina Synakiewicz, 97–120. Warszawa:

Fundacja Feminoteka. https://pl.boell.org/sites/default/files/dosc_milczenia._prze moc_seksualna_wobec_kobiet_1.pdf.

Dąbrowa, Kamil, host. 2011. *Popołudnie radia Tok FM. Rozmowa z drem Janem Faryną* [radio program]. Warszawa: Radio Tok FM.

Dąbrowska, Magdalena. 2012. "'Dać dowód miłości.' Dyskursy inicjacji seksualnej w polskiej prasie młodzieżowej lat osiemdziesiątych." In *Kultura popularna w Polsce w latach 1944–1989: problemy i perspektywy badawcze*, edited by Katarzyna Stańczak-Wiślicz, 152–74. Warszawa: Fundacja Akademia Humanistyczna, Instytut Badań Literackich PAN.

Daskalova, Krassimira. 2007. "How Should We Name the 'Women-Friendly' Actions of State Socialism?" *Aspasia: International Yearbook of Central, Eastern and Southeastern European Women's and Gender History* 1:214–19. https://doi.org/10.3167 /asp.2007.010113.

Depko, Andrzej. 2010. "Historia seksuologii." In *Podstawy seksuologii*, edited by Zbigniew Lew-Starowicz and Viletta Skrzypulec, 11–23. Warszawa: Wydawnictwo Lekarskie PZWL.

———. 2011. *Samogwałt czyli haniebny grzech samosplamienia. Historia masturbacji.* Paper presented at the meeting of the Polish Sexological Society, October 21–23, Warsaw.

Depko, Andrzej, and Sylwia Jędrzejewska. 2008. "Reformy seksualne w Europie i w Polsce w okresie międzywojennym." *Przegląd Seksuologiczny* 13:21–25.

Dębińska, Maria, 2013. "Natura, kultura i hybrydy. Prawne konstrukcje transseksualizmu i sprawy o ustalenie płci." *Lud* 97:221–244.

Długołęcka, Alicja. 2005. *Pokochałaś kobietę . . .* Warszawa: Elma Books.

———. 2008. "Tworzenie intymnych związków." In *Kiedy kobieta kocha kobietę . . . : Album relacji*, edited by Alicja Długołęcka and Agata Engel-Bernatowicz, 115–60. Warszawa: Fundacja Anka Zet Studio.

———. 2011a. "Podstawowe założenia rehabilitacji seksualnej osób z niepełnosprawnością ruchową." *Niepełnosprawność i Rehabilitacja* 4: 68–79.

———. 2011b. "Znaczenie kategorii płci w procesie rehabilitacji osób z niepełnosprawnością ruchową." *Niepełnosprawność i Rehabilitacja* 4: 52–67.

———. 2019. "Fascynujacy świat kobiet." Interview by Michał Witkowski. Accessed May 6, 2019. http://kobiety-kobietom.com/lesbijka/art.php?art=2355.

Długołęcka, Alicja, and Agata Engel-Bernatowicz, eds. 2008 *Kiedy kobieta kocha kobietę . . . Album relacji*. Warszawa: Fundacja Anka Zet Studio.

Długołęcka, Alicja, and Paulina Reiter. 2011. *Seks na wysokich obcasach*, Warszawa: Agora.

Dodson Betty. 1996. *Sex for One: The Joy of Selfloving.* New York: Three Rivers Press.

Easton, Dossie, and Janet W. Hardy. 1997. *The Ethical Slut: A Guide to Infinite Sexual Possibilities.* San Francisco, CA: Greenery Press.

Eichstaedt, Krzysztof, Piotr Gałecki, and Andrzej Depko. 2012. *Metodyka pracy biegłego psychiatry, psychologa oraz seksuologa w sprawach karnych.* Warszawa: LexisNexis Polska.

Eksner, Janusz. 1972. "Z urzędu czy na wniosek?" *Prawo i Życie*, no. 20.

Ellis, Havelock. 1894. *Man and Woman.* London: W. Scott.

———. 1897. *Sexual Inversion.* London: Wilson & Macmillan.

Ensler, Eve. 1998. *The Vagina Monologues.* New York: Villard.

FACT Book Committee. 1986. *Caught Looking. Feminism, Pornography and Censorship.* New York: Caught Looking.

Farmer, Paul. 1996. "Women, Poverty, and AIDS." In *Women, Poverty and AIDS: Sex, Drugs and Structural Violence*, edited by Paul Farmer, Margaret Connors, and Janie Simmons, 3–39. Monroe, ME: Common Courage Press.

Faulkner, Nicholas, trans. 2012. *The Criminal Code*. Bilingual ed. Warsaw: Wydawnictwo C. H. Beck.

Fidelis, Malgorzata. 2009. "Are You a Modern Girl? Consumer Culture and Young Women in 1960s Poland." In *Gender Politics and Everyday Life in State Socialist Eastern and Central Europe*, edited by Shana Penn and Jill Massimo, 171–84. New York: Palgrave.

———. 2010. *Women, Communism, and Industrialization in Postwar Poland*. Cambridge: Cambridge University Press.

Fiedotow, Agata. 2012. "Początki ruchu gejowskiego w Polsce." In *Kłopoty z seksem w PRL. Rodzenie nie całkiem po ludzku, aborcja, choroby, odmienności*, edited by Marcin Kula, 241–358. Warszawa: Wydawnictwa Uniwersytetu Warszawskiego, Instytut Pamięci Narodowej.

Fikus, Dariusz. 1979. "Van de Velde w spódnicy po polsku." *Polityka*, May 12.

Filar, Marian. 1974. *Przestępstwo zgwałcenia w polskim prawie karnym*. Warszawa: PWN.

———. 2010. "Przestępstwa przeciw wolności seksualnej i obyczajności." In *Podstawy seksuologii*, edited by Zbigniew Lew-Starowiczy, and Violetta Skrzypulec, 335–54. Warszawa: Wydawnictwo Lekarskie PZWL.

Fine, Cordelia. 2010. *Delusions of Gender: How Our Minds, Society, and Neurosexism Create Difference*. New York: Norton.

Fisher, Kate, and Jana Funke. 2015. "British Sexual Science beyond the Medical: Cross-Disciplinary, Cross-Historical, and Cross-Cultural Translations." In *Sexology and Translation. Cultural and Scientific Encounters across the Modern World*, edited by Heike Bauer, 95–114. Philadelphia: Temple University Press.

Fishman, Jennifer. 2004. "Manufacturing Desire: The Commodification of Female Sexual Dysfunction." *Social Studies of Science* 34 (2): 187–218.

Fishman, Jennifer R., and Laura Mamo. 2001. "What's in a Disorder: A Cultural Analysis of Medical and Pharmaceutical Constructions of Male and Female Sexual Dysfunction." *Women & Therapy* 24 (1/2): 179–93.

Fleck, Ludwik. (1935) 1979. *Genesis and Development of a Scientific Fact*. Translated by Fred Bradley and Thaddeus J. Trenn. Chicago: University of Chicago Press.

Flis, Andrzej. 1988. "Cracow Philosophy of the Beginning of the Twentieth Century and the Rise of Malinowski's Scientific Ideas." In *Malinowski between Two Worlds: The Polish Roots of an Anthropological Tradition*, edited by Roy F. Ellen, Ernest Gellner, Grażyna Kubica, and Janusz Mucha, 105–27. Cambridge: Cambridge University Press.

Foucault, Michel. 1978. *The History of Sexuality*, Vol. 1: *The Will to Knowledge*. Translated by R. Hurley. New York: Pantheon.

———. 1979. *Discipline and Punish: The Birth of the Prison*. Translated by Alan Sheridan. New York: Vintage.

———. 1983. "The Subject and Power." In *Michel Foucault: Beyond Structuralism and Hermeneutics*, edited by Hubert L. Dreyfus and Paul Rabinow, 208–28. Chicago: Chicago University Press.

Freidenfelds, Lara. 2009. *The Modern Period: Menstruation in Twentieth-Century America*. Baltimore: Johns Hopkins University Press.

Freud, Sigmund. (1905) 1949. *Three Essays on the Theory of Sexuality*. Translated by James Strachey. London: Imago.

Friedman, Jaclyn, and Jessica Valenti. 2008. *Yes Means Yes! Visions of Female Sexual Power and a World without Rape*. Berkeley, CA: Seal.

Frühstück, Sabine. 2003. *Colonizing Sex: Sexology and Social Control in Modern Japan*. Berkeley: University of California Press.

Fuechtner, Veronika, Douglas E. Haynes, and Ryan M Jones, eds. 2018. *A Global History of Sexual Science, 1880–1960*. Oakland: University of California.

Funk, Nanette. 2014. "A Very Tangled Knot: Official State Socialist Women's Organizations, Women's Agency and Feminism in Eastern European State Socialism." *European Journal of Women's Studies* 21 (4): 344–60. https://doi.org/10.1177/1350506814539929.

Gal, Susan, and Gail Kligman. 2000. *The Politics of Gender after Socialism: A Comparative-Historical Essay*. Princeton: Princeton University Press.

Gawin, Magdalena. 2009. "The Social Politics and Experience of Sex Education in Early Twentieth-Century Poland (1905–39)." In: *Shaping Sexual Knowledge: A Cultural History of Sex Education in Twentieth Century Europe*, edited by Lutz D. H. Sauerteig and Roger Davidson, 219–35. London: Routledge.

Gawin, Magdalena, and Ivan Crozier. 2006. "Światowa Liga Reformy Seksualnej w latach międzywojennych w Anglii i w Polsce." In *Kobieta i rewolucja obyczajowa, Społeczno-Kulturowe aspekty seksualności. Wiek XIX i XX*, edited by Anna Żarnowska and Andrzej Szwarc, 311–34, Warszawa: Wydawnictwo DiG.

Ghodsee Kristen. 2012*a*. "Rethinking State Socialist Mass Women's Organizations: The Committee of the Bulgarian Women's Movement and the United Nations Decade for Women, 1975–1985." *Journal of Women's History* 24 (4): 49–73.

———. 2012*b*. "Statistics and Sex Equality: Scientific Socialism and the Committee of the Bulgarian Women's Movement in Bulgaria, 1968–1989." Paper presented at the meeting of the European Association of Social Anthropologists, Nanterre University, July 10–13.

———. 2017. "Why Women Had Better Sex under Socialism." *New York Times*, August 12, https://www.nytimes.com/2017/08/12/opinion/why-women-had-better-sex-under-socialism.html.

———. 2018. *Why Women Have Better Sex under Socialism and Other Arguments for Economic Independence*. London: Bodley Head.

Giddens, Anthony. 1984. *The Constitution of Society: Outline of the Theory of Structuration*. Berkeley: University of California Press.

Gilman, Sander L. 1985. *Difference and Pathology: Stereotypes of Sexuality, Race, and Madness*. Ithaca, NY: Cornell University Press.

Godlewski, Julian. 1987. "Typologia zgwałceń." *Psychiatria Polska* 21 (4): 296–301.

Gonzalez, Roberto J., Laura Nader, and C. Jay Ou. 1995. "Between Two Poles: Bronislaw Malinowski, Ludwik Fleck, and the Anthropology of Science." *Current Anthropology* 36 (5): 866–69.

Górski, Henryk. 1983. "Dyskoteka." *Prawo i Życie*, no. 27.

Grabowska, Magdalena. 2011. "Pomiędzy wiedzą a stereotypem. Instytucje publiczne i organizacje pomocowe wobec problemu gwałtu. Raport z badań." In *Dość milczenia. Przemoc seksualna wobec kobiet i problem gwałtu w Polsce*, edited by Joanna Piotrowska, and Alina Synakiewicz, 121–90. Warszawa: Fundacja Feminoteka. https://pl.boell.org/sites/default/files/dosc_milczenia._przemoc_seksualna_wobec_kobiet_1.pdf.

———. 2018. *Zerwana genealogia. Działalność społeczna i polityczna kobiet po 1945 r. a współczesny ruch kobiecy*. Warszawa: Scholar.

Grabowska, Magdalena, and Agnieszka Grzybek. 2017. Introduction. In *Breaking the Taboo: Report on Sexual Violence*, edited by Magdalena Grabowska and Agnieszka Grzybek, 7–10. Warszawa: STER (Foundation for Equality and Emancipation). http://www.fundacjaster.org.pl/upload/R_ENG-final.pdf.

Grabowska, Magdalena, and Marta Rawłuszko. 2017. "Universality and Prevalence of Sexual Violence against Women." In *Breaking the Taboo: Report on Sexual Violence*, edited by Magdalena Grabowska and Agnieszka Grzybek, 11–23. Warszawa: STER (Foundation for Equality and Emancipation). http://www.fundacjaster.org.pl/upload/R_ENG-final.pdf.

Grabowska, Mirosława. 2008. "Ruchy odnowy religijnej przełomu lat siedemdziesiątych i osiemdziesiątych: społeczne przyczyny i konsekwencje." In *Pokolenie JP2. Przeszłość i przyszłość zjawiska religijnego*, edited by Tadeusz Szawiel, 22–49. Warszawa: Wydawnictwo Naukowe SCHOLAR.

Grabowska-Woźniak, Edyta. 2001. "Znieczulenie miejscowe." *Życie Warszawy*, April 7–8.

Graff, Agnieszka. 2001. *Świat bez kobiet. Płeć w polskim życiu publicznym*. Warszawa: W.A.B.

Graff, Agnieszka, and Elżbieta Korolczuk. 2017. "'Worse Than Communism and Nazism Put Together:' War on Gender in Poland." In *Anti-Gender Campaigns in Europe: Mobilizing against Equality*, edited by Roman Kuhar and David Patenotte, 175–94. London: Rowman & Littlefield.

Grębecka, Zuzanna. 2012. "Erotyka i seksualność w polskiej socjalistycznej powieści młodzieżowej." In *Kultura popularna w Polsce w latach 1944–1989: problemy i perspektywy badawcze*, edited by Katarzyna Stańczak-Wiślicz, 134–51. Warszawa: Fundacja Akademia Humanistyczna, Instytut Badań Literackich PAN.

Grzybek, Agnieszka, and Barbara Błońska. 2016. "New Procedure of Prosecuting Rape: The results of research with prosecutors and police officers." In *Breaking the Taboo: Report on Sexual Violence*, edited by Magdalena Grabowska and Agnieszka Grzybek, 43–63. Warszawa: STER (Foundation for Equality and Emancipation). http://www.fundacjaster.org.pl/upload/R_ENG-final.pdf.

Greg, Gutfeld. 2017. "*NY Times* Claims Sex Is Better under Socialism." FoxNews, August 15. https://video.foxnews.com/v/5542250823001#sp=show-clips.

GUS (Główny Urząd Statystyczny; Central Statistic Office). 2016. *Rocznik demograficzny*. Warszawa: Zakład Wydawnictw Statystycznych.

"Gwałt . . ." 1983. "Gwałt po amerykańsku." *Express Wieczorny*, December 2–4.

Hackett, Edward, Olga Amsterdamska, Michael Lynch, and Judy Wajcman, eds. 2008. *The Handbook of Science and Technology Studies*. Cambridge, MA: MIT Press.

Hall, Lesley. 1991. *Hidden Anxieties: Male Sexuality, 1900–1950*. Cambridge: Polity.

Hanausek, Tadeusz, Zdzisław Marek, and Jan Widacki. 1976. *Zgwałcenia*, Warszawa: Departament Szkolenia i Doskonalenia Zawodowego Ministerstwa Spraw Wewnętrznych.

Haraway, Donna. 1988. "Situated Knowledges: The Science Question in Feminism and the Privilege of Partial Perspective." *Feminist Studies* 14 (3): 575–99.

Harsch, Donna. 2009. "Sex, Divorce, and Women's Waged Work." In *Gender Politics and Everyday Life in State Socialist Eastern and Central Europe*, edited by Shana Penn and Jill Massimo, 97–114. New York: Palgrave.

Healey, Dan. 2009. *Bolshevik Sexual Forensics: Diagnosing Disorder in the Clinic and Courtroom, 1917–1939*. DeKalb: Northern Illinois University Press.

Herzfeld, Michael. 1997. *Cultural Intimacy: Social Poetics in the Nation-State*. New York: Routledge.

———. 2004. *The Body Impolitic: Artisans and Artifice in the Global Hierarchy of Value.* Chicago: Chicago University Press.

Herzog, Dagmar. 2005. *Sex after Fascism: Memory and Morality in Twentieth-Century Germany.* Princeton, NJ: Princeton University Press.

———. 2007. "East Germany's Sexual Evolution." In *Socialist Modern: East German Everyday Culture and Politics*, edited by Katherine Pence and Paul Betts, 71–95. Ann Arbor: University of Michigan Press.

———. 2009. "Syncopated Sex: Transforming European Sexual Cultures." *American Historical Review* 114 (5): 1287–308. https://doi.org/10.1086/ahr.114.5.1287.

Hirschfeld, Magnus. (1910) 1991. *The Transvestites: The Erotic Drive to Cross-Dress.* Buffalo, NY: Prometheus.

Hite, Shere. 1976. *The Hite Report. A Nationwide Study of Female Sexuality.* New York: Macmillan.

———. 1981. *The Hite Report on Male Sexuality.* New York: Ballantine.

———. 2006. *The Shere Hite Reader.* New York: Seven Stories.

Hołówka, Teresa, ed. 1982. *Nikt nie rodzi się kobietą.* Warszawa: Czytelnik.

Ignaciuk, Agata. 2014. "'Clueless about Contraception': The Introduction and Circulation of the Contraceptive Pill in State-Socialist Poland (1960s–1970s)." *Medicina nei Secoli. Arte e Scienza* 26 (2): 509–35.

———. 2016. "Reproductive Policies and Women's Birth Control Practices in State-Socialist Poland (1960s–1980s)." In *"Wenn die Chemie stimmt": Gender Relations and Birth Control in the Age of the "Pill,"* edited by Lutz Niethammer and Silke Satjuko, 271–94. Göttingen: Wallstein.

———. 2019. "No Man's Land? Gendering Contraception in Family Planning Advice Literature in State-Socialist Poland (1950s–1980s)." *Social History of Medicine.* https://doi.org/10.1093/shm/hkz007.

ij. 2005. "Michalina Wisłocka. Seks to nie wszystko, trzeba jeszcze miłości." *Życie na gorąco*, February 17.

Imieliński, Kazimierz. 1963. *Zagadnienia samogwałtu w świetle poglądów starszej młodzieży.* Warszawa: Państwowy Zakład Wydawnictw Lekarskich.

———. 1967a. "Analfabeci seksualni (1)." *Itd.*, no. 25.

———. 1967b. "Analfabeci seksualni (2)." *Itd.*, no. 26.

———. 1967c. "Kilka słów o seksuologii" (interview by Sławomir Kryska). *Itd*, no. 24.

———. 1967d. "Okres przedmałżeński." *Itd.*, no. 35.

———. 1967e. "Wstęp." *Itd.*, no. 24.

———. 1967f. *Życie seksualne. Psychohigiena*, Warszawa: Państwowy Zakład Wydawnictw Lekarskich.

———. 1969. "Kultura życia małżeńskiego." *Itd*, no. 11.

———. 1970. *Erotyzm.* Warszawa: Państwowe Wydawnictwo Naukowe.

———. 1974a. "O seksuologii bez emocji" (interview by Renata Wołoszczak). *Itd*, no. 6.

———. 1974b. *Życie intymne człowieka. Psychohigiena.* Warszawa: Zakład Wydawnictw Lekarskich.

———. 1982. *Zarys seksuologii i seksiatrii.* Warszawa: Państwowy Zakład Wydawnictw Lekarskich.

———, ed. (1980) 1984a. *Seksuologia kulturowa.* Warszawa: PWN.

———, ed. (1977) 1984b. *Seksuologia społeczna.* Warszawa: PWN.

———. 1985a. *Człowiek i seks.* Warszawa: Instytut Wydawniczy Związków Zawodowych.

———. 1985b. "Powstanie i działalność Zakładu Seksuologii i Patologii Więzi Międzyludzkich CMKP." In *Pamiętnik IV Konferencji Seksuologów.* Warszawa: CMKP.

———, ed. (1980) 1985c. *Seksuologia biologiczna*. Warszawa: PWN.

———. 1990. *Seksiatria*. Warszawa: PWN.

———. 1998. *Migawki z mojego życia. Wspomnienia i refleksje*. Warszawa: Polska Akademia Medycyny.

Imieliński, Kazimierz, Imieliński Chrystian, and Imieliński Andrzej. 1997. *Humanistyczne aspekty medycyny*. Warszawa: Polska Akademia Medycyny.

Irvine, Janice M. 2005. *Disorders of Desire: Sexuality and Gender in Modern American Sexology*. Philadelphia: Temple University Press.

Iwanicki, Zbigniew. 1979. "Recenzja *Sztuki kochania*." *Nowe Książki*, July 31.

Izdebski, Zbigniew. 2005. "Bo spódnica była za krótka" (interview by Sylwia Kępińska). *Pani*, January.

———. 2012. *Seksualność Polaków na początku XXI wieku. Studium badawcze*. Kraków: Wydawnictwo Uniwersytetu Jagiellońskiego.

———. 2016. "Sztuka udanej miłości." In *Sztuka kochania*, Michalina Wisłocka, 5–12. Warszawa: Agora.

Jackson, Margaret. 1987. "'Facts of Life' or the Eroticization of Women's Oppression? Sexology and the Social Construction of Heterosexuality." In *The Cultural Construction of Sexuality*, edited by Pat Caplan, 52–81. London: Tavistock.

Jackson, Stevi, and Sue Scott, eds. 1996. *Feminism and Sexuality: A Reader*. Edinburgh: Edinburgh University Press.

Jacyno, Małgorzata. 2007. *Kultura indywidualizmu*. Warszawa: Wydawnictwo Naukowe PWN.

Jaczewski, Andrzej. 1978. "Przedmowa." In *Sztuka kochania*, Michalina Wisłocka. Warszawa: Iskry.

———. 2009. *Książka moich wspomnień*. Radom: Wydawnictwo Naukowe Instytutu Technologii Eksploatacji—PIB.

Janion, Maria. 2006. *Niesamowita Słowiańszczyzna*. Kraków: Wydawnictwo Literackie.

Jarska, Natalia. 2019. "Modern Marriage and the Culture of Sexuality: Experts between the State and the Church in Poland, 1956–1970." *European History Quarterly* 49 (3): 467–90.

J.B. 1976. "Przemoc i porno" *Prawo i Życie*, no. 28.

Johnson, Ericka. 2008. "Chemistries of Love: Impotence, Erectile Dysfunction and Viagra in Läkartidningen." *Norma* 3 (1): 31–47.

Johnson, Janet Elise. 2009. *Gender Violence in Russia: The Politics of Feminist Intervention*. Bloomington: Indiana University Press.

Jordan-Young, Rebecca. 2010. *Brain Storm: The Flaws in the Science of Sex Difference*. Cambridge: Harvard University Press.

jot. 1971. "Przez nasze okulary." *Zwierciadło*, no. 21.

J.W. 1966. "Sex w wieku pojazdów kosmicznych." *Itd.*, no. 37.

Kaim, Agnieszka. 2010/2011. "Przemoc bagatelizowana. Mity na temat gwałtu." *UniGender*, 6–7. Accessed November 23, 2012. http://www.unigender.org/?page=biezacy&issue=05&article=08. Page no longer available.

———. 2011. "Polskie media wobec przemocy seksualnej." In *Dość milczenia. Przemoc seksualna wobec kobiet i problem gwałtu w Polsce*, edited by Joanna Piotrowska and Alina Synakiewicz, 72–86. Warszawa: Fundacja Feminoteka. https://pl.boell.org/sites/default/files/dosc_milczenia._przemoc_seksualna_wobec_kobiet_1.pdf.

Kaschak, Ellyn, and Leonore Tiefer, eds. 2002. *A New View of Women's Sexual Problems*. Binghamton, NY: Haworth.

Katz, Jonathan. 1995. *The Invention of Heterosexuality*. New York: Plume.

Kąkol, Kazimierz. 1966. "Jaskiniowcy." *Prawo i Życie*, no. 4.

Kelly, Liz. 1996. "'It's Everywhere': Sexual Violence as a Continuum." In *Feminism and Sexuality: A Reader*, edited by Jackson Stevi and Sue Scott, 191–206. Edinburgh: Edinburgh University Press.

Keszka, Joanna. 2011. "No Means No, Mr. Professor Starowicz!" Accessed October 16, 2011. http://barbarella.pl/. Page no longer available.

Kępiński, Antoni. 1988. *Z psychopatologii życia seksualnego*. Warszawa: Państwowy Zakład Wydawnictw Lekarskich.

Kim, Eunjung. 2010. "How Much Sex Is Healthy? The Pleasure of Asexuality." In *Against Health: How Health Became the New Morality*, edited by Jonathan M. Metzl and Anna Kirkland, 157–69. New York: New York University Press.

Kinsey, Alfred C., Wardell B. Pomeroy, and Clyde E. Martin. 1948. *Sexual Behavior in the Human Male*. Philadelphia: Saunders.

Kinsey, Alfred C., Wardell B. Pomeroy, Clyde E. Martin, and Paul H. Gebhard. 1953. *Sexual Behavior in the Human Female*. New York: Pocket.

K.J. 1966. "Eros w poliestrze." *Itd*, no. 44.

Kochanowski, Jacek. 2004. *Fantazmat zróżnicowany. Socjologiczne studium przemian tożsamości gejów*. Kraków: Universitas.

———. 2009. *Spektakl i wiedza. Perspektywa społecznej teorii queer*. Łódź: Wydawnictwo Wschód-Zachód.

———. 2013. *Socjologia seksualności. Marginesy*. Warszawa: Wydawnictwo Naukowe PWN.

Koedt Anne. 1970. *The Myth of the Vaginal Orgasm*. Somerville: New England Free Press.

Kon, Igor, and James Riordan, eds. 1993. *Sex and Russian Society*. Bloomington: Indiana University Press.

Kościańska, Agnieszka. 2009a. *Potęga ciszy. Konwersja a rekonstrukcja porządku płci na przykładzie nowego ruchu religijnego Brahma Kumaris*. Wydawnictwa Uniwersytetu Warszawskiego, Warszawa.

———. 2009b. "The 'Power of Silence:' Spirituality and Women's Agency beyond the Catholic Church in Poland." *Focaal—European Journal of Anthropology* 53:56–71. https://doi.org/10.3167/fcl.2009.530104.

———. 2012a. "Churches and Religious Communities in View of LGBT Persons." In *Situation of LGBT Persons in Poland: 2010 and 2011 Report*, edited by Mirosława Makuchowska and Michał Pawlęga, 145–65. Warszawa: Campaign against Homophobia, Lambda Warsaw, Trans-fuzja Foundation http://www.kph.org.pl/publikacje/Raport_badania_LGBT_EN_net.pdf.

———. 2012b. "Czy onanista to też Polak? Debata o masturbacji 1993–1994." *Interalia. Pismo Poświęcone Studiom Queer* 7. http://www.interalia.org.pl/pl/artykuly/aktualny_numer_2012_7/12_czy_onanista_to_tez_polak_debata_o_masturbacji_19931994.htm.

———. 2012c. "Dwóch osobników narodowości cygańskiej . . . Wątki etniczne w procesach sądowych o gwałt." *Dialog. Pheniben* 5:34–39.

———. 2012d. "'Nie' znaczy 'tak'? Dyskurs ekspercki na temat przemocy seksualnej wobec kobiet w prasie polskiej od lat 70. XX w. do dziś." *Zeszyty Etnologii Wrocławskiej* 16: 37–53. http://zew.uni.wroc.pl/files/Koscianska.pdf.

———. 2013. "Jak uchronić polskie dzieci przed demoralizacją? Dyskurs medycyny i psychologii w pewnym młodzieżowym piśmie katolickim." In *Etnograficzne wędrówki po obszarach antropologii*, edited by Łukasz Smyrski and Katarzyna Waszczyńska, 427–39. Warszawa: DiG.

———. 2014*a*. "Biedni chłopcy wykolejeni przez lekkomyślne dziewczęta" (interview by Lidia Ostałowska). *Gazeta Wyborcza, Duży Format*, July 10. http://wyborcza.pl/duzyformat/1,127290,16294906,Biedni_chlopcy_wykolejeni_przez_lekkomyslne_dziewczeta.html.

———. 2014*b*. "Violence against Women in Poland—What Tradition Has to Do with It?" *Visegrad Revue*. http://visegradrevue.eu/violence-against-women-in-poland-what-tradition-has-to-do-with-it/. Page no longer available.

———. 2016. "Moral Panic over Gender and Sexuality in Poland and Central Europe." *TCDS Shrinking of Democracy Series*. Accessed May 19, 2020. https://blogs.newschool.edu/tcds/2016/11/03/tcds-shrinking-of-democracy-series-moral-panic-over-gender-and-sexuality-in-poland-and-central-europe/.

———. 2017. *Zobaczyć łosia. Historia polskiej edukacji seksualnej od pierwszej lekcji do internetu*. Wołowiec: Czarne.

———. 2018. "Humanae Vitae, Birth Control and the Forgotten History of the Catholic Church in Poland." In *The Schism of '68: Genders and Sexualities in History*, edited by Alana Harris, 187–208. Cham: Palgrave.

———. 2020. "'Le droit de cité': Sexologie, homosexualité et le discours des droits de l'homme en Pologne socialiste dans les années 70." *Sextant* 34, Editions de l'Université de Bruxelles (forthcoming).

Kowalczyk, Robert. 2012. *Gwałt—definicje, rodzaje, przyczyny i konsekwencje*. Accessed December 2, 2012. http://www.niebieskalinia.info/artykul.php?id=1083. Page no longer available.

Krafft-Ebing, Richard von. (1886) 2011. *Psychopathia Sexualis: The Case Histories*, edited and translated by Domino Falls. Chicago: Solar.

Krastev, Ivan, and Stephen Holmes. 2018. "Explaining Eastern Europe: Imitation and Its Discontents." *Journal of Democracy* 29 (3): 117–28. https://doi.org/10.1353/jod.2018.0049.

Kratochvíl, Stanislav. 2002. *Leczenie zaburzeń seksualnych*. Translated by Andrzej Piotrowski. Warszawa: Iskry.

Krzywicka, Irena. 1998. *Wyznania gorszycielki*. Warszawa: Czytelnik.

Kubczak, Krystyna. 1986. "Wisłockiej sztuka życia." *Kontakty*, January 16.

Kuhn, Thomas. 1962. *The Structure of Scientific Revolutions*. Chicago: University of Chicago Press.

Kula, Marcin, ed. 2012. *Kłopoty z seksem w PRL. Rodzenie nie całkiem po ludzku, aborcja, choroby, odmienności*. Warszawa: Wydawnictwa Uniwersytetu Warszawskiego, Instytut Pamięci Narodowej.

Kurkiewicz, Stanisław. 1905. *Z dociekó (studyów) nad życiem płciowem: luźne osnowy (tematy)*, t. 1, *Nieświadome błądzenia i cierpienia*. *Kraków*: Drukarnia Związkowa.

———. 1906. *Z dociekó (studyów) nad życiem płciowem: luźne osnowy (tematy)*, t. 2, *Szczegółowe odróżnienie czynności płciowych*. Kraków: Drukarnia Związkowa.

Kurzępa, Bolesław. 2005. "'Inna czynność seksualna' jako znamię przestępstw." *Prokuratura i Prawo* 5:62–72.

Kuźma-Markowska, Sylwia. 2013. "Międzynarodowe aspekty działalności Towarzystwa Świadomego Macierzyństwa w latach 50. i 60. XX w." In *Problem kontroli urodzeń i antykoncepcji. Krytyczno-porównawcza analiza dyskursów*, edited by

Bożena Płonka-Syroka and Aleksandra Szlagowska, 263–82. Wrocław: Uniwersytet Medyczny im. Piastów Śląskich we Wrocławiu.

Lakoff, Andrew. 2004. "The Anxieties of Globalization: Antidepressant Sales and Economic Crisis in Argentina." *Social Studies of Science* 34 (2): 247–69.

Laqueur, Thomas W. 1990. *Making Sex: Body and Gender from the Greeks to Freud*. Cambridge, MA: Harvard University Press.

———. 2003. *Solitary Sex: A Cultural History of Masturbation*. New York: Zone.

Laszuk, Anna, host. 2011. *Komentarze radia Tok FM. Rozmowa z Aleksandrą Jodko* [radio program]. Warszawa: Radio Tok FM.

Latour, Bruno. 1987. *Science in Action*. Cambridge, MA: Harvard University Press.

Laumann, Edward O., Anthony Paik, and Raymond C. Rosen. 1999. "Sexual Dysfunction in the United States: Prevalence and Predictors." *JAMA* 281 (6): 537–44. https://doi.org/10.1001/jama.281.6.537.

Lemkin, Raphael, and Malcolm McDermontt. 1939. *The Polish Penal Code of 1932*. Durham, NC: Duke University Press.

Leszczyński, Juliusz. 1972. "Profilaktyka i represja w sprawach o zgwałcenie zbiorowe." *Prawo i Życie* no. 22.

———. 1973. *Przestępstwo zgwałcenia w Polsce*. Warszawa: Wydawnictwo Prawnicze.

Lew-Starowicz, Zbigniew. 1969a. "Czy samogwałt jest szkodliwy." *Itd*, no. 46.

———. 1969b. "O seksie, miłości i normach etycznych." Interview by Piotr Wierzbicki. *Itd*, no. 45.

———. 1970a. "Ars amandi." *Itd*, no. 33.

———. 1970b. "Emancypacja i eros." *Itd*, no. 49.

———. 1970c. "Gwałt." *Itd*, no. 38.

———. 1970d. "Homoseksualizm." *Itd*, no. 8.

———. 1970e. "Męskie nerwice płciowe." *Itd*, no. 6.

———. 1970f. "Miłość francuska." *Itd*, no. 47.

———. 1970g. "Miłość lesbijska." *Itd*, no. 17.

———. 1970h. "Model małżeństwa." *Itd*, no. 22.

———. 1970i. "Natura popędu" *Itd*, no. 9.

———. 1970j. "Oziębłość płciowa kobiet." *Itd*, no. 7.

———. 1970k. "Petting." *Itd*, no. 10.

———. 1970l. "Tabletka." *Itd*, no. 43.

———. 1970m. "Rodzina." *Itd*, no. 38.

———. 1970n. "Technika czy kultura seksualna." *Itd*, no. 24.

———. 1971a. "Akt." *Itd*, no. 8.

———. 1971b. "Antykoncepcja. *Itd*. no. 44.

———. 1971c. "Antykoncepcja." *Itd*, no. 46.

———. 1971d. "Krzywe ścieżki emancypacji kobiet." *Tygodnik Powszechny*, no. 19.

———. 1972a. "Gwałty zbiorowe." *Itd*, no. 42.

———. 1972b. "Metoda termiczna." *Itd*, no. 2.

———. 1972c. "Wspólny samogwałt." *Itd*, no. 20.

———. 1973a. "Kobiecość" *Itd*, no. 18.

———. 1973b. "Kultura współżycia 1." *Itd*, no. 33.

———. 1973c. "Kultura współżycia, 2." *Itd*, no. 35.

———. 1973d. "Listy do seksuologa." *Itd*, no. 9.

———. 1973e. "Listy do seksuologa (2)." *Itd*, no. 10.

———. 1973f. "Małżeństwo przyszłości." *Itd*, no. 46.

———. 1973g. "Męskość." *Itd*, no 19.

———. 1973*h*. "Mistyfikacje." *Itd*, no. 3.

———. 1973*i*. "Nerwica seksualna jako stres." *Itd*, no. 6.

———. 1973*j*. "Nowy cykl." *Itd*, no. 12.

———. 1973*k*. "Pacjenci erudyci." *Itd*, no. 2.

———. 1973*l*. "Postawy wobec współżycia seksualnego." *Itd*, no. 37.

———. 1973*m*. "Potrzeby seksualne." *Itd*, no. 34.

———. 1973*n*. "Samogwałt." *Itd*, no. 26.

———. 1974*a*. "Kobieta jako partner seksualny." *Itd*, no. 2.

———. 1974*b*. "Kompleks onanistyczny." *Itd*, no. 42.

———. 1975*a*. "Atrakcyjność." *Itd*, no. 43.

———. 1975*b*. "Homoseksualizm." *Itd*, no. 22.

———. 1975*c*. "Prezerwatywa." *Itd*, no. 35.

———. 1978*a*. "Igranie z ogniem." *Itd*, no. 48.

———. 1978*b*. "Inaczej." *Itd*, no. 52–53.

———. 1979. "Czy zmierzch męskości?" *Zwierciadło*, no. 49.

———. 1980*a*. "Mit Don Juana." *Itd*, no. 5.

———. 1980*b*. "Perspektywy małżeństwa." *Itd*, no. 28.

———. 1981*a*. "Leczniczy samogwałt." *Itd*, no. 40.

———. 1981*b*. "Orgazm w stosunku." *Itd*, no. 21.

———. 1981*c*. "Partnerstwo—mit czy rzeczywistość." *Itd*, no. 49.

———. 1981*d*. "Predyspozycje." *Zwierciadło*, no. 36.

———. 1982*a*. "Antyseksuologia" *Itd*, no. 23.

———. 1982*b*. "Prowokacja gwałtu." *Zwierciadło*, no. 24.

———. 1983*a*. "Aktywność kobiety." *Zwierciadło*, no. 29.

———. 1983*b*. "Cena naiwności." *Zwierciadło*, no. 45.

———. 1983*c*. "Masturbacja." no. 52.

———. 1983*d*. "Niebezpieczna antykoncepcja." *Itd*, no. 19.

———. 1983*e*. "Prowokowanie losu." *Zwierciadło*, no. 42.

———. 1983*f*. *Seks partnerki*. Warszawa: Państwowy Zakład Wydawnictw Lekarskich.

———. 1984*a*. "Masturbacja a impotencja." *Itd*, no. 35.

———. 1984*b*. "Następstwa gwałtu." *Zwierciadło*, no. 9.

———. 1984*c*. *Związki partnerskie i zachowania seksualne w populacjach pacjentów z uzależnieniem od alkoholu i z lekozależnością: praca na stopień naukowy doktora habilitowanego nauk medycznych, cz. 1 i 2*. Warszawa: Akademia Medyczna.

———. 1985*a*. *Leczenie czynnościowych zaburzeń seksualnych*. Warszawa: Państwowy Zakład Wydawnictw Lekarskich.

———. 1985*b*. "Masturbacja." *Zwierciadło*, no. 25.

———. 1985*c*. "Nietypowe problemy, cz. 3." *Itd*, no. 22.

———. 1985*d*. "Oral sex." *Itd*, no. 40.

———. 1985*e*. *Seks dojrzały*. Warszawa: Państwowy Zakład Wydawnictw Lekarskich.

———. 1985*f*. "Tyrania orgazmu." *Zwierciadło*, no. 1.

———. 1986. "Antykoncepcja pokoitalna." *Zwierciadło*, no. 3.

———. 1987*a*. "Aktywność we współżyciu." *Itd*, no. 22.

———. 1987*b*. "Homoseksualizm (lesbijstwo)." *Zwierciadło*, no. 26.

———. 1987*c*. "Pieszczoty oralne, cz. 1." *Itd*, no. 47.

———. 1987*d*. "Pieszczoty oralne, cz. 2." *Itd*, no. 48.

———. 1987*e*. "Pieszczoty oralne, cz. 3." *Itd*, no. 49.

———. 1987*f*. "Pobudzanie łechtaczki, cz. 1." *Itd*, no. 21.

———. 1987*g*. "Pobudzanie łechtaczki, cz. 2. " *Itd*, no. 22.

———. 1987*h*. "Porozumiewanie się w związku partnerskim." *Zwierciadło*, no. 1.

———. 1988*a*. "Dominanta." *Itd*, no. 49.

———. 1988*b*. "Homoseksualizm młodzież." *Itd*, no. 27.

———. 1988*c*. "Przemoc fizyczna w małżeństwie." *Zwierciadło*, no. 39.

———. 1988*d*. *Seks nietypowy*. Warszawa: Instytut Wydawniczy Związków Zawodowych.

———. 1988*e*. *Seksuologia sądowa*. Warszawa: Wydawnictwo Prawnicze.

———. 1989*a*. *Listy intymne*. Wrocław: Zakład Narodowy imienia Ossolińskich.

———. 1989*b*. "Masturbacja na Wschodzie." *Itd*, no. 7.

———. 1989*c*. "Zagrażająca kobiecość." *Zwierciadło*, no. 42.

———. 1991. *Erotyzm i techniki seksualne Wchodu*. Warszawa: Instytut Wydawniczy Związków Zawodowych.

———. 1992. *Przemoc seksualna*. Warszawa: Jacek Santorski i Co.

———. 1995. "Następstwa zgwałcenia." *Sztandar Młodych*, May 5.

———. 1997. *Leczenie zaburzeń seksualnych*, Warszawa: Wydawnictwo Lekarskie PZWL.

———. 2000. *Seksuologia sądowa*, Warszawa: Wydawnictwo Lekarskie PZWL.

———. trans. 2002*a*. "Deklaracja Praw Seksualnych." Accessed May 17, 2020. https:// spunk.pl/wp-content/uploads/2013/03/Deklaracja-Praw-Seksualnych.pdf.

———. 2002*b*. *Raport: Seksualność Polaków—Pfizer 2002—ogólnopolskie badanie przeprowadzone przez firmę SMG & KRC*. Gdańsk: Via Medica.

———. 2007. *Ona i on o seksie*. Warszawa: Świat Książki—Bertelsmann Media.

———. 2011*a*. *O kobiecie. Rozmawia Barbara Kasprzyk*. Kraków: Wydawnictwo Czerwone i Czarne.

———. 2011*b*. "Rozwój seksuologii w Polsce po II wojnie światowej." Paper presented at the meeting of the Polish Sexological Society, October 21–23, Warsaw.

———. 2012*a*. *Lew w sypialni*, Warszawa: Wydawnictwo Z/X.

———. 2012*b*. *O mężczyźnie. Rozmawia Krystyna Romanowska*. Warszawa: Czerwone i Czarne.

———. 2012*c*. *O miłości. Rozmawia Krystyna Romanowska*. Warszawa: Wydawnictwo Czerwone i Czarne.

———. 2013. *Pan od seksu*, Kraków: Znak.

Lew-Starowicz, Zbigniew, and Michał Lew-Starowicz. 1999. *Homoseksualizm*, Warszawa: Wydawnictwo Lekarskie PZWL.

Lew-Starowicz, Zbigniew, and Violetta Skrzypulec, eds. 2010. *Podstawy seksuologii*. Warszawa: Wydawnictwo Lekarskie PZWL.

Lišková, Kateřina. 2016. "Sex under Socialism: From Emancipation of Women to Normalized Families in Czechoslovakia." *Sexualities* 19 (1/2): 211–35. https://doi.org /10.1177/1363460715614246.

———. 2018. *Sexual Liberation, Socialist Style: Communist Czechoslovakia and the Science of Desire, 1945–1989*. Cambridge: Cambridge University Press.

Lloyd, Elisabeth A. 2005. *The Case of the Female Orgasm: Bias in the Science of Evolution*. Cambridge, MA: Harvard University Press.

Lubaś-Harny, Marek. 1995. "Gwałt." *Gazeta Krakowska*, December 6.

Lubicz Czerwiński, Ignacy. 1817. *Sposob szczęśliwego pożycia między mężem i żoną czyli Cnoty istotne, które ich do tego celu doprowadzać powinny*. Przemyśl: Drukarnia Jana Gołębiowskiego Typ.

Łarski, Andrzej. 1965*a*. "'Maskotki', Marlon Brando i seks." *Itd*, no. 27.

———. 1965*b*. "Młodzi Francuzi 'bez przesądów.'" *Itd*, no. 28.

Łopuski, Janusz. 1957. *Co chce wiedzieć każdy chłopiec*. Warszawa: Państwowy Zakład Wydawnictw Lekarskich.

Maciuszek, Józef. 1996. *Obraz człowieka w dziele Kępińskiego*. Wrocław: FNP, Leopoldinum.

MacKinnon, Catharine. 1996. "Francis Biddle's Sister: Pornography, Civil Rights, and Speech." In *Applications of Feminist Legal Theory to Women's Lives: Sex, Violence, Work and Reproduction*, edited by D. Kelly Weisberg, 59–79. Philadelphia: Temple University Press.

MacKinnon, Catharine A., and Andrea Dworkin. 1997. *In Harm's Way: The Pornography Civil Rights Hearings*. Cambridge, MA: Harvard University Press.

Malewska, Hanna. 1969. *Kulturowe i psychospołeczne determinanty życia seksualnego*. Warszawa: Państwowe Wydawnictwo Naukowe.

Marcinkowski, Władysław. 1973. "Przeciwko gwałtom." *Prawo i Życie* no. 3.

Marianek, Magdalena. 2003. "Pigułka od policji." *Życie Warszawy*, February 23.

Marie Claire, editorial staff. 2004. "Gwałt." *Marie Claire*, no. 10.

Marody, Mira, and Anna Giza-Poleszczuk. 2000. "Changing Images of Identity in Poland: From the Self-Sacrificing to the Self-Investing Woman?" In *Reproducing Gender: Politics, Publics, and Everyday Life after Socialism*, edited by Susan Gal and Gail Kligman, 151–75. Princeton, NJ: Princeton University Press.

Martin, Emily. 1991. "The Egg and the Sperm: How Science Has Constructed a Romance Based on Stereotypical Male-Female Roles." *Signs* 16 (3): 485–501.

Masny-Sokołowska, Urszula. 1993. "Sprawy o gwałt w Polsce." In *Prawa Kobiet. Instytucje państwowe i społeczne a przemoc wobec kobiet. Medycyna a zdrowie kobiet*. Warszawa: Polskie Stowarzyszenie Feministyczne.

Masters, William, and Virginia Johnson. 1966. *Human Sexual Response*. Boston, MA: Little, Brown.

———. 1970. *Human Sexual Inadequacy*. Boston, MA: Little, Brown.

Matoesian, Gregory M. 1993. *Reproducing Rape: Domination through Talk in the Courtroom*. Chicago: University of Chicago Press.

Matynia, Elżbieta. 2003. "Provincializing Global Feminism." *Social Research* 70 (2): 499–530.

McLellan, Josie. 2011. *Love in the Time of Communism: Intimacy and Sexuality in the GDR*. Cambridge and New York: Cambridge University Press.

McMillan, Joanna. 2006. *Sex, Science and Morality in China*, New York: Routledge.

Meier, André, dir. 2007. *Do Communists Have Better Sex?* [film]. New York: ICARUS Films.

Melody, Michale E., and Linda M. Peterson. 1999. *Teaching America about Sex: Marriage Guides and Sex Manuals from the Late Victorians to Dr. Ruth*. New York: New York University Press.

Merry, Sally Engle. 2009. *Gender Violence: A Cultural Perspective*. Oxford: Wiley-Blackwell.

Mierzejewska, Barbara. 1984. "Różne barwy gwałtu." *Dziennik Ludowy*, June 7.

Miklaszewska, Helena. 1999. "Sama sobie winna . . . Wciąż obowiązują krzywdzące stereotypy na temat gwałtu." *Życie Warszawy*, July 26.

Miller, Alice M. 2000. "Sexual but Not Reproductive: Exploring the Junction and Disjunction of Sexual and Reproductive Rights." *Health and Human Rights* 4 (2): 68–109. https://doi.org/10.2307/4065197.

Miller, Alice M., and Carole S. Vance. 2004. "Sexuality, Human Rights, Health." *Health and Human Rights* 7 (2): 5–15. https://doi.org/10.2307/4065346.

Mishtal, Joanna. 2015. *The Politics of Morality: The Church, the State, and Reproductive Rights in Postsocialist Poland*. Athens: Ohio University Press.

Misiak, Anna. 2006. *Kinematograf kontrolowany. Cenzura filmowa w kraju socjalistycznym i demokratycznym (PRL i USA). Analiza socjologiczna*. Kraków: Universitas.

MKA. 2005. "Pierwsza seksuolożka PRL." *Trybuna*, February 6.

Morgan, Robin. 1980. "Theory and Practice: Pornography and Rape." In *Take Back the Night: Women on Pornography*, edited by Laura Lederer, 134–40. New York: William Morrow.

Morgentaler, Abraham. 2003. *The Viagra Myth: The Surprising Impact on Love and Relationships*. San Francisco: Jossey-Bass.

Mosse, George L. 1985. *Nationalism and Sexuality*. New York: Howaer Ferting.

Murzynowski, Andrzej. 2005. "Criminal Procedure." In *Introduction to Polish Law*, edited by Stanisław Frankowski and Adam Bodnar, 377–407. The Hague: Kluwer Law International.

Musiał, Aleksandra. 2000. "Obojętność zamiast życzliwości." *Trybuna*, June 12.

Nawrocka, Zofia. 2011. *Przemoc seksualna w Polsce—działania rządu*. In *Dość milczenia. Przemoc seksualna wobec kobiet i problem gwałtu w Polsce*, edited by Joanna Piotrowska, and Alina Synakiewicz, 44–71. Warszawa: Fundacja Feminoteka. https://pl.boell.org/sites/default/files/dosc_milczenia._przemoc_seksualna_wobec_kobiet_1.pdf.

New View Campaign. 2000. "The New View Manifesto." Accessed May 5, 2019. http://www.newviewcampaign.org/manifesto.asp.

———. 2017 "Welcome." Accessed May 5, 2019. http://www.newviewcampaign.org/history.asp.

Nijakowski, Lech. 2010. *Pornografia. Historia, znaczenia, gatunki*. Warszawa: Iskry.

Nowacka, Violetta. 1996. "Gwałt małżeński." *Wprost*, November 24.

Nowak, Basia A. 2009. "'Where Do You Think I Learned How to Style My Own Hair?': Gender and Everyday Lives of Women Activists in Poland's League of Women." In *Gender Politics and Everyday Life in State Socialist Eastern and Central Europe*, edited by Shana Penn and Jill Massimo, 45–58. New York: Palgrave.

Nowosielski, Krzysztof. 2010. "Fizjologia reakcji seksualnej kobiety." In *Podstawy seksuologii*, edited by Zbigniew Lew-Starowicz and Violetta Skrzypulec, 101–10. Warszawa: Wydawnictwo Lekarskie PZWL.

Ołdakowski, Marek. 1965. "Czy młodzież potrafi się bawić?" *Itd*, no. 5.

Oosterhuis, Harry. 2000. *Stepchildren of Nature. Krafft-Ebing, Psychiatry, and the Making of Sexual Identity*. Chicago: University of Chicago Press.

Osiadacz, Maria. 1975a. "Bilans zbrodni." *Prawo i Życie*, no. 31.

———. 1975b. "'Wampir' z Zagłębia." *Prawo i Życie*, no. 10.

———. 1977. "Dziewczyna i mercedes." *Prawo i Życie*, no. 15.

Ostrowska, Elżbieta. 2004. "Matki Polki i ich synowie. Kilka uwag o genezie obrazów kobiecości i męskości w kulturze polskiej." In *Gender. Konteksty*, edited by Małgorzata Radkiewicz, 215–27. Kraków: Rapid.

Oudshoorn, Nelly. 1994. *Beyond the Natural Body: An Archeology of Sex Hormones*. New York: Routledge.

Owczarzak, Jill. 2009a. "Defining HIV Risk and Determining Responsibility in Postsocialist Poland." *Medical Anthropology Quarterly* 23 (4): 417–35. https://doi.org/10.1111/j.1548-1387.2009.01071.x.

———. 2009b. "Introduction: Postcolonial Studies and Postsocialism in Eastern Europe." *Focaal* 53:3–19. https://doi.org/10.3167/fcl.2009.530101.

Peperkamp, Esther. 2008. "The Fertile Body and the Cross-Fertilization of Disciplinary Regimes: Technologies of Self in a Polish Catholic Youth Movement." In *Exploring Regimes of Discipline: The Dynamics of Restraint*, edited by Noel Dyck, 113–34. Oxford: Berghahn.

Perkowski, Piotr. 2011. "Przemoc seksualna i niuanse wrażliwości społecznej względem kobiet w świetle źródeł okresu PRL." In *Zapisy cierpienia*, edited by Katarzyna Stańczak-Wiślicz, 283–301. Wrocław: Wydawnictwo Chronicon.

Petryna, Adriana. 2009. *When Experiments Travel: Clinical Trials and the Global Search for Human Subjects*. Princeton, NJ: Princeton University Press.

Pietkiewicz, Barbara. 2005. "Pornografia pod płaszczykiem." *Polityka*, February 19. Accessed May 6, 2020. https://www.polityka.pl/archiwumpolityki/1859406,1,pornografia -pod-plaszczykiem.read.

Pine, Frances. 2001. "Retreat to the Household? Gendered Domains in Post-socialist Poland." In *Postsocialism: Ideals, Ideologies and Practice in Eurasia*, edited by Chris M. Hann, 95–113. London: Routledge.

Pinkwart, Maciej. 1972. "Gwałt zbiorowy (Sprawozdanie z posiedzenia Klubu Publicystów Społeczno-Prawnych SDP)." *Prawo i Życie*, no. 20.

Piotrowska, Joanna, and Alina Synakiewicz eds. 2011. *Dość milczenia. Przemoc seksualna wobec kobiet i problem gwałtu w Polsce*. Warszawa: Fundacja Feminoteka. https:// pl.boell.org/sites/default/files/dosc_milczenia._przemoc_seksualna_wobec _kobiet_1.pdf.

Płatek, Monika. 2005. "Gwałt-przestępstwo w cieniu Temidy." In *Gaudium In Litteris est. Księga Jubileuszowa ofiarowana Pani Profesor Genowefie Rejman*, edited by Lech Gardocki, Michał Królikowski, and Anna Walczak-Żochowska, 289–307. Warszawa: Liber.

———. 2010. "Kryminologiczno-epistemologiczne i genderowe aspekty przestępstwa zgwałcenia." *Archiwum kryminologii* 32:349–82.

———. 2011. "Przestępstwo zgwałcenia w świetle prawa i z perspektywy osób poszkodowanych." In *Dość milczenia. Przemoc seksualna wobec kobiet i problem gwałtu w Polsce*, edited by Joanna Piotrowska, and Alina Synakiewicz, 23–43. Warszawa: Fundacja Feminoteka. https://pl.boell.org/sites/default/files/dosc _milczenia._przemoc_seksualna_wobec_kobiet_1.pdf.

———. 2014. "Zgwałcenie." In *Płeć w kulturze. Encyklopedia*, edited by Monika Rudaś-Grodzka, Katarzyna Nadana-Sokołowska, Agnieszka Mrozik, Kazimierza Szczuka, Katarzyna Czeczot, Barbara Smoleń, Anna Nasiłowska, Ewa Serafin, and Agnieszka Wróbel, 591–95. Warszawa: Wydawnictwo Czarna Owca.

Podgórska, Joanna, 2008. "Gwałty i mity." *Polityka*, August 2. Accessed May 17, 2020. https://www.polityka.pl/tygodnikpolityka/spoleczenstwo/262894,1,gwalty -randkowe---problem-niestety-powszechny.read.

Pol, Zuzanna. 2002. ". . . sama się prosiła." *Marie Claire*, no. 4.

Polish Ministry of Health (Ministerstwo Zdrowia). 2018. "Konsultanci krajowi." Accessed January 28, 2019. https://www.gov.pl/web/zdrowie/konsultanci-krajowi.

Polish Ministry of Justice (Ministerstwo Sprawiedliwości). 2007a. *Średni wymiar kary pozbawienia wolności prawomocnie skazanych dorosłych wg rodzajów przestępstw—czyn główny w 2005r*. Wydział Statystyki DO II 0350-04/07. Warszawa: Ministerstwo Sprawiedliwości.

———. 2007b. *Informacja statystyczna o ewidencji spraw i orzecznictwie w sądach powszechnych oraz o więziennictwie w 2005 roku*. Warszawa: Ministerstwo Sprawiedliwości.

Polish Sexological Society (Polskie Towarzystwo Seksuologiczne). 2016. "Stanowisko Polskiego Towarzystwa Seksuologicznego na temat zdrowia osób o orientacji homoseksualnej." Accessed May 13, 2020. http://pts-seksuologia.pl/sites/strona /59/stanowiskopts-na-temat-zdrowia-osob-o-orientacji-homoseksualnej.

————. 2017. "Stanowisko Polskiego Towarzystwa Seksuologicznego w sprawie związków i rodzicielstwa osób homoseksualnych i biseksualnych." Accessed May 13, 2020. http://pts-seksuologia.pl/sites/strona/66/stanowisko-pts-w-sprawie-zwiazkow-i -rodzicielstwa-osob-homoseksualnych-i-biseksualnych.

Ponton. 2009. *Jaka naprawdę wygląda edukacja seksualna w polskich szkołach? Raport.* Warszawa: Grupa Edukatorów Seksualnych Ponton. Accessed May 13, 2020. http://ponton.org.pl/wp-content/uploads/2018/08/Raport2009.pdf.

Ponton. 2020. "Wolontariat." Warszawa: Grupa Edukatorów Seksualnych Ponton. Accessed May 13, 2020. http://ponton.org.pl/wolontariat/.

Popkowicz-Tajchert, Renata. 1971. "Gwałt i naiwność." *Prawo i Życie*, no. 17.

Porter, Roy, and Lesley Hall. 1995. *The Facts of Life: The Creation of Sexual Knowledge in Britain, 1650–1950.* New Haven, CT: Yale University Press.

Potts, Annie. 2000. "Coming, Coming, Gone: A Feminist Deconstruction of Heterosexual Orgasm." *Sexualities* 3 (1): 55–76. https://doi.org/10.1177/136346000003001003.

Radcliffe Institute for Advanced Study. 2011. *Our Bodies, Ourselves: The Collective Goes Global* (exhibition), Cambridge, MA: Schlesinger Library, Harvard University.

Radkowska Walkowicz, Magdalena. 2013. *Doświadczenie in vitro. Niepłodność i nowe technologie reprodukcyjne w perspektywie antropologicznej.* Warszawa: Wydawnictwa Uniwersytetu Warszawskiego.

Reinharz, Sulamith. 1992. *Feminist Methods in Social Research.* Oxford: Oxford University Press.

Renkin, Hadley Z. 2009. "Homophobia and Queer Belonging in Hungary." *Focaal* 53:20–37. https://doi.org/10.3167/fcl.2009.530102.

————. 2016. "Biopolitical Mythologies: Róheim, Freud, (Homo)phobia, and the Sexual Science of Eastern European Otherness." *Sexualities* 19 (1/2): 168–89. https://doi .org/10.1177/1363460714550908.

Renkin, Hadley Z., and Agnieszka Kościańska. 2016. "The Science of Sex in a Space of Uncertainty: Naturalizing and Modernizing Europe's East, Past and Present." *Sexualities* 19 (1/2): 159–67. https://doi.org/10.1177/1363460715614235.

Richardson, Sarah S. 2010. "Sexes, Species, and Genomes: Why Males and Females Are Not Like Humans and Chimpanzees." *Biology and Philosophy* 25 (5): 823–41. https://doi.org/10.1007/s10539-010-9207-5.

Rivkin-Fish, Michele. 1999. "Sexuality Education in Russia: Defining Pleasure and Danger for a Fledging Democratic Society." *Social Science and Medicine* 49:801–14. https://doi.org/10.1016/S0277-9536(99)00168-9.

Robinson, Paul. 1989. *The Modernization of Sex.* Ithaca, NY: Cornell University Press.

Rose, Nikolas. 2006. "Disorders without Borders? The Expanding Scope of Psychiatric Practice." *BioSocieties* 1 (4): 465–84. https://doi.org/10.1017/S1745855206004078.

Różycki, Marek. 1995. *Wisłocka w pigułce.* Warszawa: Oficyna Wydawnicza Szczepan Szymański.

Rubin, Gayle. 1984. "Thinking Sex: Notes for a Radical Theory of the Politics." In *Pleasure and Danger: Exploring Female Sexuality*, edited by Carole Vance, 267–319. London: Routledge & Kegan Paul.

Rymuszko, Marek. 1972. "Czy musimy czekać?" *Prawo i Życie*, no. 21.

————. 1976. "Incydent." *Prawo i Życie*", nos. 32–36.

Sadowska, Maria, dir. 2017. *Sztuka kochania. Historia Michaliny Wisłockiej* [film]. Warsaw: Watchout Studio.

Schnelle, Thomas. 1986. "Microbiology and Philosophy of Science, Lwów and the German Holocaust: Stations of a Life—Ludwik Fleck 1896–1961." In *Cognition and*

Fact: Materials on Ludwik Fleck, edited by Robert S. Cohen and Thomas Schnelle, 3–36. Dordrecht: Springer Netherlands.

Sharp, Ingrid. 2004. "The Sexual Unification of Germany." *Journal of the History of Sexuality* 13 (3): 348–65.

Shcheglov, Lev. 1993. "Medical Sexology." In *Sex and Russian Society,* edited by Igor Kon and James Riordan, 152–64. Bloomington: Indiana University Press.

Sherfey, Jane. 1970. "A Theory of Female Sexuality." In *Sisterhood Is Powerful: An Anthology of Writings from the Women's Liberation Movement,* edited by Robin Morgan, 245–56. New York: Random House.

Siedlecka, Joanna. 2005. "Ireneusz Iredyński. Zbaletowany." *Rzeczpospolita,* March 19.

Siemaszko, Andrzej. 2011. *2.10.Zgwałcenie: art. 197 § 1 i 2 (art.168 § 1 k.k. z 1969 r.). 2.11. Zgwałcenie ze szczególnym okrucieństwem lub zbiorowe art. 197 § 3 (art.168 § 2 k.k. z 1969 r.).* Accessed February 25, 2011. http://www.bezpiecznepanstwo.pl/?a =articles_get&id=38&c=2. Page no longer available.

Sierakowska, Katarzyna. 2004. "Elementy kobiecego dyskursu o seksualności na łamach międzywojennych periodyków dla kobiet." In *Kobieta i małżeństwo. Społeczno-kulturowe aspekty seksualności. Wiek XIX i XX,* edited by Anna Żarnowska and Andrzej Szwarc, 365–80. Warszawa: Wydawnictwo DiG.

Sierzpowska, Anna. 1993. "Seksualność kobiety." In *Prawa Kobiet. Instytucje państwowe i społeczne a przemoc wobec kobiet. Medycyna a zdrowie kobiet,* 5–8. Warszawa: Polskie Stowarzyszenie Feministyczne.

Skultans, Vieda. 2007. "The Appropriation of Suffering. Psychiatric Practice in the Post-Soviet Clinic." *Theory, Culture & Society,* 24 (3): 27–48. https://doi.org/10.1177 /0263276407077625.

Smith, Olivia. 2018. *Rape Trials in England and Wales: Observing Justice and Rethinking Rape Myths.* Cham: Palgrave Macmillan.

Sokoluk, Wiesław, Dagmara Andziak, and Maria Trawińska. 1987. *Przysposobienie do życia w rodzinie.* Warszawa: Wydawnictwa Szkolne i Pedagogiczne.

Somerville, Siobhan. 1994. "Scientific Racism and the Emergence of the Homosexual Body." *Journal of the History of Sexuality* 5 (2): 243–66.

Synowiecka, Sylwia. 1999. "Czego chcesz, kobieto?" *Nowa Trybuna Opolska,* March 4.

Szołajski, Kondad, dir. 2001. *Sztuka kochania według Wisłockiej* [film]. Telewizja Polska.

Szpakowska, Małgorzata. 2003. *Chcieć i mieć. Samowiedza obyczajowa w Polsce czasu przemian.* Warszawa: W.A.B.

———. 2012. *"Wiadomości Literackie" prawie dla wszystkich.* Warszawa: Wydawnictwo W.A.B.

Szulc, Lukasz. 2017. *Transnational Homosexuals in Communist Poland: Cross-Border Flows in Gay and Lesbian Magazines.* Cham: Palgrave Macmillan.

Szymańska, Anna. 1972. "Jaskiniowcy nadal wśród nas." *Prawo i Życie,* no. 17.

Szymańska, Monika, Lew-Starowicz Zbigniew, and Mastalerz Ewelina. 2012. "Problemy młodych zgłaszających się do seksuologa." *Przegląd seksuologiczny* 29: 12–16.

Środa, Magdalena. 1992. "Kobieta: wychowanie, role, tożsamość." In *Głos mają kobiety,* edited by Sławomira Walczewska, 9–17. Kraków: Convivium.

———. 2007. "Kobiety, Kościół, katolicyzm." In *Czarna księga kobiet,* edited by Christine Ockrant, 654–662. Warszawa: W.A.B.

Terry, Jennifer. 1999. *An American Obsession. Science, Medicine, and Homosexuality in Modern Society.* Chicago: University of Chicago Press.

Tiefer, Leonore. 2000. "Sexology and the Pharmaceutical Industry: The Threat of Co-option." *Journal of Sex Research* 37 (3): 273–83.

———. 2001. "Arriving at a 'New View' of Women's Sexual Problems: Background, Theory, and Activism." *Women & Therapy* 24 (1/2): 63–98. https://doi.org/10.1300/J015v24n01_12.

———. 2004. *Sex Is Not a Natural Act and Other Essays.* Boulder, CO: Westview. Kindle.

———. 2006. "The Viagra Phenomenon." *Sexualities* 9 (3): 273–94. https://doi.org/10.1177/1363460706065049.

Tin, Louis-Georges. 2012. *The Invention of Heterosexual Culture.* Cambridge, MA: MIT Press.

Tissot, Samuel Auguste. (1760) 1832. *Onanism.* New York: Collins & Hannay.

TNS OBOP. 2002. *Jak karać przestępców.* Warszawa: TNS OBOP.

Tomasik, Krzysztof. 2012. *Gejerel. Mniejszości seksualne w PRL-u.* Warszawa: Krytyka Polityczna.

Turkowicz, Beata. 2005. "Tabletka ideologiczna." *Trybuna*, August 8.

Urbanek, Bożena. 2004. "Poradniki medyczne o seksualności kobiet i mężczyzn w XIX w." In *Kobieta i małżeństwo. Społeczno-kulturowe aspekty seksualności. Wiek XIX i XX*, edited by Anna Żarnowska, Andrzej Szwarc, 61–72. Warszawa: Wydawnictwo DiG.

Vance, Carole S. 1983. "Gender Systems, Ideology, and Sex Research." In *The Powers of Desire. The Politics of Sexuality*, edited in Ann Snitow, Christine Stansell, and Sharon Thompson, 371–84. New York: Monthly Review Press.

———, ed. 1984a. *Pleasure and Danger: Exploring Female Sexuality.* Boston: Routledge & Kegan Paul.

———. 1984b. "Pleasure and Danger: Towards a Politics of Sexuality." In *Pleasure and Danger: Exploring Female Sexuality*, edited by Carole S. Vance, 1–28. Boston: Routledge & Kegan Paul.

———. 1989. "Social Construction Theory: Problems in the History of Sexuality." *Homosexuality, Which Homosexuality?* edited by Dennis Altman, 13–33. Amsterdam: Uitgeverij An Dekker/Schorer.

———. 2011. "Thinking Trafficking, Thinking Sex." *GLQ* 17 (1): 135–43. https://doi.org/10.1215/10642684-2010-024.

Vance, Carole S., and Ann Barr Snitow. 1984. "Toward a Conversation about Sex in Feminism: A Modest Proposal." *Signs* 10 (1): 126–35.

Van De Velde, Theodoor Hendrik. 1926. *Ideal Marriage: Its Physiology and Technique.* London: Frayser & Whitby.

Wasilewski, Bohdan, and Stanisław Dulko. 2011. "30-lecie Zakładu Seksuologii i Patologii Więzi Międzyludzkich CMKP." Paper presented at Polish Sexology: The Past and the Future. Zakład Seksuologii Medycznej i Psychoterapii, Centrum Medyczne Kształcenia Podyplomowego, Warsaw, December 20.

Waters, Chris. 2006. "Sexology." In *The Modern History of Sexuality*, edited by H. G. Cocks and Matt Houlbrrok, 41–93. New York: Palgrave.

Weeks, Jeffrey. 1985. *Sexuality and Its Discontents: Meanings, Myths, and Modern Sexualities*: London: Routledge.

———. 2011. *The Languages of Sexuality.* New York: Routledge.

Widera-Wysoczańska, Agnieszką. 2000. "Uznaj swoją niewinność" (interview by Martyna Głębocka). *Słowo Ludu*, June 14.

Wisłocka, Michalina. 1978. *Sztuka kochania.* Warszawa: Iskry.

———. 1979. "Sztuka kochania" (interview by Janina Pałęcka). *Zwierciadło*, no. 12.

———. 1987. "Oskarżam kapitana Nemo" (interview by Magdalena Rulska). *Sztandar Młodych*, December 4–6.

———. 1988. *Sztuka kochania dwadzieścia lat później.* Warszawa: Iskry.

———. 1993a. "Pogoń za wiatrem" (interview by Ewa Mazgal). *Gazeta Olsztyńska*, March 26–28.

———. 1993b. *Sukces w miłości. Jak kochać jak być kochanym.* Warszawa: Rytm.

———. 1993c. "Uroda polskiego erotyzmu" (interview by Monika Pieras). *Głos Poranny*, March 13–14.

———. (1978) 1995. *Sztuka kochania*, extended edition. Warszawa: Graf-Punkt.

———. 1997. "Jak scyzoryk" (interview by Leszek Kalinowski). *Gazeta Lubuska*, July 12–13.

———. 1998. *Malinka, Bratek i Jaś.* Warszawa: Prószyński i S-ka.

———. 2000. "Ja jestem od dziewczyn, od chłopców są inni" (interview by Agnieszka Grzybek and Barbara Limanowska). *Biuletyn OŚKI* nr 1 (10).

———. 2004. "Seksualistka" (interview by Darek Zaborek). *Gazeta Wyborcza*, September 20. http://wyborcza.pl/duzyformat/1,127291,2291497.html.

Wiśniewska-Roszkowska, Kinga. 1980. *Asceza, moralność, zdrowie.* Warszawa: PAX.

Wolfe, Leanna. 2011. "The Sexual Culture of Baby Boomers." Paper presented at the Society for the Scientific Study of Sexuality, Western Region Annual Meeting, April 14–17, San Francisco.

Wolff, Charlotte. 1986. *Magnus Hirschfeld: A Portrait of a Pioneer in Sexology.* London: Quartet.

Wolff, Larry. 1994. *Inventing Eastern Europe: The Map of Civilization on the Mind of the Enlightenment.* Stanford, CA: Stanford University Press.

Wołosik, Anna, and Ewa Majewska. 2011. *Napastowanie seksualne. Głupia zabawa czy poważana sprawa.* Warszawa: Difin.

Wyka, Anna. 1993. *Badacz społeczny wobec doświadczenia.* Warszawa: IFiS PAN.

Yanagisako, Sylvia J., and Jane Collier. 1987. "Toward a Unified Analysis of Gender and Kinship." In *Gender and Kinship: Essays toward Unified Analysis*, edited by Jane Collier and Sylvia J. Yanagisako, 14–50. Stanford, CA: Stanford University Press.

Z.B. 1973. "Przeciwko gwałtom." *Prawo i Życie* no. 6.

Zielińska, Eleonora. 2000. "Between Ideology, Politics and Common Sense: The Discourse of Reproductive Rights in Poland." In *Reproducing Gender: Politics, Publics, and Everyday Life after Socialism*, edited by Susan Gal and Gail Kligman, 23–57. Princeton, NJ: Princeton University Press.

Zimmerman, Jonathan. 2015. *Too Hot to Handle: A Global History of Sex Education.* Princeton, NJ: Princeton University Press.

Zola, Irving K. 1972. "Medicine as an Institution of Social Control." *Sociological Review* 20:487–504.

———. 1991. "Bringing Our Bodies and Ourselves Back In: Reflections on a Past, Present, and Future 'Medical Sociology.'" *Journal of Health and Social Behavior* 32 (1): 1–16.

INDEX

AGNIESZKA KOŚCIAŃSKA is Associate Professor at the Department of Ethnology and Cultural Anthropology, University of Warsaw. She is the author and (co)editor of several volumes on gender and sexuality, including the monographs, *The Power of Silence: Gender and Religious Conversion* (in Polish; University of Warsaw Press, 2009) and *To See a Moose: The History of Polish Sex Education from the First Class to the Internet* (forthcoming with Berghahn Books; Polish version with Czarne, 2017).

www.ingramcontent.com/pod-product-compliance
Lightning Source LLC
Chambersburg PA
CBHW022306280326
41932CB00010B/996